Android NDK Beginner's Guide

Second Edition

Discover the native side of Android and inject the power of C/C++ in your applications

Sylvain Ratabouil

BIRMINGHAM - MUMBAI

Android NDK Beginner's Guide
Second Edition

First published: January 2012

Second Edition: April 2015

Production reference: 1240415

Published by Packt Publishing Ltd.
Livery Place
35 Livery Street
Birmingham B3 2PB, UK.

ISBN 978-1-78398-964-5

www.packtpub.com

Credits

Author

Sylvain Ratabouil

Reviewers

Guy Cole

Krzysztof Fonał

Sergey Kosarevsky

Raimon Ràfols

Commissioning Editor

Ashwin Nair

Acquisition Editor

Vinay Argekar

Content Development Editor

Rohit Singh

Technical Editor

Ryan Kochery

Copy Editors

Hiral Bhat

Adithi Shetty

Sameen Siddiqui

Project Coordinator

Mary Alex

Proofreaders

Simran Bhogal

Safis Editing

Indexer

Monica Ajmera Mehta

Graphics

Disha Haria

Production Coordinator

Conidon Miranda

Cover Work

Conidon Miranda

About the Author

Sylvain Ratabouil is an IT consultant, experienced in Android, Java, and C/C++. He has contributed to the development of digital and mobile applications for large companies as well as industrial projects for the space and aeronautics industries. As a technology lover, he is passionate about mobile technologies and cannot live without his Android smartphone.

About the Reviewers

Guy Cole is a veteran Silicon Valley contractor with engagements in many well-known companies such as Facebook, Cisco, Motorola, Cray Research, Hewlett-Packard, Wells Fargo Bank, Barclays Global Investments, DHL Express, and many smaller, less-famous companies. You can contact him via LinkedIn for your next project.

Krzysztof Fonał is passionate about computer science. He fell in love with this field when he was eleven. He strongly believes that technology doesn't matter; problem solving skills matters, as well as the passion to absorb knowledge. He currently works with Trapeze Group, which is a world leader in providing IT solutions. He plans to work with machine learning books and also on the Corona SDK.

Sergey Kosarevsky is a software engineer with experience in C++ and 3D graphics. He worked for mobile industry companies and was involved in mobile projects at SPB Software, Yandex, and Layar. He has more than 12 years of software development experience and more than 6 years of Android NDK experience. Sergey earned his PhD in the field of mechanical engineering from St.Petersburg Institute of Machine-Building in Saint-Petersburg, Russia. He is a coauthor of *Android NDK Game Development Cookbook*. In his spare time, Sergey maintains and develops an open source multiplatform gaming engine, Linderdaum Engine (http://www.linderdaum.com), and a multi-platform open source file manager, WCM Commander (http://wcm.linderdaum.com).

Raimon Ràfols has been developing for mobile devices since 2004. He has experience in developing on several technologies, specializing in UI, build systems, and client-server communications. He is currently working as a mobile software engineering manager at Imagination Technologies near London. In his spare time, he enjoys programming, photography, and giving talks at mobile conferences about Android performance optimization and Android custom views.

I would like to express my gratitude to my beloved girlfriend, Laia, for her support and understanding.

www.PacktPub.com

Support files, eBooks, discount offers, and more

For support files and downloads related to your book, please visit www.PacktPub.com.

Did you know that Packt offers eBook versions of every book published, with PDF and ePub files available? You can upgrade to the eBook version at www.PacktPub.com and as a print book customer, you are entitled to a discount on the eBook copy. Get in touch with us at service@packtpub.com for more details.

At www.PacktPub.com, you can also read a collection of free technical articles, sign up for a range of free newsletters and receive exclusive discounts and offers on Packt books and eBooks.

https://www2.packtpub.com/books/subscription/packtlib

Do you need instant solutions to your IT questions? PacktLib is Packt's online digital book library. Here, you can search, access, and read Packt's entire library of books.

Why subscribe?

- ◆ Fully searchable across every book published by Packt
- ◆ Copy and paste, print, and bookmark content
- ◆ On demand and accessible via a web browser

Free access for Packt account holders

If you have an account with Packt at www.PacktPub.com, you can use this to access PacktLib today and view 9 entirely free books. Simply use your login credentials for immediate access.

Table of Contents

Preface

Android NDK is all about injecting high performance and portable code into your mobile apps by exploiting the maximum speed of these mobile devices. Android NDK allows you to write fast code for intensive tasks and port existing code to Android and non-Android platforms. Alternatively, if you have an application with multiple lines of C code, using NDK can considerably reduce the project development process. This is one of the most efficient operating systems for multimedia and games.

This Beginner's Guide will show you how to create applications enabled by C/C++ and integrate them with Java. By using this practical step-by-step guide, and gradually practicing your new skills using the tutorials, tips, and tricks, you will learn how to run C/C++ code embedded in a Java application or in a standalone application.

The books starts by teaching you how to access native API and port libraries used in some of the most successful Android applications. Next, you will move on to create a real native application project through the complete implementation of a native API and porting existing third-party libraries. As we progress through the chapters, you will gain a detailed understanding of rendering graphics and playing sound with OpenGL ES and OpenSL ES, which are becoming the new standard in mobility. Moving forward, you will learn how to access the keyboard and input peripherals, and read accelerometer or orientation sensors. Finally, you will dive into more advanced topics, such as RenderScript.

By the end of the book, you will be familiar enough with the key elements to start exploiting the power and portability of native code.

What this book covers

Chapter 1, Setting Up Your Environment, covers all the prerequisite packages installed on our system. This chapter also covers installing the Android Studio bundle, which contains both the Android Studio IDE and the Android SDK.

Chapter 2, Starting a Native Android Project, discusses how to build our first sample application using command-line tools and how to deploy it on an Android device. We also create our first native Android projects using Eclipse and Android Studio.

Chapter 3, Interfacing Java and C/C++ with JNI, covers how to make Java communicate with C/C++. We also handle Java object references in native code using Global references, and we learn the differences of Local references. Finally, we raise and check Java exceptions in native code.

Chapter 4, Calling Java Back from Native Code, calls Java code from native code with the JNI Reflection API. We also process bitmaps natively with the help of JNI and decode a video feed by hand.

Chapter 5, Writing a Fully Native Application, discusses creating `NativeActivity` that polls activity events to start or stop native code accordingly We also access the display window natively, such as a bitmap to display raw graphics. Finally, we retrieve time to make the application adapt to device speed using a monotonic clock.

Chapter 6, Rendering Graphics with OpenGL ES, covers how to initialize an OpenGL ES context and bind it to an Android window. Then, we see how to turn `libpng` into a module and load a texture from a PNG asset.

Chapter 7, Playing Sound with OpenSL ES, covers how to initialize OpenSL ES on Android. Then, we learn how to play background music from an encoded file and in-memory sounds with a sound buffer queue. Finally, we discover how to record and play a sound in a way that is thread-safe and non-blocking.

Chapter 8, Handling Input Devices and Sensors, discusses multiple ways to interact with Android from native code. More precisely, we discover how to attach an input queue to the Native App Glue event loop.

Chapter 9, Porting Existing Libraries to Android, covers how to activate the STL with a simple flag in the NDK makefile system. We port the Box2D library into an NDK module that is reusable among Android projects.

Chapter 10, Intensive Computing with RenderScript, introduces RenderScript, an advanced technology to parallelize intensive computation tasks. We also see how to use predefined RenderScript with built-in Intrinsics, which is currently mainly dedicated to image processing.

What you need for this book

To run the examples in the book, the following software will be required:

- ◆ System: Windows, Linux or Mac OS X
- ◆ JDK: Java SE Development Kit 7 or 8
- ◆ Cygwin: On Windows only

Who this book is for

Are you an Android Java programmer who needs more performance? Are you a C/C++ developer who doesn't want to bother with the complexity of Java and its out-of-control garbage collector? Do you want to create fast, intensive multimedia applications or games? If you've answered yes to any of these questions, then this book is for you. With some general knowledge of C/C++ development, you will be able to dive head first into native Android development.

Sections

In this book, you will find several headings that appear frequently (Time for action, What just happened?, Pop quiz, and Have a go hero).

To give clear instructions on how to complete a procedure or task, we use these sections as follows:

Time for action – heading

1. Action 1
2. Action 2
3. Action 3

Instructions often need some extra explanation to ensure they make sense, so they are followed with these sections:

What just happened?

This section explains the working of the tasks or instructions that you just completed.

You will also find some other learning aids in the book, for example:

Have a go hero – heading

These are practical challenges that give you ideas to experiment with what you have learned.

Conventions

You will also find a number of text styles that distinguish between different kinds of information. Here are some examples of these styles and an explanation of their meaning.

Code words in text, database table names, folder names, filenames, file extensions, pathnames, dummy URLs, user input, and Twitter handles are shown as follows: "Finally, create a new Gradle task ndkBuild that will manually trigger the ndk-build command."

A block of code is set as follows:

```
#include <unistd.h>
...
sleep(3); // in seconds
```

When we wish to draw your attention to a particular part of a code block, the relevant lines or items are set in bold:

```
if (mGraphicsManager.start() != STATUS_OK) return STATUS_KO;

mAsteroids.initialize();
mShip.initialize();

mTimeManager.reset();
return STATUS_OK;
```

Any command-line input or output is written as follows:

```
adb shell stop
adb shell setprop dalvik.vm.checkjni true
```

New terms and **important words** are shown in bold. Words that you see on the screen, in menus or dialog boxes for example, appear in the text like this: "If everything works properly, a message **Late-enabling – Xcheck:jni** appears in the Logcat when your application starts."

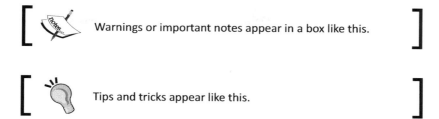

Warnings or important notes appear in a box like this.

Tips and tricks appear like this.

Reader feedback

Feedback from our readers is always welcome. Let us know what you think about this book—what you liked or disliked. Reader feedback is important for us as it helps us develop titles that you will really get the most out of.

To send us general feedback, simply e-mail feedback@packtpub.com, and mention the book's title in the subject of your message.

If there is a topic that you have expertise in and you are interested in either writing or contributing to a book, see our author guide at www.packtpub.com/authors.

Customer support

Now that you are the proud owner of a Packt book, we have a number of things to help you to get the most from your purchase.

Downloading the example code

You can download the example code files from your account at http://www.packtpub.com for all the Packt Publishing books you have purchased. If you purchased this book elsewhere, you can visit http://www.packtpub.com/support and register to have the files e-mailed directly to you.

Errata

Although we have taken every care to ensure the accuracy of our content, mistakes do happen. If you find a mistake in one of our books—maybe a mistake in the text or the code—we would be grateful if you could report this to us. By doing so, you can save other readers from frustration and help us improve subsequent versions of this book. If you find any errata, please report them by visiting http://www.packtpub.com/submit-errata, selecting your book, clicking on the **Errata Submission Form** link, and entering the details of your errata. Once your errata are verified, your submission will be accepted and the errata will be uploaded to our website or added to any list of existing errata under the Errata section of that title.

To view the previously submitted errata, go to https://www.packtpub.com/books/content/support and enter the name of the book in the search field. The required information will appear under the **Errata** section.

Piracy

Piracy of copyrighted material on the Internet is an ongoing problem across all media. At Packt, we take the protection of our copyright and licenses very seriously. If you come across any illegal copies of our works in any form on the Internet, please provide us with the location address or website name immediately so that we can pursue a remedy.

Please contact us at copyright@packtpub.com with a link to the suspected pirated material.

We appreciate your help in protecting our authors and our ability to bring you valuable content.

Questions

If you have a problem with any aspect of this book, you can contact us at questions@packtpub.com, and we will do our best to address the problem.

1
Setting Up Your Environment

Are you ready to take up the mobile challenge? Is your computer switched on, mouse and keyboard plugged in, and screen illuminating your desk? Then let's not wait a minute more!

Developing Android applications requires a specific set of tools. You may already know about the Android Software Development Kit for pure Java applications. However, getting full access to the power of Android devices requires more: the Android Native Development Kit.

Setting up a proper Android environment is not that complicated, however it can be rather tricky. Indeed, Android is still an evolving platform and recent additions, such as Android Studio or Gradle, are not well supported when it comes to NDK development. Despite these annoyances, anybody can have a ready-to-work environment in an hour.

In this first chapter, we are going to:

- Install prerequisites packages
- Set up an Android development environment
- Launch an Android emulator
- Connect an Android device for development

Getting started with Android development

What differentiates mankind from animals is the use of tools. Android developers, the authentic species you belong to, are no different!

To develop applications on Android, we can use any of the following three platforms:

◆ Microsoft Windows (XP and later)

◆ Apple OS X (Version 10.4.8 or later)

◆ Linux (distributions using GLibc 2.7 or later, such as latest versions of Ubuntu)

These systems are supported on x86 platforms (that is, PCs with processors such as Intel or AMD) in both 32- and 64-bit versions, except for Windows XP (32-bit only).

This is a good start but, unless you are able to read and write binary code as well as speak your mother tongue, having a raw OS is not enough. We also need software dedicated to Android development:

◆ A **JDK (Java Development Kit)**

◆ An Android SDK (Software Development Kit)

◆ An Android NDK (Native Development Kit)

◆ An **IDE (Integrated Development Environment)** such as Eclipse or Visual Studio (or vi for hard-core coders). Android Studio and IntelliJ are not yet well-suited for NDK development, although they provide basic support for native code.

◆ A good old command-line shell to manipulate all these tools. We will use Bash.

Now that we know what tools are necessary to work with Android, let's start with the installation and setup process.

 The following section is dedicated to Windows. If you are a Mac or Linux user, you can jump to *Setting up an OS X* or *Setting up Linux* section.

Setting up Windows

Before installing the necessary tools, we need to set up Windows to host our Android development tools properly. Although it is not the most natural fit for Android development, Windows still provides a fully functional environment.

The following section explains how to set up the prerequisite packages on Windows 7. The process is the same for Windows XP, Vista, or 8.

Time for action – preparing Windows for Android development

To develop with the Android NDK on Windows, we need to set up a few prerequisites:
Cygwin, a JDK, and Ant.

1. Go to `http://cygwin.com/install.html` and download the Cygwin setup
   program suitable for your environment. Once downloaded, execute it.

2. In the installation window, click on **Next** and then **Install from Internet**.

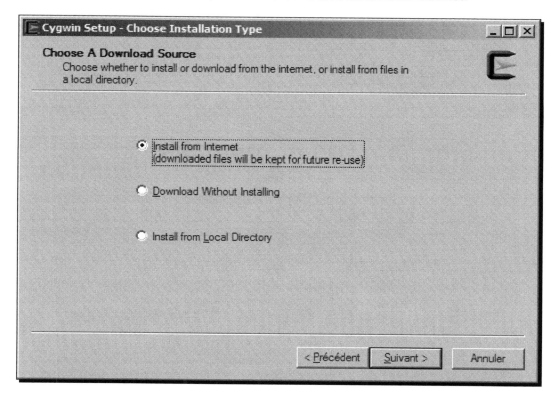

Follow the installation wizard screens. Consider selecting a download site from
where Cygwin packages are downloaded in your country.

Then, when proposed, include the **Devel**, **Make**, **Shells**, and **bash** packages:

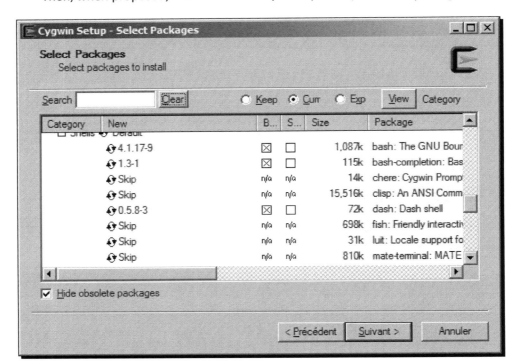

Follow the installation wizard until the end. This may take some time depending on your Internet connection.

3. Download Oracle JDK 7 from the Oracle website at http://www.oracle.com/technetwork/java/javase/downloads/index.html (or JDK 8, although it is not officially supported at the time this book is written). Launch and follow the installation wizard until the end.

4. Download Ant from its website at http://ant.apache.org/bindownload.cgi and unzip its binary package in the directory of your choice (for example, C:\Ant).

5. After installation, define JDK, Cygwin, and Ant locations in environment variables. To do so, open Windows **Control Panel** and go to the **System** panel (or right-click on the **Computer** item in the Windows Start menu and select **Properties**).

Then, go to **Advanced system settings**. The **System Properties** window appears. Finally, select the **Advanced** tab and click on the **Environment Variables** button.

6. In the Environment Variables window, inside the System variables list, add:

- ❑ The CYGWIN_HOME variable with the Cygwin installation directory as the value (for example, C:\Cygwin)

- ❑ The JAVA_HOME variable with the JDK installation directory as the value

- ❑ The ANT_HOME variable with the Ant installation directory as the value (for example, C:\Ant)

Prepend %CYGWIN_HOME%\bin;%JAVA_HOME%\bin;%ANT_HOME%\bin;, all separated by a semicolon, at the beginning of your PATH environment variable.

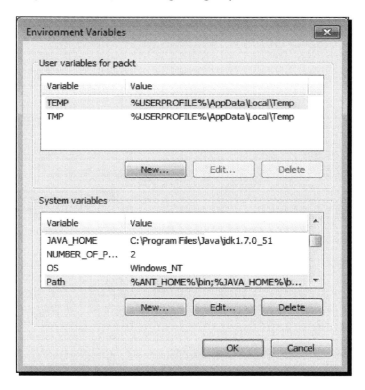

7. Finally, launch a Cygwin terminal. Your profile files get created on the first launch. Check the make version to ensure Cygwin works:

```
make -version
```

You will see the following output:

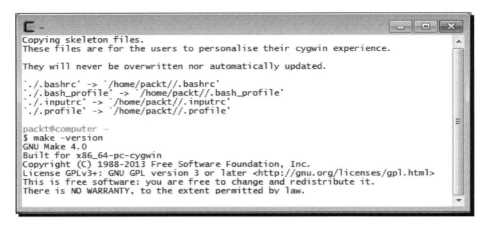

8. Ensure JDK is properly installed by running Java and checking its version. Check carefully to make sure the version number corresponds to the newly installed JDK:

```
java -version
```

You will see the following output on the screen:

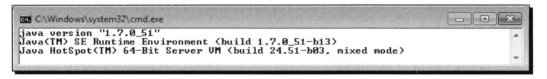

9. From a classic Windows terminal, check the Ant version to make sure it is properly working:

```
ant -version
```

You will see the following on the terminal:

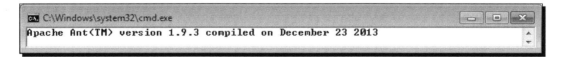

What just happened?

Windows is now set up with all the necessary packages to host Android development tools:

◆ Cygwin, which is an open source software collection, allows the Windows platform to emulate a Unix-like environment. It aims at natively integrating software based on the POSIX standard (such as Unix, Linux, and so on) into Windows. It can be considered as an intermediate layer between applications originated from Unix/Linux (but natively recompiled on Windows) and the Windows OS itself. Cygwin includes Make, which is required by the Android NDK compilation system to build native code.

 Even if Android NDK R7 introduced native Windows binaries, which does not require a Cygwin runtime, it is still recommended to install the latter for debugging purpose.

◆ A JDK 7, which contains the runtime and tools necessary to build Java applications on Android and run the Eclipse IDE as well as Ant. The only real trouble that you may encounter when installing a JDK is some interferences from a previous installation, such as an existing **Java Runtime Environment (JRE)**. Proper JDK use can be enforced through the JAVA_HOME and PATH environment variables.

 Defining the JAVA_HOME environment variable is not required. However, JAVA_HOME is a popular convention among Java applications, Ant being one of them. It first looks for the java command in JAVA_HOME (if defined) before looking in PATH. If you install an up-to-date JDK in another location later on, do not forget to update JAVA_HOME.

◆ Ant, which is a Java-based build automation utility. Although not a requirement, it allows building Android applications from the command line, as we will see in *Chapter 2, Starting a Native Android Project*. It is also a good solution to set up a continuous integration chain.

The next step consists of setting up the Android development kits.

Installing Android development kits on Windows

Android requires specific development kits to develop applications: the Android SDK and NDK. Hopefully, Google has thought about the developer community and provides all the necessary tools for free.

In the following part, we will install these kits to start developing native Android applications on Windows 7.

Time for action – installing Android SDK and NDK on Windows

The Android Studio bundle already contains the Android SDK. Let's install it.

1. Open your web browser and download the Android Studio bundle from `http://developer.android.com/sdk/index.html`.

Run the downloaded program and follow the installation wizard. When requested, install all Android components.

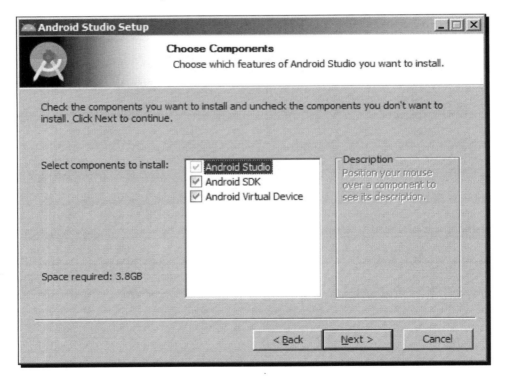

Then, choose the installation directories for Android Studio and the Android SDK (for example, `C:\Android\android-studio` and `C:\Android\sdk`).

2. Launch Android Studio to ensure it is properly working. If Android Studio proposes to import settings from a previous installation, select your preferred option and click on **OK**.

The Android Studio welcome screen should then appear. Close it.

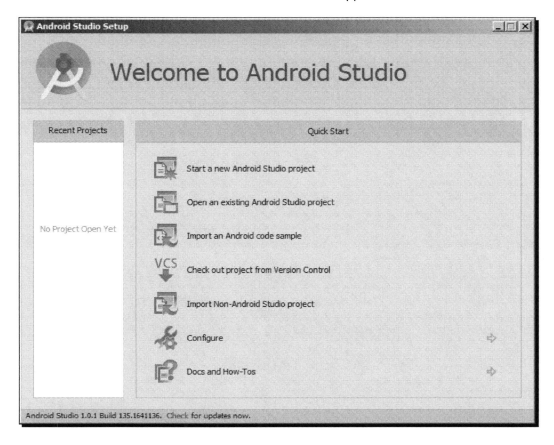

3. Go to http://developer.android.com/tools/sdk/ndk/index.html and download the Android NDK (not SDK!) suitable for your environment. Extract the archive inside the directory of your choice (for example, C:\Android\ndk).

4. To easily access Android utilities from the command line, let's declare the Android SDK and NDK as environment variables. From now on, we will refer to these directories as $ANDROID_SDK and $ANDROID_NDK.

Open the **Environment Variables** system window, as we did previously. Inside the System variables list, add the following:

- The ANDROID_SDK variable with the SDK installation directory (for example, C:\Android\sdk)

- The ANDROID_NDK variable with the NDK installation directories (for example, C:\Android\ndk)

Prepend %ANDROID_SDK%\tools;%ANDROID_SDK%\platform-tools;%ANDROID_NDK%;, all separated by a semicolon, at the beginning of your PATH environment variable.

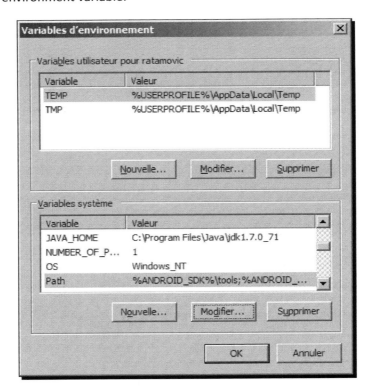

5. All Windows environment variables should be imported automatically by Cygwin when launched. Open a Cygwin terminal and list the Android devices connected to your computer (even if none are currently) with `adb` to check whether SDK is working. No error should appear:

```
adb devices
```

6. Check the `ndk-build` version to ensure that NDK is working. If everything works, the `Make` version should appear:

```
ndk-build -version
```

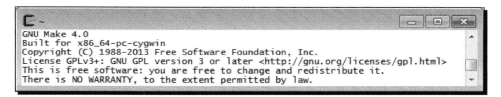

7. Open **Android SDK Manager**, located in the ADB bundle directory's root.

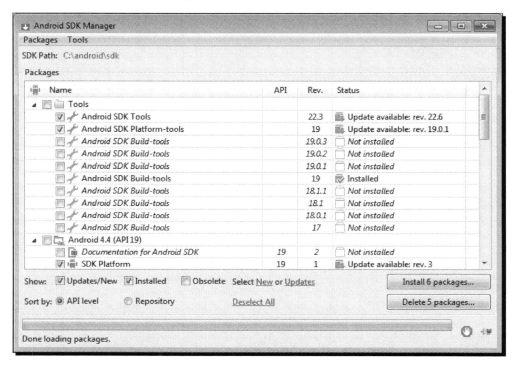

In the opened window, click on **New** to select all the packages and then click on the **Install packages...** button. Accept the licenses in the popup that appears and start the installation of Android development packages by clicking on the **Install** button.

After a few long minutes, all packages are downloaded and a confirmation message indicating that the Android SDK manager has been updated appears.

Validate and close the manager.

What just happened?

Android Studio is now installed on the system. Although it is now the official Android IDE, we are not going to use it much throughout the book because of its lack of support of the NDK. It is, however, absolutely possible to use Android Studio for Java development, and command line or Eclipse for C/C++.

The Android SDK has been set up through the Android Studio package. An alternative solution consists of manually deploying the SDK standalone package provided by Google. On the other hand, the Android NDK has been deployed manually from its archive. Both the SDK and NDK are made available through the command line thanks to a few environment variables.

To get a fully functional environment, all Android packages have been downloaded thanks to the Android SDK manager, which aims at managing all the platforms, sources, samples, and emulation features available through the SDK. This tool greatly simplifies the update of your environment when new SDK API and components are released. There is no need to reinstall or overwrite anything!

However, the Android SDK Manager does not manage the NDK, which explains why we downloaded it separately, and why you will need to update it manually in the future.

Installing all Android packages is not strictly necessary. Only the SDK platform (and possibly Google APIs) releases targeted by your application are really required. Installing all packages may avoid troubles when importing other projects or samples though.

The installation of your Android development environment is not over yet. We still need one more thing to develop comfortably with the NDK.

 This is the end of the section dedicated to the Windows setup. The following section is dedicated to OS X.

Setting up OS X

Apple computers have a reputation for being simple and easy to use. I must say that this adage is rather true when it comes to Android development. Indeed, as a Unix-based system, OS X is well adapted to run the NDK toolchain.

The following section explains how to set up the prerequisite packages on Mac OS X Yosemite.

Time for action – preparing OS X for Android development

To develop with the Android NDK on OS X, we need to set up a few prerequisites: a JDK, Developer Tools, and Ant.

1. A JDK is preinstalled on OS X 10.6 Snow Leopard and below. On these systems, Apple's JDK is in version 6. Since this version is deprecated, it is advised to install an up-to-date JDK 7 (or JDK 8, although it is not officially supported at the time this book is written).

    On the other hand, OS X 10.7 Lion and above does not have a default JDK installed. Installing the JDK 7 is thus mandatory.

To do so, download Oracle JDK 7 from the Oracle website at `http://www.oracle.com/technetwork/java/javase/downloads/index.html`. Launch the DMG and follow the installation wizard until the end.

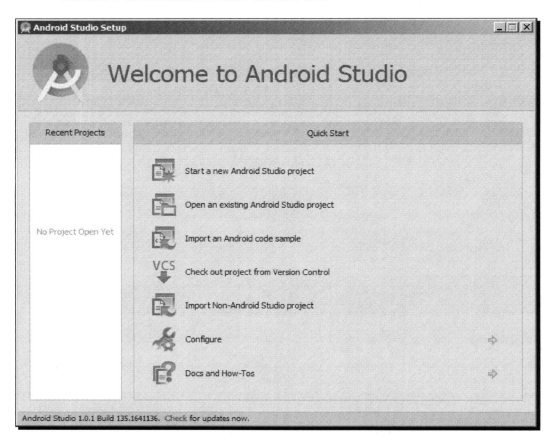

Check the Java version to ensure that the JDK is properly installed.

```
java -version
```

```
Mac-mini:~ packt$ java -version
java version "1.7.0_71"
Java(TM) SE Runtime Environment (build 1.7.0_71-b14)
Java HotSpot(TM) 64-Bit Server VM (build 24.71-b01, mixed mode)
Mac-mini:~ packt$ 
```

To know if a JDK 6 is installed, check **Java Preferences.app** located by going to **Applications | Utilities** on your Mac. If you have JDK 7, check whether you have the **Java** icon under **System Preferences**.

2. All Developer Tools are included in the XCode installation package (Version 5, at the time this book is written). XCode is provided on the AppStore for free. Starting from OS X 10.9, the Developer Tools package can be installed separately from a terminal prompt with the following command:

```
xcode-select --install
```

Then, from the popup window that appears, select **Install**.

3. To build native code with the Android NDK, whether XCode or the single Developer Tools package is installed, we need Make. Open a terminal prompt and check the Make version to ensure that it correctly works:

```
make -version
```

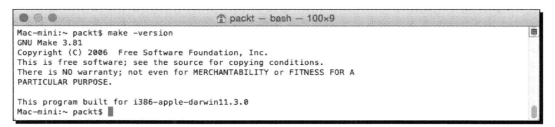

4. On OS X 10.9 and later, Ant must be installed manually. Download Ant from its website at http://ant.apache.org/bindownload.cgi and unzip its binary package in the directory of your choice (for example, /Developer/Ant).

Then, create or edit the file ~/.profile and make Ant available on the system path by appending the following:

```
export ANT_HOME="/Developer/Ant"
export PATH=${ANT_HOME}/bin:${PATH}
```

Log out from your current session and log in again (or restart your computer) and check whether Ant is correctly installed by checking its version from the command line:

```
ant -version
```

```
● ● ●                        Developer — bash — 101×5
Mac-mini:Developer packt$
Mac-mini:Developer packt$
Mac-mini:Developer packt$ ant -version
Apache Ant(TM) version 1.9.4 compiled on April 29 2014
Mac-mini:Developer packt$ █
```

What just happened?

Our OS X system is now set up with the necessary packages to host Android development tools:

◆ A JDK 7, which contains the runtime and tools necessary to build Java applications on Android and to run the Eclipse IDE as well as Ant.

◆ Developer Tools package, which packages various command-line utilities. It includes Make, which is required by the Android NDK compilation system to build native code.

◆ Ant, which is a Java-based build automation utility. Although not a requirement, it allows building Android applications from the command line, as we will see in *Chapter 2*, *Starting a Native Android Project*. It is also a good solution to set up a continuous integration chain.

The next step consists of setting up the Android Development Kit.

Installing Android development kits on OS X

Android requires specific development kits to develop applications: the Android SDK and NDK. Hopefully, Google has thought about the developer community and provides all the necessary tools for free.

In the following part, we are going to install these kits to start developing native Android applications on Mac OS X Yosemite.

Time for action – installing Android SDK and NDK on OS X

The Android Studio bundle already contains the Android SDK. Let's install it.

1. Open your web browser and download the Android Studio bundle from `http://developer.android.com/sdk/index.html`.

2. Run the downloaded DMG file. In the window that appears, drag the **Android Studio** icon into **Applications** and wait for Android Studio to be fully copied on the system.

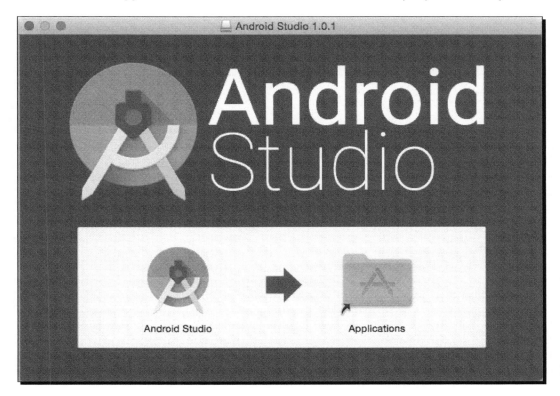

3. Run Android Studio from Launchpad.

If an error **Unable to find a valid JVM** appears (because Android Studio cannot find a suitable JRE when launched), you can run Android Studio from the command line as follows (using the appropriate JDK path):

```
export
STUDIO_JDK=/Library/Java/JavaVirtualMachines/jdk1.7.0_71.jdk
open /Applications/Android\ Studio.apps
```

To solve the Android Studio startup issue, you can also install the former JDK 6 package provided by Apple. Beware! This version is outdated and thus, deprecated.

If Android Studio proposes to import settings from a previous installation, select your preferred option and click on **OK**.

In the next **Setup Wizard** screen that appears, select the **Standard** installation type and continue the installation.

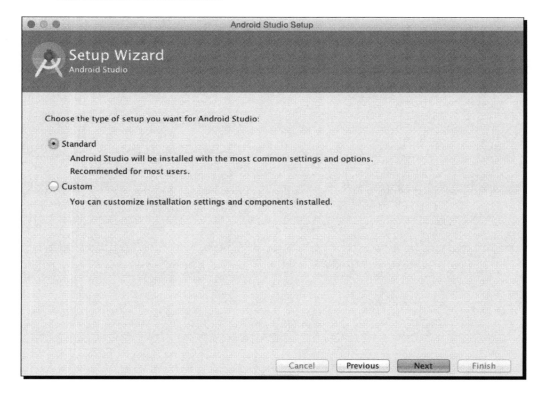

Complete the installation until the Android Studio welcome screen appears. Then, close Android Studio.

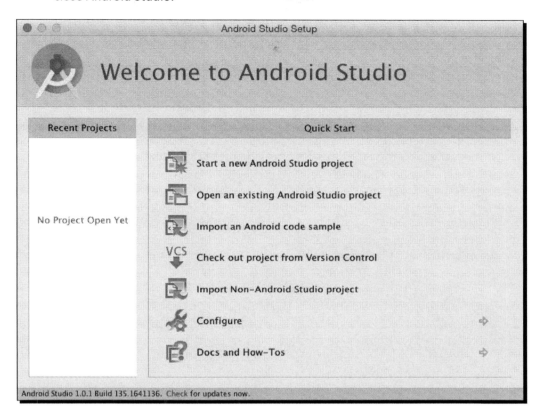

4. Go to `http://developer.android.com/tools/sdk/ndk/index.html` and download the Android NDK (not SDK!) archive suitable for your environment. Extract it inside the directory of your choice (for example, `~/Library/Android/ndk`).

5. To easily access Android utilities from the command line, let's declare the Android SDK and NDK as environment variables. From now on, we will refer to these directories as `$ANDROID_SDK` and `$ANDROID_NDK`. Assuming you use the default `Bash` command-line shell, create or edit `.profile` (which is a hidden file!) in your home directory and append the following instructions (adapt paths according to your installation):

```
export ANDROID_SDK="~/Library/Android/sdk"
export ANDROID_NDK="~/Library/Android/ndk"
export PATH="${ANDROID_SDK}/tools:${ANDROID_SDK}/platform-
tools:${ANDROID_NDK}:${PATH}"
```

6. Log out from your current session and log in again (or restart your computer). List the Android devices connected to your computer (even if none currently are) with `adb` to check whether Android SDK is working. No error should appear:

`adb devices`

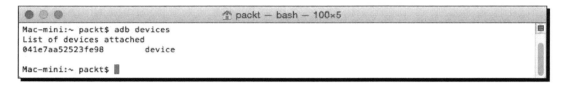

7. Check the `ndk-build` version to ensure that NDK is working. If everything works, the `Make` version should appear:

`ndk-build -version`

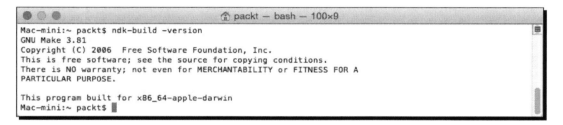

8. Open a terminal and start the Android SDK manager with the following command:

`android`

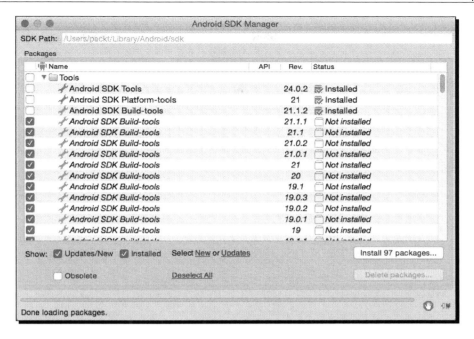

In the opened window, click on **New** to select all the packages and then click on the **Install packages...** button. Accept the licenses in the popup that appears and start the installation of all Android packages by clicking on the **Install** button.

After a few long minutes, all packages are downloaded and a confirmation message indicating that the Android SDK manager has been updated appears.

Validate and close the manager.

What just happened?

Android Studio is now installed on the system. Although it is now the official Android IDE, we will not use it much through the book because of its lack of support of the NDK. It is, however, absolutely possible to use Android Studio for Java development, and command line or Eclipse for C/C++.

The Android SDK has been set up through the Android Studio package. An alternative solution consists of manually deploying the SDK standalone package provided by Google. On the other hand, the Android NDK has been deployed manually from its archive. Both the SDK and NDK are made available through the command line, thanks to a few environment variables.

OS X is tricky when it comes to environment variables. They can be easily declared in `.profile` for applications launched from a terminal, as we just did. They can also be declared using an `environment.plist` file for GUI applications, which are not launched from Spotlight.

To get a fully functional environment, all Android packages have been downloaded thanks to the Android SDK manager, which aims at managing all the platforms, sources, samples, and emulation features available through the SDK. This tool greatly simplifies the update of your environment when new SDK API and components are released. There is no need to reinstall or overwrite anything!

However, the Android SDK manager does not manage the NDK, which explains why we downloaded it separately, and why you will need to update it manually in the future.

 Installing all Android packages is not strictly necessary. Only the SDK platform (and possibly Google APIs) releases targeted by your application are really required. Installing all packages may avoid troubles importing other projects or samples though.

The installation of your Android development environment is not over yet. We still need one more thing to develop comfortably with the NDK.

 This is the end of the section dedicated to the OS X setup. The following section is dedicated to Linux.

Setting up Linux

Linux is naturally suited for Android development as the Android toolchain is Linux-based. Indeed, as a Unix-based system, Linux is well adapted to run the NDK toolchain. Beware, however, that commands to install packages may vary depending on your Linux distribution.

The following section explains how to set up the prerequisite packages on Ubuntu 14.10 Utopic Unicorn.

Time for action – preparing Ubuntu for Android development

To develop with the Android NDK on Linux, we need to set up a few prerequisites: Glibc, Make, OpenJDK, and Ant.

1. From Command Prompt, check whether Glibc (the GNU C standard library) 2.7 or later, usually shipped with Linux systems by default, is installed:

```
ldd --version
```

```
packt@computer: ~
ldd (Ubuntu EGLIBC 2.17-93ubuntu4) 2.17
Copyright (C) 2012 Free Software Foundation, Inc.
This is free software; see the source for copying conditions.  There is NO
warranty; not even for MERCHANTABILITY or FITNESS FOR A PARTICULAR PURPOSE.
Written by Roland McGrath and Ulrich Drepper.
```

2. Make is also required to build native code. Install it from the build-essential package (requires administrative privilege):

```
sudo apt-get install build-essential
```

Run the following command to ensure Make is correctly installed, in which case its version is displayed:

```
make –version
```

```
packt@computer: ~
GNU Make 3.81
Copyright (C) 2006  Free Software Foundation, Inc.
This is free software; see the source for copying conditions.
There is NO warranty; not even for MERCHANTABILITY or FITNESS FOR A
PARTICULAR PURPOSE.

This program built for x86_64-pc-linux-gnu
```

3. On 64-bit Linux systems, install the 32-bit libraries compatibility package, as Android SDK has binaries compiled for 32 bits only. To do so on Ubuntu 13.04 and earlier, simply install the `ia32-libs` package:

```
sudo apt-get install ia32-libs
```

On Ubuntu 13.10 64 bits and later, this package has been removed. So, install the required packages manually:

```
sudo apt-get install lib32ncurses5 lib32stdc++6 zlib1g:i386 libc6-i386
```

4. Install Java OpenJDK 7 (or JDK 8, although it is not officially supported at the time this book is written). Oracle JDK is also fine:

```
sudo apt-get install openjdk-7-jdk
```

Ensure JDK is properly installed by running Java and checking its version:

```
java -version
```

```
packt@computer: ~
java version "1.7.0_51"
OpenJDK Runtime Environment (IcedTea 2.4.4) (7u51-2.4.4-0ubuntu0.13.10.1)
```

5. Install Ant with the following command (requires administrative privilege):

```
sudo apt-get install ant
```

Check whether Ant is properly working:

```
ant -version
```

```
packt@computer: ~
Apache Ant(TM) version 1.9.2 compiled on July 14 2013
```

What just happened?

Our Linux system is now prepared with the necessary packages to host Android development tools:

◆ The build-essential package, which is a minimal set of tools for compilation and packaging on Linux Systems. It includes Make, which is required by the Android NDK compilation system to build native code. **GCC** (the **GNU C Compiler**) is also included but is not required as Android NDK already contains its own version.

◆ 32-bit compatibility libraries for 64-bit systems, since the Android SDK still uses 32-bit binaries.

◆ A JDK 7, which contains the runtime and tools necessary to build Java applications on Android and run the Eclipse IDE as well as Ant.

◆ Ant, which is a Java-based build automation utility. Although not a requirement, it allows building Android applications from the command line, as we will see in *Chapter 2, Starting a Native Android Project*. It is also a good solution to set up a continuous integration chain.

The next step consists of setting up the Android development kits.

Installing Android development kits on Linux

Android requires specific development kits to develop applications: the Android SDK and NDK. Hopefully, Google has thought about the developer community and provides all the necessary tools for free.

In the following part, we will install these kits to start developing native Android applications on Ubuntu 14.10 Utopic Unicorn.

Time for action – installing Android SDK and NDK on Ubuntu

The Android Studio bundle already contains the Android SDK. Let's install it.

1. Open your web browser and download the Android Studio bundle from `http://developer.android.com/sdk/index.html`. Extract the downloaded archive in the directory of your choice (for example, `~/Android/Android-studio`).

2. Run the Android Studio script `bin/studio.sh`. If Android Studio proposes to import settings from a previous installation, select your preferred option and click on **OK**.

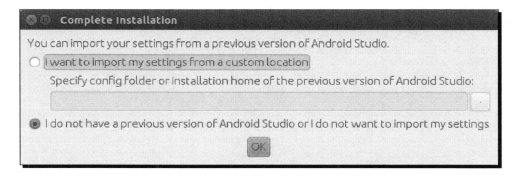

In the next **Setup Wizard** screen that appears, select a **Standard** installation type and continue installation.

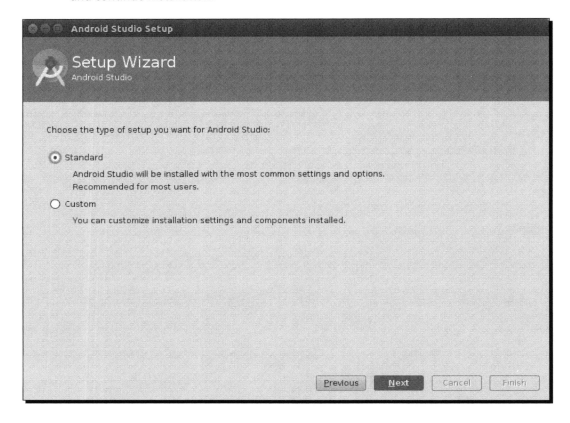

Complete installation until the Android Studio welcome screen. Then, close Android Studio.

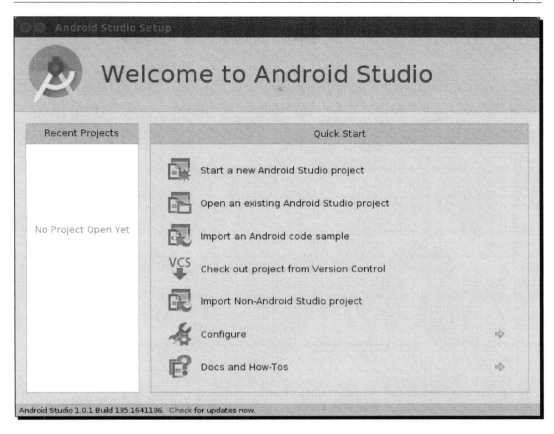

3. Go to `http://developer.android.com/tools/sdk/ndk/index.html` and download the Android NDK (not SDK!) archive suitable for your environment. Extract it inside the directory of your choice (for example, `~/Android/Ndk`).

4. To easily access Android utilities from the command line, let's declare the Android SDK and NDK as environment variables. From now on, we will refer to these directories as $ANDROID_SDK and $ANDROID_NDK. Edit your .profile file (beware since this is a hidden file!) in your home directory and add the following variables at the end (adapt their path according to your installation directories):

```
export ANDROID_SDK="~/Android/Sdk"
export ANDROID_NDK="~/Android/Ndk"
export PATH="${ANDROID_SDK}/tools:${ANDROID_SDK}/platform-
tools:${ANDROID_NDK}:${PATH}"
```

5. Log out from your current session and log in again (or restart your computer). List the Android devices connected to your computer (even if none currently are) with adb to check whether Android SDK is working. No error should appear:

adb devices

```
packt@computer: ~
List of devices attached
```

6. Check the ndk-build version to ensure that NDK is working. If everything works, the Make version should appear:

ndk-build -version

```
packt@computer: ~
GNU Make 3.81
Copyright (C) 2006  Free Software Foundation, Inc.
This is free software; see the source for copying conditions.
There is NO warranty; not even for MERCHANTABILITY or FITNESS FOR A
PARTICULAR PURPOSE.

This program built for x86_64-pc-linux-gnu
```

7. Open a terminal and start the Android SDK manager with the following command:

android

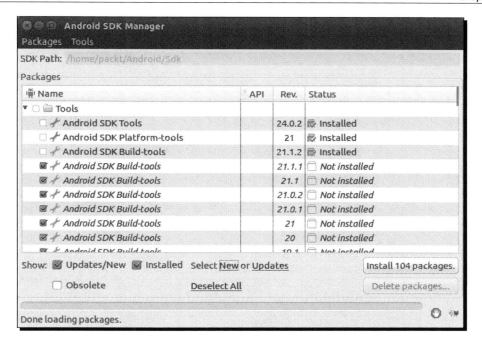

In the opened window, click on **New** to select all the packages, and then click on the **Install packages...** button. Accept the licenses in the popup that appears and start the installation of all Android package by clicking on the **Install** button.

After a few long minutes, all packages are downloaded and a confirmation message indicating that the Android SDK manager has been updated appears.

Validate and close the manager.

What just happened?

Android Studio is now installed on the system. Although it is now the official Android IDE, we are not going to use it much throughout the book because of its lack of support of the NDK. It is, however, absolutely possible to use Android Studio for Java development, and the command line or Eclipse for C/C++.

The Android SDK has been set up through the Android Studio package. An alternative solution consists of manually deploying the SDK standalone package provided by Google. On the other hand, the Android NDK has been deployed manually from its archive. Both the SDK and NDK are made available through the command line, thanks to a few environment variables.

To get a fully functional environment, all Android packages have been downloaded thanks to the Android SDK manager, which aims at managing all the platforms, sources, samples, and emulation features available through the SDK. This tool greatly simplifies the update of your environment when new SDK API and components are released. There is no need to reinstall or overwrite anything!

However, the Android SDK manager does not manage the NDK, which explains why we downloaded it separately, and why you will need to update it manually in the future.

 Installing all Android packages is not strictly necessary. Only the SDK platform (and possibly Google APIs) releases targeted by your application are really required. Installing all packages may avoid trouble when importing other projects or samples though.

The installation of not or Android development environment is not over yet. We still need one more thing to develop comfortably with the NDK.

 This is the end of the section dedicated to the Linux setup. The following section is for all operating systems.

Installing the Eclipse IDE

Because of Android Studio limitations, Eclipse is still one of the most appropriate IDEs to develop native code on Android. Using an IDE is not required though; command-line lovers or `vi` fanatics can skip this part!

In the following section, we will see how to set up Eclipse.

Time for action – installing Eclipse with ADT on your OS

Since the latest Android SDK releases, Eclipse and its plugins (ADT and CDT) need to be installed manually. To do so execute the following steps:

1. Go to `http://www.eclipse.org/downloads/` and download Eclipse for Java developers. Extract the downloaded archive in the directory of your choice (for example, `C:\Android\eclipse` on Windows, `~/ Android/Eclipse` on Linux, and `~/Library/Android/eclipse` on Mac OS X).

Then, run Eclipse. If Eclipse asks for a workspace (which contains Eclipse settings and projects) when starting up, define the directory of your choice or leave the default settings and then click on **OK**.

When Eclipse has finished loading, close the welcome page. The following window should appear:

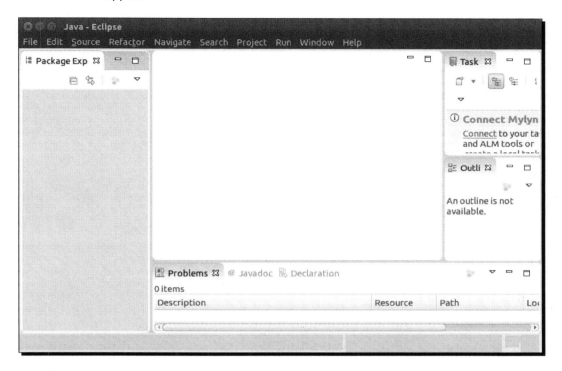

2. Go to **Help** | **Install New Software…**. Enter `https://dl-ssl.google.com/android/eclipse` in the **Work with:** field and validate. After a few seconds, a **Developer Tools** plugin appears. Select it and click on the **Next** button.

In case this step fails while accessing update sites, check your Internet connection. You may be either disconnected or connected behind a proxy. In the latter case, you can download the ADT plugin as a separate archive from the ADT web page and install it manually, or configure Eclipse to connect through a proxy.

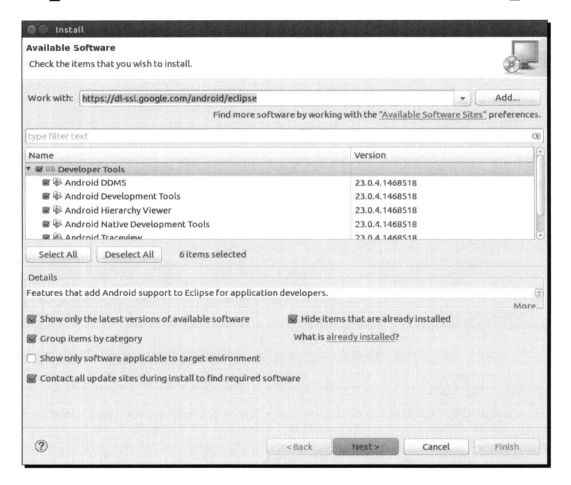

Follow the wizard and accept conditions when asked. On the last wizard page, click on **Finish** to install ADT. A warning may appear indicating that the plugin content is unsigned. Ignore it and click on **OK**. When finished, restart Eclipse as requested.

3. Go back to **Help | Install New Software....** Open the **Work with** combobox and select the item containing the Eclipse version name (here, Luna). Then, check the **Show only software applicable to target environment** option. Find **Programming Languages** in the plugin tree and unfold it. Finally, check all C/C++ plugins and click on **Next**.

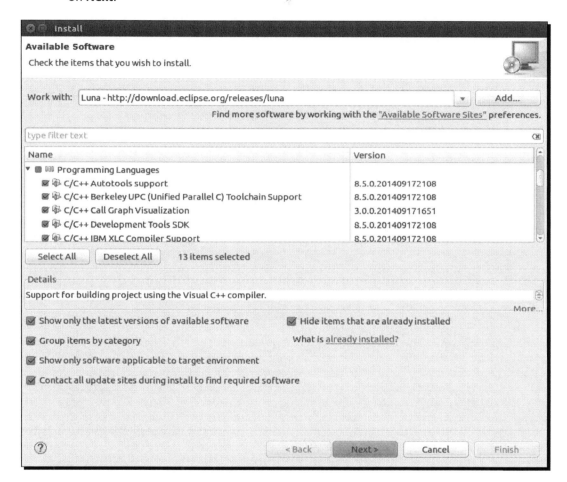

Follow the wizard and accept conditions when asked. On the last wizard page, click on **Finish**. Wait until the installation is complete and restart Eclipse.

4. Go to **Windows | Preferences... (Eclipse | Preferences...** on Mac OS X) and then select **Android** on the left tree. If everything is fine, the SDK Location should be filled with the Android SDK path.

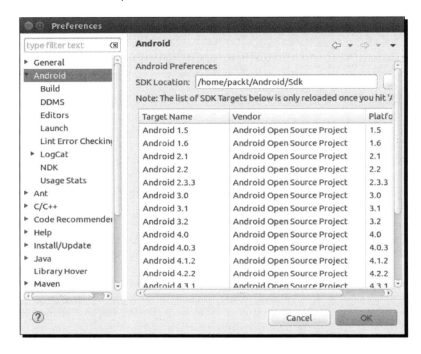

Then, on the same window, go to **Android | NDK**. The **NDK Location** field should be empty. Fill it with the Android NDK path and validate. If the path is wrong, Eclipse complains that the directory is not valid.

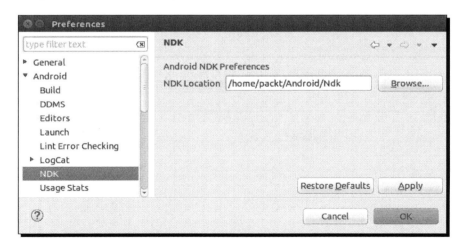

What just happened?

Eclipse is now up and running with the appropriate SDK and NDK configuration. Since the ADT package is no longer provided by Google, the Android development plugin ADT and the C/C++ Eclipse plugin CDT have to be installed manually in Eclipse.

Please note that Eclipse has been deprecated by Google and replaced by Android Studio. Sadly, Android Studio C/C++ and NDK support is rather limited for the moment. The only way to build native code is through Gradle, the new Android build system, whose NDK features are still unstable. If a comfortable IDE is essential to you, you can still use Android Studio for Java development and Eclipse for C/C++ though.

If you work on Windows, maybe you are Visual Studio adept. In that case, I advise you that a few projects, shown as follows, bring Android NDK development to Visual Studio:

- ◆ Android++, which is a free extension for Visual Studio that can be found at `http://android-plus-plus.com/`. Although still in Beta at the time this book is written, Android++ looks quite promising.

- ◆ NVidia Nsight, which can be downloaded with a developer account from the Nvidia developer website at `https://developer.nvidia.com/nvidia-nsight-tegra` (if you have a Tegra device). It packages together the NDK, a slightly customized version of Visual Studio, and a nice debugger.

- ◆ VS-Android, which can be found at `https://github.com/gavinpugh/vs-android`, is an interesting Open Source project, which brings NDK tools to Visual Studio.

Our development environment is now almost ready. The last piece is missing though: an environment to run and test our applications.

Setting up the Android emulator

The Android SDK provides an emulator to help developers who want to speed up their deploy-run-test cycle or want to test, for example, different kinds of resolutions and OS versions. Let's see how to set it up.

Time for action – creating an Android virtual device

The Android SDK provides everything we need to easily create a new emulator **Android Virtual Device (AVD)**:

1. Open **Android SDK Manager** from a terminal by running the following command:

```
android
```

2. Go to **Tools | Manage AVDs...**. Alternatively, click on the dedicated **Android Virtual Device Manager** button in the main toolbar of Eclipse.

   Then, click on the **New** button to create a new Android emulator instance. Fill the form with the following information and click on **OK**:

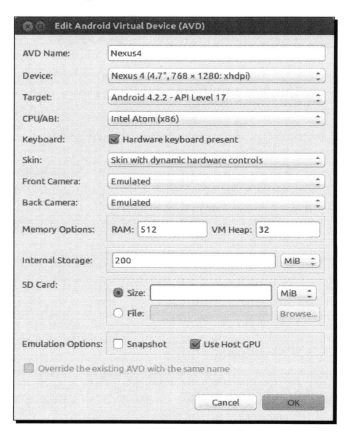

3. The newly created virtual device now appears in the **Android Virtual Device Manager** list. Select it and click on **Start...**.

If you get an error related to libGL on Linux, open a command prompt and run the following command to install the Mesa graphics library: sudo apt-get install libgl1-mesa-dev.

4. The **Launch Options** window appears. Tweak the display size depending on your screen size if needed and then click on **Launch**. The emulator starts up and after some time, your virtual device is loaded:

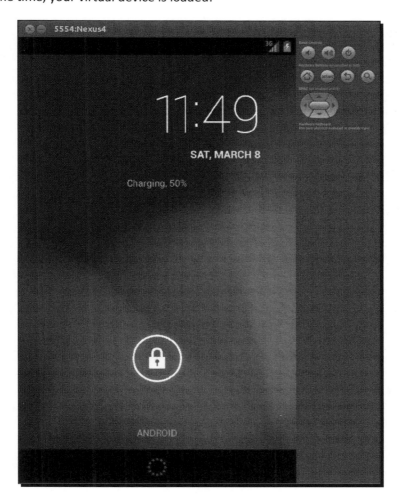

5. By default, the emulator SD card is read only. Although this is optional, you can set it in write mode by issuing the following command from a prompt:

```
adb shell
su
mount -o rw,remount rootfs /
chmod 777 /mnt/sdcard
exit
```

What just happened?

Android emulators can be easily managed through the Android Virtual Device manager. We are now able to test the applications we will develop in a representative environment. Even better, we can now test them in several conditions and resolutions without requiring a costly device. However, if emulators are useful development tools, take into account that emulation is not always perfectly representative and lacks some features, especially hardware sensors, which can be partially emulated.

Android Virtual Device manager is not the only place where we can manage emulators. We can also use the command-line tool emulator provided with the Android SDK. For example, to launch the Nexus4 emulator created earlier directly from a terminal prompt, enter the following:

```
emulator -avd Nexus4
```

While creating the Nexus4 AVD, acute readers might have been surprised to see we set CPU/ABI to Intel Atom (x86), whereas most Android devices run on ARM processors. Indeed, since Windows, OS X, and Linux all run on x86, only x86 Android emulator images can benefit from hardware and GPU acceleration. On the other hand, ARM ABI can run rather slow without it, but it may be more representative of the devices your application may run on.

 To benefit from full hardware acceleration with an X86 AVD, you will need to install the Intel **Hardware Accelerated Execution Manager (HAXM)** on your Windows or Mac OS X system. On Linux, you can install KVM instead. These programs can work only if your CPU benefits from a Virtualization Technology (which is the case most of the time nowadays).

Acuter readers may be even more surprised that we have not selected the latest Android platform. The reason is simply that x86 images are not available for all Android platforms.

 The Snapshot option allows saving the emulator state before closing it. Sadly, this open is incompatible with GPU acceleration. You have to select either one.

As a final note, know that customizing additional options, such as the presence of a GPS, camera, and so on, is also possible when creating an AVD to test an application in limited hardware conditions. The screen orientation can be switched with *Ctrl + F11* and *Ctrl + F12* shortcuts. For more information on how to use and configure the emulator, check out the Android website at http://developer.android.com/tools/devices/emulator.html.

Developing with an Android device

Although emulators can be of help, they are obviously nothing compared to a real device. So, take your Android device in hand, switch it on and let's try to connect it to our development platform. Any of the following steps may change depending on your manufacturer and phone language. So, please refer to your device documentation for specific instructions.

Time for action – setting up an Android device

Device configuration is dependent on your target OS. To do so:

1. Configure your device driver on your OS if applicable:

    ❑ If you use Windows, installation of a development device is manufacturer-specific. More information can be found at `http://developer.android.com/tools/extras/oem-usb.html` with a full list of device manufacturers. If you have a driver CD with your Android device, you can use it. Note that the Android SDK also contains some Windows drivers under `$ANDROID_SDK\extras\google\usb_driver`. Specific instructions are available for Google development phones, Nexus One, and Nexus S at `http://developer.android.com/sdk/win-usb.html`.

    ❑ If you use OS X, simply connecting your development device to your Mac should be enough to get it working! Your device should be recognized immediately without installing anything. Mac's ease of use is not a legend.

    ❑ If you are a Linux user, connecting your development device to your Distribution (at least on Ubuntu) should be enough to get it working too!

2. If your mobile device runs Android 4.2 or later, from the application list screen, go to **Settings | About phone** and tap several times on **Build Number** at the end of the list. After some efforts, **Developer options** will magically appear in your application list screen.

    On Android 4.1 devices and earlier, **Developer options** should be visible by default.

3. Still on your device, from the application list screen, go to **Settings | Developer options** and enable **Debugging** and **Stay awake**.

4. Plug your device into your computer using a data connection cable. Beware! Some cables are charge-only cables and will not work for development! Depending on your device manufacturer, it may appear as a USB disk.

    On Android 4.2.2 devices and later, a dialog **Allow USB debugging?** appears on the phone screen. Select **Always allow from this computer** to permanently allow debugging and then click on **OK**.

5. Open Command Prompt and execute the following:

   ```
   adb devices
   ```

```
packt@computer: ~
List of devices attached
HT03VPL07956     device
```

On Linux, if **?????????** appears instead of your device name (which is likely), then `adb` does not have proper access rights. A solution might be to restart `adb` as root (at your own risk!):

```
sudo $ANDROID_SDK/platform-tools/adb kill-server
```

```
sudo $ANDROID_SDK/platform-tools/adb devices
```

Another solution to find your Vendor ID and Product ID may be needed. Vendor ID is a fixed value for each manufacturer that can be found on the Android developer website at `http://developer.android.com/tools/device.html` (for example, HTC is `0bb4`). The device's Product ID can be found using the result of the `lsusb` command in which we look for the Vendor ID (for example, here 0c87 is HTC Desire product ID):

```
lsusb | grep 0bb4
```

```
packt@computer: ~
Bus 002 Device 007: ID 0bb4:0c87 HTC (High Tech Computer Corp.) Desire (debug)
```

Then, with root privilege, create a file `/etc/udev/rules.d/51-android.rules` with your Vendor ID and Product ID and change file rights to 644:

```
sudo sh -c 'echo SUBSYSTEM==\"usb\", SYSFS{idVendor}==\"<Your
Vendor ID>\", ATTRS{idProduct}=\"<Your Product ID>\",
GROUP=\"plugdev\", MODE=\"0666\" > /etc/udev/rules.d/52-
android.rules'
```

```
sudo chmod 644 /etc/udev/rules.d/52-android.rules
```

Finally, restart the `udev` service and `adb`:

```
sudo service udev restart
```

```
adb kill-server
```

```
adb devices
```

6. Launch Eclipse and open the **DDMS** perspective (**Window | Open Perspective | Other...**). If working properly, your phone should be listed in the **Devices** view.

> Eclipse is a compound of many views, such as the Package Explorer View, the Debug View, and so on. Usually, most of them are already visible, but sometimes they are not. In that case, open them through the main menu by navigating to **Window | Show View | Other...**. Views in Eclipse are grouped in **Perspectives**, which store workspace layout. They can be opened by going to **Window | Open Perspective | Other...**. Beware that some contextual menus may be available only in some perspectives.

What just happened?

Our Android device has been switched into development mode and connected to our workstation through the Android Debug Bridge daemon. ADB gets started automatically the first time it is called, either from Eclipse or the command line.

We also enabled the **Stay awake** option to stop automatic screen shutdown when the phone charges, or when developing with it! And, more important than anything, we discovered that HTC means High Tech Computer! Jokes apart, connection process can be tricky on Linux, although little trouble should be encountered nowadays.

Still having trouble with a reluctant Android device? That could mean any of the following:

◆ ADB is malfunctioning. In that case, restart the ADB deamon or execute it with administrative privilege.

◆ Your development device is not working properly. In that case, try restarting your device or disabling and re-enabling development mode. If that still does not work, then buy another one or use the emulator.

◆ Your host system is not properly set up. In that case, check your device manufacturer instructions carefully to make sure the necessary driver is correctly installed. Check hardware properties to see whether it is recognized and turn on USB storage mode (if applicable) to see whether it is properly detected. Please refer to your device documentation.

> When the charge-only mode is activated, SD card files and directories are visible to the Android applications installed on your phone but not to your computer. On the opposite side, when disk drive mode is activated, those are visible only from your computer. Check your connection mode when your application cannot access its resource files on an SD card.

More about ADB

ADB is a multi-facet tool which is used as a mediator between the development environment and devices. It is composed of:

- ◆ A background process running on emulators and devices to receive orders or requests from your workstation.

- ◆ A background server on your workstation communicating with connected devices and emulators. When listing devices, the ADB server is involved. When debugging, the ADB server is involved. When any communication with a device happens, the ADB server is involved!

- ◆ A client running on your workstation and communicating with devices through the ADB server. The ADB client is what we interacted with to list devices.

ADB offers many useful options among which some are in the following table:

Command	Description
`adb help`	To get an exhaustive help with all options and flags available
`adb bugreport`	To print the whole device state
`adb devices`	To list all Android devices currently connected including emulators
`adb install [-r] <apk path>`	To install an application package. Append `-r` to reinstall an already deployed application and keep its data
`adb kill-server`	To terminate the ADB daemon
`adb pull <device path> <local path>`	To transfer a file to your computer
`adb push <local path> <device path>`	To transfer a file to your device or emulator
`adb reboot`	To restart an Android device programmatically
`adb shell`	To start a shell session on an Android device (more on this in *Chapter 2, Starting a Native Android Project*)
`adb start-server`	To launch the ADB daemon
`adb wait-for-device`	To sleep until a device or emulator is connected to your computer (for example, in a script)

ADB also provides optional flags to target a specific device when several are connected simultaneously:

`-s <device id>`	To target a specific device by its name (device name can be found with adb devices)
`-d`	To target the current physical device if only one is connected (or an error message is raised)
`-e`	To target the currently running emulator if only one is connected (or an error message is raised)

For example, to dump the emulator state when a device is connected at the same time, execute the following command:

```
adb -e bugreport
```

This is only an overview of what ADB can do. More information can be found on the Android developer website at `http://developer.android.com/tools/help/adb.html`.

Summary

Setting up our Android development platform is a bit tedious but is hopefully performed once and for all!

In summary, we installed all the prerequisite packages on our system. Some of them are specific to the target OS, such as Cygwin on Windows, Developer Tools on OS X, or build-essential packages on Linux. Then, we installed the Android Studio bundle, which contains both the Android Studio IDE and the Android SDK. The Android NDK has to be downloaded and set up separately.

Even if we will not use it much throughout this book, Android Studio remains one of the best choices for pure Java development. It is guaranteed to be maintained by Google and may become a good choice when Gradle NDK's integration gets more mature.

Meanwhile, the simplest solution is to go with Eclipse for NDK development. We installed Eclipse with the ADT and CDT plugin. These plugins integrate well together. They allow combining the power of Android Java and native C/C++ code into one single IDE.

Finally, we launched an Android emulator and connected an Android device to our development platform through the Android Debug Bridge.

 With the Android NDK being "open", anybody can build its own version. The Crystax NDK is a special NDK package built by Dmitry Moskalchuk. It brings advanced features unsupported by the NDK (latest toolchains, Boost out of the box... exceptions were first supported by the CrystaxNDK). Advanced users can find it on the Crystax website at https://www.crystax. net/en/android/ndk.

We now have the necessary tools in our hands to shape our mobile ideas. In the next chapter, we will tame them to create, compile, and deploy our first Android project!

2

Starting a Native Android Project

A man with the most powerful tools in hand is unarmed without the knowledge of their usage. Make, GCC, Ant, Bash, Eclipse...—any new Android programmer needs to deal with this technological ecosystem. Luckily, some of these names may already sound familiar. Indeed, Android is based on many open source components, laid together by the Android Development Kits and their specific tool-set: ADB, AAPT, AM, NDK-Build, NDK-GDB... Mastering them will give us the power to create, build, deploy and debug our own Android applications.

Before diving deeper into native code in the next chapter, let's discover these tools by starting a new concrete Android project that includes native C/C++ code. Despite Android Studio being the new official Android IDE, its lack of support for native code encourages us to focus mainly on Eclipse.

Therefore, in this chapter, we are going to:

- ◆ Build an official sample application and deploy it on an Android device
- ◆ Create our first native Android project using Eclipse
- ◆ Interface Java with C/C++ using Java Native Interfaces
- ◆ Debug a native Android application
- ◆ Analyze a native crash dump
- ◆ Set up a Gradle project with native code

By the end of this chapter, you should know how to start a new native Android project on your own.

Building NDK sample applications

The simplest way to get started with your new Android development environment is to compile and deploy some of the samples provided with the Android NDK. A possible (and *polygonful*!) choice is the **San Angeles** demo, created in 2004 by Jetro Lauha and later ported to OpenGL ES (more information at `http://jet.ro/visuals/4k-intros/san-angeles-observation/`).

Time for action – compiling and deploying San Angeles sample

Let's use Android SDK and NDK tools to build a working APK:

1. Open a command-line prompt and go to the San Angeles sample directory inside the Android NDK. All further steps have to be performed from this directory.

    Generate San Angeles project files with the `android` command:

    ```
    cd $ANDROID_NDK/samples/san-angeles
    android update project -p ./
    ```

    ```
    packt@computer: ~/android/ndk/samples/san-angeles
    packt@computer:~/android/ndk/samples/san-angeles$ android update project -p ./
    Updated and renamed default.properties to project.properties
    Updated local.properties
    No project name specified, using Activity name 'DemoActivity'.
    If you wish to change it, edit the first line of build.xml.
    Added file ./build.xml
    Added file ./proguard-project.txt
    ```

    You may get the following error upon executing this command:

    `Error: The project either has no target set or the target is invalid.`

    `Please provide a --target to the 'android update' command.`

    This means that you have not installed all the Android SDK platforms as specified in *Chapter 1, Setting Up Your Environment*. In which case, either install them using the `Android manager tool` or specify your own project target, for example, `android update project --target 18 -p ./`.

2. Compile San Angeles native library with `ndk-build`:

```
packt@computer: ~/android/ndk/samples/san-angeles
Updated and renamed default.properties to project.properties
Updated local.properties
No project name specified, using Activity name 'DemoActivity'.
If you wish to change it, edit the first line of build.xml.
Added file ./build.xml
Added file ./proguard-project.txt
```

3. Build and package San Angeles application in **Debug** mode:

```
ant debug
```

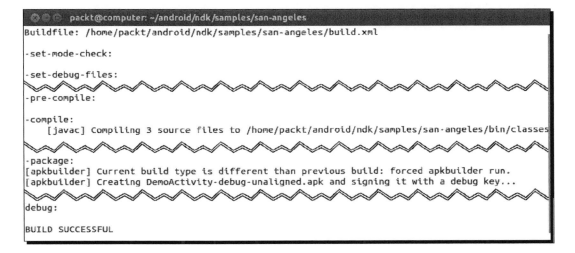

```
packt@computer: ~/android/ndk/samples/san-angeles
Buildfile: /home/packt/android/ndk/samples/san-angeles/build.xml

-set-mode-check:

-set-debug-files:

-pre-compile:

-compile:
    [javac] Compiling 3 source files to /home/packt/android/ndk/samples/san-angeles/bin/classes

-package:
[apkbuilder] Current build type is different than previous build: forced apkbuilder run.
[apkbuilder] Creating DemoActivity-debug-unaligned.apk and signing it with a debug key...

debug:

BUILD SUCCESSFUL
```

4. Make sure your Android device is connected or the emulator is started. Then deploy the generated package:

```
ant installd
```

```
packt@computer: ~/android/ndk/samples/san-angeles
File Edit View Search Terminal Help
Buildfile: /opt/android-ndk/samples/san-angeles/build.xml

-set-mode-check:

-set-debug-files:

install:
     [echo] Installing /opt/android-ndk/samples/san-angeles/bin/DemoActivity-debug.apk onto
default emulator or device...
     [exec] 480 KB/s (20341 bytes in 0.041s)
     [exec]     pkg: /data/local/tmp/DemoActivity-debug.apk
     [exec] Success

installd:

BUILD SUCCESSFUL
Total time: 4 seconds
```

5. Launch SanAngeles application on your device or emulator:

```
adb shell am start -a android.intent.action.MAIN -n
com.example.SanAngeles/com.example.SanAngeles.DemoActivity
```

```
packt@computer: ~/android/ndk/samples/san-angeles
Starting: Intent { act=android.intent.action.MAIN cmp=com.example.SanAngeles/.DemoActivity }
```

Downloading the example code

You can download the example code files from your account at
http://www.packtpub.com for all the Packt Publishing
books you have purchased. If you purchased this book
elsewhere, you can visit http://www.packtpub.com/
support and register to have the files e-mailed directly to you.

What just happened?

The old-school San Angeles demo, full of flat-shaded polygons and nostalgia, is now running on your device. With only a few command lines, involving most of the tools needed for the Android development, a full application including native C/C++ code has been generated, compiled, built, packaged, deployed, and launched.

Let's see this process in detail.

Generating project files with Android manager

We generated project files from an existing code base thanks to the Android manager. The following bullet points give more information regarding this process:

◆ `build.xml`: This is the Ant file that describes how to compile and package the final application APK file (which stands for *Android PacKage*). This build file contains mainly links to properties and core Android Ant build files.

◆ `local.properties`: This file contains the Android SDK location. Every time your SDK location changes, this file should be regenerated.

◆ `proguard-project.txt`: This file contains a default configuration for **Proguard**, a code optimizer and obfuscator for Java code. More information about it can be found at `http://developer.android.com/tools/help/proguard.html`.

♦ `project.properties`: This file contains the application target Android SDK version. This file is generated by default from a pre-existing `default.properties` file in the `project` directory. If no `default.properties` exists, then an additional `-target <API Target>` flag (for example, `--target 4` for Android 4 Donut) must be appended to the `android create` command.

> Target SDK version is different from the minimum SDK version. The first version describes the latest Android version for which an application is built, whereas the latter indicates the minimum Android version on which the application is allowed to run. Both can be declared optionally in `AndroidManifest.xml` file (clause `<uses-sdk>`) but only the target SDK version is "duplicated" in `project.properties`.

> When creating an Android application, choose carefully the minimum and target Android API you want to support, as this can dramatically change your application capabilities as well as your audience wideness. Indeed, as a result of fragmentation, targets tend to move a lot and faster in Android!
>
> An application that does not target the latest Android version does not mean it will not run on it. However, it will not have access to all the latest features nor all of the latest optimizations.

The Android manager is the main entry point for an Android developer. Its responsibilities are bound to SDK version updates, virtual devices management, and projects management. They can be listed exhaustively from the command line by executing `android -help`. Since we have already looked at SDK and AVD management in *Chapter 1, Setting Up Your Environment*, let's focus on its project management capabilities:

1. `android create project` allows creating new Android projects ex-nihilo from the command line. Generated projects contain only Java files but no NDK-related files. A few additional options must be specified to allow for proper generation, such as:

Option	Description
`-a`	Main activity name
`-k`	Application package
`-n`	Project name
`-p`	Project path
`-t`	Target SDK version
`-g` and `-v`	To generate Gradle build file instead of Ant and specifying its plugin version

An example of command line to create a new project is as follows:

```
android create project -p ./MyProjectDir -n MyProject -t android-8
-k com.mypackage -a MyActivity
```

2. `android update project` creates project files from existing sources, as shown in the previous tutorial. However, if they already exist it can also upgrade the project target to new SDK versions (that is, the `project.properties` file) and update the Android SDK location (that is, the `local.properties` file). The available flags are slightly different:

Option	Description
-l	Library projects to add
-n	Project name
-p	Project path
-t	Target SDK version
-s	To update projects in subfolders

We can also append a new library project with the -l flag, for example:

```
android update project -p ./ -l ../MyLibraryProject
```

3. `android create lib-project` and `android update lib-project` manage library projects. These kinds of projects are not well adapted for native C/C++ development, especially when it comes to debugging, since NDK has its own way of reusing native libraries.

4. `android create test-project`, `android update test-project`, and `android create uitest-project` manage unit test and UI test projects.

More details about all these options can be found on the Android developer website at `http://developer.android.com/tools/help/android.html`.

Compiling native code with NDK-Build

After generating project files, we then compile our first native C/C++ library (also called *module*) using `ndk-build`. This command, the most essential one to know for NDK development, is basically a Bash script, which:

♦ Sets up the Android native compilation toolchain based on either GCC or CLang.

♦ Wraps `Make` to control native code construction with the help of user-defined `Makefiles`: `Android.mk` and optional `Application.mk`. By default, NDK-

♦ `Build` looks for in the `jni` project directory, where native C/C++ are often located by convention.

NDK-Build generates intermediate object files from C/C++ source files (in the `obj` directory) and produces the final binary library (`.so`) in the `libs` directory. NDK-related build files can be erased with the following command:

```
ndk-build clean
```

For more information about NDK-Build and Makefiles, see *Chapter 9*, *Porting Existing Libraries to Android*.

Building and packaging an application with Ant

An Android application is not composed of native C/C++ code only, but also of Java code. Thus, we have:

◆ Built Java sources located in the `src` directory with `Javac`(Java Compiler).

◆ Dexed generated Java bytecode, that is, transforming it into Android Dalvik or ART bytecode with DX. Indeed, both Dalvik and ART Virtual Machines (more about these later in this chapter) operate on a specific bytecode, which is stored in an optimized format called **Dex**.

◆ Packaged Dex files, Android manifest, resources (images, and so on), and native libraries in the final APK file with AAPT, also known as the **Android Asset Packaging Tool**.

All these operations are summarized in one call to Ant: `ant debug`. The result is an APK packaged in debug mode and generated in the `bin` directory. Other build modes are available (for example, release mode) and can be listed with `ant help`. If you would like to erase temporary Java-related build files (for example, the `Java .class`), then simply run the following command line:

```
ant clean
```

Deploying an application package with Ant

A packaged application can be deployed as is with Ant through **ADB**. The available options for deployment are as follows:

◆ `ant installd` for debug mode
◆ `ant installr` for release mode

Beware that an APK cannot overwrite an older APK of the same application if they come from a different source. In such a case, remove the previous application first by executing the following command line:

```
ant uninstall
```

Installation and uninstallation can also be performed directly through ADB, for example:

- ◆ adb install <path to application APK>: For installing an application for the first time (for example, bin/DemoActivity-debug.apk for our sample).

- ◆ adb install -r <path to application APK>: For reinstalling an application and to keep its data stored on the device.

- ◆ adb uninstall <application package name>: For uninstalling an application identified by its Application package name (for example, com.example.SanAngeles for our sample).

Launching an application with ADB Shell

Finally, we launched the application thanks to the **Activity Manager** (**AM**). AM command parameters that are used to start San Angeles come from the AndroidManifest.xml file:

- ◆ com.example.SanAngeles is the application package name (the same we use to uninstall an application as previously shown).

- ◆ com.example.SanAngeles.DemoActivity is the launched Activity canonical class name (that is, a simple class name concatenated to its package). Here is a brief example of how these are used:

```
<?xml version="1.0" encoding="utf-8"?>
<manifest xmlns:android="http://schemas.android.com/apk/res/android"
       package="com.example.SanAngeles"
       android:versionCode="1"
       android:versionName="1.0">
...
       <activity android:name=".DemoActivity"
                android:label="@string/app_name">
```

Because it is located on your device, AM needs to be run through ADB. To do so, the latter features a limited Unix-like shell, which features some classic commands such as ls, cd, pwd, cat, chmod, or ps as well as a few Android specific ones as shown in the following table:

am	The Activity Manager which not only starts Activities but can also kill them, broadcast intent, start/stop profiler, and so on.
dmesg	To dump kernel messages.
dumpsys	To dump the system state.
logcat	To display device log messages.

run-as <user id> <command>	To run a command with the user id privilege. user id can be an application package name, which gives access to application files (for example, run-as com.example.SanAngeles ls).
sqlite3 <db file>	To open an SQLite Database (it can be combined with run-as).

ADB can be started in one of the following ways:

◆ With a command in parameter, as shown in step 5 with AM, in which case Shell runs a single command and immediately exits.

◆ With the adb shell command without a parameter, in which case you can use it as a classic Shell (and, for example, call am and any other command).

ADB Shell is a real '*Swiss Army knife*', which allows advanced manipulations on your device, especially with the root access. For example, it becomes possible to observe applications deployed in their "sandbox" directory (that is, the /data/data directory) or to list and kill the currently running processes. Without root access to your phone, possible actions are more limited. For more information, have a look at http://developer.android.com/tools/help/adb.html.

If you know a bit about the Android ecosystem, you may have heard about rooted phones and non-rooted phones. **Rooting** a phone means getting administrative privilege, generally using hacks. Rooting a phone is useful to install a custom ROM version (optimized or modified, for example, **Cyanogen**) or to perform any sort of (especially dangerous) manipulations that a root user can do (for example, accessing and deleting any file). Rooting is not an illegal operation as such, as you are modifying YOUR device. However, not all manufacturers appreciate this practice, which usually voids the warranty.

More about Android tooling

Building San Angeles sample application gives you a glimpse of what Android tools can do. However, behind their somewhat 'rustic' look, more is possible. Information can be found on the Android developer website at http://developer.android.com/tools/help/index.html.

Creating your first native Android project

In the first part of the chapter, we saw how to use Android command-line tools. However, developing with Notepad or VI is not really attractive. Coding should be fun! And to make it so, we need our preferred IDE to perform boring or unpractical tasks. So now we will see how to create a native Android project using Eclipse.

 The resulting project is provided with this book under the name Store_Part1.

Time for action – creating a native Android project

Eclipse provides a wizard to help us set up our project:

1. Launch Eclipse. In the main menu, go to **File** | **New** | **Project**....

2. Then, in the opened **New project** wizard, **go to Android | Android Application Project** and click on **Next**.

3. In the next screen, enter project properties as follows and click on **Next** again:

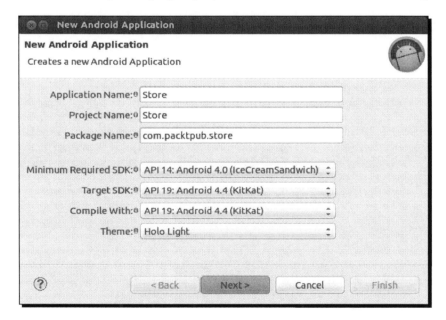

4. Click on **Next** twice, leaving default options, to go to the **Create activity** wizard screen. Select **Blank activity with Fragment** and click on **Next**.

5. Finally, in the **Blank Activity** screen, enter activity properties as follows:

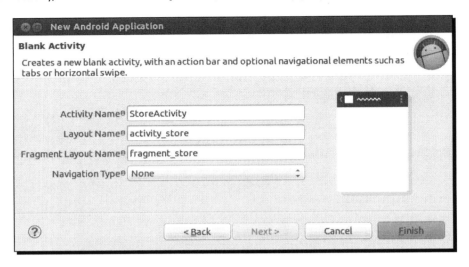

6. Click on **Finish** to validate. After a few seconds, the wizard disappears and the project **Store** is displayed in Eclipse.

7. Add native C/C++ support to the project. Select the project **Store** in the **Package Explorer** view and from its right-click context menu, go to **Android Tools | Add Native Support...**.

8. In the opened **Add Android Native Support** popup, set the library name to com_packtpub_store_Store and click on **Finish**.

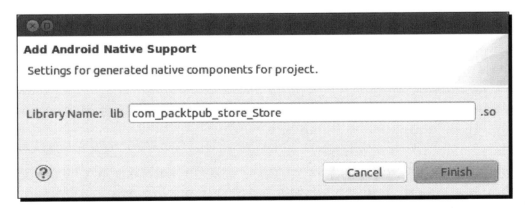

9. The `jni` and `obj` directories are created in the project directory. The first directory contains one makefile `Android.mk` and one C++ source file `com_packtpub_store_Store.cpp`.

 After adding native support, Eclipse may automatically switch your perspective to C/C++. Therefore, in case your development environment does not look as usual, simply check your perspective in the Eclipse's top-right corner. You can work on an NDK project from either a Java or C/C++ perspective without any trouble.

10. Create a new Java class `Store` in `src/com/packtpub/store/Store.java`. From within a static block, load the `com_packtpub_store_Store` native library:

```
package com.packtpub.store;

public class Store {
    static {
        System.loadLibrary("com_packtpub_store_Store");
    }
}
```

11. Edit `src/com/packtpub/store/StoreActivity.java`. Declare and initialize a new instance of `Store` in activity's `onCreate()`. Since we do not need them, remove the `onCreateOptionsMenu()` and `onOptionsItemSelected()` methods that may have been created by the Eclipse project creation wizard:

```
package com.packtpub.store;
...
public class StoreActivity extends Activity {
    private Store mStore = new Store();

    @Override
    protected void onCreate(Bundle savedInstanceState) {
        super.onCreate(savedInstanceState);
        setContentView(R.layout.activity_store);

        if (savedInstanceState == null) {
            getFragmentManager().beginTransaction()
                            .add(R.id.container,
                                new PlaceholderFragment())
                            .commit();
        }
```

```
        }

        public static class PlaceholderFragment extends Fragment {
            public PlaceholderFragment() {
            }

            @Override
            public View onCreateView(LayoutInflater inflater,
                                     ViewGroup container,
                                     Bundle savedInstanceState)
            {
                View rootView = inflater.inflate(R.layout.fragment_store,
                                                 container, false);
                return rootView;
            }
        }
    }
```

12. Connect your device or emulator and launch the application. Select `Store` in the **Package Explorer** view and then navigate to **Run | Run As | Android Application** from the Eclipse main menu. Alternatively, click on the **Run** button in the Eclipse toolbar.

13. Select the application type **Android Application** and click on **OK** to get the following screen:

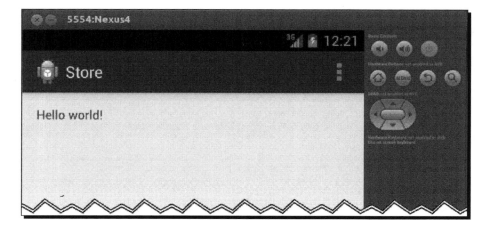

What just happened?

In only a few steps, our first native Android project has been created and launched thanks to Eclipse.

1. The Android project creation wizard helps get you started quickly. It generates the minimum code for a simple Android application. However, by default, new Android projects support Java and only Java.

2. With the help of ADT, an Android Java project is easily turned into a hybrid project with native C/C++ support. It generates the minimum files necessary for an NDK-Build to compile a native library:

    `Android.mk` is a Makefile describing which source files to compile and how to generate the final native library.

    `com_packtpub_store_Store.cpp` is an almost empty file containing a single include. We are going to explain this in the next part of this chapter.

3. Once the project is set up, dynamically loading a native library is done in a single call to `System.loadLibrary()`. This is easily done in a static block, which ensures that the library is loaded once and for all, before a class is initialized. Beware that this works only if the container class is loaded from a single Java ClassLoader (which is usually the case).

Working with an IDE like Eclipse really offers a huge productivity boost and makes programming much more comfortable! But if you are a command-line aficionado or would like to train your command-line skills, the first part, *Building NDK sample applications*, can easily be applied here.

Introducing Dalvik and ART

It is not possible to talk about Android without mentioning a few words about **Dalvik** and **ART**.

Dalvik is a **Virtual Machine** on which the Dex bytecode is interpreted (not native code!). It is at the core of any application running on Android. Dalvik has been conceived to fit the constrained requirements of mobile devices. It is specifically optimized to use less memory and CPU. It sits on top of the Android kernel, which provides the first layer of abstraction over the hardware (process management, memory management, and so on).

ART is the new Android runtime environment, which has replaced Dalvik since the Android 5 Lollipop. It has improved performances a lot compared to Dalvik. Indeed, where Dalvik interprets bytecode `Just-In-Time` upon application startup, ART, on the other hand, precompiles bytecode `Ahead-Of-Time` into native code during application installation. ART is backward compatible with applications packaged for former Dalvik VMs.

Android has been designed with speed in mind. Because most users do not want to wait for their application to be loaded while others are still running, the system is able to instantiate multiple Dalvik or ART VMs quickly, thanks to the **Zygote** process. Zygote, (whose name comes from the very first biologic cell of an organism from which daughter cells get reproduced), starts when the system boots up. It preloads (or "warms up") all core libraries shared among applications as well as the Virtual Machine instance. To launch a new application, Zygote is simply forked and the initial Dalvik instance gets copied as a consequence. Memory consumption is lowered by sharing as many libraries as possible between processes.

Dalvik and ART are themselves made of native C/C++ code compiled for the target Android platform (ARM, X86, and so on). This means that interfacing these VMs with native C/C++ libraries is easily possible provided that it is compiled with the same **Application Binary Interface (ABI)** (which basically describes the application or library binary format). This is the role devoted to the Android NDK. For more information, have a look at the **Android Open Source Project (AOSP)**, that is, the Android source code at `https://source.android.com/`.

Interfacing Java with C/C++

Native C/C++ code has the ability to unleash the power of your application. To do so, Java code needs to invoke and run its native counterpart. In this part, we are going to interface Java and native C/C++ code together.

 The resulting project is provided with this book under the name `Store_Part2`.

Time for action – calling C code from Java

Let's create our first native method and call it from the Java side:

1. Open `src/com/packtpub/store/Store.java` and declare one native method to query the `Store`. This method returns `int` with the number of entries in it. There is no need to define a method body:

```java
package com.packtpub.store;

public class Store {
    static {
        System.loadLibrary("com_packtpub_store_Store");
    }

    public native int getCount();
}
```

2. Open `src/com/packtpub/store/StoreActivity.java` and initialize the store. Use its `getCount()` method value to initialize the application title:

```java
public class StoreActivity extends Activity {
    ...
    public static class PlaceholderFragment extends Fragment {
        private Store mStore = new Store();
    ...
        public PlaceholderFragment() {
        }

        @Override
        public View onCreateView(LayoutInflater inflater,
                                 ViewGroup container,
                                 Bundle savedInstanceState)
        {
            View rootView = inflater.inflate(R.layout.fragment_store,
                                             container, false);
            updateTitle();
            return rootView;
        }

        private void updateTitle() {
            int numEntries = mStore.getCount();
            getActivity().setTitle(String.format("Store (%1$s)",
                                                 numEntries));
        }
    }
}
```

3. Generate a JNI header file from the `Store` class. Go to the Eclipse main menu and go to **Run | External Tools | External Tools Configurations...**. Create a new **Program** configuration with the following parameters described in the following screenshot:

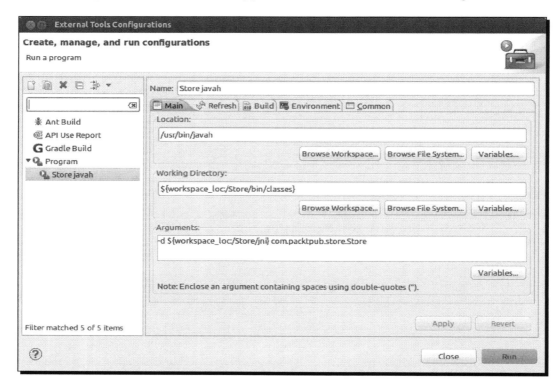

Location refers to the `javah` absolute path, which is OS specific. On Windows, you can enter `${env_var:JAVA_HOME}\bin\javah.exe`. On Mac OS X and Linux, it is usually `/usr/bin/javah`.

4. In the **Refresh** tab, check **Refresh resources upon completion** and select **Specific resources**. Using the **Specify Resources...** button, select the `jni` folder. Finally, click on **Run** to execute `javah`. A new file `jni/com_packtpub_store_Store.h` will then be generated. This contains a prototype for the native method `getCount()` expected on the Java side:

```
/* DO NOT EDIT THIS FILE - it is machine generated */
#include <jni.h>
/* Header for class com_packtpub_store_Store */

#ifndef _Included_com_packtpub_store_Store
```

```
#define _Included_com_packtpub_store_Store
#ifdef __cplusplus
extern "C" {
#endif
/*
 * Class:      com_packtpub_store_Store
 * Method:     getCount
 * Signature:  ()I
 */
JNIEXPORT jint JNICALL Java_com_packtpub_store_Store_getCount
  (JNIEnv *, jobject);

#ifdef __cplusplus
}
#endif
#endif
```

5. We can now implement `jni/com_packtpub_store_Store.cpp` so that it returns `0` when invoked. The method signature originates from the generated header file (you can replace any previous code) except that the parameter names have been explicitly specified:

```
#include "com_packtpub_store_Store.h"

JNIEXPORT jint JNICALL Java_com_packtpub_store_Store_getCount
  (JNIEnv* pEnv, jobject pObject) {
    return 0;
}
```

6. Compile and run the application.

What just happened?

Java now talks C/C++! In the previous part, we created a hybrid Android project. In this part, we interfaced Java with native code. This cooperation is established through **Java Native Interfaces (JNI)**. JNI is the bridge, which binds Java to C/C++. This occurs in three main steps.

Defining native method prototypes on the Java side, marked with the native keyword. Such methods have no body, like an abstract method, because they are implemented on the native side. Native methods can have parameters, a return value, visibility (private, protected, package protected, or public), and can be static: such as the usual Java methods.

Native methods can be called from anywhere in Java code, provided that containing a native library has been loaded before they are called. Failure to do so results in an exception of type `java.lang.UnsatisfiedLinkError`, which is raised when the native method is invoked for the first time.

Using `javah` to generate a header file with corresponding native C/C++ prototypes. Although it is not compulsory, the `javah` tool provided by the JDK is extremely useful to generate native prototypes. Indeed, the JNI convention is tedious and error-prone (more about this in *Chapter 3, Interfacing Java and C/C++ with JNI*). The JNI code is generated from the `.class` file, which means your Java code must be compiled first.

Writing native C/C++ code implementation to perform expected operations. Here, we simply return 0 when the `Store` library is queried. Our native library is compiled in the `libs/armeabi` directory (the one for ARM processors) and is named `libcom_packtpub_store_Store.so`. Temporary files generated during compilation are located in the `obj/local` directory.

Despite its apparent simplicity, interfacing Java with C/C++ is much more involved than what it seems superficially. How to write JNI code on the native side is explored in more detail in *Chapter 3, Interfacing Java and C/C++ with JNI*.

Debugging native Android applications

Before diving deeper into JNI, there is one last important tool that any Android developer needs to know how to use: the **Debugger**. The official NDK one is the GNU Debugger also known as **GDB**.

The resulting project is provided with this book under the name `Store_Part3`.

Time for action – debugging a native Android application

1. Create file `jni/Application.mk` with the following content:

```
APP_PLATFORM := android-14
APP_ABI := armeabi armeabi-v7a x86
```

These are not the only ABIs provided by the NDK; more processor architectures such as MIPS or variants such as 64 bits or hard floats exist. The ones used here are the main ones you should be concerned with. They can easily be tested on an emulator.

2. Open **Project Properties**, go to **C/C++ Build**, uncheck **Use default build command** and enter `ndk-build NDK_DEBUG=1`:

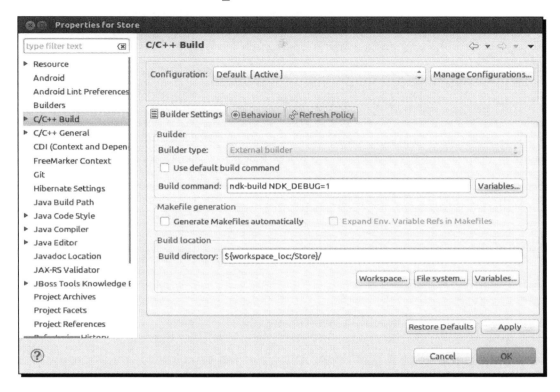

3. In `jni/com_packtpub_store_Store.cpp`, place a breakpoint inside the `Java_com_packtpub_store_Store_getCount()` method by double-clicking on the Eclipse editor gutter.

4. Select the `Store` project in the **Package Explorer** or **Project Explorer** view and go to **Debug As | Android Native Application**. The application starts, but you will probably find that nothing happens. Indeed, the breakpoint is likely to be reached before the GDB Debugger could attach to the application process.

5. Leave the application and reopen it from your device application menu. This time, Eclipse stops at the native breakpoint. Look at your device screen. The UI should be frozen because the main application thread is paused in native code.

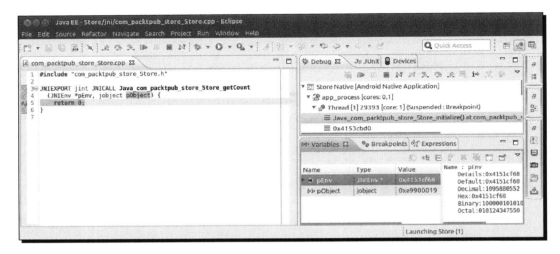

6. Inspect variables in the **Variables** view and check the call stack in the **Debug** view. In the **Expressions** view, enter *pEnv.functions and open result expression to see the various functions provided by the JNIEnv object.

7. **Step Over** current instruction from the Eclipse toolbar or with the shortcut, *F6* (you can also use **Step Into** with the shortcut, *F7*). The following instructions will be highlighted:

  ❑ **Resume** the execution from the Eclipse toolbar or with the shortcut, *F8*. The application screen is displayed on your device again.

  ❑ **Terminate** the application from the Eclipse toolbar or with the shortcut, *Ctrl+F2*. The application is killed and the **Debug** view is emptied.

What just happened?

This useful productivity tool that is a debugger is now an asset in our toolbox. We can easily stop or resume program execution at any point, step into, over or out of native instructions, and inspect any variable. This ability is made available to developers thanks to NDK-GDB, which is a wrapper script around the command-line debugger GDB (which can be cumbersome to use by hand). Hopefully, GDB is supported by Eclipse CDT and by extension Eclipse ADT.

On Android, and more generally on embedded devices, GDB is configured in client/server mode, while a program runs on a device as a server (gdbserver, which is generated by NDK-Build in the libs directory). A remote client, that is, a developer's workstation with Eclipse, connects and sends remote debugging commands to it.

Defining NDK application-wide settings

To help NDK-Build and NDK-GDB do their work, we created a new Application.mk file. This file should be considered as a global Makefile defining application-wide compilation settings, such as the following:

◆ APP_PLATFORM: Android API that the application targets. This information should be a duplication of minSdkVersion in the AndroidManifest.xml file.

◆ APP_ABI: CPU architectures that the application targets. An Application Binary Interface specifies the binary code format (instruction set, calling conventions, and so on) that makes executable and library binaries. ABIs are thus strongly related to processors. ABI can be tweaked with additional settings such as LOCAL_ARM_CODE.

The main ABIs that are currently supported by the Android NDK are as shown in the following table:

armeabi	This is the default option, which should be compatible with all ARM devices. Thumb is a special instruction set that encodes instructions on 16 bits instead of 32 to improve code size (useful for devices with constrained memory). The instruction set is severely restricted compared to ArmEABI.
armeabi **with LOCAL_ARM_CODE = arm**	(Or Arm v5) Should run on all ARM devices. Instructions are encoded on 32 bits but may be more concise than Thumb code. Arm v5 does not support advanced extensions such as floating point acceleration and is thus slower than Arm v7.
armeabi-v7a	Supports extensions such as Thumb-2 (similar to Thumb but with additional 32-bit instructions) and VFP, plus some optional extensions such as NEON. Code compiled for Arm V7 will not run on Arm V5 processors.
armeabi-v7a-hard	This ABI is an extension of the armeabi-v7a that supports hardware floats instead of soft floats.
arm64-v8a	This is dedicated to the new 64-bit processor architecture. 64-bit ARM processors are backward compatible with older ABIs.

x86 and x86_64	For "PC-like" processor architectures (that is, Intel/AMD). These are the ABIs used on the emulator in order to get hardware acceleration on a PC. Although most Android devices are ARM, some of them are now X86-based. The x86 ABI is for 32-bit processors and x86_64 is for 64-bit processors.
mips and mips 64	For processors made by MIPS Technologies, now property of Imagination Technologies well-known for the PowerVR graphics processors. Almost no device uses these at the time of writing this book. The mips ABI is for 32-bit processors and mips64 is for 64-bit processors.
all, all32 and all64	This is a shortcut to build an ndk library for all 32-bit or 64-bit ABIs.

Each library and intermediate object file is recompiled for each ABI. They are stored in their own respective directory which can be found in the `obj` and `libs` folders.

A few more flags can be used inside `Application.mk`. We will discover more about this in detail in *Chapter 9, Porting Existing Libraries to Android*.

The `Application.mk` flags are not the only ones necessary to ensure the NDK debugger work; `NDK_DEBUG=1` must also be passed manually to NDK-Build so that it compiles Debug binaries and generates GDB setup files (`gdb.setup` and `gdbserver`) correctly. Note that this should probably be considered more as a defect in Android development tools rather than a real configuration step, since it should normally handle the debugging flag automatically.

NDK-GDB day-to-day

Debugger support in the NDK and Eclipse is quite recent and has improved a lot among NDK releases (for example, debugging purely native threads was not working before). However, although it is now quite usable, debugging on Android can sometimes be buggy, unstable, and rather slow (because it needs to communicate with the remote Android device).

 NDK-GDB might sometimes appear crazy and stop at a breakpoint with a completely unusual stack trace. This could be related to GDB not being able to correctly determine current ABI while debugging. To fix this issue, put only your corresponding device ABI in the `APP_ABI` clause and remove or comment any other.

NDK Debugger can also be tricky to use, such as when debugging native startup code. Indeed, GDB does not start fast enough to activate breakpoints. A simple way to overcome this problem is to make native code sleep for a few seconds when an application starts. To leave GDB enough time to attach an application process, we can do, for example, the following:

```
#include <unistd.h>
...
sleep(3); // in seconds.
```

Another solution is to launch a Debug session and then simply leave and re-launch the application from your device, as we have seen in the previous tutorial. This is possible because the Android application life cycle is such that an application survives when it is in the background, until the memory is needed. This trick only works if your application does not crash during startup though.

Analyzing native crash dumps

Every developer has one day experienced an unexpected crash in its application. Do not be ashamed, it has happened to all of us. And as a newcomer in Android native development, this situation will happen again, many times. Debuggers are a tremendous tool to look for problems in your code. Sadly, however they work in "real-time", when a program runs. They become sterile with fatal bugs that cannot be reproduced easily. Hopefully, there is a tool for that: **NDK-Stack**. NDK-Stack helps you read a crash dump to analyze an application's stack-trace at the moment it crashed.

 The resulting project is provided with this book under the name `Store_Crash`.

Time for action – analyzing a native crash dump

Let's make our application crash to see how to read a crash dump:

1. Simulate a fatal bug in `jni/com_packtpub_store_Store.cpp`:

```
#include "com_packtpub_store_Store.h"

JNIEXPORT jint JNICALL Java_com_packtpub_store_Store_getCount
  (JNIEnv* pEnv, jobject pObject) {
    pEnv = 0;
    return pEnv->CallIntMethod(0, 0);
}
```

2. Open the **LogCat** view in Eclipse, select the **All Messages (no filter)** option, and then run the application. A crash dump appears in the logs. This is not pretty! If you look carefully through it, you should find a `backtrace` section with a snapshot of the call-stack at the moment the application crashed. However, it does not give the line of code involved:

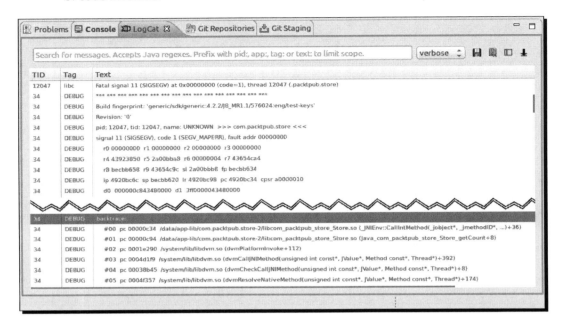

3. From a command-line prompt, go to the project directory. Find the line of code implied in the crash by running NDK-Stack with `logcat` as the input. NDK-Stack needs the `obj` files corresponding to the device ABI on which the application crashed, for example:

```
cd <projet directory>
adb logcat | ndk-stack -sym obj/local/armeabi-v7a
```

```
packt@computer: ~/Project/Store
File Edit View Search Terminal Help
********** Crash dump: **********
Build fingerprint: 'generic/sdk/generic:4.2.2/JB_MR1.1/576024:eng/test-keys'
pid: 1500, tid: 1500, name: UNKNOWN  >>> com.packtpub.store <<<
signal 11 (SIGSEGV), code 1 (SEGV_MAPERR), fault addr 00000000
Stack frame #00  pc 00000c34  /data/app-lib/com.packtpub.store-2/libcom_packtpub_store_Store.so (_JNIEnv
::CallIntMethod(_jobject*, _jmethodID*, ...)+36): Routine _JNIEnv::CallIntMethod(_jobject*, _jmethodID*,
...) at /opt/android-ndk/platforms/android-14/arch-arm/usr/include/jni.h:641
Stack frame #01  pc 00000c94  /data/app-lib/com.packtpub.store-2/libcom_packtpub_store_Store.so (Java_co
m_packtpub_store_Store_initialize+40): Routine Java_com_packtpub_store_Store_getCount at /home/packtpub/
Project/Store/jni/com_packtpub_store_Store.cpp:6
Stack frame #02  pc 0001e290  /system/lib/libdvm.so (dvmPlatformInvoke+112)
Stack frame #03  pc 0004d1f9  /system/lib/libdvm.so (dvmCallJNIMethod(unsigned int const*, JValue*, Meth
od const*, Thread*)+392)
Stack frame #04  pc 00038b45  /system/lib/libdvm.so (dvmCheckCallJNIMethod(unsigned int const*, JValue*,
 Method const*, Thread*)+8)
Stack frame #05  pc 0004f357  /system/lib/libdvm.so (dvmResolveNativeMethod(unsigned int const*, JValue*
, Method const*, Thread*)+174)
```

What just happened?

NDK-Stack utility provided with the Android NDK can help you locate the source of an application crash. This tool is an inestimable help and should be considered as your first-aid kit when a bad crash happens. However, if it can point you toward the *where*, it is another kettle of fish to find out the *why*.

Stack-trace is only a small part of a crash dump. Deciphering the rest of a dump is rarely necessary but understanding its meaning is good for general culture.

Deciphering crash dumps

Crash dumps are not only dedicated to overly talented developers seeing a red-dressed girl in binary code, but also to those who have a minimum knowledge of assemblers and the way processors work. The goal of this trace is to give as much information as possible on the current state of the program at the time it crashed. It contains:

- 1st line: **Build Fingerprint** is a kind of identifier indicating the device/Android release currently running. This information is interesting when analyzing dumps from various origins.

- 3rd line: The **PID** or process identifier uniquely identifies an application on the Unix system, and the **TID**, which is the thread identifier. The thread identifier can be the same as the process identifier when a crash occurs on the main thread.

- 4th line: The crash origin represented as a **Signal** is a classic segmentation fault (**SIGSEGV**).

- ◆ **Processor Register** values. A register holds values or pointers on which the processor can work immediately.

- ◆ **Backtrace** (that is the stack-trace) with the method calls that lead to the crash.

- ◆ **Raw stack** is similar to the backtrace but with stack parameters and variables.

- ◆ Some **Memory Words** around the main register (provided for ARM processors only). The first column indicates memory-line locations, while others columns indicate memory values represented in hexadecimal.

Processor registers are different between processor architectures and versions. ARM processors provide:

rX	**Integer Registers** where a program puts values it works on.
dX	**Floating Point Registers** where a program puts values it works on.
fp (or r11)	**Frame Pointer** holds the current stack frame location during a routine call (in conjunction with the Stack Pointer).
ip (or r12)	**Intra Procedure Call Scratch Register** may be used with some sub-routine calls; for example, when the linker needs a veneer (a small piece of code) to aim at a different memory area when branching. Indeed, a branch instruction to jump somewhere else in memory requires an offset argument relative to the current location, allowing a branching range of a few MB only, not the full memory.
sp (or r13)	**Stack Pointer** holds the location of the top of the stack.
lr (or r14)	**Link Register** saves a program counter value temporarily so that it can restore it later. A typical example of its use is as a function call, which jumps somewhere in the code and then goes back to its previous location. Of course, several chained sub-routine calls require the Link Register to be stacked.
pc (or r15)	**Program Counter** holds the address of the next instruction to be executed. The program counter is just incremented when executing a sequential code to fetch the next instruction but it is altered by branching instructions (if/else, a C/C++ function calls, and so on).
cpsr	**Current Program Status Register** contains a few flags about the current processor working mode and some additional bit flags for condition codes (such as N for an operation that resulted in a negative value, Z for a 0 or equality result, and so on), interrupts, and instruction sets (Thumb or ARM).

 Remember that the use of registers is mainly a convention. For example, Apple iOS uses `r7` as a Frame Pointer instead of `r12` on ARMs. So always be very careful when writing or reusing assembly code!

On the other hand, X86 processors provide:

eax	**Accumulator Register** is used, for example, for arithmetic or I/O operations.
ebx	**Base Register** is a data pointer for memory access.
ecx	**Counter Register** is used for iterative operations such as loop counter.
edx	**Data Register** is a secondary Accumulator Register used in conjunction with `eax`.
esi	**Source Index Register** is used for memory array copying in conjunction with `edi`.
edi	**Destination Index Register** is used for memory array copying in conjunction with `esi`.
eip	**Instruction Pointer** holds offset of the next instruction.
ebp	**Base Pointer** holds the current stack frame location during a routine call (in conjunction with the Stack Pointer).
esp	**Stack Pointer** holds the location of the top of the stack.
xcs	**Code Segment** helps in addressing the memory segment in which the program runs.
xds	**Data Segment** helps addressing a data memory segment.
xes	**Extra Segment** is an additional register to address a memory segment.
xfs	**Additional Segment** which is a general purpose data segment.
xss	**Stack segment** holds the Stack memory segment.

 Many X86 registers are a **legacy**, which means that they lost the initial purpose they were created for. Take their descriptions with some caution.

Deciphering stack-traces is not an easy task and requires time and expertise. Don't bother too much if you do not understand every part of it yet. This is necessary as a last resort only.

Setting up a Gradle project to compile native code

Android Studio is now the new officially supported Android IDE, in place of Eclipse. It comes with **Gradle**, which is the new official Android build system. Gradle introduces a Groovy-based specific language to define the project configuration easily. Although its support of the NDK is still preliminary, it keeps improving and is becoming more and more useable.

Let's now see how to create an Android Studio project with Gradle that compiles native code.

 The resulting project is provided with this book under the name `Store_Gradle_Auto`.

Time for action – creating a native Android project

Gradle-based projects can be created easily through Android Studio:

1. Launch Android Studio. On the welcome screen, select **New Project...** (or go to **File | New Project...** if a project is already opened).

2. From the **New Project** wizard, enter the following configuration and click on **Next**:

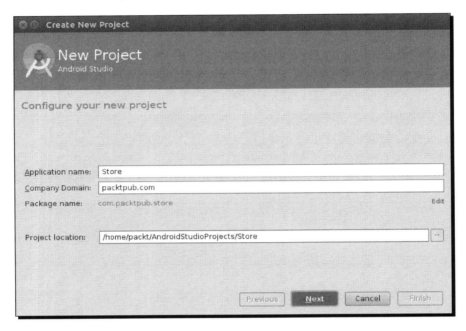

3. Then, select the minimum SDK (for example, API 14: Ice Scream Sandwich) and click on **Next**.

4. Select **Blank Activity with Fragment** and click on **Next**.

5. Finally, enter **Activity Name** and **Layout Name** names as follows and click on **Finish**:

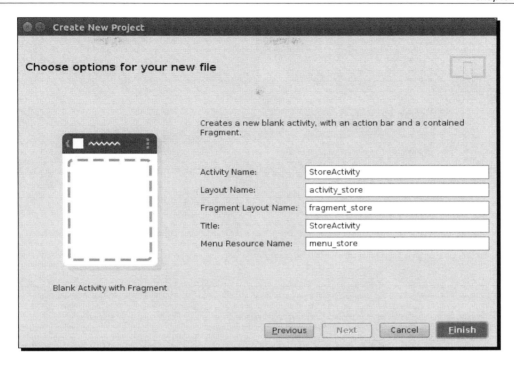

6. Android Studio should then open the project:

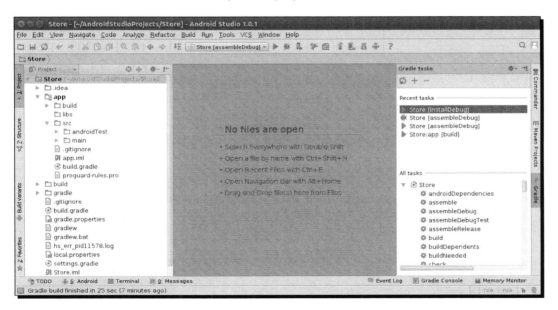

7. Modify `StoreActivity.java` and create `Store.java` in the same way as we did in the *Interfacing Java with C/C++* section in this chapter (Step 1 and 2).

8. Create the `app/src/main/jni` directory. Copy the C and Header files we created in the *Interfacing Java with C/C++* section in this chapter (Step 4 and 5).

9. Edit `app/build.gradle` that has been generated by Android Studio. In `defaultConfig`, insert a `ndk` section to configure the module (that is, a library) name:

```
apply plugin: 'com.android.application'

android {
    compileSdkVersion 21
    buildToolsVersion "21.1.2"

    defaultConfig {
        applicationId "com.packtpub.store"
        minSdkVersion 14
        targetSdkVersion 21
        versionCode 1
        versionName "1.0"
        ndk {
            moduleName "com_packtpub_store_Store"
        }
    }
    buildTypes {
        release {
            minifyEnabled false
            proguardFiles getDefaultProguardFile('proguard-android.
txt'), 'proguard-rules.pro'
        }
    }
}

dependencies {
    compile fileTree(dir: 'libs', include: ['*.jar'])
    compile 'com.android.support:appcompat-v7:21.0.3'
}
```

10. Compile and install the project on your device by clicking on **installDebug** in the **Gradle tasks** view of Android Studio.

If Android Studio complains that it cannot find the NDK, make sure the `local.properties` file in the project's root directory contains both `sdk.dir` and `ndk.dir` properties that can point to your Android SDK and NDK location.

What just happened?

We created our first Android Studio project that compiles native code through Gradle. NDK properties are configured in a section specific to `ndk` in the `build.gradle` file (for example, the module name).

Multiple settings are available as shown in the following table:

Property	Description
abiFilter	The list of ABIs to compile for; by default, all.
cFlags	Custom flags to pass to the compiler. More about this in *Chapter 9, Porting Existing Libraries to Android*.
ldLibs	Custom flags to pass to the linker. More about this in *Chapter 9, Porting Existing Libraries to Android*.
moduleName	This is the name of the module to be built.
stl	This is the STL library to use for compilation. More about this in *Chapter 9, Porting Existing Libraries to Android*.

You might have noticed that we have not reused the `Android.mk` and `Application.mk` files. This is because Gradle generates the build files automatically if given an input to `ndk-build` at compilation time. In our example, you can see the generated `Android.mk` for the `Store` module in the `app/build/intermediates/ndk/debug` directory.

NDK automatic Makefile generation makes it easy to compile native NDK code on simple projects. However, if you want more control on your native build, you can create your own Makefiles like the ones created in the Interfacing Java with C/C++ section in this chapter. Let's see how to do this.

 The resulting project is provided with this book under the name `Store_Gradle_Manual`.

Time for action – using your own Makefiles with Gradle

Using your own handmade makefiles with Gradle is a bit tricky but not too complicated:

1. Copy the Android.mk and Application.mk files we created in the *Interfacing Java with C/C++* section in this chapter into the app/src/main/jni directory.

2. Edit app/build.gradle.

3. Add an import for the OS "Class" and remove the first ndk section we created in the previous section:

```
import org.apache.tools.ant.taskdefs.condition.Os

apply plugin: 'com.android.application'

android {
    compileSdkVersion 21
    buildToolsVersion "21.1.2"

    defaultConfig {
        applicationId "com.packtpub.store"
        minSdkVersion 14
        targetSdkVersion 21
        versionCode 1
        versionName "1.0"
    }
    buildTypes {
        release {
            minifyEnabled false
            proguardFiles getDefaultProguardFile('proguard-android.
txt'), 'proguard-rules.pro'
        }
    }
```

4. Still in the android section of app/build.gradle., insert a sourceSets.main section with the following:

❑ jniLibs.srcDir, which defines where Gradle will find the generated libraries.

❑ jni.srcDirs, which is set to an empty array to disable native code compilation through Gradle.

```
        ...
        sourceSets.main {
            jniLibs.srcDir 'src/main/libs'
            jni.srcDirs = []
        }
```

5. Finally, create a new Gradle task `ndkBuild` that will manually trigger the `ndk-build` command, specifying the custom directory `src/main` as the compilation directory.

Declare a dependency between the `ndkBuild` task and the Java compilation task to automatically trigger native code compilation:

```
...

task ndkBuild(type: Exec) {
    if (Os.isFamily(Os.FAMILY_WINDOWS)) {
        commandLine 'ndk-build.cmd', '-C', file('src/main').absolutePath
    } else {
        commandLine 'ndk-build', '-C', file('src/main').absolutePath
    }
}

tasks.withType(JavaCompile) {
    compileTask -> compileTask.dependsOn ndkBuild
}
}

dependencies {
    compile fileTree(dir: 'libs', include: ['*.jar'])
    compile 'com.android.support:appcompat-v7:21.0.3'
}
```

6. Compile and install the project on your device by clicking on **installDebug** in the **Gradle tasks** view of Android Studio.

What just happened?

The Makefile generation and native source compilation performed by the Android Gradle plugin can easily be disabled. The trick is to simply indicate that no native source directory is available. We can then use the power of Gradle, which allows defining easily custom build tasks and dependencies between them, to execute the `ndk-build` command. This trick allows using our own NDK makefiles, giving us more flexibility in the way we build native code.

Summary

Creating, compiling, building, packaging, and deploying an application project are not the most exciting tasks, but they cannot be avoided. Mastering them will allow you to be productive and focused on the real objective: **producing code**.

In summary, we built our first sample application using command-line tools and deploying it on an Android device. We also created our first native Android project using Eclipse and interfaced Java with C/C++ using Java Native Interfaces. We debugged a native Android application with NDK-GDB and analyzed a native crash dump to find its origin in the source code. Finally, we created a similar project using Android Studio and built it with Gradle.

This first experiment with the Android NDK gives you a good overview of the way native development works. In the next chapter, we are going to focus on the code and dive more deeply into the JNI protocol.

3

Interfacing Java and C/C++ with JNI

Android is inseparable from Java. Its kernel and core libraries are native, but the Android application framework is almost entirely written in Java or at least wrapped inside a thin layer of Java. Do not expect to build your Android GUI directly in C/C++! Most APIs are available only from Java. At best, we can hide it under the cover... Thus, native C/C++ code on Android would be nonsense if it was not possible to tie Java and C/C++ together.

This role is devoted to the Java Native Interface API. JNI is a standardized specification allowing Java to call native code and native code to call Java back. It is a two-way bridge between the Java and native side; the only way to inject the power of C/C++ into your Java application.

Thanks to JNI, one can call C/C++ functions from Java like any Java method, passing Java primitives or objects as parameters and receiving them as result of native calls. In turn, native code can access, inspect, modify, and call Java objects or raise exceptions with a reflection-like API. JNI is a subtle framework which requires care as any misuse can result in a dramatic ending...

In this chapter, we will implement a basic key/value store to handle various data types. A simple Java GUI will allow defining an *entry* composed of a key (a character string), a type (an integer, a string, and so on), and a value related to the selected type. Entries are retrieved, inserted, or updated (remove will not be supported) inside a simple fixed size array of entries, which will reside on the native side.

To implement this project, we are going to:

- Initialize a native JNI library
- Convert Java Strings in native code
- Pass Java primitives to native code
- Handle Java object references in native code
- Manage Java Arrays in native code
- Raise and check Java exceptions in native code.

By the end of this chapter, you should be able perform native calls with any Java type and use exceptions.

JNI is a very technical framework that requires care, as any misuse can result in a dramatic ending. This chapter does not pretend to cover it exhaustively but rather focuses on the essential knowledge to bridge the gap between Java and C++.

Initializing a native JNI library

Before accessing their native methods, native libraries must be loaded through a Java call to `System.loadLibrary()`. JNI provides a hook, `JNI_OnLoad()`, to plug your own initialization code. Let's override it to initialize our native store.

 The resulting project is provided with this book under the name `Store_Part4`.

Time for action – defining a simple GUI

Let's create a Java Graphical User Interface for our `Store` and bind it to the native store structure that we will create:

1. Rewrite the `res/fragment_layout.xml` layout to define the graphical interface as follows. It defines:

   - A **Key** `TextView` label and `EditText` to enter the key
   - A **Value** `TextView` label and `EditText` to enter the value matching the key
   - A **Type** `TextView` label and `Spinner` to define the type of the value

❑ A **Get Value** and a **Set Value** Button to retrieve and change a value in the store

```xml
<LinearLayout
xmlns:a="http://schemas.android.com/apk/res/android"
  xmlns:tools="http://schemas.android.com/tools"
  a:layout_width="match_parent" a:layout_height="match_parent"
  a:orientation="vertical"
tools:context="com.packtpub.store.StoreActivity$PlaceholderFrag
ment">
  <TextView
    a:layout_width="match_parent"
a:layout_height="wrap_content"
    a:text="Save or retrieve a value from the store:" />
  <TableLayout
    a:layout_width="match_parent"
a:layout_height="wrap_content"
    a:stretchColumns="1" >
    <TableRow>
      <TextView a:id="@+id/uiKeyLabel" a:text="Key : " />
      <EditText a:id="@+id/uiKeyEdit" ><requestFocus
/></EditText>
    </TableRow>
    <TableRow>
      <TextView a:id="@+id/uiValueLabel" a:text="Value : " />
      <EditText a:id="@+id/uiValueEdit" />
    </TableRow>
    <TableRow>
      <TextView a:id="@+id/uiTypeLabel"
a:layout_height="match_parent"
                a:gravity="center_vertical" a:text="Type : " />
      <Spinner a:id="@+id/uiTypeSpinner" />
    </TableRow>
  </TableLayout>
  <LinearLayout
    a:layout_width="wrap_content"
a:layout_height="wrap_content"
    a:layout_gravity="right" >
    <Button a:id="@+id/uiGetValueButton"
a:layout_width="wrap_content"
            a:layout_height="wrap_content" a:text="Get Value" />
    <Button a:id="@+id/uiSetValueButton" a:layout_width="wrap_
content"
            a:layout_height="wrap_content" a:text="Set Value" />
  </LinearLayout>
</LinearLayout>
```

The end result should look as follows:

2. Create a new class in `StoreType.java` with an empty enumeration:

```
package com.packtpub.store;

public enum StoreType {
}
```

3. The GUI and native store need to be bound together. This is the role undertaken by the `StoreActivity` class. To do this, when `PlaceholderFragment` is created in `onCreateView()`, initialize all the GUI components defined earlier in the layout file:

```
public class StoreActivity extends Activity {
    ...
    public static class PlaceholderFragment extends Fragment {
        private Store mStore = new Store();
        private EditText mUIKeyEdit, mUIValueEdit;
        private Spinner mUITypeSpinner;
```

```
private Button mUIGetButton, mUISetButton;
private Pattern mKeyPattern;

...

@Override
public View onCreateView(LayoutInflater inflater,
                         ViewGroup container,
                         Bundle savedInstanceState)
{
    View rootView =
inflater.inflate(R.layout.fragment_store,
                                  container, false);
    updateTitle();

    // Initializes text components.
    mKeyPattern = Pattern.compile("\\p{Alnum}+");
    mUIKeyEdit = (EditText) rootView.findViewById(
                                    R.id.uiKeyEdit);
    mUIValueEdit = (EditText) rootView.findViewById(
                                    R.id.uiValueEdit);
```

4. Spinner content is bound to the StoreType enum. Use ArrayAdapter to bind together the Spinner and enum values.

```
...
ArrayAdapter<StoreType> adapter =
    new ArrayAdapter<StoreType>(getActivity(),
                    android.R.layout.simple_spinner_item,
                    StoreType.values());
adapter.setDropDownViewResource(
            android.R.layout.simple_spinner_dropdown_item);
mUITypeSpinner = (Spinner) rootView.findViewById(
                                    R.id.uiTypeSpinner);
mUITypeSpinner.setAdapter(adapter);
...
```

5. The **Get Value** and **Set Value** buttons trigger the private methods onGetValue() and onSetValue(), which respectively pull data from and push data to the store. Use OnClickListener to bind buttons and methods together:

```
...
mUIGetButton = (Button) rootView.findViewById(
                                    R.id.uiGetValueButton);
mUIGetButton.setOnClickListener(new OnClickListener() {
    public void onClick(View pView) {
        onGetValue();
```

```
                }
            });
            mUISetButton = (Button) rootView.findViewById(
                                          R.id.uiSetValueButton);
            mUISetButton.setOnClickListener(new OnClickListener() {
                public void onClick(View pView) {
                    onSetValue();
                }
            });
            return rootView;
        }
        ...
```

6. In `PlaceholderFragment`, define the `onGetValue()` method, which will retrieve entries from the store according to `StoreType` selected in the GUI. Leave the switch empty as it will not handle any kind of entries for now:

```
        ...
        private void onGetValue() {
            // Retrieves key and type entered by the user.
            String key = mUIKeyEdit.getText().toString();
            StoreType type = (StoreType) mUITypeSpinner
                                            .getSelectedItem();
            // Checks key is correct.
            if (!mKeyPattern.matcher(key).matches()) {
                displayMessage("Incorrect key.");
                return;
            }

            // Retrieves value from the store and displays it.
            // Each data type has its own access method.
            switch (type) {
                // Will retrieve entries soon...
            }
        }
        ...
```

7. Then, still in `PlaceholderFragment`, define the `onSetValue()` method in `StoreActivity` to insert or update entries in the store. If the value format is incorrect, a message is displayed:

```
        ...
        private void onSetValue() {
            // Retrieves key and type entered by the user.
            String key = mUIKeyEdit.getText().toString();
```

```
            String value = mUIValueEdit.getText().toString();
            StoreType type = (StoreType) mUITypeSpinner
                                            .getSelectedItem();
        // Checks key is correct.
        if (!mKeyPattern.matcher(key).matches()) {
            displayMessage("Incorrect key.");
            return;
        }

        // Parses user entered value and saves it in the store.
        // Each data type has its own access method.
        try {
            switch (type) {
                // Will put entries soon...
            }
        } catch (Exception eException) {
            displayMessage("Incorrect value.");
        }
        updateTitle();
    }
    ...
```

8. Finally, a little helper method displayMessage() in PlaceholderFragment
will help warn the user when a problem occurs. It displays a simple Android
Toast message:

```
        ...
        private void displayMessage(String pMessage) {
            Toast.makeText(getActivity(), pMessage, Toast.LENGTH_LONG)
                .show();
        }
    }
}
```

What just happened?

We created a basic Graphical User Interface in Java with a few visual components from the
Android framework. As you can see, there is nothing specific to the NDK here. The moral of
the story is that native code can be integrated with any existing Java code.

Obviously, we still have some work to do to make our native code perform some useful
things for the Java application. Let's now switch to the native side.

Time for action – initializing the native store

We need to create and initialize all the structures we will use for the next section of the chapter:

1. Create the `jni/Store.h` file, which defines store data structures:

   ❑ The `StoreType` enumeration will reflect the corresponding Java enumeration. Leave it empty for now.

   ❑ The `StoreValue` union will contain any of the possible store values. Leave it empty for now too.

   ❑ The `StoreEntry` structure contains one piece of data in the store. It is composed of a key (a raw C string made from `char*`), a type (`StoreType`), and a value (`StoreValue`).

> Note that we will see how to set up and use C++ STL strings in *Chapter 9, Porting Existing Libraries to Android*.

   ❑ `Store` is the main structure that defines a fixed size array of entries and a length (that is, the number of allocated entries):

```
#ifndef _STORE_H_
#define _STORE_H_

#include <cstdint>

#define STORE_MAX_CAPACITY 16

typedef enum {
} StoreType;

typedef union {
} StoreValue;

typedef struct {
    char* mKey;
    StoreType mType;
    StoreValue mValue;
} StoreEntry;

typedef struct {
```

```
        StoreEntry mEntries[STORE_MAX_CAPACITY];
        int32_t mLength;
    } Store;
    #endif
```

 Include guards (that is, #ifndef, #define, and #endif), which ensure that a header file is included only once during compilation, and can be replaced by the non-standard (but widely supported) preprocessor instruction, #pragma once.

2. In jni/com_packtpub_Store.cpp, implement the JNI_OnLoad() initialization hook. Inside, initialize the unique instance of the Store data structure store into a static variable:

```
#include "com_packtpub_store_Store.h"
#include "Store.h"

static Store gStore;

JNIEXPORT jint JNI_OnLoad(JavaVM* pVM, void* reserved) {
    // Store initialization.
    gStore.mLength = 0;
    return JNI_VERSION_1_6;
}
...
```

3. Update the native store getCount() method accordingly to reflect the store allocated entry count:

```
...
JNIEXPORT jint JNICALL Java_com_packtpub_store_Store_getCount
    (JNIEnv* pEnv, jobject pObject) {
        return gStore.mLength;
}
```

What just happened?

We built the foundation of our store project with a simple GUI and a native in-memory data array. The containing native library is loaded with either a call to:

◆ System.load(), which takes the library full path in parameter.

◆ System.loadLibrary(), which requires only the library name without the path, prefix (that is, lib), or extension.

The native code initialization occurs in the `JNI_OnLoad()` hook, which is called only once during the lifetime of the native code. It is a perfect place to initialize and cache global variables. JNI elements (classes, methods, fields, and so on) are also often cached in `JNI_OnLoad()` to improve the performance. We will see more about this throughout this chapter and the next one.

Please note that the pendent call `JNI_OnUnload()` defined in the JNI specification is almost useless in Android since there is no way to guarantee that a library is unloaded before process termination.

The `JNI_OnLoad()` signature is systematically defined as follows:

```
JNIEXPORT jint JNICALL JNI_OnLoad(JavaVM* vm, void* reserved);
```

What makes `JNI_OnLoad()` so useful is its `JavaVM` parameter. From it, you can retrieve the **JNIEnv interface pointer** as follows:

```
JNIEXPORT jint JNI_OnLoad(JavaVM* pVM, void* reserved) {
    JNIEnv *env;
    if (pVM->GetEnv((void**) &env, JNI_VERSION_1_6) != JNI_OK) {
        abort();
    }
    ...
    return JNI_VERSION_1_6;
}
```

> The `JNI_OnLoad()` definition in a JNI library is optional. However, if omitted, you may notice that a warning **No JNI_OnLoad found in <mylib>. so** is displayed in the **Logcat** when you start your application. This has absolutely no consequence and can be safely ignored.

`JNIEnv` is the main entry point for all JNI calls, which explains why it is passed to all native methods. It provides a set of methods to access Java primitives and arrays from native code. It is complemented with a reflection-like API to give full access to Java objects from native code. We are going to discover its features in more detail throughout this chapter and the next one.

> The `JNIEnv` interface pointer is thread-specific. You must not share it between threads! Use it only on the thread it was retrieved from. Only a JavaVM element is thread-safe and can be shared among threads.

Converting Java strings in native code

The first kind of entry we will handle is strings. Strings, which are represented as (almost) classic objects in Java, can be manipulated on the native side and translated to native strings, that is, raw character arrays, thanks to JNI. Strings are a first-class citizen despite their complexity inherent to their heterogeneous representations.

In this part, we will send Java strings to the native side and translate them to their native counterpart. We will also convert them back to a Java string.

 The resulting project is provided with this book under the name `Store_Part5`.

Time for action – handling strings in the native store

Let's handle String values in our store:

1. Open `StoreType.java` and specify the new String type our store handles in the enumeration:

```
public enum StoreType {
    String
}
Open Store.java and define the new functionalities our native key/
value store provides (for now, only strings):
public class Store {
    ...
    public native int getCount();

    public native String getString(String pKey);
    public native void setString(String pKey, String pString);
}
```

2. In `StoreActivity.java`, retrieve string entries from the native `Store` in the `onGetValue()` method. Do it according to the type `StoreType` currently selected in the GUI (even if there is only one possible type for now):

```
public class StoreActivity extends Activity {
    ...
    public static class PlaceholderFragment extends Fragment {
        ...
        private void onGetValue() {
            ...
            switch (type) {
```

```
        case String:
            mUIValueEdit.setText(mStore.getString(key));
            break;
    }
}
...
```

3. Insert or update string entries in the store in the onSetValue() method:

```
...
private void onSetValue() {
    ...
    try {
        switch (type) {
        case String:
            mStore.setString(key, value);
            break;
        }
    } catch (Exception eException) {
        displayMessage("Incorrect value.");
    }
    updateTitle();
}
...
}
}
```

4. In jni/Store.h, include a new header jni.h to access the JNI API.

```
#ifndef _STORE_H_
#define _STORE_H_

#include <cstdint>
#include "jni.h"
...
```

5. Next, integrate strings into the native StoreType enumeration and the StoreValue union:

```
...
typedef enum {
    StoreType_String
} StoreType;

typedef union {
    char*       mString;
} StoreValue;
...
```

6. Terminate by declaring utility methods to check, create, find, and destroy entries. JNIEnv and jstring are JNI types defined in the jni.h header:

```
...
bool isEntryValid(JNIEnv* pEnv, StoreEntry* pEntry, StoreType pType);

StoreEntry* allocateEntry(JNIEnv* pEnv, Store* pStore, jstring pKey);

StoreEntry* findEntry(JNIEnv* pEnv, Store* pStore, jstring pKey);

void releaseEntryValue(JNIEnv* pEnv, StoreEntry* pEntry);
#endif
```

7. Create a new file jni/Store.cpp to implement all these utility methods. First, isEntryValid() simply checks whether an entry is allocated and has the expected type:

```
#include "Store.h"
#include <cstdlib>
#include <cstring>

bool isEntryValid(JNIEnv* pEnv, StoreEntry* pEntry, StoreType pType) {
    return ((pEntry != NULL) && (pEntry->mType == pType));
}
...
```

8. The findEntry() method compares the key passed as a parameter with every key in the store until a match is found. Instead of working with classic native strings (that is, a char*), it receives a jstring parameter, which is the direct representation of a Java String on the native side.

9. To recover a native string from a Java String, use GetStringUTFChars() from the JNI API to get a temporary character buffer containing the converted Java string. Its content can then be manipulated using standard C routines. GetStringUTFChars() must be systematically coupled with a call to ReleaseStringUTFChars() to release the temporary buffer allocated in GetStringUTFChars():

 Java strings are stored in memory as UTF-16 strings. When their content is extracted in native code, the returned buffer is encoded in Modified UTF-8. Modified UTF-8 is compatible with standard C String functions, which usually works on string buffers composed of 8 bits per characters.

```
...
StoreEntry* findEntry(JNIEnv* pEnv, Store* pStore, jstring pKey) {
    StoreEntry* entry = pStore->mEntries;
```

```
        StoreEntry* entryEnd = entry + pStore->mLength;

        // Compare requested key with every entry key currently stored
        // until we find a matching one.
        const char* tmpKey = pEnv->GetStringUTFChars(pKey, NULL);
        while ((entry < entryEnd) && (strcmp(entry->mKey, tmpKey) != 0)) {
            ++entry;
        }
        pEnv->ReleaseStringUTFChars(pKey, tmpKey);

        return (entry == entryEnd) ? NULL : entry;
}
...
```

JNI does not forgive any mistakes. If, for example, you pass NULL as the first parameter in GetStringUTFChars(), VM will abort immediately. In addition, Android JNI does not respect JNI specification perfectly. Although the JNI Specification indicates that GetStringUTFChars() might return NULL if the memory could not be allocated, Android VMs will simply abort in such cases.

10. Implement allocateEntry(), which either creates a new entry (that is, increments the store length and returns the last element) or returns an existing one if the key already exists (after releasing its previous value).

If the entry is a new one, convert its key to a native string that can be kept in the memory. Indeed, raw JNI objects live for the duration of a native method call and must not be kept outside its scope:

```
...
StoreEntry* allocateEntry(JNIEnv* pEnv, Store* pStore, jstring pKey) {
    // If entry already exists in the store, releases its content
    // and keep its key.
    StoreEntry* entry = findEntry(pEnv, pStore, pKey);
    if (entry != NULL) {
        releaseEntryValue(pEnv, entry);
    }
    // If entry does not exist, create a new entry
    // right after the entries already stored.
    else {
        entry = pStore->mEntries + pStore->mLength;

        // Copies the new key into its final C string buffer.
        const char* tmpKey = pEnv->GetStringUTFChars(pKey, NULL);
```

```
        entry->mKey = new char[strlen(tmpKey) + 1];
        strcpy(entry->mKey, tmpKey);
        pEnv->ReleaseStringUTFChars(pKey, tmpKey);

        ++pStore->mLength;
    }
    return entry;
}
...
```

11. Write the last method `releaseEntryValue()`, which frees the memory allocated for a value if needed:

```
...
void releaseEntryValue(JNIEnv* pEnv, StoreEntry* pEntry) {
    switch (pEntry->mType) {
    case StoreType_String:
        delete pEntry->mValue.mString;
        break;
    }
}
```

12. Refresh the JNI header file `jni/com_packtpub_Store.h` with `javah` as seen in the previous chapter. You should see two new methods `Java_com_packtpub_store_Store_getString()` and `Java_com_packtpub_store_Store_setString()` in it.

13. In `jni/com_packtpub_Store.cpp`, insert the `cstdlib` header file:

```
#include "com_packtpub_store_Store.h"
#include <cstdlib>
#include "Store.h"
...
```

14. With the help of the previously generated JNI header, implement the native method `getString()`. This method looks for the key passed to the store and returns its corresponding string value. If any problem occurs, a default `NULL` value is returned.

15. Java strings are not real primitives. Types `jstring` and `char*` cannot be used interchangeably as we already saw. To create a Java `String` object from a native string, use `NewStringUTF()` from the JNI API:

```
...
JNIEXPORT jstring JNICALL Java_com_packtpub_store_Store_getString
  (JNIEnv* pEnv, jobject pThis, jstring pKey) {
    StoreEntry* entry = findEntry(pEnv, &gStore, pKey);
```

```
        if (isEntryValid(pEnv, entry, StoreType_String)) {
            // Converts a C string into a Java String.
            return pEnv->NewStringUTF(entry->mValue.mString);
        } else {
            return NULL;
        }
    }
    ...
```

16. Then, implement the `setString()` method, which allocates an entry (that is, creates a new entry in the store or reuses an existing one if it has the same key) and stores the converted Java string value in it.

17. The string value is translated from a Java string directly to our own string buffer using the `GetStringUTFLength()` and `GetStringUTFRegion()` methods from the JNI API. This is an alternative to `GetStringUTFChars()` used earlier. Finally, we must not forget to append the `null` character, which is the standard for a raw C string:

```
...
JNIEXPORT void JNICALL Java_com_packtpub_store_Store_setString
    (JNIEnv* pEnv, jobject pThis, jstring pKey, jstring pString) {
    // Turns the Java string into a temporary C string.
    StoreEntry* entry = allocateEntry(pEnv, &gStore, pKey);
    if (entry != NULL) {
        entry->mType = StoreType_String;
        // Copy the temporary C string into its dynamically allocated
        // final location. Then releases the temporary string.
        jsize stringLength = pEnv->GetStringUTFLength(pString);
        entry->mValue.mString = new char[stringLength + 1];
        // Directly copies the Java String into our new C buffer.
        pEnv->GetStringUTFRegion(pString, 0, stringLength,
                                 entry->mValue.mString);
        // Append the null character for string termination.
        entry->mValue.mString[stringLength] = '\0';    }
}
```

18. Finally, update the `Android.mk` file to compile `Store.cpp`:

```
LOCAL_PATH := $(call my-dir)

include $(CLEAR_VARS)

LOCAL_MODULE    := com_packtpub_store_Store
LOCAL_SRC_FILES := com_packtpub_store_Store.cpp Store.cpp

include $(BUILD_SHARED_LIBRARY)
```

What just happened?

Run the application. Try to save a few entries with different keys and values. Then try to get them back from the native store. We managed to pass and retrieve strings from Java to C/C++. These values are saved in a native memory as native strings. Entries can then be retrieved as Java strings from the store according to their key.

Java and C strings are completely different beasts. Java strings need a concrete conversion to native strings to allow processing of their content using standard C string routines. Indeed, `jstring` is not a representation of a classic `char*` array but of a reference to a Java `String` object, accessible from the Java code only.

We discovered two ways to convert Java strings to native strings in this part:

◆ By pre-allocating a memory buffer in which the converted Java string is copied.

◆ By retrieving a converted Java string in a memory buffer managed by JNI.

Choosing either solution depends on how memory is handled by the client code.

Native character encoding

JNI provides two kinds of methods to deal with strings:

◆ The ones with UTF in their name that work with Modified UTF-8 strings

◆ The ones without UTF in their name that work with UTF-16 encoding

Modified UTF-8 and UTF-16 strings are two different character encodings:

◆ **Modified UTF-8** is a slightly different flavor of UTF-8 specific to Java. This encoding can represent standard ASCII characters (each on one byte) or can grow up to 4 bytes to represent extended characters (Ararbic, Cyrilic, Greek, Hebrew, and so on). The difference between standard UTF-8 and Modified UTF-8 resides in the different representation of the `null` character, which simply does not exist in the latter encoding. In this way, such strings can be processed with a standard C routine for which the `null` character is used as an ending sentinel.

◆ **UTF-16** is the real encoding employed for Java strings. Each character is represented with two bytes, hence the Java `char` size. As a consequence, it is more efficient to work with UTF-16 in native code rather than Modified UTF-8 since they do not require conversion. The drawback is that classic C string routines will not work with them since they are not `null` terminated.

Character encoding is a complex subject for which you can find more information at `http://www.oracle.com/technetwork/articles/javase/supplementary-142654.html` and in the Android documentation at `http://developer.android.com/training/articles/perf-jni.html#UTF_8_and_UTF_16_strings`.

JNI String API

JNI provides several methods to handle a Java string on the native side:

◆ `GetStringUTFLength()` computes the Modified UTF-8 string length in *byte* (indeed UTF-8 strings have varying character sizes), whereas `GetStringLength()` computes UTF-16 string *number of characters* (not bytes, since UTF-16 characters are of a fixed size):

```
jsize GetStringUTFLength(jstring string)
jsize GetStringLength(jstring string)
```

◆ `GetStringUTFChars()` and `GetStringChars()` allocate a new memory buffer managed by JNI to store the result of Java to native (respectively Modified UTF-8 and UTF-16) string conversion. Use it when you want to convert an entire string without bothering with memory allocation. The last parameter `isCopy`, when not `null`, indicates whether the string has been internally copied by JNI or whether the returned buffer points to the real Java string memory. In Android, the returned `isCopy` value is generally `JNI_TRUE` for `GetStringUTFChars()` and `JNI_FALSE` for `GetStringChars()` (indeed the latter does not require encoding conversion):

```
const char* GetStringUTFChars(jstring string, jboolean* isCopy)
const jchar* GetStringChars(jstring string, jboolean* isCopy)
```

> Although JNI specification indicates that `GetStringUTFChars()` can return NULL (which means that the operation has failed because, for example, memory could not be allocated), in practice, this check is useless because the Dalvik or ART VMs generally abort in this case. So simply avoid getting into that situation! You should still keep NULL-checks if your code aims at being portable to other Java Virtual Machines.

◆ `ReleaseStringUTFChars()` and `ReleaseStringChars()` free the memory buffer allocated by `GetStringUTFChars()` and `GetStringChars()` when the client has finished processing it. These methods must always be called in pairs:

```
void ReleaseStringUTFChars(jstring string, const char* utf)
void ReleaseStringChars(jstring string, const jchar* chars)
```

◆ `GetStringUTFRegion()` and `GetStringRegion()` retrieve all or only a region of the Java string. It works on a string buffer provided and managed by the client code. Use it when you want to manage memory allocation (for example, to reuse an existing memory buffer) or need to access small sections of a string:

```
void GetStringRegion(jstring str, jsize start, jsize len, jchar* buf)
void GetStringUTFRegion(jstring str, jsize start, jsize len, char* buf)
```

♦ GetStringCritical() and ReleaseStringCritical() are similar to GetStringChars() and ReleaseStringChars() but are only available for UTF-16 strings. According to the JNI specification, GetStringCritical() is more likely to return a direct pointer without making any copy. In exchange, the caller must not perform blocking or JNI calls and should not hold the string for a long time (like a critical section with threads). In practice, Android seems to behave similarly whether you use critical functions or not (but this may change):

```
const jchar* GetStringCritical(jstring string, jboolean* isCopy)
void ReleaseStringCritical(jstring string, const jchar* carray)
```

This is the essential knowledge you need to know to deal with Java strings through JNI.

Passing Java primitives to native code

The simplest kinds of elements we can handle with JNI are Java primitive types. Indeed, both the Java and native side use practically the same representation for this kind of data which, does not require any specific memory management.

In this part, we will see how to pass integers to the native side and send them back to the Java side.

 The resulting project is provided with this book under the name Store_Part6.

Time for action – handling primitives in the native store

1. In StoreType.java, add the newly managed integer type to the enumeration:

```
public enum StoreType {
    Integer,
    String
}
```

2. Open Store.java and define the new integer functionalities our native store provides:

```
public class Store {
    ...
    public native int getCount();

    public native int getInteger(String pKey);
```

```
    public native void setInteger(String pKey, int pInt);

    public native String getString(String pKey);
    public native void setString(String pKey, String pString);
}
```

3. In the `StoreActivity` class, update the `onGetValue()` method to retrieve
integer entries from the store when they are selected in the GUI:

```
public class StoreActivity extends Activity {
    . . .
    public static class PlaceholderFragment extends Fragment {
        . . .
        private void onGetValue() {
            . . .
            switch (type) {
            case Integer:
                mUIValueEdit.setText(Integer.toString(mStore
                                .getInteger(key)));
                break;
            case String:
                mUIValueEdit.setText(mStore.getString(key));
                break;
            }
        }
        . . .
```

4. Also, insert or update integer entries in the store in the `onSetValue()` method.
The entry data needs to be parsed before being passed to the native side:

```
        . . .
        private void onSetValue() {
            . . .
            try {
                switch (type) {
                case Integer:
                    mStore.setInteger(key, Integer.parseInt(value));
                    break;
                case String:
                    mStore.setString(key, value);
                    break;
                }
            } catch (Exception eException) {
                displayMessage("Incorrect value.");
```

```
                }
                updateTitle();
            }
            . . .
        }
    }
```

5. In `jni/Store.h`, append the integer type in the native `StoreType` enumeration and the `StoreValue` union:

```
. . .
typedef enum {
    StoreType_Integer,
    StoreType_String
} StoreType;
typedef union {
    int32_t    mInteger;
    char*      mString;
} StoreValue;
. . .
```

6. Refresh the JNI header file `jni/com_packtpub_Store.h` with `javah`. Two new methods `Java_com_packtpub_store_Store_getInteger()` and `Java_com_packtpub_store_Store_getInteger()` should appear.

7. In `jni/com_packtpub_Store.cpp`, implement `getInteger()` with the help of the generated JNI header. This method simply returns the integer value of an entry without doing any specific conversion other than an implicit cast from `int32_t` to `jint`. If any problem occurs, during retrieval, a default value is returned:

```
. . .
JNIEXPORT jint JNICALL Java_com_packtpub_store_Store_getInteger
    (JNIEnv* pEnv, jobject pThis, jstring pKey) {
        StoreEntry* entry = findEntry(pEnv, &gStore, pKey);
        if (isEntryValid(pEnv, entry, StoreType_Integer)) {
            return entry->mValue.mInteger;
        } else {
            return 0;
        }
}
. . .
```

8. The second method `setInteger()` stores the given integer value in the allocated entry. Note how here too that the passed JNI integer can be reversely cast to a C/C++ integer:

```
...
JNIEXPORT void JNICALL Java_com_packtpub_store_Store_setInteger
   (JNIEnv* pEnv, jobject pThis, jstring pKey, jint pInteger) {
      StoreEntry* entry = allocateEntry(pEnv, &gStore, pKey);
      if (entry != NULL) {
          entry->mType = StoreType_Integer;
          entry->mValue.mInteger = pInteger;
      }
}
```

What just happened?

Run the application. Try to save a few entries with different keys, types, and values. Then try to get them back from the native store. We have this time managed to pass and retrieve integer primitives from Java to C/C++.

Integer primitives wear several dresses during native calls; first, `int` in Java code, then `jint` during transfer from/to Java code, and finally, `int` or `int32_t` in native code. Obviously, we could have kept the JNI representation `jint` in native code if we wanted to, since all of these types are simply equivalent. In other words, `jint` is simply an alias.

 The `int32_t` type is `typedef` introduced by the C99 standard library with the aim at more portability. The difference with the standard `int` type is that its size-in-bytes is fixed for all compilers and platforms. More numeric types are defined in `stdint.h` (in C) or `cstdint` (in C++).

All primitive types have their proper alias in JNI:

Java type	JNI type	C type	Stdint C type
boolean	Jboolean	unsigned char	uint8_t
byte	Jbyte	signed char	int8_t
char	Jchar	unsigned short	uint16_t
double	Jdouble	double	N/A
float	jfloat	float	N/A
int	jint	Int	int32_t
long	jlong	long long	int64_t
short	jshort	Short	int16_t

You can use them exactly the same way we used integers in this part. More information about primitive types in JNI can be found at `http://docs.oracle.com/javase/6/docs/technotes/guides/jni/spec/types.html`

Have a go hero – passing and returning other primitive types

The current store deals only with integers and strings. Based on this model, try to implement store methods for other primitive types: `boolean`, `byte`, `char`, `double`, `float`, `long`, and `short`.

 The resulting project is provided with this book under the name `Store_Part6_Full`.

Referencing Java objects from native code

We know from the previous section that a string is represented in JNI as `jstring`, which is in fact a Java object, which means that it is possible to exchange any Java object through JNI! However, because native code cannot understand or access Java directly, all Java objects have the same representation, `jobject`.

In this part, we will focus on how to save an object on the native side and how to send it back to Java. As an example, we will work with a custom object `Color`, although any other type of object would work too.

 The resulting project is provided with this book under the name `Store_Part7`.

Time for action – saving references to Objects in native Store

1. Create a new Java class `com.packtpub.store.Color` encapsulating an integer representation of a color. This integer is parsed from `String` containing HTML code (for example, `#FF0000`) thanks to the `android.graphics.Color` class:

```
package com.packtpub.store;
import android.text.TextUtils;
public class Color {
    private int mColor;
```

```java
        public Color(String pColor) {
            if (TextUtils.isEmpty(pColor)) {
                throw new IllegalArgumentException();
            }
            mColor = android.graphics.Color.parseColor(pColor);
        }
        @Override
        public String toString() {
            return String.format("#%06X", mColor);
        }
    }
```

2. In `StoreType.java`, append the new Color data type to the enumeration:

```java
public enum StoreType {
    Integer,
    String,
    Color
}
```

3. In the `Store` class, append two new native methods to retrieve and save a `Color` object:

```java
public class Store {
    ...
    public native Color getColor(String pKey);
    public native void setColor(String pKey, Color pColor);
}
```

4. Open `StoreActivity.java` and update methods `onGetValue()` and `onSetValue()` to parse and display `Color` instances:

```java
public class StoreActivity extends Activity {
    ...
    public static class PlaceholderFragment extends Fragment {
        ...
        private void onGetValue() {
            ...
            switch (type) {
            ...
            case Color:
                mUIValueEdit.setText(mStore.getColor(key)
                                .toString());
                break;
            }
        }
```

```
        private void onSetValue() {
            ...
            try {
                switch (type) {
                ...
                case Color:
                    mStore.setColor(key, new Color(value));
                    break;
                }
            } catch (Exception eException) {
                displayMessage("Incorrect value.");
            }
            updateTitle();
        }
        ...
    }
}
```

5. In `jni/Store.h`, append the new color type to the `StoreType` enumeration and add a new member to the `StoreValue` union. But what type should you use, `Color` is an object known only from Java? In JNI, all java objects have the same type; `jobject`, an (indirect) object reference:

```
...
typedef enum {
    ...
    StoreType_String,
    StoreType_Color
} StoreType;
typedef union {
    ...
    char*     mString;
    jobject   mColor;
} StoreValue;
...
```

6. Regenerate the JNI header file `jni/com_packtpub_Store.h` with `javah`. You should see two new methods `Java_com_packtpub_store_Store_getColor()` and `Java_com_packtpub_store_Store_setColor()` in it.

7. Open `jni/com_packtpub_Store.cpp` and implement the two freshly generated methods `getColor()` and `setColor()`. The first one simply returns the Java Color object kept in the store entry as shown in the following code:

```
...
JNIEXPORT jobject JNICALL Java_com_packtpub_store_Store_getColor
   (JNIEnv* pEnv, jobject pThis, jstring pKey) {
      StoreEntry* entry = findEntry(pEnv, &gStore, pKey);
      if (isEntryValid(pEnv, entry, StoreType_Color)) {
          return entry->mValue.mColor;
      } else {
          return NULL;
      }
}
...
```

The real subtleties are introduced in the second method `setColor()`. Indeed, at first sight, simply saving the `jobject` value in the store entry would seem sufficient. However, this assumption is wrong. Objects passed in parameters or created inside a JNI method are Local references. Local references cannot be kept in native code outside of the native method scope (such as for strings).

8. To be allowed to keep a Java object reference in native code after native method returns, they must be turned into Global references in order to inform the Dalvik VM that they must not be garbage collected. To do so, the JNI API provides the `NewGlobalRef()` method:

```
...
JNIEXPORT void JNICALL Java_com_packtpub_store_Store_setColor
   (JNIEnv* pEnv, jobject pThis, jstring pKey, jobject pColor) {
      // Save the Color reference in the store.
      StoreEntry* entry = allocateEntry(pEnv, &gStore, pKey);
      if (entry != NULL) {
          entry->mType = StoreType_Color;
          // The Java Color is going to be stored on the native side.
          // Need to keep a global reference to avoid a potential
          // garbage collection after method returns.
          entry->mValue.mColor = pEnv->NewGlobalRef(pColor);
      }
}
```

9. In `Store.cpp`, modify `releaseEntryValue()` to delete the global
reference when the entry is replaced by a new one. This is done with the
`DeleteGlobalRef()` method, which is the counterpart of `NewGlobalRef()`:

```
...
void releaseEntryValue(JNIEnv* pEnv, StoreEntry* pEntry) {
    switch (pEntry->mType) {
    case StoreType_String:
        delete pEntry->mValue.mString;
        break;
    case StoreType_Color:
        // Unreferences the object for garbage collection.
        pEnv->DeleteGlobalRef(pEntry->mValue.mColor);
        break;
    }
}
```

What just happened?

Run the application. Enter and save a color value such as **#FF0000** or **red**, which is a
predefined value allowed by the Android color parser. Get the entry back from the store. We
managed to reference a Java object on the native side! Java objects are not and cannot be
converted to C++ objects. Both are inherently different. Thus, to keep Java objects on the
native side, we must keep references to them using the JNI API.

All objects coming from Java are represented by `jobject`, even `jstring` (which is in fact a
`typedef` over `jobject` internally). A `jobject` is just a dumb "pointer" without any smart
garbage collection mechanism (after all, we want to get rid of Java, at least partially). It does
not give you a direct reference to the Java object memory but rather an indirect one. Indeed,
Java objects do not have a fixed location in memory on the opposite to C++ objects. They
may be moved during their lifetime. Regardless, it would be a bad idea to mess with a Java
object representation in the memory.

Local references

Native calls have a scope limited to a method, which means that as soon as a native method
ends, the VM becomes in charge again. The JNI specification uses this fact to its advantage
in order to keep object references local to method boundaries. This means that `jobject`
can only be used safely inside the method it was given to. Once native method returns, the
Dalvik VM has no way to know if native code still holds object references and can decide to
collect them at any time.

These kinds of references are called **Local** references. They are automatically freed (the reference, not the object although the garbage collector might too) when native method returns to allow proper garbage collection later in the Java code. For example, the following piece of code should be strictly prohibited. Keeping such a reference outside the JNI method will eventually lead to an undefined behavior (a memory corruption, a crash, and so on):

```
static jobject gMyReference;
JNIEXPORT void JNICALL Java_MyClass_myMethod(JNIEnv* pEnv,
                                    jobject pThis, jobject pRef) {
    gMyReference = pRef;
    ...
}

// Later on...
env->CallVoidMethod(gMyReference, ...);
```

Objects are passed to native methods as Local references. Every `jobject` returned by JNI functions (except `NewGlobalRef()`) is a Local reference. Just remember that everything is a Local reference by default.

JNI provides several methods for managing Local references:

1. `NewLocalRef()` to create one explicitly (from a Global references, for example), although this is rarely needed in practice:

   ```
   jobject NewLocalRef(jobject ref)
   ```

2. `DeleteLocalRef()` to delete one when it is no longer needed:

   ```
   void DeleteLocalRef(jobject localRef)
   ```

Local references cannot be used outside the method scope and cannot be shared between threads, even during a single native call!

You are not required to delete Local references explicitly. However, according to the JNI specification, a JVM is only required to store 16 Local references at the same time and may refuse to create more (this is implementation-specific). It is thus good practice to release unused Local references as soon as possible, especially when working with arrays.

Hopefully, JNI provides a few more methods to help working with Local references.

1. `EnsureLocalCapacity()` informs the VM that it needs more Local references. This method return `-1` and throws a Java `OutOfMemoryError` when it cannot guarantee the requested capacity:

   ```
   jint EnsureLocalCapacity(jint capacity)
   ```

2. `PushLocalFrame()` and `PopLocalFrame()` offer a second way to allocate more Local references. It can be understood as a way to batch Local slot allocation and Local references deletion. This method also returns `-1` and throws a Java `OutOfMemoryError` when it cannot guarantee the requested capacity:

   ```
   jint PushLocalFrame(jint capacity)
   jobject PopLocalFrame(jobject result)
   ```

> Until Android 4.0 Ice Cream Sandwich, Local references were actually direct pointers, which means they could be kept beyond their natural scope and still be working. This is not the case anymore and such buggy code must be avoided.

Global references

To be able to use an object reference outside the method scope or keep it for a long period of time, references must be made **Global**. Global references also allow sharing objects between threads, which is not the case with Local references.

JNI provides two methods for this purpose:

1. `NewGlobalRef()` to create Global references preventing garbage collection of the pointed object and allowing it to be shared between threads. It is possible for two references for the same object to be different:

   ```
   jobject NewGlobalRef(jobject obj)
   ```

2. `DeleteGlobalRef()` to delete Global references when they are no longer needed. Without it, the Dalvik VM would consider that objects are still referenced and would never collect them:

   ```
   void DeleteGlobalRef(jobject globalRef)
   ```

3. `IsSameObject()` to compare two object references, instead of using `==`, which is not a correct way to compare references:

```
jboolean IsSameObject(jobject ref1, jobject ref2)
```

> Never forget to pair `New<Reference Type>Ref()` with `Delete<Reference Type>Ref()`. Failure to do so results in a memory leak.

Weak references

Weak references are the last kind of reference available in JNI. They are similar to Global references in that they can be kept between JNI calls and shared between threads. However, unlike Global references, they do not prevent garbage collection. Thus, this kind of reference must be used with care as it can become invalid at any moment, unless you create a Global or Local reference from them before use each time you need it (and release it right after!).

> When used appropriately, Weak references are useful to prevent memory leaks. If you have already done some Android development, you may already know one of the most common leaks: keeping a "hard" reference to an Activity from a background thread (typically, an `AsyncTask`) to notify the Activity later on when processing is over. Indeed, the Activity might be destroyed (because the user rotated the screen, for example) before a notification is sent. When using a Weak reference, the Activity can still be garbage collected and memory freed.

`NewWeakGlobalRef()` and `DeleteWeakGlobalRef()` are the only methods necessary to create and delete a Weak reference:

```
jweak NewWeakGlobalRef(JNIEnv *env, jobject obj);
void DeleteWeakGlobalRef(JNIEnv *env, jweak obj);
```

These methods return a `jweak` reference, which can be cast to the input object if needed (for example, if you create a reference to `jclass`, then the returned `jweak` can be cast into `jclass` or `jobject`).

However, you should not use it directly but rather pass it to `NewGlobalRef()` or `NewLocalRef()` and use their result as usual. To ensure a local or Global reference issued from a Weak reference is valid, simply check whether the reference returned by `NewGlobalRef()` or `NewLocalRef()` is `NULL`. Once you are finished with the object, you can delete the Global or Local reference. Restart the process every time you work with that Weak object again. For example:

```
jobject myObject = ...;
// Keep a reference to that object until it is garbage collected.
jweak weakRef = pEnv->NewWeakGlobalRef(myObject);
...

// Later on, get a real reference, hoping it is still available.
jobject localRef = pEnv->NewLocalRef(weakRef);
if (!localRef) {
// Do some stuff...
pEnv->DeleteLocalRef(localRef);
} else {
    // Object has been garbage collected, reference is unusable...
}


...
// Later on, when weak reference is no more needed.
pEnv->DeleteWeakGlobalRef(weakRef);
```

To check whether a Weak reference itself points to an object, compare `jweak` to `NULL` using `IsSameObject()` (do not use `==`):

```
jboolean IsSameObject(jobject ref1, jobject ref2)
```

Do not try to check the Weak reference state before creating a Global or Local reference because the pointed object might be collected concurrently.

 Prior to Android 2.2 Froyo, Weak references simply did not exist. Until Android 4.0 Ice Cream Sandwich, they could not be used in JNI calls except `NewGlobalRef()` or `NewLocalRef()`. Although this is not an obligation anymore, using weak references directly in other JNI calls should be considered a bad practice.

For more information on the subject, have a look at the JNI specification at `http://docs.oracle.com/javase/6/docs/technotes/guides/jni/spec/jniTOC.html`.

Managing Java arrays

There is one last type of data we have not talked about yet: **arrays**. Arrays have a specific place in Java as well as in JNI. They have their proper types and APIs, although Java arrays are also objects at their root.

In this part, we will improve our store by letting users enter a set of values simultaneously in an entry. This set is going to be communicated to the native store as a Java array, which in turn is going to be stored as a classic C array.

 The resulting project is provided with this book under the name Store_Part8.

Time for action – handling Java arrays in native Store

To help us handle operations on arrays, let's download a helper library, **Google Guava** (release 18.0 at the time of writing this book) available at http://code.google.com/p/guava-libraries/. Guava offers many useful methods to deal with primitives and arrays, and perform "pseudo-functional" programming.

Copy guava jar in the project libs directory. Open the **Properties** project and go to **Java Build Path | Libraries**. Reference Guava jar by clicking on the **Add JARs...** button and validate.

1. Edit the StoreType.java enumeration and add three new values: IntegerArray, StringArray, and ColorArray:

```
public enum StoreType {
    ...
    Color,
    IntegerArray,
    StringArray,
    ColorArray
}
```

2. Open Store.java and add new methods to retrieve and save int, String, and Color arrays:

```
public class Store {
    ...
    public native int[] getIntegerArray(String pKey);
    public native void setIntegerArray(String pKey, int[] pIntArray);
    public native String[] getStringArray(String pKey);
    public native void setStringArray(String pKey,
                                      String[] pStringArray);
```

```
    public native Color[] getColorArray(String pKey);
    public native void setColorArray(String pKey,Color[] pColorArray);
}
```

3. Edit `StoreActivity.java` to connect native methods to the GUI.

Modify the `onGetValue()` method so that it retrieves an array from the store depending on its type, concatenates its values with a semicolon separator (thanks to Guava joiners), and finally, displays them:

```
public class StoreActivity extends Activity {
    ...
    public static class PlaceholderFragment extends Fragment {
        ...
        private void onGetValue() {
            ...
            switch (type) {
            ...
            case IntegerArray:
                mUIValueEdit.setText(Ints.join(";", mStore
                                .getIntegerArray(key)));
                break;
            case StringArray:
                mUIValueEdit.setText(Joiner.on(";").join(
                                mStore.getStringArray(key)));
                break;
            case ColorArray:
                mUIValueEdit.setText(Joiner.on(";").join(mStore
                                .getColorArray(key)));
                break;                  case IntegerArray:
            }
        }
    ...
```

4. Improve `onSetValue()` to convert a list of values into an array before transmitting it to `Store` (thanks to the Guava transformation feature):

```
        ...
        private void onSetValue() {
            ...
            try {
                switch (type) {
                ...
                case IntegerArray:
                    mStore.setIntegerArray(key, Ints.toArray(
                        stringToList(new Function<String, Integer>() {
```

```
                        public Integer apply(String pSubValue) {
                            return Integer.parseInt(pSubValue);
                        }
                    }, value)));
                    break;
                case StringArray:
                    String[] stringArray = value.split(";");
                    mStore.setStringArray(key, stringArray);
                    break;
                case ColorArray:
                    List<Color> idList = stringToList(
                        new Function<String, Color>() {
                            public Color apply(String pSubValue) {
                                return new Color(pSubValue);
                            }
                        }, value);
                    mStore.setColorArray(key, idList.toArray(
                                         new Color[idList.size()]));
                    break;
                }
            } catch (Exception eException) {
                displayMessage("Incorrect value.");
            }
            updateTitle();
        }
        ...
```

5. Write a helper method `stringToList()` to help you convert a string into a list of the target type:

```
        ...
        private <TType> List<TType> stringToList(
                        Function<String, TType> pConversion,
                        String pValue) {
            String[] splitArray = pValue.split(";");
            List<String> splitList = Arrays.asList(splitArray);
            return Lists.transform(splitList, pConversion);
        }
    }
}
```

6. In `jni/Store.h`, add the new array types to the `StoreType` enumeration. Also, declare the new fields `mIntegerArray`, `mStringArray`, and `mColorArray` in the `StoreValue` union. Store arrays are represented as raw C arrays (that is, a pointer):

```
...
typedef enum {
    ...
    StoreType_Color,
    StoreType_IntegerArray,
    StoreType_StringArray,
    StoreType_ColorArray
} StoreType;

typedef union {
    ...
    jobject   mColor;
    int32_t*  mIntegerArray;
    char**    mStringArray;
    jobject*  mColorArray;
} StoreValue;
...
```

7. We also need to remember the length of these arrays. Enter this information in a new field `mLength` in `StoreEntry`:

```
...
typedef struct {
    char* mKey;
    StoreType mType;
    StoreValue mValue;
    int32_t mLength;
} StoreEntry;
...
```

8. In `jni/Store.cpp`, insert cases in `releaseEntryValue()` for the new arrays types. Indeed, allocated arrays have to be freed when the corresponding entry is released. As colors are Java objects, delete the Global references saved within each array item, else garbage collection will never happen (causing a memory leak):

```
void releaseEntryValue(JNIEnv* pEnv, StoreEntry* pEntry) {
    switch (pEntry->mType) {
    ...
    case StoreType_IntegerArray:
        delete[] pEntry->mValue.mIntegerArray;
        break;
    case StoreType_StringArray:
        // Destroys every C string pointed by the String array
```

```cpp
                // before releasing it.
                for (int32_t i = 0; i < pEntry->mLength; ++i) {
                    delete pEntry->mValue.mStringArray[i];
                }
                delete[] pEntry->mValue.mStringArray;
                break;
            case StoreType_ColorArray:
                // Unreferences every Id before releasing the Id array.
                for (int32_t i = 0; i < pEntry->mLength; ++i) {
                    pEnv->DeleteGlobalRef(pEntry->mValue.mColorArray[i]);
                }
                delete[] pEntry->mValue.mColorArray;
                break;
        }
    }
    ...
```

9. Regenerate the JNI header `jni/com_packtpub_Store.h` with `Javah`. In `jni/com_packtpub_Store.cpp`, implement all these new methods. To do so, first add the `csdtint` include.

```cpp
#include "com_packtpub_store_Store.h"
#include <cstdint>
#include <cstdlib>
#include "Store.h"
...
```

10. Then, cache the `String` and `Color` JNI Classes to be able to create, in the following steps, object arrays of these types. Classes are accessible by reflection from `JNIEnv` itself, and are retrievable from the `JavaVM` given to `JNI_OnLoad()`.

We need to check whether the found classes are null in case they cannot be loaded. If that happens, an exception is raised by the VM so that we can return immediately:

```cpp
...
static jclass StringClass;
static jclass ColorClass;

JNIEXPORT jint JNI_OnLoad(JavaVM* pVM, void* reserved) {
    JNIEnv *env;
    if (pVM->GetEnv((void**) &env, JNI_VERSION_1_6) != JNI_OK) {
        abort();
    }
    // If returned class is null, an exception is raised by the VM.
    jclass StringClassTmp = env->FindClass("java/lang/String");
    if (StringClassTmp == NULL) abort();
```

```
StringClass = (jclass) env->NewGlobalRef(StringClassTmp);
env->DeleteLocalRef(StringClassTmp);
jclass ColorClassTmp = env->FindClass("com/packtpub/store/Color");
if (ColorClassTmp == NULL) abort();
ColorClass = (jclass) env->NewGlobalRef(ColorClassTmp);
env->DeleteLocalRef(ColorClassTmp);
// Store initialization.
gStore.mLength = 0;
return JNI_VERSION_1_6;
}
...
```

11. Write a `getIntegerArray()` implementation. A JNI array of integers is represented with the `jintArray` type. If an int is equivalent to `jint`, an `int *` array is absolutely not equivalent to `jintArray`. The first is a pointer to a memory buffer, whereas the second is a reference to an object.

Thus, to return `jintArray` here, instantiate a new Java integer array with the `NewIntArray()` JNI API method. Then, use `SetIntArrayRegion()` to copy the native int buffer content into `jintArray`:

```
...
JNIEXPORT jintArray JNICALL
Java_com_packtpub_store_Store_getIntegerArray
  (JNIEnv* pEnv, jobject pThis, jstring pKey) {
    StoreEntry* entry = findEntry(pEnv, &gStore, pKey);
    if (isEntryValid(pEnv, entry, StoreType_IntegerArray)) {
        jintArray javaArray = pEnv->NewIntArray(entry->mLength);
        pEnv->SetIntArrayRegion(javaArray, 0, entry->mLength,
                                entry->mValue.mIntegerArray);
        return javaArray;
    } else {
        return NULL;
    }
}
...
```

12. To save a Java array in native code, the inverse operation `GetIntArrayRegion()` exists. The only way to allocate a suitable memory buffer is to measure the array size with `GetArrayLength()`:

```
...
JNIEXPORT void JNICALL Java_com_packtpub_store_Store_setIntegerArray
  (JNIEnv* pEnv, jobject pThis, jstring pKey,
   jintArray pIntegerArray) {
    StoreEntry* entry = allocateEntry(pEnv, &gStore, pKey);
```

```
        if (entry != NULL) {
            jsize length = pEnv->GetArrayLength(pIntegerArray);
            int32_t* array = new int32_t[length];
            pEnv->GetIntArrayRegion(pIntegerArray, 0, length, array);

            entry->mType = StoreType_IntegerArray;
            entry->mLength = length;
            entry->mValue.mIntegerArray = array;
        }
    }
    ...
```

Java object arrays are different than Java primitive arrays. They are instantiated with a class type (here, the cached `String jclass`) because Java arrays are monotype. Object arrays themselves are represented with the `jobjectArray` type and can be created with the `NewObjectArray()` JNI API method.

Unlike primitive arrays, it is not possible to work on all elements at the same time. Instead, objects are set one by one with `SetObjectArrayElement()`. Here, the native array is filled with `String` objects stored on the native side, which keeps Global references to them. So there is no need to delete or create any reference here except the reference to the newly allocated string.

```
    ...
JNIEXPORT jobjectArray JNICALL
Java_com_packtpub_store_Store_getStringArray
    (JNIEnv* pEnv, jobject pThis, jstring pKey) {
    StoreEntry* entry = findEntry(pEnv, &gStore, pKey);
    if (isEntryValid(pEnv, entry, StoreType_StringArray)) {
        // An array of String in Java is in fact an array of object.
        jobjectArray javaArray = pEnv->NewObjectArray(entry->mLength,
                StringClass, NULL);
        // Creates a new Java String object for each C string stored.
        // Reference to the String can be removed right after it is
        // added to the Java array, as the latter holds a reference
        // to the String object.
        for (int32_t i = 0; i < entry->mLength; ++i) {
            jstring string = pEnv->NewStringUTF(
                    entry->mValue.mStringArray[i]);
            // Puts the new string in the array
            pEnv->SetObjectArrayElement(javaArray, i, string);
            // Do it here to avoid holding many useless local refs.
            pEnv->DeleteLocalRef(string);
        }
```

```
            return javaArray;
        } else {
            return NULL;
        }
    }
    ...
```

In `setStringArray()`, array elements are retrieved one by one with
`GetObjectArrayElement()`. Returned references are local and should be made global to
store them safely on the native side.

```
    ...
    JNIEXPORT void JNICALL Java_com_packtpub_store_Store_setStringArray
      (JNIEnv* pEnv, jobject pThis, jstring pKey,
       jobjectArray pStringArray) {
        // Creates a new entry with the new String array.
        StoreEntry* entry = allocateEntry(pEnv, &gStore, pKey);
        if (entry != NULL) {
            // Allocates an array of C string.
            jsize length = pEnv->GetArrayLength(pStringArray);
            char** array = new char*[length];
            // Fills the C array with a copy of each input Java string.
            for (int32_t i = 0; i < length; ++i) {
                // Gets the current Java String from the input Java array.
                // Object arrays can be accessed element by element only.
                jstring string = (jstring)
                            pEnv->GetObjectArrayElement(pStringArray, i);
                jsize stringLength = pEnv->GetStringUTFLength(string);
                array[i] = new char[stringLength + 1];
                // Directly copies the Java String into our new C buffer.
                pEnv->GetStringUTFRegion(string,0,stringLength, array[i]);
                // Append the null character for string termination.
                array[i][stringLength] = '\0';
                // No need to keep a reference to the Java string anymore.
                pEnv->DeleteLocalRef(string);
            }
            entry->mType = StoreType_StringArray;
            entry->mLength = length;
            entry->mValue.mStringArray = array;
        }
    }
```

Implement the same operations for colors, starting with `getColorArray()`. Since strings
and colors are both objects on the Java side, the returned array can be created in the same
way with `NewObjectArray()`.

Place each `Color` reference saved inside the array using the JNI method
`SetObjectArrayElement()`. Since colors have been stored on the native side as
global Java references, no Local reference needs to be created or deleted:

```
...
JNIEXPORT jobjectArray JNICALL
Java_com_packtpub_store_Store_getColorArray
  (JNIEnv* pEnv, jobject pThis, jstring pKey) {
    StoreEntry* entry = findEntry(pEnv, &gStore, pKey);
    if (isEntryValid(pEnv, entry, StoreType_ColorArray)) {
        // Creates a new array with objects of type Id.
        jobjectArray javaArray = pEnv->NewObjectArray(entry->mLength,
                ColorClass, NULL);
        // Fills the array with the Color objects stored on the native
        // side, which keeps a global reference to them. So no need
        // to delete or create any reference here.
        for (int32_t i = 0; i < entry->mLength; ++i) {
            pEnv->SetObjectArrayElement(javaArray, i,
                                        entry->mValue.mColorArray[i]);
        }
        return javaArray;
    } else {
        return NULL;
    }
}
...
```

In `setColorArray()`, color elements are also retrieved one by one with
`GetObjectArrayElement()`. Here, again, returned references are local and should be
made global to store them safely on the native side:

```
...
JNIEXPORT void JNICALL Java_com_packtpub_store_Store_setColorArray
  (JNIEnv* pEnv, jobject pThis, jstring pKey,
   jobjectArray pColorArray) {
    // Saves the Color array in the store.
    StoreEntry* entry = allocateEntry(pEnv, &gStore, pKey);
    if (entry != NULL) {
        // Allocates a C array of Color objects.
        jsize length = pEnv->GetArrayLength(pColorArray);
        jobject* array = new jobject[length];
        // Fills the C array with a copy of each input Java Color.
        for (int32_t i = 0; i < length; ++i) {
            // Gets the current Color object from the input Java array.
```

```
            // Object arrays can be accessed element by element only.
            jobject localColor = pEnv->GetObjectArrayElement(
                    pColorArray, i);
            // The Java Color is going to be stored on the native side
            // Need to keep a global reference to avoid a potential
            // garbage collection after method returns.
            array[i] = pEnv->NewGlobalRef(localColor);
            // We have a global reference to the Color, so we can now
            // get rid of the local one.
            pEnv->DeleteLocalRef(localColor);
        }
        entry->mType = StoreType_ColorArray;
        entry->mLength = length;
        entry->mValue.mColorArray = array;
    }
}
```

What just happened?

We transmitted Java arrays from the Java to the native side and vice versa. Java arrays are Java objects that can only be manipulated through a dedicated JNI API. They cannot be cast into native C/C++ arrays and are not usable the same way.

We also saw how to leverage the JNI_OnLoad() callback to cache JNI class descriptors. Class descriptors, of type jclass (which is also jobject behind the scenes), are equivalent to Class<?> in Java. They allow to define the type of array we want, a bit like the reflection API in Java. We will come back to this subject in the next chapter.

Primitive arrays

Primitives array types available are jbooleanArray, jbyteArray, jcharArray, jdoubleArray, jfloatArray, jlongArray, and jshortArray. These types represent references to real Java arrays.

These arrays can be manipulated with several methods provided by JNI:

1. New<Primitive>Array() to create a new Java array:

   ```
   jintArray NewIntArray(jsize length)
   ```

2. GetArrayLength() retrieves the length of an array:

   ```
   jsize GetArrayLength(jarray array)
   ```

3. `Get<Primitive>ArrayElements()` retrieves a whole array into a memory buffer allocated by JNI. The last parameter `isCopy`, when not null, indicates whether an array has been internally copied by JNI or it has returned buffer points to the real Java string memory:

```
jint* GetIntArrayElements(jintArray array, jboolean* isCopy)
```

4. `Release<Primitive>ArrayElements()` releases the memory buffer allocated by `Get<Primitive>ArrayElements()`. Always use both in pairs. The last parameter mode is related to the `isCopy` parameter and indicates the following:

   ❑ If 0, then JNI should copy the modified array back into the initial Java array and tell JNI to release its temporary memory buffer. This is the most common flag.

   ❑ If `JNI_COMMIT`, then JNI should copy the modified array back into the initial array but without releasing the memory. That way, the client code can transmit the result back to Java while still pursuing its work on the memory buffer.

   ❑ If `JNI_ABORT`, then JNI must discard any change made in the memory buffer and leave the Java array unchanged. This will not work correctly if the temporary native memory buffer is not a copy.

   ```
   void ReleaseIntArrayElements(jintArray array, jint* elems, jint
   mode)
   ```

5. `Get<Primitive>ArrayRegion()` retrieves all or part of an array into a memory buffer allocated by the client code. For example for integers:

```
void GetIntArrayRegion(jintArray array, jsize start, jsize len,
                    jint* buf)
```

6. `Set<Primitive>ArrayRegion()` initializes all or part of a Java array from a native buffer managed by the client code. For example for integers:

```
void SetIntArrayRegion(jintArray array, jsize start, jsize len,
                    const jint* buf)
```

7. `Get<Primitive>ArrayCritical()` and `Release<Primitive>ArrayCriti cal()` are similar to `Get<Primitive>ArrayElements()` and `Release<Primi tive>ArrayElements()` but are only available to provide a direct access to the target array (instead of a copy). In exchange, the caller must not perform blocking or JNI calls and should not hold the array for a long time (like a critical section with threads). Not that the same two methods are featured for all primitives:

```
void* GetPrimitiveArrayCritical(jarray array, jboolean* isCopy)
void ReleasePrimitiveArrayCritical(jarray array, void* carray,
jint mode)
```

Have a go hero – handling other array types

With the knowledge freshly acquired, you can implement store methods for other array types: jbooleanArray, jbyteArray, jcharArray, jdoubleArray, jfloatArray, jlongArray, and jshortArray.

As an example, you can write the setBooleanArray() method for the jbooleanArray type using GetBooleanArrayElements() and ReleaseBooleanArrayElements() instead of GetBooleanArrayRegion(). The result should look like the following, with both methods called in a pair with memcpy() in between:

```
...
JNIEXPORT void JNICALL Java_com_packtpub_store_Store_setBooleanArray
  (JNIEnv* pEnv, jobject pThis, jstring pKey,
   jbooleanArray pBooleanArray) {
    // Finds/creates an entry in the store and fills its content.
    StoreEntry* entry = allocateEntry(pEnv, &gStore, pKey);
    if (entry != NULL) {
        entry->mType = StoreType_BooleanArray;
        jsize length = pEnv->GetArrayLength(pBooleanArray);
        uint8_t* array = new uint8_t[length];
        // Retrieves array content.
        jboolean* arrayTmp = pEnv->GetBooleanArrayElements(
                pBooleanArray, NULL);
        memcpy(array, arrayTmp, length * sizeof(uint8_t));
        pEnv->ReleaseBooleanArrayElements(pBooleanArray,
          arrayTmp, 0);
        entry->mType = StoreType_BooleanArray;
        entry->mValue.mBooleanArray = array;
        entry->mLength = length;
    }
}
...
```

 The resulting project is provided with this book under the name Store_Part8_Full.

Object arrays

Object arrays are named `jobjectArray` in JNI and represent a reference to a Java Object array. Objects arrays are specific because unlike primitive arrays, each array element is a reference to an object. As a consequence, a new Global reference is automatically registered each time an object is inserted in the array. That way, when native calls end, references do not get garbage collected. Note that object arrays cannot be converted to "native" arrays like primitives.

Object arrays can be manipulated with several methods provided by JNI:

1. `NewObjectArray()` creates a new object array instance:

    ```
    jobjectArray NewObjectArray(jsize length, jclass elementClass,
                                jobject initialElement);
    ```

2. `GetArrayLength()` retrieves the length of an array (same method as primitives):

    ```
    jsize GetArrayLength(jarray array)
    ```

3. `GetObjectArrayElement()` retrieves one single object reference from a Java array. The returned reference is Local:

    ```
    jobject GetObjectArrayElement(jobjectArray array, jsize index)
    ```

4. `SetObjectArrayElement()` puts one single object reference into a Java array. A Global reference is created implicitly:

    ```
    void SetObjectArrayElement(jobjectArray array, jsize index,
    jobject value)
    ```

See `http://docs.oracle.com/javase/6/docs/technotes/guides/jni/spec/functions.html` for a more exhaustive list of JNI functions.

Raising and checking Java exceptions

Error handling in the Store project is not really satisfying. If the requested key cannot be found or if the retrieved value type does not match the requested type, a default value is returned. Do not even try with a Color entry. We definitely need a way to indicate that an error occurred! And what better way to indicate an error than an exception?

JNI provides the necessary API to raise an exception at the JVM level. These exceptions are the ones you can then catch in Java. They have nothing in common, neither the syntax nor the flow, with the usual C++ exceptions you can find in other programs (we will see more about them in *Chapter 9, Porting Existing Libraries to Android*).

In this part, we will see how to raise JNI exceptions from the native to the Java side.

 The resulting project is provided with this book under the name Store_Part9.

Time for action – raising & catching exceptions in native Store

1. Create the Java exception com.packtpub.exception.InvalidTypeException of type Exception as follows:

```
package com.packtpub.exception;

public class InvalidTypeException extends Exception {
    public InvalidTypeException(String pDetailMessage) {
        super(pDetailMessage);
    }
}
```

Repeat the operation for two other exceptions: NotExistingKeyException of type Exception and StoreFullException of type RuntimeException.

2. Open Store.java and declare thrown exceptions on getInteger() in class Store (StoreFullException is RuntimeException and does not need declaration):

```
public class Store {
    ...
    public native int getInteger(String pKey)
        throws NotExistingKeyException, InvalidTypeException;
    public native void setInteger(String pKey, int pInt);
    ...
```

Repeat the operation for all other getter prototypes (strings, colors, and so on).

3. These exceptions need to be caught. Catch NotExistingKeyException and InvalidTypeException in onGetValue():

```
public class StoreActivity extends Activity {
    ...
    public static class PlaceholderFragment extends Fragment {
        ...
        private void onGetValue() {
            ...
            try {
                switch (type) {
                ...
```

```
            }
            // Process any exception raised while retrieving data.
            catch (NotExistingKeyException eNotExistingKeyException) {
                displayMessage(eNotExistingKeyException.getMessage());
            } catch (InvalidTypeException eInvalidTypeException) {
                displayMessage(eInvalidTypeException.getMessage());
            }
        }
```

4. Catch StoreFullException in onSetValue() in case the entry cannot be inserted because the store capacity is exhausted:

```
        private void onSetValue() {
            ...
            try {
                ...
            } catch (NumberFormatException eNumberFormatException) {
                displayMessage("Incorrect value.");
            } catch (StoreFullException eStoreFullException) {
                displayMessage(eStoreFullException.getMessage());
            } catch (Exception eException) {
                displayMessage("Incorrect value.");
            }
            updateTitle();
        }
        ...
    }
}
```

5. Open jni/Store.h created in previous parts and define three new helper methods to throw exceptions:

```
...
void throwInvalidTypeException(JNIEnv* pEnv);

void throwNotExistingKeyException(JNIEnv* pEnv);

void throwStoreFullException(JNIEnv* pEnv);
#endif
```

6. Edit the `jni/Store.cpp` file to throw `NotExistingKeyException` and `InvalidTypeException` when getting an inappropriate entry from the store. A good place to raise them is when checking an entry with `isEntryValid()`:

```
...
bool isEntryValid(JNIEnv* pEnv, StoreEntry* pEntry, StoreType pType) {
    if (pEntry == NULL) {
        throwNotExistingKeyException(pEnv);
    } else if (pEntry->mType != pType) {
        throwInvalidTypeException(pEnv);
    }
    return !pEnv->ExceptionCheck();
}
...
```

7. `StoreFullException` is obviously raised when a new entry is inserted. Modify `allocateEntry()` in the same file to check entry insertions:

```
...
StoreEntry* allocateEntry(JNIEnv* pEnv, Store* pStore, jstring pKey) {
    // If entry already exists in the store, releases its content
    // and keep its key.
    StoreEntry* entry = findEntry(pEnv, pStore, pKey);
    if (entry != NULL) {
        releaseEntryValue(pEnv, entry);
    }
    // If entry does not exist, create a new entry
    // right after the entries already stored.
    else {
        // Checks store can accept a new entry.
        if (pStore->mLength >= STORE_MAX_CAPACITY) {
            throwStoreFullException(pEnv);
            return NULL;
        }
        entry = pStore->mEntries + pStore->mLength;
        // Copies the new key into its final C string buffer.
        ...
    }
    return entry;
}
...
```

Implement `throwNotExistingException()`. To throw a Java exception, the first task is to find the corresponding class (like with the Java reflection API). Since we can assume these exceptions will not be raised frequently, we can keep from caching class reference. Then, raise the exception with `ThrowNew()`. Once we no longer need the exception class reference, we can get rid of it with `DeleteLocalRef()`:

```
...
void throwNotExistingKeyException(JNIEnv* pEnv) {
    jclass clazz = pEnv->FindClass(
                    "com/packtpub/exception/NotExistingKeyException");
    if (clazz != NULL) {
        pEnv->ThrowNew(clazz, "Key does not exist.");
    }
    pEnv->DeleteLocalRef(clazz);
}
```

Repeat the operation for the two other exceptions. The code is identical (even to throw a runtime exception) and only the class name changes.

What just happened?

Launch the application and try to get an entry with a non-existing key. Repeat the operation with an entry, which exists in the store but with a different type than the one selected in the GUI. In both cases, there is an error message. Try to save more than 16 references in the store and you will get an error again. In each case, an exception has been raised on the native side and caught on the Java side.

Raising exceptions in native code is not a complex task, but it is not trivial either. An exception is instantiated with a class descriptor of type `jclass`. This class descriptor is required by JNI to instantiate the proper kind of exception. JNI exceptions are not declared on JNI method prototypes since they are not related to C++ exceptions (exceptions which cannot be declared in C anyway). This explains why we have not regenerated the JNI header to accommodate the changes in the `Store.java file`.

Executing code in Exception state

Once an exception is raised, be really careful with the JNI call you make. Indeed, any subsequent call fails until either of the following events occur:

1. The method is returned and an exception is propagated.

2. The exception is cleared. Clearing an exception means that the exception is handled and thus not propagated to Java. For example:

```
// Raise an exception
jclass clazz = pEnv->FindClass("java/lang/RuntimeException");
if (clazz != NULL) {
  pEnv->ThrowNew(clazz, "Oups an exception.");
}
pEnv->DeleteLocalRef(clazz);

...

// Detect and catch the exception by clearing it.
jthrowable exception = pEnv->ExceptionOccurred();
if (exception) {
  // Do something...
  pEnv->ExceptionDescribe();
  pEnv->ExceptionClear();
  pEnv->DeleteLocalRef(exception);
}
```

Only a few JNI methods are still safe to call after an exception is raised:

DeleteGlobalRef	PopLocalFrame
DeleteLocalRef	PushLocalFrame
DeleteWeakGlobalRef	Release<Primitive>ArrayElements
ExceptionCheck	ReleasePrimitiveArrayCritical
ExceptionClear	ReleaseStringChars
ExceptionDescribe	ReleaseStringCritical
ExceptionOccurred	ReleaseStringUTFChars
MonitorExit	

Do not try to call any other JNI method. Native code should clean its resources and give control back to Java as soon as possible (or handle the exception itself). Indeed, JNI exceptions have nothing in common with C++ exceptions. Their execution flow is completely different. When a Java exception is raised from native code, the latter can still pursue its processing. However, as soon as native call returns hand back to the Java VM, the latter propagates the exception as usual. In other words, JNI exceptions raised from native code affect Java code only (and JNI calls others then the one listed previously).

Exception handling API

JNI offers several methods to manage exceptions among which:

1. `ThrowNew()` to raise the exception itself, allocating a new instance:

    ```
    jint ThrowNew(jclass clazz, const char* message)
    ```

2. `Throw()` to raise an exception that has already been allocated (for example, to rethrow):

    ```
    jint Throw(jthrowable obj)
    ```

3. `ExceptionCheck()` to check whether an exception is pending, whoever raised it (native code or a Java callback). A simple `jboolean` is returned, which makes it appropriate for simple checks:

    ```
    jboolean ExceptionCheck()
    ```

4. `ExceptionOccurred()` to retrieve a `jthrowable` reference to the raised exception:

    ```
    jthrowable ExceptionOccurred()
    ```

5. `ExceptionDescribe()` is equivalent to `printStackTrace()` in Java:

    ```
    void ExceptionDescribe()
    ```

6. An exception can be marked as caught on the native side with `ExceptionClear()`:

    ```
    void ExceptionClear()
    ```

It is essential to learn how to use these methods to write robust code, especially when calling back Java from native code. We will learn more about this subject in the next chapter.

Summary

In this chapter, we saw how to make Java communicate with C/C++. Android is now almost bilingual! Java can call C/C++ code with any type of data or object.

We first initialized a native JNI library using the `JNI_OnLoad` hook. Then, we converted Java Strings inside native code and saw the difference between Modified UTF-8 and UTF-16 character encoding. We also passed Java primitives to native code. Each of these primitives has their C/C++ equivalent type they can be cast to.

We also handled Java object references in native code using Global references and learned the difference between these and Local references. The first must be carefully deleted to ensure proper garbage collection, while the latter has native method scope and must be managed with care as their number is limited by default.

We also discussed how to manage Java arrays in native code so that we could access their content as native arrays. Arrays may or may not be copied by the VM when manipulated in native code. This performance penalty has to be taken into account.

Finally, we raised and checked Java exceptions in native code. We saw that they have a different flows from the standard C++ exceptions. When an exception occurs, only a few cleaning JNI methods are safe to call. JNI exceptions are JVM-level exceptions, which means their flow is completely different from standard C++ exceptions.

However, there is still more to come. Any Java object, method, or field can be called or retrieved by native code. Let's see how to call Java from C/C++ code in the next chapter.

4
Calling Java Back from Native Code

To reach its full potential, JNI allows calling back Java code from C/C++. "Back" because native code is first invoked from Java, which in turn calls it back. Such calls are performed through a reflective API, which allows doing almost anything that can be done directly in Java.

Another important matter to consider with JNI is threading. Native code can be run on a Java thread, managed by the Dalvik VM, and also from a native thread created with standard POSIX primitives. Obviously, a native thread cannot call JNI code unless it is turned into a managed Java thread! Programming with JNI necessitates knowledge of all these subtleties. This chapter will guide you through the main ones.

The last topic, which is specific to Android and not JNI, other: the Android-specific Bitmap API aims at giving full processing power to graphics applications running on these tiny (but powerful) devices.

The Android NDK also proposes a new API to access natively an important type of object: bitmaps. The Bitmap API, which is Android-specific, gives full processing power to graphics applications running on these tiny (but powerful) devices.

The `Store` project we started in the previous chapter is going to be our canvas to demonstrate JNI callbacks and synchronization. To illustrate Bitmap processing, we are going to create a new project that decodes a device's camera feed inside native code.

To summarize, in this chapter, we are going to learn how to:

◆ Call Java back from native code

◆ Attach a native thread to the Dalvik VM and handle synchronization with Java threads

◆ Process Java bitmaps in native code

By the end of this chapter, you should be able to make Java and C/C++ communicate and synchronize reciprocally.

Calling Java back from native code

In the previous chapter, we discovered how to get a Java class descriptor with the JNI method `FindClass()`. However, we can get much more! Actually, if you are a regular Java developer, this should remind you of something: the Java Reflection API. JNI is similar in that it can modify Java object fields, run Java methods, and access static members, but from native code!

For this last part with the `Store` project, let's enhance our store application so that it notifies Java when an entry has been successfully inserted.

 The resulting project is provided with this book under the name `Store_Part10`.

Time for action – determining JNI method signatures

Let's define a Java interface that native C/C++ code will call back through JNI:

1. Create a `StoreListener.java`, which contains an interface defining a few callbacks, one for integers, one for strings, and one for colors, as follows:

```
package com.packtpub.store;

public interface StoreListener {
    void onSuccess(int pValue);

    void onSuccess(String pValue);

    void onSuccess(Color pValue);
}
```

2. Open `Store.java` and make a few changes.

- Declare a member delegate `StoreListener`, to which success callbacks are sent

- Change the `Store` constructor to inject the delegate listener, which is going to be `StoreActivity`

```
Public class Store implements StoreListener {
    private StoreListener mListener;


    public Store(StoreListener pListener) {
        mListener = pListener;
    }
    ...
```

Finally, implement the `StoreListener` interface and its corresponding methods, which simply forwards calls to the delegate:

```
    ...
    public void onSuccess(int pValue) {
        mListener.onSuccess(pValue);
    }

    public void onSuccess(String pValue) {
        mListener.onSuccess(pValue);
    }

    public void onSuccess(Color pValue) {
        mListener.onSuccess(pValue);
    }
}
```

3. Open `StoreActivity.java` and implement the `StoreListener` interface in `PlaceholderFragment`.

Also, change the `Store` construction accordingly:

```
public class StoreActivity extends Activity {
    ...
    public static class PlaceholderFragment extends Fragment
    implements StoreListener {
        private Store mStore = new Store(this);
        ...
```

When a success callback is received, a simple toast message is raised:

```
. . .
public void onSuccess(int pValue) {
    displayMessage(String.format(
        "Integer '%1$d' successfuly saved!", pValue));
}

public void onSuccess(String pValue) {
    displayMessage(String.format(
        "String '%1$s' successfuly saved!", pValue));
}

public void onSuccess(Color pValue) {
    displayMessage(String.format(
        "Color '%1$s' successfuly saved!", pValue));
    }
  }
}
```

4. Open a terminal in the `Store` project's directory and run the `javap` command to determine method signatures.

    ```
    javap -s -classpath bin/classes com.packtpub.store.Store
    ```

```
packt@computer: ~/Project/Store
File  Edit  View  Search  Terminal  Help

  public void onSuccess(int);
    Signature: (I)V

  public void onSuccess(java.lang.String);
    Signature: (Ljava/lang/String;)V

  public void onSuccess(com.packtpub.store.Color);
    Signature: (Lcom/packtpub/store/Color;)V
}
```

What just happened?

Calling back Java methods with the JNI API requires **descriptors**, as we will see in the next part. To determine a Java method descriptor, we need a **signature**. Indeed, methods in Java can be **overloaded**, which means that there can be two methods with the same name but different parameters. This is why a signature is required.

We can determine a method's signature with `javap`, a JDK utility to disassemble `.class` files. This signature can then be given to the JNI Reflection API. Formally speaking, a signature is declared in the following way:

```
(<Parameter 1 Type Code>[<Parameter 1 Class>];...)<Return Type Code>
```

For example, the signature for the method `boolean myFunction(android.view.View pView, int pIndex)` would be `(Landroid/view/View;I)Z`. Another example, `(I)V`, means an integer is expected and a void is returned. A last example, `(Ljava/lang/String;)V`, means a String is passed in parameter.

The following table summarizes the various types available in JNI with their code:

Java type	Native type	Native array type	Type code	Array type code
boolean	jboolean	jbooleanArray	Z	[Z
byte	jbyte	jbyteArray	B	[B
char	jchar	jcharArray	C	[C
double	jdouble	jdoubleArray	D	[D
float	jfloat	jfloatArray	F	[F
int	jint	jintArray	I	[I
long	jlong	jlongArray	J	[J
Short	jshort	jshortArray	S	[S
Object	jobject	jobjectArray	L	[L
String	jstring	N/A	L	[L
Class	jclass	N/A	L	[L
Throwable	jthrowable	N/A	L	[L
void	void	N/A	V	N/A

All these values correspond to the one dumped by `javap`. For more information about descriptors and signatures, have a look at the Oracle documentation at `http://docs.oracle.com/javase/specs/jvms/se7/html/jvms-4.html#jvms-4.3`.

Now that we have the proper signature, we can start calling Java from C/C++.

Time for action – calling back Java from native code

Let's continue our `Store` by calling back the interface we defined from native code:

1. In `com_packtpub_store_Store.cpp`, declare method descriptors with type `jmethodID` for each callback, which is going to be cached:

    ```
    ...
    static Store gStore;

    static jclass StringClass;
    static jclass ColorClass;

    static jmethodID MethodOnSuccessInt;
    static jmethodID MethodOnSuccessString;
    static jmethodID MethodOnSuccessColor;
    ...
    ```

2. Then, cache all the callback descriptors in `JNI_OnLoad()`. This can be done in two main steps:

    Getting a Class descriptor with the JNI method `FindClass()`. One can find a class descriptor, thanks to its absolute package path, here: `com./packtpub/store/Store`.

    Retrieving a method descriptor from the class descriptor with `GetMethodID()`. To differentiate several overloaded methods, the signatures retrieved earlier with `javap` must be specified:

    ```
    ...
    JNIEXPORT jint JNI_OnLoad(JavaVM* pVM, void* reserved) {
        JNIEnv *env;
        if (pVM->GetEnv((void**) &env, JNI_VERSION_1_6) != JNI_OK) {
            abort();
        }
        ...
        // Caches methods.
        jclass StoreClass = env->FindClass("com/packtpub/store/Store");
        if (StoreClass == NULL) abort();

        MethodOnSuccessInt = env->GetMethodID(StoreClass, "onSuccess",
                "(I)V");
    ```

```
if (MethodOnSuccessInt == NULL) abort();

MethodOnSuccessString = env->GetMethodID(StoreClass, "onSuccess",
        "(Ljava/lang/String;)V");
if (MethodOnSuccessString == NULL) abort();

MethodOnSuccessColor = env->GetMethodID(StoreClass, "onSuccess",
        "(Lcom/packtpub/store/Color;)V");
if (MethodOnSuccessColor == NULL) abort();
env->DeleteLocalRef(StoreClass);


// Store initialization.

gStore.mLength = 0;

return JNI_VERSION_1_6;

}

...
```

3. Notify the Java Store (that is, `pThis`) when an integer is successfully inserted in `setInteger()`. To invoke a Java method on a Java object, simply use `CallVoidMethod()` (which means that the called Java method returns void). To do so, we need:

- ❏ An object instance

- ❏ A method signature

- ❏ Effective parameters to pass, if applicable (here, an integer value)

```
...
JNIEXPORT void JNICALL Java_com_packtpub_store_Store_setInteger
  (JNIEnv* pEnv, jobject pThis, jstring pKey, jint pInteger) {
    StoreEntry* entry = allocateEntry(pEnv, &gStore, pKey);
    if (entry != NULL) {
        entry->mType = StoreType_Integer;
        entry->mValue.mInteger = pInteger;

        pEnv->CallVoidMethod(pThis, MethodOnSuccessInt,
                (jint) entry->mValue.mInteger);
    }
}
...
```

4. Repeat the operation for strings. There is no need to generate a Global reference when allocating the returned Java string as it is used immediately in the Java callback. We can also destroy the Local reference to this string right after usage, but JNI will take care of that when returning from the native callback:

```
. . .
JNIEXPORT void JNICALL Java_com_packtpub_store_Store_setString
    (JNIEnv* pEnv, jobject pThis, jstring pKey, jstring pString) {
        // Turns the Java string into a temporary C string.
        StoreEntry* entry = allocateEntry(pEnv, &gStore, pKey);
        if (entry != NULL) {
            entry->mType = StoreType_String;
            . . .

            pEnv->CallVoidMethod(pThis, MethodOnSuccessString,
                    (jstring) pEnv->NewStringUTF(entry->mValue.mString));
        }
    }
    . . .
```

5. Finally, repeat the operation for colors:

```
. . .
JNIEXPORT void JNICALL Java_com_packtpub_store_Store_setColor
    (JNIEnv* pEnv, jobject pThis, jstring pKey, jobject pColor) {
        // Save the Color reference in the store.
        StoreEntry* entry = allocateEntry(pEnv, &gStore, pKey);
        if (entry != NULL) {
            entry->mType = StoreType_Color;
            entry->mValue.mColor = pEnv->NewGlobalRef(pColor);

            pEnv->CallVoidMethod(pThis, MethodOnSuccessColor,
                    (jstring) entry->mValue.mColor);
        }
    }
    . . .
```

What just happened?

Launch the application and insert an integer, a string, or color entry. A successful message is displayed with the inserted value. The native code called the Java side thanks to the JNI Reflection API. This API is not only useful to execute a Java method, it is also the only way to process `jobject` parameters passed to a native method. However, if calling C/C++ code from Java is rather easy, performing Java operations from C/C++ is a bit more involving!

Although a bit repetitive and verbose, calling any Java method should always be as trivial as this:

- Retrieve the class descriptor from those we want to call methods (here, the `Store` Java object):

  ```
  jclass StoreClass = env->FindClass("com/packtpub/store/Store");
  ```

- Retrieve the method descriptors for the callback we want to call (such as the `Method` class in Java). These method descriptors are retrieved from the class descriptor, which owns it (like a `Class` in Java):

  ```
  jmethodID MethodOnSuccessInt = env->GetMethodID(StoreClass,
                                      "onSuccess", "(I)V");
  ```

- Optionally, cache the descriptors so that they can be used immediately in future native calls. Again, `JNI_OnLoad()` makes it easy to cache JNI descriptors before any native call is made. Descriptors whose names end with `Id`, such as `jmethodID`, can be freely cached. They are not references that can be leaked, or have to be made global on the opposite to `jclass` descriptors.

   Caching descriptors is definitely good practice, as retrieving Fields or Methods through the JNI reflection may cause some overhead.

- Invoke methods with the necessary parameters on an object. The same method descriptor can be reused on any object instance of the corresponding class:

  ```
  env->CallVoidMethod(pThis, MethodOnSuccessInt, (jint) myInt);
  ```

Whatever method you need to call on a Java object, the same process always applies.

More on the JNI Reflection API

Once you know the Reflection API, you know most of the JNI. Here are some of the provided methods that may be useful:

- FindClass() retrieves a (Local) reference to a Class descriptor object according to its absolute path:

  ```
  jclass FindClass(const char* name)
  ```

- GetObjectClass() has the same purpose, except that FindClass() finds class definitions according to their absolute path, whereas the other finds the class directly from an object instance (such as getClass() in Java):

  ```
  jclass GetObjectClass(jobject obj)
  ```

- The following methods allow you to retrieve JNI descriptors for methods and fields, and either static or instance members. These descriptors are IDs and not references to Java objects. There is no need to turn them into Global references. These methods require the method or field name and a signature to differentiate overloads. Constructor descriptors are retrieved in the same way as methods, except that their name is always <init> and they have a void return value:

  ```
  jmethodID GetMethodID(jclass clazz, const char* name,
                        const char* sig)
  jmethodID GetStaticMethodID(jclass clazz, const char* name,
                              const char* sig)

  jfieldID GetStaticFieldID(jclass clazz, const char* name,
                            const char* sig)
  jfieldID GetFieldID(jclass clazz, const char* name, const char* sig)
  ```

- There is a second set of methods to retrieve field values using their corresponding descriptors. There is one getter and one setter method per primitive type, plus another for objects:

  ```
  jobject GetObjectField(jobject obj, jfieldID fieldID)
  <primitive> Get<Primitive>Field(jobject obj, jfieldID fieldID)

  void SetObjectField(jobject obj, jfieldID fieldID, jobject value)
  void Set<Primitive>Field(jobject obj, jfieldID fieldID,
                           <jprimitive> value)
  ```

- The same goes for methods according to their return values:

  ```
  jobject CallObjectMethod(JNIEnv*, jobject, jmethodID, ...)

  <jprimitive> Call<Primitive>Method(JNIEnv*, jobject, jmethodID, ...);
  ```

- Variants of these methods exist with an A and V postfix. The behavior is identical, except that arguments are specified respectively using a va_list (that is, variable argument list) or jvalue array (jvalue being a union of all JNI types):

```
jobject CallObjectMethodV(JNIEnv*, jobject, jmethodID, va_list);
jobject CallObjectMethodA(JNIEnv*, jobject, jmethodID, jvalue*);
```

Have a look at jni.h in the Android NDK include directory to see all the possibilities by the JNI reflective API.

Debugging JNI

The goal of JNI calls is often performance. Thus, JNI does not perform advanced checking when its API methods are invoked. Hopefully, there exists an **extended checking** mode, which performs advanced checks and gives feedback in the Android Logcat.

To activate it, run the following command from a command prompt:

```
adb shell setprop debug.checkjni 1
```

The extended checking mode is available for applications started after this flag is set, until it is set to 0, or until the device is rebooted. For rooted devices, the whole device can be started with this mode with the following commands:

```
adb shell stop
adb shell setprop dalvik.vm.checkjni true
adb shell start
```

If everything works properly, a message **Late-enabling – Xcheck:jni** appears in the Logcat when your application starts. Then, check the Logcat regularly to find its JNI warning or error.

```
packt@packt: ~
File Edit View Search Terminal Help
I/art     ( 2280): Late-enabling -Xcheck:jni
F/art     ( 2280): art/runtime/check_jni.cc:65] JNI DETECTED ERROR IN APPLICATION: DeleteGlobalRef on
local reference: 0xf6600019
F/art     ( 2280): art/runtime/check_jni.cc:65]    in call to DeleteGlobalRef
```

Synchronizing Java and native threads

Parallel programming is a mainstream subject nowadays. Android makes no exception since the introduction of multicore processors. You can do the threading entirely on the Java side (with the Java Thread and Concurrency APIs), on the native side (with the **POSIX PThread** API, which is provided by the NDK), and, more interestingly, between the Java and native side using JNI.

In this part, we will create a background thread, the watcher, which keeps a constant eye on what is inside the data store. It iterates through all entries and then sleeps for a fixed amount of time. When the watcher thread finds a key of a specific type predefined in the code, it acts accordingly. For this first part, we are just going to clip integer values to a predefined range.

Of course, threads need synchronization. The native thread is going to access and update the store only when a user understands the UI thread, and does not modify it. The native thread is created in C/C++ but the UI thread is a Java thread. We are going to use JNI monitors to synchronize both of them.

Time for action – allocating an object with JNI

Let's define a background Watcher that will use an object shared between Java and C/C++ as a lock:

1. In `Store.java`, add two new methods to start and stop a watcher thread. These methods respectively return and take a `long` as parameter. This value helps us hold a native pointer on the Java side:

    ```
    public class Store implements StoreListener {
        ...
        public native long startWatcher();
        public native void stopWatcher(long pPointer);
    }
    ```

2. Create a new file, `StoreThreadSafe.java`. The `StoreThreadSafe` class inherits from the `Store` class and aims at making the `Store` instances thread-safe using `synchronized` Java blocks. Declare a static member field `LOCK` of type `Object` and define a default constructor:

    ```
    package com.packtpub.store;

    import com.packtpub.exception.InvalidTypeException;
    ```

```
import com.packtpub.exception.NotExistingKeyException;

public class StoreThreadSafe extends Store {
    protected static Object LOCK;

    public StoreThreadSafe(StoreListener pListener) {
        super(pListener);
    }
    ...
```

3. Override the `Store` methods, such as `getCount()`, `getInteger()`, and `setInteger()` using Java blocks synchronized with the `LOCK` object:

```
    ...
    @Override
    public int getCount() {
        synchronized (LOCK) {
            return super.getCount();
        }
    }
    ...
    @Override
    public int getInteger(String pKey)
        throws NotExistingKeyException, InvalidTypeException
    {
        synchronized (LOCK) {
            return super.getInteger(pKey);
        }
    }

    @Override
    public void setInteger(String pKey, int pInt) {
        synchronized (LOCK) {
            super.setInteger(pKey, pInt);
        }
    }
    ...
```

4. Do the same for all other methods, such as `getString()`, `setString()`, `getColor()`, `setColor()`, etc., and the `stopWatcher()` method. Do not override the `onSuccess` callbacks and the `startWatcher()` method:

```
...
@Override
public void stopWatcher(long pPointer) {
    synchronized (LOCK) {
        super.stopWatcher(pPointer);
    }
}
}
```

Do *not* override the `onSuccess` callbacks and the `startWatcher()` method.

5. Open `StoreActivity.java` and replace the previous `Store` instance with an instance of `StoreThreadSafe`. Also, create a member field of type `long` to hold a native pointer to the watcher thread. When the fragment is resumed, start the watcher thread and save its pointer. When the fragment is paused, stop the watcher thread with the previously saved pointer:

```
public class StoreActivity extends Activity {
    ...
    public static class PlaceholderFragment extends Fragment
    implements StoreListener {
        private StoreThreadSafe mStore = new StoreThreadSafe(this);
        private long mWatcher;
        private EditText mUIKeyEdit, mUIValueEdit;
        private Spinner mUITypeSpinner;
        private Button mUIGetButton, mUISetButton;
        private Pattern mKeyPattern;

        ...
        @Override
        public void onResume() {
            super.onResume();
            mWatcher = mStore.startWatcher();
        }
        @Override
        public void onPause() {
            super.onPause();
            mStore.stopWatcher(mWatcher);
        }
        ...
    }
}
```

6. Edit `jni/Store.h` and include a new header `pthread.h`:

```
#ifndef _STORE_H_
#define _STORE_H_

#include <cstdint>
#include <pthread.h>
#include "jni.h"
```

7. The watcher works on a `Store` instance updated at regular intervals of time. It needs:

- The instance of the `Store` structure it watches
- A `JavaVM`, which is the only object safely shareable among threads and from which `JNIEnv` can be safely retrieved
- A Java object to synchronize on (corresponding to the `LOCK` object we defined on the Java side)
- A `pthread` variable dedicated to native thread management
- An indicator to stop the watcher thread

```
. . .
typedef struct {
    Store* mStore;
    JavaVM* mJavaVM;
    jobject mLock;
    pthread_t mThread;
    int32_t mRunning;
} StoreWatcher;
. . .
```

8. Finally, define three methods to start and stop the watcher thread, run its main loop, and process an entry:

```
. . .
StoreWatcher* startWatcher(JavaVM* pJavaVM, Store* pStore,
        jobject pLock);
void stopWatcher(StoreWatcher* pWatcher);
void* runWatcher(void* pArgs);
void processEntry(StoreEntry* pEntry);
#endif
```

9. Refresh the JNI header file `jni/com_packtpub_Store.h` with `javah`. You should
see two new methods, `Java_com_packtpub_store_Store_startWatcher()`
and `Java_com_packtpub_store_Store_stopWatcher()`, in it.

In `com_packtpub_store_Store.cpp`, create a new static variable `gLock` that is
going to hold the Java synchronization object.

```
...
static Store gStore;
static jobject gLock;
...
```

10. Create an instance of the `Object` class in `JNI_OnLoad()` using the JNI
Reflection API:

- ❑ First, find its `Object` constructor with `GetMethodID()`. Constructors in JNI
  are named `<init>` and have no result.

- ❑ Then, invoke the constructor to create an instance and make it global.

- ❑ Finally, remove local references when they become useless:

```
JNIEXPORT jint JNI_OnLoad(JavaVM* pVM, void* reserved) {
    JNIEnv *env;
    if (pVM->GetEnv((void**) &env, JNI_VERSION_1_6) != JNI_OK) {
        abort();
    }
    ...
    jclass ObjectClass = env->FindClass("java/lang/Object");
    if (ObjectClass == NULL) abort();
    jmethodID ObjectConstructor = env->GetMethodID(ObjectClass,
            "<init>", "()V");
    if (ObjectConstructor == NULL) abort();
    jobject lockTmp = env->NewObject(ObjectClass, ObjectConstructor);
    env->DeleteLocalRef(ObjectClass);
    gLock = env->NewGlobalRef(lockTmp);
    env->DeleteLocalRef(lockTmp);
    ...
```

11. Save the created `Object` instance in the `StoreThreadSafe.LOCK` field. This
object is going to be used during the lifetime of the application to synchronize:

- ❑ First, retrieve the `StoreThreadSafe` class and its `LOCK` field using the JNI
  Reflection methods `FindClass()` and `GetStaticFieldId()`

- ❑ Then, save the value into the `LOCK` static field with the JNI method
  `SetStaticObjectField()`, which requires a field signature (such
  as methods)

❑ Finally, remove the local reference to the `StoreThreadSafe` class when it becomes useless:

```
. . .
jclass StoreThreadSafeClass = env->FindClass(
        "com/packtpub/store/StoreThreadSafe");
if (StoreThreadSafeClass == NULL) abort();
jfieldID lockField = env->GetStaticFieldID(StoreThreadSafeClass,
        "LOCK", "Ljava/lang/Object;");
if (lockField == NULL) abort();
env->SetStaticObjectField(StoreThreadSafeClass, lockField, gLock);
env->DeleteLocalRef(StoreThreadSafeClass);

return JNI_VERSION_1_6;
}
. . .
```

12. Implement `startWatcher()`, which calls the corresponding method defined earlier. It requires JavaVM, which can be retrieved from the `JNIEnv` object with `GetJavaVM()`. The pointer (that is, the memory address) to the created `Store` is returned as a `long` value to the Java side, which can then store it for alter use:

```
. . .
JNIEXPORT jlong JNICALL
Java_com_packtpub_store_Store_startWatcher
    (JNIEnv *pEnv, jobject pThis) {
      JavaVM* javaVM;
      // Caches the VM.
      if (pEnv->GetJavaVM(&javaVM) != JNI_OK) abort();

      // Launches the background thread.
      StoreWatcher* watcher = startWatcher(javaVM, &gStore, gLock);
      return (jlong) watcher;
}
. . .
```

13. Terminate by implementing `stopWatcher()`, which casts the given `long` value back to a native pointer. Pass it to the corresponding method:

```
. . .
JNIEXPORT void JNICALL
Java_com_packtpub_store_Store_stopWatcher
    (JNIEnv *pEnv, jobject pThis, jlong pWatcher) {
      stopWatcher((StoreWatcher*) pWatcher);
}
```

What just happened?

We used JNI to allocate a Java object from native code and save it in a static Java field. This example shows the power of the JNI Reflection API; almost anything that can be done in Java, can be done from native code with JNI.

To allocate Java objects, JNI provides the following methods:

- `NewObject()` to instantiate a Java object using the specified constructor method:
  ```
  jobject NewObject(jclass clazz, jmethodID methodID, ...)
  ```

- Variants of this method exist with an `A` and `V` postfix. Behavior is identical, except that arguments are specified respectively using a `va_list` or a `jvalue` array:
  ```
  jobject NewObjectV(jclass clazz, jmethodID methodID, va_list args)
  jobject NewObjectA(jclass clazz, jmethodID methodID, jvalue* args)
  ```

- `AllocObject()` allocates a new object but does not invoke its constructor. A possible usage would be the allocation of many of the objects, which does not require initialization to get some performance gains. Use it only if you know what you are doing:
  ```
  jobject AllocObject(jclass clazz)
  ```

In the previous chapter, we used static variables for the native store because its life cycle was tied to the application. We want to remember values until the application exits. If a user leaves the activity and comes back to it later, values are still available while the process remains alive.

For the watcher thread we used a different strategy because its life cycle is tied to the activity. When the activity gains focus, the thread is created and started. When activity loses focus, the thread is stopped and destroyed. Since this thread may need time to stop, several occurrences may run temporarily at the same time (if you turn the screen quickly multiple times in the `Store` example).

Thus, it is not safe to use static variables as it could be concurrently overwritten (leading to a memory leak), or, even worse, released (leading to memory corruption). These kind of problems can also arise when an activity starts another one. In that case, `onStop()` and `onDestroy()` of the first activity occurs after `onCreate()` and `onStart()` of the second activity, as defined in the Android Activity life cycle.

Instead, a better solution to handle this situation is to allow the Java side to manage the native memory. In our example, a pointer to a native structure allocated on the native side is returned to the Java side as a `long` value. Any further JNI calls must be performed with this pointer as a parameter. This pointer can then be given back to the native side when the life cycle of this piece of data ends.

> The use of a `long` value (represented on 64-bit) to save a native pointer is necessary in order to remain compatible with 64-bit versions of Android (with 64-bit memory addresses) that arrived with Android Lollipop.

To summarize, use native static variables with care. If your variables are tied to the application life cycle, static variables are fine. If your variables are tied to the activity lifecycle, you should allocate an instance of them in your activity and manage them from there to avoid problems.

Now that we have a shared lock between the Java and the native side, let's continue our example by implementing the Watcher thread.

Time for action – running and synchronizing a thread

Let's create a native thread using the POSIX PThread API and attach it to the VM:

1. In `Store.cpp`, include `unistd.h`, which gives access to the `sleep()` function:

    ```
    #include "Store.h"
    #include <cstdlib>
    #include <cstring>
    #include <unistd.h>
    ...
    ```

    Implement `startWatcher()`. This method is executed from the UI thread. To do so, first instantiate and initialize a `StoreWatcher` structure.

2. Then, initialize and launch a native thread with the `pthread` POSIX API:

    ```
    StoreWatcher* startWatcher(JavaVM* pJavaVM, Store* pStore,
            jobject pLock) {
        StoreWatcher* watcher = new StoreWatcher();
        watcher->mJavaVM = pJavaVM;
        watcher->mStore = pStore;
        watcher->mLock = pLock;
        watcher->mRunning = true;
    ...
    ```

Then, initialize and launch a native thread with the PThread POSIX API:

- ❏ `pthread_attr_init()` initializes the necessary data structure
- ❏ `pthread_create()` starts the thread

```
. . .
    pthread_attr_t lAttributes;
    if (pthread_attr_init(&lAttributes)) abort();
    if (pthread_create(&watcher->mThread, &lAttributes,
                            runWatcher, watcher)) abort();
    return watcher;
}
. . .
```

3. Implement `stopWatcher()`, which turns off the running indicator to request the watcher thread to stop:

```
. . .
void stopWatcher(StoreWatcher* pWatcher) {
    pWatcher->mRunning = false;
}
. . .
```

4. Implement the thread's main loop in `runWatcher()`. Here, we are not on the UI thread anymore, but on the watcher thread.

- ❏ So first, attach the thread as a daemon to the Dalvik VM using `AttachCurrentThreadAsDaemon()`. This operation returns `JNIEnv` from the given `JavaVM`. This gives us direct access to the Java side from this new thread. Remember that `JNIEnv` is thread-specific and cannot be shared between threads directly.

- ❏ Then, make this thread loop and take a nap for a few seconds during each iteration using `sleep()`:

```
. . .
void* runWatcher(void* pArgs) {
    StoreWatcher* watcher = (StoreWatcher*) pArgs;
    Store* store = watcher->mStore;

    JavaVM* javaVM = watcher->mJavaVM;
    JavaVMAttachArgs javaVMAttachArgs;
    javaVMAttachArgs.version = JNI_VERSION_1_6;
    javaVMAttachArgs.name = "NativeThread";
    javaVMAttachArgs.group = NULL;

    JNIEnv* env;
```

```
        if (javaVM->AttachCurrentThreadAsDaemon(&env,
                &javaVMAttachArgs) != JNI_OK) abort();
    // Runs the thread loop.
    while (true) {
        sleep(5); // In seconds.
            . . .
```

5. While in a loop iteration, delimit a critical section (where only one thread can go at the same time) with JNI methods `MonitorEnter()` and `MonitorExit()`. These methods require an object to synchronize on (like a `synchronized` block in Java).

Then, you can safely:

❑ Check whether the thread should be stopped, and leave the loop in that case

❑ Process each entry from the store

```
            . . .
        // Critical section beginning, one thread at a time.
        // Entries cannot be added or modified.
        env->MonitorEnter(watcher->mLock);
        if (!watcher->mRunning) break;
        StoreEntry* entry = watcher->mStore->mEntries;
        StoreEntry* entryEnd = entry + watcher->mStore->mLength;
        while (entry < entryEnd) {
            processEntry(entry);
            ++entry;
        }
        // Critical section end.
        env->MonitorExit(watcher->mLock);
    }
    . . .
```

Before exiting, detach the thread when it is going to end and exit. It is very important to always detach an attached thread so that the Dalvik or ART VM stop managing it.

6. Finally, terminate the thread using the `pthread_exit()` API method:

```
    . . .
    javaVM->DetachCurrentThread();
    delete watcher;
    pthread_exit(NULL);
}
. . .
```

7. Finally, write the `processEntry()` method, which does nothing more than check the boundaries of integer entries and limit them to the arbitrary range `[-100000,100000]`. You can also process any of the other entries you wish:

```
...
void processEntry(StoreEntry* pEntry) {
    switch (pEntry->mType) {
    case StoreType_Integer:
        if (pEntry->mValue.mInteger > 100000) {
            pEntry->mValue.mInteger = 100000;
        } else if (pEntry->mValue.mInteger < -100000) {
            pEntry->mValue.mInteger = -100000;
        }
        break;
    }
}
```

What just happened?

Compile and run the application in Debug mode using the Eclipse Java debugger (not the native one). When the application starts, a native background thread is created and attached to the Dalvik VM. You can see it in the **Debug** view. Then, the UI thread and the native background thread are synchronized together with the JNI Monitor API to handle concurrency issues properly. Finally, when leaving the application, the background thread is detached and destroyed. Thus, it disappears from the **Debug** view:

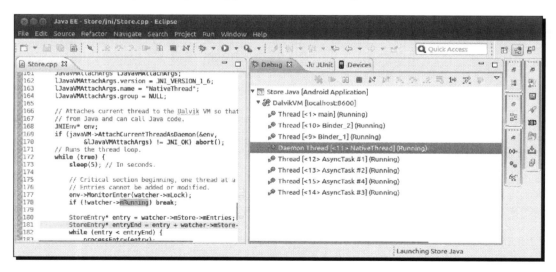

Now, from the `Store` interface on your Android device, define a key and enter an integer value greater than `100,000`. Wait a few seconds and retrieve the value using the same key. It should appear clamped to `100,000` by the Watcher thread. This Watcher looks for each value in the store and changes it if needed.

The Watcher is running on a native thread (that is, not created directly by the Java VM). The NDK allows creating native threads using the PThread POSIX API. This API is a standard used commonly on Unix systems for multithreading. It defines a set of functions and data structures, all prefixed with `pthread_`, to create not only threads, but also **Mutexes** (which stands for Mutual Exclusion) or **Condition variables** (to make a thread wait for a specific condition).

The PThread API is a whole subject in itself and is outside the scope of this book. You will need to know it to master native multithreading on Android. For more information on this subject, have a look at `https://computing.llnl.gov/tutorials/pthreads/` and `http://randu.org/tutorials/threads/`.

Synchronizing Java and C/C++ with JNI Monitors

On the Java side, we synchronize threads using `synchronized` blocks with an arbitrary lock object. Java also allows methods, whether native or not, to be `synchronized`. The lock object, in that case, is implicitly the one on which native methods are defined. For example, we could define a native method as follows:

```
public class MyNativeClass {
        public native synchronized int doSomething();
    ...
}
```

This would not have worked in our case, since there is a single static instance of the store on the native side. We need a single static instance of our lock object.

> Please note that the pattern used here, that is, making `StoreThreadSafe` inherit from the `Store` class, override its methods and use static variables, should not be considered specifically as the best practice. It has been used for simplicity purposes in this book because the `Store` and the `lock` object are static.

On the native side, synchronization is performed with a JNI monitor, which is equivalent to the `synchronized` keyword in Java:

◆ `MonitorEnter()` delimits the start of a critical section. The monitor is associated with an object, which can be considered as a kind of identifier. Only one thread at a time can go inside the section defined by this object:

```
jint MonitorEnter(jobject obj)
```

◆ `MonitorExit()` delimits the end of a critical section. It must be called, along with `MonitorEnter()`, to ensure the monitor is released and other threads can go:

```
jint MonitorExit(jobject obj)
```

Because Java threads are based on POSIX primitives internally, it is also possible to implement thread synchronization entirely natively with the POSIX API. You can find more information about it at `https://computing.llnl.gov/tutorials/pthreads/`.

 Java and C/C++ are different languages with similar, but somewhat different semantics. Thus, always be careful not to expect C/C++ to behave like Java. As an example, the volatile has a different semantic in Java and C/C++, since both follow a different memory model.

Attaching and detaching native threads

By default, the Dalvik VM is unaware of the native threads that run in the same process. In return, the native threads cannot access the VM either... unless it is attached to it. The attachment is handled in JNI with the following methods:

◆ `AttachCurrentThread()` to tell the VM to manage the current thread. Once attached, a pointer to the `JNIEnv` for the current thread is returned at the specified location:

```
jint AttachCurrentThread(JNIEnv** p_env, void* thr_args)
```

◆ `AttachCurrentThreadAsDaemon()` to attach a thread as a daemon. Java specification defines that the JVM does not have to wait for a daemon thread to exit before leaving, the opposite to normal threads. This distinction has no real meaning on Android, since an application can be killed at any time by the system:

```
jint AttachCurrentThreadAsDaemon(JNIEnv** p_env, void* thr_args)
```

◆ `DetachCurrentThread()` indicates to the VM that a thread does not need to be managed anymore. An attached thread like the Watcher thread must be eventually unattached before exiting. Dalvik detects threads that are not detached and reacts by aborting and leaving a dirty crash dump in your logs! When getting detached, any monitor held is released, and any waiting thread is notified:

```
jint DetachCurrentThread()
```

 Since Android 2.0, a technique to make sure a thread is systematically detached is to bind a destructor callback to the native thread with `pthread_key_create()` and call `DetachCurrentThread()` in it. A `JNIEnv` instance can be saved into thread local storage with `pthread_setspecific()` to pass it as an argument to the destructor.

After a thread is attached, the **ClassLoader** JNI uses Java classes to correspond to the first object it finds on the call stack. For purely native threads, no `ClassLoader` might be found. In that case, JNI uses the system `ClassLoader`, which might not be able to find your own application classes, that is, `FindClass()` fails. In that case, either cache the necessary JNI elements globally in `JNI_OnLoad()` or share an application class loader with the needing thread.

Processing bitmaps natively

The Android NDK proposes an API dedicated to bitmap processing, which gives direct access to the surface of Android bitmaps. This API is specific to Android and is not related to the JNI specification. However, bitmaps are Java objects and will need to be treated as such in native code.

To see more concretely how bitmaps can be modified from native code, let's try to decode a camera feed from native code. Raw video frames recorded on Android are generally encoded in a specific format, **YUV**, which is not compatible with classic RGB images. This is a situation where native code comes to the rescue to help us decode such images. In the following example, we are going to extract each color component (that is, red, green, and blue) into a separate bitmap.

 The resulting project is provided with this book under the name `LiveCamera`.

Time for action – decoding a camera's feed

Let's write the necessary Java code to record and display pictures in a fresh new project:

1. Create a new hybrid Java/C++ project as shown in *Chapter 2*, *Starting a Native Android Project*:

   - Name it `LiveCamera`
   - The main package is `com.packtpub.livecamera`
   - The main activity is `LiveCameraActivity`
   - The main activity layout name is `activity_livecamera`
   - Use the **Blank Activity** template

2. Once created, turn the project into a native project as already seen. In the `AndroidManifest.xml` file, request access permission to the camera. Then, set the activity style to `fullscreen` and its orientation to `landscape`. Landscape orientation avoids most camera orientation problems that are met on Android devices:

```xml
<?xml version="1.0" encoding="utf-8"?>
<manifest xmlns:android="http://schemas.android.com/apk/res/android"
  package="com.packtpub.livecamera"
  android:versionCode="1" android:versionName="1.0" >
  <uses-sdk android:minSdkVersion="14" android:targetSdkVersion="19"/>
  <uses-permission android:name="android.permission.CAMERA" />
  <application
    android:allowBackup="false"
    android:icon="@drawable/ic_launcher"
    android:label="@string/app_name" >
    <activity
      android:name=".LiveCameraActivity"
      android:label="@string/app_name"
      android:screenOrientation="landscape"
      android:theme="@android:style/Theme.NoTitleBar.Fullscreen" >
      <intent-filter>
        <action android:name="android.intent.action.MAIN" />
        <category android:name="android.intent.category.LAUNCHER" />
      </intent-filter>
    </activity>
  </application>
</manifest>
```

3. Define the `activity_livecamera.xml` layout as follows. It represents a 2x2 grid containing one `TextureView` and three `ImageView` elements:

```xml
<?xml version="1.0" encoding="utf-8"?>
<LinearLayout
  xmlns:a="http://schemas.android.com/apk/res/android"
  a:baselineAligned="true" a:orientation="horizontal"
  a:layout_width="fill_parent" a:layout_height="fill_parent" >
  <LinearLayout
    a:layout_width="fill_parent" a:layout_height="fill_parent"
    a:layout_weight="1" a:orientation="vertical" >
    <TextureView
      a:id="@+id/preview" a:layout_weight="1"
      a:layout_width="fill_parent"
a:layout_height="fill_parent" />
    <ImageView
      a:id="@+id/imageViewR" a:layout_weight="1"
      a:layout_width="fill_parent" a:layout_height="fill_parent" />
  </LinearLayout>
  <LinearLayout
    a:layout_width="fill_parent" a:layout_height="fill_parent"
    a:layout_weight="1" a:orientation="vertical" >
    <ImageView
      a:id="@+id/imageViewG" a:layout_weight="1"
      a:layout_width="fill_parent" a:layout_height="fill_parent" />
    <ImageView
      a:id="@+id/imageViewB" a:layout_weight="1"
      a:layout_width="fill_parent" a:layout_height="fill_parent" />
  </LinearLayout>
</LinearLayout>
```

4. Open `LiveCameraActivity.java` and implement it as follows:

 ❑ First, extend `SurfaceTextureListener`, which is going to help us initialize and close the camera feed

 ❑ Then, extend the `PreviewCallback` interface to listen for new camera frames

Do not forget to load the native static library, as follows:

```java
package com.packtpub.livecamera;
...
public class LiveCameraActivity extends Activity implements
TextureView.SurfaceTextureListener, Camera.PreviewCallback {
    static {
        System.loadLibrary("livecamera");
    }
    ...
```

5. Create a few member variables:

- ❏ mCamera is the Android camera API
- ❏ mTextureView displays the raw camera feed
- ❏ mVideoSource captures camera frames into a byte buffer
- ❏ mImageViewR, G, and B display processed images, one for each color component
- ❏ mImageR, G, and B are the bitmaps backing the ImageView (the "back buffers")

```
. . .
private Camera mCamera;
private TextureView mTextureView;
private byte[] mVideoSource;
private ImageView mImageViewR, mImageViewG, mImageViewB;
private Bitmap mImageR, mImageG, mImageB;
. . .
```

In onCreate(), specify the layout defined in the previous step.

Then, retrieve the views to show images.

6. Finally, listen for TextureView events with setSurfaceTextureListener(). You can ignore some of the callbacks that are not necessary in this example:

```
. . .
@Override
protected void onCreate(Bundle savedInstanceState) {
    super.onCreate(savedInstanceState);
    setContentView(R.layout.activity_livecamera);
    mTextureView = (TextureView) findViewById(R.id.preview);
    mImageViewR = ((ImageView)findViewById(R.id.imageViewR));
    mImageViewG = ((ImageView)findViewById(R.id.imageViewG));
    mImageViewB = ((ImageView)findViewById(R.id.imageViewB));

    mTextureView.setSurfaceTextureListener(this);
}
@Override
public void onSurfaceTextureSizeChanged(SurfaceTexture pSurface,
    int pWidth, int pHeight) {}

@Override
public void onSurfaceTextureUpdated(SurfaceTexture pSurface) {}
. . .
```

7. The `onSurfaceTextureAvailable()` callback in `LiveCameraActivity.java` is triggered after the `TextureView` surface is created. This is the place where surface dimensions and pixel formats get known.

So, open the Android camera and set up `TextureView` as its preview target. Listen for new camera frames with `setPreviewCallbackWithBuffer()`:

```
...
@Override
public void onSurfaceTextureAvailable(SurfaceTexture pSurface,
                                      int pWidth, int pHeight) {
    mCamera = Camera.open();
    try {
        mCamera.setPreviewTexture(pSurface);
        mCamera.setPreviewCallbackWithBuffer(this);
        // Sets landscape mode to avoid complications related to
        // screen orientation handling.
        mCamera.setDisplayOrientation(0);
        ...
```

8. Then, call `findBestResolution()`, which we will implement next to find a suitable resolution for the camera feed. Set up the latter accordingly with the `YCbCr_420_SP` format (which should be the default on Android).

```
        ...
        Size size = findBestResolution(pWidth, pHeight);
        PixelFormat pixelFormat = new PixelFormat();
        PixelFormat.getPixelFormatInfo(mCamera.getParameters()
                        .getPreviewFormat(), pixelFormat);
        int sourceSize = size.width * size.height
                        * pixelFormat.bitsPerPixel / 8;
        // Set-up camera size and video format.
        // should be the default on Android anyway.
        Camera.Parameters parameters = mCamera.getParameters();
        parameters.setPreviewSize(size.width, size.height);
        parameters.setPreviewFormat(PixelFormat.YCbCr_420_SP);
        mCamera.setParameters(parameters);
        ...
```

9. After that, set up the video buffer and the bitmaps that display camera frames:

```
        ...
        mVideoSource = new byte[sourceSize];
        mImageR = Bitmap.createBitmap(size.width, size.height,
                        Bitmap.Config.ARGB_8888);
```

```
            mImageG = Bitmap.createBitmap(size.width, size.height,
                                        Bitmap.Config.ARGB_8888);
            mImageB = Bitmap.createBitmap(size.width, size.height,
                                        Bitmap.Config.ARGB_8888);
            mImageViewR.setImageBitmap(mImageR);
            mImageViewG.setImageBitmap(mImageG);
            mImageViewB.setImageBitmap(mImageB);
            ...
```

Finally, enqueue the video frame buffer and start the camera preview:

```
            ...
            mCamera.addCallbackBuffer(mVideoSource);
            mCamera.startPreview();
        } catch (IOException ioe) {
            mCamera.release();
            mCamera = null;
            throw new IllegalStateException();
        }
    }
    ...
```

10. Still in `LiveCameraActivity.java`, implement `findBestResolution()`. An Android camera can support various resolutions, which are highly dependent on the device. As there is no rule on what could be the default resolution, we need to look for a suitable one. Here, we select the biggest resolution that fits the display surface, or the default one if none can be found.

```
    ...
    private Size findBestResolution(int pWidth, int pHeight) {
        List<Size> sizes = mCamera.getParameters()
                        .getSupportedPreviewSizes();
        // Finds the biggest resolution which fits the screen.
        // Else, returns the first resolution found.
        Size selectedSize = mCamera.new Size(0, 0);
        for (Size size : sizes) {
            if ((size.width <= pWidth)
              && (size.height <= pHeight)
              && (size.width >= selectedSize.width)
              && (size.height >= selectedSize.height)) {
                selectedSize = size;
            }
        }
        // Previous code assume that there is a preview size smaller
        // than screen size. If not, hopefully the Android API
```

```
        // guarantees that at least one preview size is available.
        if ((selectedSize.width == 0) || (selectedSize.height == 0)) {
            selectedSize = sizes.get(0);
        }
        return selectedSize;
    }
    ...
```

11. Release the camera when the `TextureView` surface is destroyed in `onSurfaceTextureDestroyed()`, as it is a shared resource. Bitmap buffers can also be recycled and nullified to ease garbage collector work.

```
    ...
    @Override
    public boolean onSurfaceTextureDestroyed(SurfaceTexture pSurface)
    {
        // Releases camera which is a shared resource.
        if (mCamera != null) {
            mCamera.stopPreview();
            mCamera.release();
            // These variables can take a lot of memory. Get rid of
            // them as fast as we can.
            mCamera = null;
            mVideoSource = null;
            mImageR.recycle(); mImageR = null;
            mImageG.recycle(); mImageG = null;
            mImageB.recycle(); mImageB = null;
        }
        return true;
    }
    ...
```

12. Finally, decode raw video frames in `onPreviewFrame()`. This handler is triggered by the `Camera` class each time a new frame is ready.

Raw video bytes are passed to the native method `decode()`, along with the backing bitmap, and a filter to select each color component.

Once decoded, invalidate the surface to redraw it.

Finally, "re-enqueue" the raw video buffer to request the capture of a new video frame.

```
    ...
    @Override
    public void onPreviewFrame(byte[] pData, Camera pCamera) {
        // New data has been received from camera. Processes it and
```

```
                // requests surface to be redrawn right after.
                if (mCamera != null) {
                    decode(mImageR, pData, 0xFFFF0000);
                    decode(mImageG, pData, 0xFF00FF00);
                    decode(mImageB, pData, 0xFF0000FF);
                    mImageViewR.invalidate();
                    mImageViewG.invalidate();
                    mImageViewB.invalidate();

                    mCamera.addCallbackBuffer(mVideoSource);
                }
            }

            public native void decode(Bitmap pTarget, byte[] pSource,
                                    int pFilter);
        }
```

What just happened?

We captured live images from our device's camera thanks to the Android Camera API. After setting up the camera capture format and definition, we created all the necessary capture buffer and output images to display onscreen. Captures are saved in a buffer enqueued by the application when it requires a new frame. Then, this buffer is given with a bitmap to a native method, which we will write in the next section. Finally, the output image is displayed onscreen.

The video feed is encoded in the YUV NV21 format. YUV is a color format originally invented in the old days of electronics to make black and white video receivers compatible with color transmissions and is still commonly used nowadays. The default frame format is guaranteed by the Android specification to be **YCbCr 420 SP** (or **NV21**) on Android.

 Although YCbCr 420 SP is the default video format on Android, the emulator only supports YCbCr 422 SP. This defect should not cause much trouble as it basically swaps colors. This problem should not occur on real devices.

Now that our live image is captured, let's process it on the native side.

Time for action – processing pictures with the Bitmap API

Let's continue our application by decoding and filtering images on the native side by the color channel:

1. Create native C source, `jni/CameraDecoder.c` (not a C++ file, so that we can see the difference with JNI code written in C++).

Include `android/bitmap.h`, which defines the NDK bitmap processing API and `stdlib.h` (not `cstdlib` as this file is written in C):

```
#include <android/bitmap.h>
#include <stdlib.h>
...
```

Write a few utility macros to help decode a video.

- ❑ `toInt()` converts a jbyte to an integer, erasing all useless bits with a mask
- ❑ `max()` gets the maximum between two values
- ❑ `clamp()` clamps a value inside a defined interval
- ❑ `color()` builds an ARGB color from each color component

```
...
#define toInt(pValue) \
    (0xff & (int32_t) pValue)
#define max(pValue1, pValue2) \
    (pValue1 < pValue2) ? pValue2 : pValue1
#define clamp(pValue, pLowest, pHighest) \
    ((pValue < 0) ? pLowest : (pValue > pHighest) ? pHighest : pValue)
#define color(pColorR, pColorG, pColorB) \
    (0xFF000000 | ((pColorB << 6)  & 0x00FF0000) \
                | ((pColorG >> 2)  & 0x0000FF00) \
                | ((pColorR >> 10) & 0x000000FF))
...
```

2. Implement the native method `decode()`.

First, retrieve bitmap information and check whether its pixel format is a 32-bit RGBA. Then, lock it to allow drawing operations.

After this, gain access to the input video frame content passed as a Java byte array with `GetPrimitiveArrayCritical()`:

```
...
void JNICALL decode(JNIEnv * pEnv, jclass pClass, jobject pTarget,
        jbyteArray pSource, jint pFilter) {
    // Retrieves bitmap information and locks it for drawing.
    AndroidBitmapInfo bitmapInfo;
    uint32_t* bitmapContent;
    if (AndroidBitmap_getInfo(pEnv,pTarget, &bitmapInfo) < 0) abort();
    if (bitmapInfo.format != ANDROID_BITMAP_FORMAT_RGBA_8888) abort();
    if (AndroidBitmap_lockPixels(pEnv, pTarget,
            (void**)&bitmapContent) < 0) abort();

    // Accesses source array data.
    jbyte* source = (*pEnv)->GetPrimitiveArrayCritical(pEnv,
            pSource, 0);
    if (source == NULL) abort();
    ...
```

3. Decode the raw video frame into the output bitmap. The video frame is encoded in the YUV format, which is quite different from RGB. The YUV format encodes a color in three components:

- One luminance component, that is, the grayscale representation of a color.

- Two chrominance components, which encode the color information (also called **Cb** and **Cr** as they represent the blue-difference and red-difference).

- There are many frame formats based on YUV colors. Here, we convert frames by following the YCbCr 420 SP (or NV21) format. This kind of image frame is composed of a buffer of 8-bit Y luminance samples, followed by a second buffer of interleaved 8-bit V and U chrominance samples. The VU buffer is subsampled, which means that there are less U and V samples compared to Y samples (1 U sample and 1 V sample for 4 Y samples). The following algorithm processes each pixel and converts each YUV pixel to RGB using the appropriate formula (see `http://www.fourcecc.org/fccyvrgb.php` for more information):

```
...
    int32_t frameSize = bitmapInfo.width * bitmapInfo.height;
    int32_t yIndex, uvIndex, x, y;
    int32_t colorY, colorU, colorV;
    int32_t colorR, colorG, colorB;
    int32_t y1192;

    // Processes each pixel and converts YUV to RGB color.
```

```
// Algorithm originates from the Ketai open source project.
// See http://ketai.googlecode.com/.
for (y = 0, yIndex = 0; y < bitmapInfo.height; ++y) {
    colorU = 0; colorV = 0;
    // Y is divided by 2 because UVs are subsampled vertically.
    // This means that two consecutives iterations refer to the
    // same UV line (e.g when Y=0 and Y=1).
    uvIndex = frameSize + (y >> 1) * bitmapInfo.width;

    for (x = 0; x < bitmapInfo.width; ++x, ++yIndex) {
        // Retrieves YUV components. UVs are subsampled
        // horizontally too, hence %2 (1 UV for 2 Y).
        colorY = max(toInt(source[yIndex]) - 16, 0);
        if (!(x % 2)) {
            colorV = toInt(source[uvIndex++]) - 128;
            colorU = toInt(source[uvIndex++]) - 128;
        }

        // Computes R, G and B from Y, U and V.
        y1192 = 1192 * colorY;
        colorR = (y1192 + 1634 * colorV);
        colorG = (y1192 - 833  * colorV - 400 * colorU);
        colorB = (y1192 + 2066 * colorU);

        colorR = clamp(colorR, 0, 262143);
        colorG = clamp(colorG, 0, 262143);
        colorB = clamp(colorB, 0, 262143);

        // Combines R, G, B and A into the final pixel color.
        bitmapContent[yIndex] = color(colorR,colorG,colorB);
        bitmapContent[yIndex] &= pFilter;
    }
}
...
```

To finish, release the Java byte buffer acquired earlier and unlock the backing bitmap.

```
...
(*pEnv)-> ReleasePrimitiveArrayCritical(pEnv,pSource,source,0);
if (AndroidBitmap_unlockPixels(pEnv, pTarget) < 0) abort();
}
...
```

4. Instead of relying on a naming convention to find native methods, JNI allows native methods to be registered manually in `JNI_OnLoad()`.

So, define a table that describes the native methods to register their name, signature, and address. Here, only `decode()` needs to be specified.

Then, in `JNI_OnLoad()`, find the Java on which the native method `decode()` is declared (here, `LiveCameraActivity`), and tell JNI which method to use with `RegisterNatives()`:

```
...
static JNINativeMethod gMethodRegistry[] = {
  { "decode", "(Landroid/graphics/Bitmap;[BI)V", (void *) decode }
};
static int gMethodRegistrySize = sizeof(gMethodRegistry)
                        / sizeof(gMethodRegistry[0]);

JNIEXPORT jint JNI_OnLoad(JavaVM* pVM, void* reserved) {
    JNIEnv *env;
    if ((*pVM)->GetEnv(pVM, (void**) &env, JNI_VERSION_1_6) != JNI_OK)
    { abort(); }

    jclass LiveCameraActivity = (*env)->FindClass(env,
            "com/packtpub/livecamera/LiveCameraActivity");
    if (LiveCameraActivity == NULL) abort();
    (*env)->RegisterNatives(env, LiveCameraActivity,
            gMethodRegistry, 1);
    (*env)->DeleteLocalRef(env, LiveCameraActivity);

    return JNI_VERSION_1_6;
}
```

5. Write the `Application.mk` makefile as follows:

```
APP_PLATFORM := android-14
APP_ABI := all
```

6. Write the `Android.mk` makefile as follows (link it to the `jnigraphics` module, which defines the Android Bitmap API):

```
LOCAL_PATH := $(call my-dir)

include $(CLEAR_VARS)

LOCAL_MODULE    := livecamera
LOCAL_SRC_FILES := CameraDecoder.c
LOCAL_LDLIBS    := -ljnigraphics

include $(BUILD_SHARED_LIBRARY)
```

What just happened?

Compile and run the application. The raw video feed is displayed in the top-left corner without any transformation. The raw video frame is decoded in native code and each color channel is extracted into three Java bitmaps. These bitmaps are displayed inside three `ImageView` elements in each of the corners of the screen.

The algorithm used to decode the YUV frame originates from the Ketai open source project, an image and sensor processing library for Android. See `http://ketai.googlecode.com/` for more information. Beware that YUV to RGB is an expensive operation that is likely to remain a point of contention in your program (**RenderScript**, which we will discover in *Chapter 10, Intensive Computing with RenderScript*, can help in that task).

The code presented here is far from being optimal (the decoding algorithm can be optimized, the video frames, captured with multiple buffers, memory accesses can be reduced, and code can be multithreaded) but it gives an overview of how bitmap can be processed natively with the NDK.

Native code is given direct access to the bitmap surface thanks to the Android NDK Bitmap API defined in the `jnigraphics` module. This API, which can be considered as an Android specific extension to JNI, defines the following methods:

- `AndroidBitmap_getInfo()` to retrieve bitmap information. The returned value is negative when a problem occurs, or else 0:

  ```
  int AndroidBitmap_getInfo(JNIEnv* env, jobject jbitmap,
                            AndroidBitmapInfo* info);
  ```

- Bitmap information is retrieved in the `AndroidBitmapInfo` structure, which is defined as follows:

  ```
  typedef struct {
      uint32_t    width;  // Width in pixels
      uint32_t    height; // Height in pixels
      uint32_t    stride; // Number of bytes between each line
      int32_t     format; // Pixel structure (see AndroidBitmapFormat)
      uint32_t    flags;  // Unused for now
  } AndroidBitmapInfo;
  ```

- `AndroidBitmap_lockPixels()` gives exclusive access to the bitmap while processing it. The returned value is negative when a problem occurs, or else 0:

  ```
  int AndroidBitmap_lockPixels(JNIEnv* env, jobject jbitmap, void**
  addrPtr);
  ```

- `AndroidBitmap_unlockPixels()` releases the exclusive lock on the bitmap. The returned value is negative when a problem occurs, or else 0:

  ```
  int AndroidBitmap_unlockPixels(JNIEnv* env, jobject jbitmap);
  ```

Drawing operations on any bitmap occurs systematically in three main steps:

1. First, the bitmap surface is acquired.

2. Then, bitmap pixels are modified. Here, video pixels are converted to RGB and written to the bitmap surface.

3. Finally, the bitmap surface is released.

Bitmaps must be systematically locked and then unlocked when accessed natively. Drawing operations must occur imperatively between a lock/unlock pair. Have a look at the `bitmap.h` header file for more information.

Registering native methods manually

In our store example, native method prototypes have been generated automatically by `Javah` using a specific name and parameter convention. The Dalvik VM can then load them at runtime by "guessing" their names. However, this convention is easy to break and has no runtime flexibility. Hopefully, JNI lets you manually register native methods that are going to be called from Java. And what better place than `JNI_OnLoad()` to do that?

Registration is performed with the following JNI method:

```
jint RegisterNatives(jclass clazz, const JNINativeMethod* methods,
                     jint nMethods)
```

  ◆ `jclass` is a reference to the Java class hosting the native method. We will see more about it through this chapter and the next one.

  ◆ `methods` is an array of `JNINativeMethod`, a structure describing the native methods to register.

  ◆ `nMethods` indicates how many methods are described inside the `methods` array.

The `JNINativeMethod` structure is defined as follows:

```
typedef struct {
    const char* name;
    const char* signature;
    void*       fnPtr;
} JNINativeMethod;
```

The first and second elements are `name` and `signature` of the corresponding Java method, and the third parameter `fnPtr`, is a pointer to the corresponding method on the native side. That way, you can get rid of `javah` and its annoying naming convention and choose at runtime which method to call.

JNI in C versus JNI in C++

The NDK allows writing applications in either C (like our `LiveCamera` example) or C++ (like our `Store` example). So does JNI.

C is not an object-oriented language but C++ is. This is why you do not write JNI in C like in C++. In C, `JNIEnv` is in fact a structure containing function pointers. Of course, when `JNIEnv` is given to you, all these pointers are initialized so that you can call them a bit like an object. However, this parameter, which is implicit in an object-oriented language, is given as the first parameter in C (`env` in the following code). Also, `JNIEnv` needs to be dereferenced the first time to run a method:

```
JNIEnv *env = ...;
(*env)->RegisterNative(env, ...);
```

The C++ code is more natural and simple. This parameter is implicit, and there is no need to dereference JNIEnv, as methods are not declared as function pointers anymore, but as real member methods:

```
JNIEnv *env = ...;
env->RegisterNative(env, ...);
```

Thus, despite being really similar, you do not write JNI code in C in exactly the same way you write it in C++.

Summary

Thanks to JNI, Java and C/C++ can be tightly integrated together. Android is now fully bilingual! Java can call C/C++ code with any type of data or object, and native code can call Java back.

We also discovered how to call Java code from native code with the JNI Reflection API. Practically any Java operation can be performed from native code thanks to it. However, for best performance, class, method, or field descriptors must be cached.

We also saw how to attach and detach a thread to the VM and synchronize Java and native threads together with JNI monitors. Multithreaded code is probably one of the most difficult subjects in programming. Do it with care!

Finally, we also natively processed bitmaps thanks to JNI, and decoded a video feed by hand. However, an expensive conversion is needed from the default YUV format (which should be supported on every device according to Android specifications) to RGB.

When dealing with native code on Android, JNI is almost always in the way. It is a verbose and very technical API, not to mention cumbersome, which requires care. Its subtleties would require a whole book for an in-depth understanding. Instead, this chapter has given you the essential knowledge to integrate your own C/C++ module in your own Java application.

In the next chapter, we will see how to create a fully native application, which completely gets rid of JNI.

Writing a Fully Native Application

*In previous chapters, we have breached Android NDK's surface using JNI. But there is much more to find inside! The NDK includes its own set of specific features, one of them being **Native Activities**. Native activities allow creating applications based only on native code, without a single line of Java. No more JNI! No more references! No more Java!*

*In addition to native activities, the NDK brings some APIs for native access to Android resources, such as **display windows**, **assets**, **device configuration**... These APIs help in getting rid of the tortuous JNI bridge often necessary to embed native code. Although there is a lot still missing, and not likely to be available (Java remains the main platform language for GUIs and most frameworks), multimedia applications are a perfect target to apply them...*

This chapter initiates a native C++ project developed progressively throughout this book: **DroidBlaster**. Based on a top-down viewpoint, this sample scrolling shooter will feature 2D graphics, and, later on, 3D graphics, sound, input, and sensor management. In this chapter, we will create its base structure and main game components.

Let's now enter the heart of the Android NDK by:

- ◆ Creating a fully native activity
- ◆ Handling main activity events
- ◆ Accessing display window natively
- ◆ Retrieving time and calculating delays

Creating a native Activity

The `NativeActivity` class provides a facility to minimize the work necessary to create a native application. It lets the developer get rid of all the boilerplate code to initialize and communicate with native code and concentrate on core functionalities. This *glue* Activity is the simplest way to write applications, such as games without a line of Java code.

 The resulting project is provided with this book under the name `DroidBlaster_Part1`.

Time for action – creating a basic native Activity

We are now going to see how to create a minimal native activity that runs an event loop.

1. Create a new hybrid Java/C++ project, as shown in *Chapter 2, Starting a Native Android Project*.

  ❑ Name it `DroidBlaster`.

  ❑ Turn the project into a native project, as already seen in the previous chapter. Name the native module `droidblaster`.

  ❑ Remove the native source and header files that have been created by ADT.

  ❑ Remove the reference to the Java `src` directory in **Project Properties | Java Build Path | Source**. Then, remove the directory itself on disk.

  ❑ Get rid of all layouts in the `res/layout` directory.

  ❑ Get rid of `jni/droidblaster.cpp` if it has been created.

2. In `AndroidManifest.xml`, use `Theme.NoTitleBar.Fullscreen` as the application theme.

Declare a `NativeActivity` that refers to the native module named `droidblaster` (that is, the native library we will compile) using the meta-data property `android.app.lib_name`:

```
<?xml version="1.0" encoding="utf-8"?>
<manifest xmlns:android="http://schemas.android.com/apk/res/android"
    package="com.packtpub.droidblaster2d" android:versionCode="1"
    android:versionName="1.0">
    <uses-sdk
        android:minSdkVersion="14"
        android:targetSdkVersion="19"/>

    <application android:icon="@drawable/ic_launcher"
        android:label="@string/app_name"
```

```
            android:allowBackup="false"
            android:theme
            ="@android:style/Theme.NoTitleBar.Fullscreen">
            <activity android:name="android.app.NativeActivity"
                android:label="@string/app_name"
                android:screenOrientation="portrait">
                <meta-data android:name="android.app.lib_name"
                    android:value="droidblaster"/>
                <intent-filter>
                    <action android:name ="android.intent.action.MAIN"/>
                    <category
                        android:name="android.intent.category.LAUNCHER"/>
                </intent-filter>
            </activity>
        </application>
</manifest>
```

3. Create the file `jni/Types.hpp`. This header will contain common types and the header `cstdint`:

```
#ifndef _PACKT_TYPES_HPP_
#define _PACKT_TYPES_HPP_

#include <cstdint>

#endif
```

4. Let's write a logging class to get some feedback in the Logcat.

- ❑ Create `jni/Log.hpp` and declare a new class `Log`.

- ❑ Define the `packt_Log_debug` macro to allow the activating or deactivating of debug messages with a simple compile flag:

```
#ifndef _PACKT_LOG_HPP_
#define _PACKT_LOG_HPP_

class Log {
public:
    static void error(const char* pMessage, ...);
    static void warn(const char* pMessage, ...);
    static void info(const char* pMessage, ...);
    static void debug(const char* pMessage, ...);
};

#ifndef NDEBUG
    #define packt_Log_debug(...) Log::debug(__VA_ARGS__)
```

```
#else
    #define packt_Log_debug(...)
#endif

#endif
```

5. Implement the jni/Log.cpp file and implement the info() method. To write messages to Android logs, the NDK provides a dedicated logging API in the android/log.h header, which can be used similarly as printf() or vprintf() (with varArgs) in C:

```
#include "Log.hpp"

#include <stdarg.h>
#include <android/log.h>

void Log::info(const char* pMessage, ...) {
    va_list varArgs;
    va_start(varArgs, pMessage);
    __android_log_vprint(ANDROID_LOG_INFO, "PACKT", pMessage,
        varArgs);
    __android_log_print(ANDROID_LOG_INFO, "PACKT", "\n");
    va_end(varArgs);
}
...
```

Write other log methods, error(), warn(), and debug(), which are almost identical, except the level macro, which are respectively ANDROID_LOG_ERROR, ANDROID_LOG_WARN, and ANDROID_LOG_DEBUG instead.

6. Application events in NativeActivity can be processed with an event loop. So, create jni/EventLoop.hpp to define a class with a unique method run().

Include the android_native_app_glue.h header, which defines the android_app structure. It represents what could be called an **applicative context**, where all the information is related to the native activity; its state, its window, its event queue, and so on:

```
#ifndef _PACKT_EVENTLOOP_HPP_
#define _PACKT_EVENTLOOP_HPP_

#include <android_native_app_glue.h>

class EventLoop {
```

```
public:
    EventLoop(android_app* pApplication);

    void run();

private:
    android_app* mApplication;
};
#endif
```

7. Create `jni/EventLoop.cpp` and implement the activity event loop in the `run()`
method. Include a few log events to get some feedback in Android logs.

During the whole activity lifetime, the `run()` method loops continuously over
events until it is requested to terminate. When an activity is about to be destroyed,
the `destroyRequested` value in the `android_app` structure is changed internally
to indicate to the client code that it must exit.

Also, call `app_dummy()` to ensure the glue code that ties native code to
`NativeActivity` is not stripped by the linker. We will see more about this in
Chapter 9, Porting Existing Libraries to Android.

```
#include "EventLoop.hpp"
#include "Log.hpp"

EventLoop::EventLoop(android_app* pApplication):
        mApplication(pApplication)
{}

void EventLoop::run() {
    int32_t result; int32_t events;
    android_poll_source* source;

    // Makes sure native glue is not stripped by the linker.
    app_dummy();

    Log::info("Starting event loop");
    while (true) {
        // Event processing loop.
        while ((result = ALooper_pollAll(-1, NULL, &events,
                (void**) &source)) >= 0) {
            // An event has to be processed.
            if (source != NULL) {
                source->process(mApplication, source);
            }
```

```
                // Application is getting destroyed.
                if (mApplication->destroyRequested) {
                    Log::info("Exiting event loop");
                    return;
                }
            }
        }
    }
```

8. Finally, create `jni/Main.cpp` to define the program entry point `android_main()`, which runs the event loop in a new file `Main.cpp`:

```cpp
#include "EventLoop.hpp"
#include "Log.hpp"

void android_main(android_app* pApplication) {
    EventLoop(pApplication).run();
}
```

9. Edit the `jni/Android.mk` file to define the `droidblaster` module (the LOCAL_MODULE directive).

Describe the C++ files to compile the LOCAL_SRC_FILES directive with the help of the LS_CPP macro (more about this in *Chapter 9, Porting Existing Libraries to Android*).

Link `droidblaster` with the `native_app_glue` module (the LOCAL_STATIC_LIBRARIES directive) and android (required by the **Native App Glue** module), as well as the `log` libraries (the LOCAL_LDLIBS directive):

```makefile
LOCAL_PATH := $(call my-dir)

include $(CLEAR_VARS)

LS_CPP=$(subst $(1)/,,$(wildcard $(1)/*.cpp))
LOCAL_MODULE := droidblaster
LOCAL_SRC_FILES := $(call LS_CPP,$(LOCAL_PATH))
LOCAL_LDLIBS := -landroid -llog
LOCAL_STATIC_LIBRARIES := android_native_app_glue

include $(BUILD_SHARED_LIBRARY)

$(call import-module,android/native_app_glue)
```

10. Create `jni/Application.mk` to compile the native module for multiple `ABI`s. We will use the most basic ones, as shown in the following code:

```
APP_ABI := armeabi armeabi-v7a x86
```

What just happened?

Build and run the application. Of course, you will not see anything tremendous when starting this application. Actually, you will just see a black screen! However, if you look carefully at the **LogCat** view in Eclipse (or the `adb logcat` command), you will discover a few interesting messages that have been emitted by your native application in reaction to activity events:

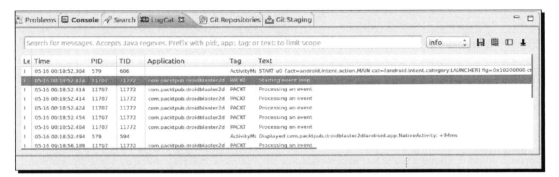

We initiated a Java Android project without a single line of Java code! Instead of referencing a child of `Activity` in `AndroidManifest`, we referenced the `android.app.NativeActivity` class provided by the Android framework.

`NativeActivity` is a Java class, launched like any other Android activity and interpreted by the Dalvik Virtual Machine like any other Java class. However, we never faced it directly. `NativeActivity` is in fact a helper class provided with Android SDK, which contains all the necessary glue code to handle application events (lifecycle, input, sensors, and so on) and broadcasts them transparently to native code. Thus, a native activity does not eliminate the need for JNI. It just hides it under the cover! However, the native C/C++ module run by `NativeActivity` is executed outside Dalvik boundaries in its own thread, entirely natively (using the Posix Thread API)!

`NativeActivity` and native code are connected together through the `native_app_glue` module. The Native App Glue has the responsibility of:

◆ Launching the native thread, which runs our own native code

◆ Receiving events from `NativeActivity`

◆ Routing these events to the native thread event loop for further processing

The `Native glue` module code is located in `${ANDROID_NDK}/sources/android/native_app_glue` and can be analyzed, modified, or forked at will (see *Chapter 9, Porting Existing Libraries to Android*, for more information). The headers related to native APIs such as, `looper.h`, can be found in `${ANDROID_NDK}/platforms/<Target Platform>/<Target Architecture>/usr/include/android/`. Let's see in more detail how it works.

More about the Native App Glue

Our own native code entry point is declared inside the `android_main()` method, which is similar to the main methods in desktop applications. It is called only once when `NativeActivity` is instantiated and launched. It loops over application events until `NativeActivity` is terminated by the user (for example, when pressing a device's back button) or until it exits by itself (more about this in the next part).

The `android_main()` method is not the real native application entry point. The real entry point is the `ANativeActivity_onCreate()` method hidden in the `android_native_app_glue` module. The event loop we implemented in `android_main()` is in fact a delegate event loop, launched in its own native thread by the glue module. This design decouples native code from the `NativeActivity` class, which is run on the UI thread on the Java side. Thus, even if your code takes a long time to handle an event, `NativeActivity` is not blocked and your Android device still remains responsive.

The delegate native event loop in `android_main()` is itself composed, in our example, of two nested while loops. The outer one is an infinite loop, terminated only when activity destruction is requested by the system (indicated by the `destroyRequested` flag). It executes an inner loop, which processes all pending application events.

```
...
int32_t result; int32_t events;
android_poll_source* source;
while (true) {
    while ((result = ALooper_pollAll(-1, NULL, &events,
            (void**) &source)) >= 0) {
        if (source != NULL) {
            source->process(mApplication, source);
        }
        if (mApplication->destroyRequested) {
            return;
        }
    }
}
...
```

The inner `For` loop polls events by calling `ALooper_pollAll()`. This method is part of the `Looper` API, which can be described as a general-purpose event loop manager provided by Android. When timeout is set to `-1`, like in the preceding example, `ALooper_pollAll()` remains blocked while waiting for events. When at least one is received, `ALooper_pollAll()` returns and the code flow continues.

The `android_poll_source` structure describing the event is filled and is then used by client code for further processing. This structure looks as follows:

```
struct android_poll_source {
    int32_t id; // Source identifier
    struct android_app* app; // Global android application context
    void (*process)(struct android_app* app,
        struct android_poll_source* source); // Event processor
};
```

The `process()` function pointer can be customized to process application events manually, as we will see in the next section.

As we saw in this part, the event loop receives an `android_app` structure in parameter. This structure, described in `android_native_app_glue.h`, contains some contextual information as shown in the following table:

`void* userData`	Pointer to any data you want. This is essential in giving some contextual information to the activity or input event callbacks.
`void (*pnAppCmd) (...)` and `int32_t (*onInputEvent) (...)`	These member variables represent the event callbacks triggered by the Native App Glue when an activity or an input event occurs. We will see more about this in the next section.
`ANativeActivity* activity`	Describes the Java native activity (its class as a JNI object, its data directories, and so on) and gives the necessary information to retrieve a JNI context.
`AConfiguration* config`	Describes the current hardware and system state, such as the current language and country, the current screen orientation, density, size, and so on.
`void* savedState size_t and savedStateSize`	Used to save a buffer of data when an activity (and thus its native thread) is destroyed and later restored.
`AInputQueue* inputQueue`	Provides input events (used internally by the native glue). We will see more about input events in *Chapter 8, Handling Input Devices and Sensors*.
`ALooper* looper`	Allows attaching and detaching event queues used internally by the native glue. Listeners poll and wait for events sent on a communication pipe.

`ANativeWindow* window` and `ARect contentRect`	Represents the "drawable" area on which graphics can be drawn. The `ANativeWindow` API, declared in `native_window.h`, allows retrieval of the window width, height, and pixel format, and the changing of these settings.
`int activityState`	Current activity state, that is, `APP_CMD_START`, `APP_CMD_RESUME`, `APP_CMD_PAUSE`, and so on.
`int destroyRequested`	When equal to `1`, it indicates that the application is about to be destroyed and the native thread must be terminated immediately. This flag has to be checked in the event loop.

The `android_app` structure also contains some additional data for internal use only, which should not be changed.

Knowing all these details is not essential to program native programs but can help you understand what's going on behind your back. Let's now see how to handle these activity events.

Handling Activity events

In the first part, a native event loop was run, which flushes events without really processing them. In this second part, we are going to discover more about these events occurring during the activity lifecycle, and how to process them, spending the remaining time stepping our application.

> The resulting project is provided with this book under the name `DroidBlaster_Part2`.

Time for action – stepping the event loop

Let's extend the previous example to step our application when events are processed.

1. Open `jni/Types.hpp` and define a new type status to represent return codes:

```
#ifndef _PACKT_TYPES_HPP_
#define _PACKT_TYPES_HPP_

#include <cstdlib>

typedef int32_t status;

const status STATUS_OK   = 0;
```

```
const status STATUS_KO   = -1;
const status STATUS_EXIT = -2;

#endif
```

2. Create the `jni/ActivityHandler.hpp` header and define an "interface" to observe native activity events. Each possible event has its own handler method: `onStart()`, `onResume()`, `onPause()`, `onStop()`, `onDestroy()`, and so on. However, we are generally interested in three specific moments in the activity life cycle:

   ❑ `onActivate()`, invoked when the activity is resumed and its window is available and focused

   ❑ `onDeactivate()`, invoked when the activity is paused or the display window loses its focus or is destroyed

   ❑ `onStep()`, invoked when no event has to be processed and computations can take place

```cpp
#ifndef _PACKT_ACTIVITYHANDLER_HPP_
#define _PACKT_ACTIVITYHANDLER_HPP_

#include "Types.hpp"

class ActivityHandler {
public:
    virtual ~ActivityHandler() {};

    virtual status onActivate() = 0;
    virtual void onDeactivate() = 0;
    virtual status onStep() = 0;

    virtual void onStart() {};
    virtual void onResume() {};
    virtual void onPause() {};
    virtual void onStop() {};
    virtual void onDestroy() {};

    virtual void onSaveInstanceState(void** pData, size_t* pSize) {};
    virtual void onConfigurationChanged() {};
    virtual void onLowMemory() {};

    virtual void onCreateWindow() {};
    virtual void onDestroyWindow() {};
    virtual void onGainFocus() {};
    virtual void onLostFocus() {};
};
#endif
```

3. Enhance `jni/EventLoop.hpp` with the following methods:

- ❏ `activate()` and `deactivate()`, executed when an activity availability changes

- ❏ `callback_appEvent()`, which is static and routes events to `processActivityEvent()`

Also, define some member variables as follows:

- ❏ `mActivityHandler` observes activity events. This instance is given as a constructor parameter and requires the inclusion of `ActivityHandler.hpp`

- ❏ `mEnabled` saves the application state when the application is active/paused

- ❏ `mQuit` indicates the event loop needs to exit

```cpp
#ifndef _PACKT_EVENTLOOP_HPP_
#define _PACKT_EVENTLOOP_HPP_

#include "ActivityHandler.hpp"
#include <android_native_app_glue.h>

class EventLoop {
public:
    EventLoop(android_app* pApplication,
            ActivityHandler& pActivityHandler);

    void run();

private:
    void activate();
    void deactivate();

    void processAppEvent(int32_t pCommand);

    static void callback_appEvent(android_app* pApplication,
        int32_t pCommand);

private:
    android_app* mApplication;
    bool mEnabled;
    bool mQuit;

    ActivityHandler& mActivityHandler;
};
#endif
```

4. Edit `jni/EventLoop.cpp`. The constructor initialization list itself is trivial to implement. Then, fill the `android_app` application context with additional information:

❏ `userData` points to any data you want. It is the only information accessible from `callback_appEvent()` declared previously. In our case, this is the `EventLoop` instance (that is, `this`).

❏ `onAppCmd` points to an internal callback triggered each time an event occurs. In our case, this is the role devoted to the static method `callback_appEvent()`.

```
#include "EventLoop.hpp"
#include "Log.hpp"

EventLoop::EventLoop(android_app* pApplication,
        ActivityHandler& pActivityHandler):
        mApplication(pApplication),
        mEnabled(false), mQuit(false),
        mActivityHandler(pActivityHandler) {
    mApplication->userData = this;
    mApplication->onAppCmd = callback_appEvent;
}
...
```

❏ Update the `run()` main event loop. Instead of blocking when there is no more activity event to process, `ALooper_pollAll()` must let the program flow continue to perform the recurrent processing. Here, processing is performed by the listener in `mActivityHandler.onStep()`. This behavior is obviously only needed when the application is enabled.

❏ Also, allow the activity to be terminated programmatically using the `AnativeActivity_finish()` method.

```
...
void EventLoop::run() {
    int32_t result; int32_t events;
    android_poll_source* source;

    // Makes sure native glue is not stripped by the linker.
    app_dummy();

    Log::info("Starting event loop");
```

```
        while (true) {
            // Event processing loop.
            while ((result = ALooper_pollAll(mEnabled ? 0 : -1,
            NULL,
                    &events, (void**) &source)) >= 0) {
                // An event has to be processed.
                if (source != NULL) {
                    Log::info("Processing an event");
                    source->process(mApplication, source);
                }
                // Application is getting destroyed.
                if (mApplication->destroyRequested) {
                    Log::info("Exiting event loop");
                    return;
                }
            }

            // Steps the application.
            if ((mEnabled) && (!mQuit)) {
                if (mActivityHandler.onStep() != STATUS_OK) {
                    mQuit = true;
                    ANativeActivity_finish(mApplication->activity);
                }
            }
        }
    }
    ...
```

What just happened?

We changed our event loop to update our application, instead of blocking uselessly, when there are no more events to process. This behavior is specified in ALooper_pollAll() by its first parameter, timeout:

♦ When timeout is -1, as defined previously, call is blocking until events are received.

♦ When timeout is 0, call is non-blocking so that, if nothing remains in the queue, the program flow continues (the inner while loop is terminated) and makes it possible to perform recurrent processing.

♦ When timeout is greater than 0, we have a blocking call, which remains until an event is received or the duration is elapsed.

Here, we want to step the activity (that is, perform computations) when it is in active state (mEnabled is `true`); in that case, timeout is `0`. When the activity is in deactivated state (mEnabled is `false`), events are still processed (for example, to resurrect the activity) but nothing needs to get computed. The thread has to be blocked to avoid consuming battery and processor time uselessly; in that case, timeout is `-1`.

Once all pending events are processed, the listener is stepped. It can request the application to be terminated, for example, if the game is finished. To leave the application programmatically, the NDK API provides the `ANativeActivity_finish()` method to request activity termination. Termination does not occur immediately but after the last few events (pause, stop, and so on) are processed.

Time for action – handling Activity events

We are not done yet. Let's continue our example to handle activity events and log them to the **LogCat** view:

1. Continue editing `jni/EventLoop.cpp`. Implement `activate()` and `deactivate()`.Check both activity states before notifying the listener (to avoid untimely triggering). We consider an activity as activated only if a display window is available:

```
...
void EventLoop::activate() {
    // Enables activity only if a window is available.
    if ((!mEnabled) && (mApplication->window != NULL)) {
        mQuit = false; mEnabled = true;
        if (mActivityHandler.onActivate() != STATUS_OK) {
            goto ERROR;
        }
    }
    return;

ERROR:
    mQuit = true;
    deactivate();
    ANativeActivity_finish(mApplication->activity);
}

void EventLoop::deactivate() {
    if (mEnabled) {
        mActivityHandler.onDeactivate();
```

```
                           mEnabled = false;
            }
    }
    . . .
```

□   Route activity events from the static callback `callback_appEvent()` to the member method `processAppEvent()`.

□   To do so, retrieve the `EventLoop` instance, thanks to the `userData` pointer (this being unavailable from a static method). Effective event processing is then delegated to `processAppEvent()`, which brings us back to the object-oriented world. The command, that is the activity event, given by the native glue is passed at the same time.

```
    . . .
    void EventLoop::callback_appEvent(android_app* pApplication,
        int32_t pCommand) {
        EventLoop& eventLoop = *(EventLoop*) pApplication->userData;
        eventLoop.processAppEvent(pCommand);
    }
    . . .
```

2.   Process the forwarded events in `processAppEvent()`. The pCommand parameter contains an enumeration value (`APP_CMD_*`), which describes the occurring event (`APP_CMD_START`, `APP_CMD_GAINED_FOCUS`, and so on).

Depending on the event, activate or deactivate the event loop and notify the listener:

Activation occurs when the activity gains focus. This event is always the last event that occurs after the activity is resumed and the window is created. Getting focus means that the activity can receive input events.

Deactivation occurs when the window loses focus or the application is paused (both can occur first). For security, deactivation is also performed when the window is destroyed, although this should always occur after the focus is lost. Losing focus means that the application does not receive input events anymore.

```
    . . .
    void EventLoop::processAppEvent(int32_t pCommand) {
        switch (pCommand) {
        case APP_CMD_CONFIG_CHANGED:
            mActivityHandler.onConfigurationChanged();
            break;
        case APP_CMD_INIT_WINDOW:
            mActivityHandler.onCreateWindow();
```

```
        break;
    case APP_CMD_DESTROY:
        mActivityHandler.onDestroy();
        break;
    case APP_CMD_GAINED_FOCUS:
        activate();
        mActivityHandler.onGainFocus();
        break;
    case APP_CMD_LOST_FOCUS:
        mActivityHandler.onLostFocus();
        deactivate();
        break;
    case APP_CMD_LOW_MEMORY:
        mActivityHandler.onLowMemory();
        break;
    case APP_CMD_PAUSE:
        mActivityHandler.onPause();
        deactivate();
        break;
    case APP_CMD_RESUME:
        mActivityHandler.onResume();
        break;
    case APP_CMD_SAVE_STATE:
        mActivityHandler.onSaveInstanceState(
            &mApplication->savedState, &mApplication->savedStateSize);
          break;
    case APP_CMD_START:
        mActivityHandler.onStart();
        break;
    case APP_CMD_STOP:
        mActivityHandler.onStop();
        break;
    case APP_CMD_TERM_WINDOW:
        mActivityHandler.onDestroyWindow();
        deactivate();
        break;
    default:
        break;
    }
}
```

 A few events, such as APP_CMD_WINDOW_RESIZED, are available but never triggered. Do not listen to them unless you are ready to stick your hands in the glue.

3. Create `jni/DroidBlaster.hpp`, which implements the `ActivityHandler` interface and all its methods (some have been skipped here for conciseness). This class will run the game logic as follows:

```
#ifndef _PACKT_DROIDBLASTER_HPP_
#define _PACKT_DROIDBLASTER_HPP_

#include "ActivityHandler.hpp"
#include "EventLoop.hpp"
#include "Types.hpp"

class DroidBlaster : public ActivityHandler {
public:
    DroidBlaster(android_app* pApplication);
    void run();

protected:
    status onActivate();
    void onDeactivate();
    status onStep();

    void onStart();
    ...

private:
    EventLoop mEventLoop;
};
#endif
```

4. Implement `jni/DroidBlaster.cpp` with all the required handlers. To keep this introduction to the activity lifecycle simple, we are just going to log each event that occurs. Use `onStart()` as a model for all the handlers that have been skipped in the following code.

Steps are limited to a simple thread sleep (to avoid flooding the Android log), which requires the inclusion of `unistd.h`.

Note that the event loop is now run directly by the `DroidBlaster` class:

```
#include "DroidBlaster.hpp"
#include "Log.hpp"

#include <unistd.h>

DroidBlaster::DroidBlaster(android_app* pApplication):
    mEventLoop(pApplication, *this) {
```

```
    Log::info("Creating DroidBlaster");
}

void DroidBlaster::run() {
    mEventLoop.run();
}

status DroidBlaster::onActivate() {
    Log::info("Activating DroidBlaster");
    return STATUS_OK;
}

void DroidBlaster::onDeactivate() {
    Log::info("Deactivating DroidBlaster");
}

status DroidBlaster::onStep() {
    Log::info("Starting step");
    usleep(300000);
    Log::info("Stepping done");
    return STATUS_OK;
}

void DroidBlaster::onStart() {
    Log::info("onStart");
}
...
```

5. Finally, initialize and run the `DroidBlaster` game in the `android_main()` entry point:

```
#include "DroidBlaster.hpp"
#include "EventLoop.hpp"
#include "Log.hpp"

void android_main(android_app* pApplication) {
    DroidBlaster(pApplication).run();
}
```

What just happened?

If you like a black screen, you are served! Again, this time, everything happens in the Eclipse **LogCat** view. All messages that have been emitted in reaction to application events are displayed here, as shown in the following screenshot:

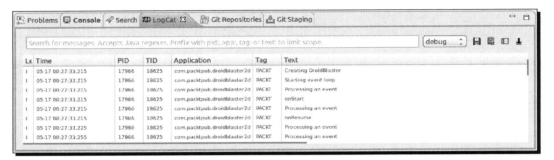

We created a minimalist framework, which handles application events in the native thread using an event-driven approach. Events (which are named commands) are redirected to a listener object, which performs its own specific computations.

Native activity events correspond mostly to classic Java activity events. Events are a critical and rather tricky point that any application needs to handle. They occur generally in pairs, such as `start/stop`, `resume/pause`, `create/destroy`, `create window/destroy window`, or `gain/lose focus`. Although they occur most of the time in a predetermined order, some specific cases may cause different behaviors, for example:

- Leaving the application using the back button destroys the activity and native thread.

- Leaving the application using the home button stops the activity and releases the window. The native thread is kept on hold.

- Pressing the device's home button for a long time and then getting back should cause a loss and gain of focus only. The native thread is kept on hold.

- Shutting down the phone screen and switching it back should terminate and reinitialize the window right after the activity is resumed. The native thread is kept on hold.

- When changing screen orientation (not applicable here), the whole activity may not lose its focus, although the recreated activity will regain it.

Understanding the activity lifecycle is essential to develop Android applications. Have a look at `http://developer.android.com/reference/android/app/Activity.html` in the official Android documentation for a detailed description.

The Native App Glue gives you a chance to save your activity state before it is destroyed by triggering `APP_CMD_SAVE_STATE`. The state must be saved in the `android_app` structure in `savedState`, which is a pointer to a memory buffer to save, and in `savedStateSize`, which is the size of the memory buffer to save. The buffer must be allocated by ourselves, using `malloc()` (deallocation being automatic), and must not contain pointers, only "raw" data.

Accessing window surface natively

Application events are essential to understand, but not very exciting. An interesting feature of the Android NDK is the ability to access the display window natively. With this privileged access, applications can draw any graphics they want onscreen.

We will now exploit this feature to get a graphic feedback in our application: a red square on screen. This square is going to represent the spaceship the user will control during the game.

 The resulting project is provided with this book under the name `DroidBlaster_Part3`.

Time for action – displaying raw graphics

Let's make `DroidBlaster` more interactive with some graphics and game components.

1. Edit `jni/Types.hpp` and create a new structure `Location` to hold entity positions. Also, define a macro to generate a random value in the requested range as follows:

```
#ifndef _PACKT_TYPES_HPP_
#define _PACKT_TYPES_HPP_
...
struct Location {
    Location(): x(0.0f), y(0.0f) {};

    float x; float y;
};

#define RAND(pMax) (float(pMax) * float(rand()) /
float(RAND_MAX))
#endif
```

2. Create a new file, `jni/GraphicsManager.hpp`. Define a structure `GraphicsElement`, which contains the location and dimensions of the graphical element to display:

```
#ifndef _PACKT_GRAPHICSMANAGER_HPP_
#define _PACKT_GRAPHICSMANAGER_HPP_

#include "Types.hpp"

#include <android_native_app_glue.h>

struct GraphicsElement {
    GraphicsElement(int32_t pWidth, int32_t pHeight):
        location(),
        width(pWidth), height(pHeight) {
    }

    Location location;
    int32_t width;  int32_t height;
};
...
```

Then, in the same file, define a `GraphicsManager` class as follows:

- ❑ `getRenderWidth()` and `getRenderHeight()` to return the display size
- ❑ `registerElement()` is a `GraphicsElement` factory method that tells the manager what element to draw
- ❑ `start()` and `update()` `initialize` the manager and render the screen for each frame respectively

A few member variables are needed:

- ❑ `mApplication` stores the application context needed to access the display window
- ❑ `mRenderWidth` and `mRenderHeight` for the display size
- ❑ `mElements` and `mElementCount` for a table of all the elements to draw

```
    ...
    class GraphicsManager {
    public:
        GraphicsManager(android_app* pApplication);
        ~GraphicsManager();

        int32_t getRenderWidth() { return mRenderWidth; }
```

```
        int32_t getRenderHeight() { return mRenderHeight; }

        GraphicsElement* registerElement(int32_t pHeight, int32_t
        pWidth);

        status start();
        status update();

    private:
        android_app* mApplication;

        int32_t mRenderWidth; int32_t mRenderHeight;
        GraphicsElement* mElements[1024]; int32_t mElementCount;
    };
    #endif
```

3. Implement `jni/GraphicsManager.cpp`, starting with the constructor, destructor, and registration methods. They manage the list of `GraphicsElement` to update:

```cpp
#include "GraphicsManager.hpp"
#include "Log.hpp"

GraphicsManager::GraphicsManager(android_app* pApplication) :
    mApplication(pApplication),
    mRenderWidth(0), mRenderHeight(0),
    mElements(), mElementCount(0) {
    Log::info("Creating GraphicsManager.");
}

GraphicsManager::~GraphicsManager() {
    Log::info("Destroying GraphicsManager.");
    for (int32_t i = 0; i < mElementCount; ++i) {
        delete mElements[i];
    }
}

GraphicsElement* GraphicsManager::registerElement(int32_t pHeight,
        int32_t pWidth) {
    mElements[mElementCount] = new GraphicsElement(pHeight, pWidth);
    return mElements[mElementCount++];
}
...
```

4. Implement the start() method to initialize the manager.

First, use the ANativeWindow_setBuffersGeometry() API method to force the window depth format to 32 bits. The two zeros passed in parameters are the required window width and height. They are ignored unless initialized with a positive value. In such a case, the requested window area defined by width and height is scaled to match the screen size.

Then, retrieve all the necessary window dimensions in an ANativeWindow_ Buffer structure. To fill this structure, the window must be first locked with ANativeWindow_lock(), and then unlocked with AnativeWindow_ unlockAndPost() once done.

```
...
status GraphicsManager::start() {
    Log::info("Starting GraphicsManager.");

    // Forces 32 bits format.
    ANativeWindow_Buffer windowBuffer;
    if (ANativeWindow_setBuffersGeometry(mApplication->window,
    0, 0,
        WINDOW_FORMAT_RGBX_8888) < 0) {
        Log::error("Error while setting buffer geometry.");
        return STATUS_KO;
    }

    // Needs to lock the window buffer to get its properties.
    if (ANativeWindow_lock(mApplication->window,
            &windowBuffer, NULL) >= 0) {
        mRenderWidth = windowBuffer.width;
        mRenderHeight = windowBuffer.height;
        ANativeWindow_unlockAndPost(mApplication->window);
    } else {
        Log::error("Error while locking window.");
        return STATUS_KO;
    }
    return STATUS_OK;
}
...
```

5. Write the update() method, which renders raw graphics each time an application is stepped.

The window surface must be locked before any draw operation takes place with AnativeWindow_lock(). Again, the AnativeWindow_Buffer structure is filled with window information for width and height, but more importantly, the stride and bits pointer.

> The stride gives the distance in "pixels" between two successive pixel lines in the window.

> The bits pointer gives direct access to the window surface, in much the same way as the Bitmap API, as seen in the previous chapter.

With these two pieces of information, any pixel-based operations can be performed natively.

For example, clear the window memory area with 0 to get a black background. A brute-force approach using memset() can be applied for that purpose.

```
. . .
status GraphicsManager::update() {
    // Locks the window buffer and draws on it.
    ANativeWindow_Buffer windowBuffer;
    if (ANativeWindow_lock(mApplication->window,
            &windowBuffer, NULL) < 0) {
        Log::error("Error while starting GraphicsManager");
        return STATUS_KO;
    }

    // Clears the window.
    memset(windowBuffer.bits, 0, windowBuffer.stride *
            windowBuffer.height * sizeof(uint32_t*));
. . .
```

> ❏ Once cleared, draw all elements registered with GraphicsManager. Each element is represented as a red square onscreen.

> ❏ First, compute the coordinates (upper-left and bottom-right corners) of the elements to draw.

❏   Then, clip their coordinates to avoid drawing outside the window memory area. This operation is rather important as going beyond window limits might result in a segmentation fault:

```
...
// Renders graphic elements.
int32_t maxX = windowBuffer.width - 1;
int32_t maxY = windowBuffer.height - 1;
for (int32_t i = 0; i < mElementCount; ++i) {
    GraphicsElement* element = mElements[i];

    // Computes coordinates.
    int32_t leftX = element->location.x - element->width / 2;
    int32_t rightX = element->location.x + element->width / 2;
    int32_t leftY = windowBuffer.height - element->location.y
                        - element->height / 2;
    int32_t rightY = windowBuffer.height - element->location.y
                        + element->height / 2;

    // Clips coordinates.
    if (rightX < 0 || leftX > maxX
     || rightY < 0 || leftY > maxY) continue;

    if (leftX < 0) leftX = 0;
    else if (rightX > maxX) rightX = maxX;
    if (leftY < 0) leftY = 0;
    else if (rightY > maxY) rightY = maxY;
...
```

6.   After that, draw each pixel of the element on screen. The `line` variable points to the beginning of the first line of pixels on which the element is drawn. This pointer is computed using the stride (distance between two lines of pixels) and the top `Y` coordinate of the element.

Then, we can loop over window pixels to draw a red square representing the element. Start from the left `X` coordinate to the right `X` coordinate of the element, switching from one pixel line to another (that is, on the `Y` axis) when the end of each is reached.

```
...
// Draws a rectangle.
uint32_t* line = (uint32_t*) (windowBuffer.bits)
                + (windowBuffer.stride * leftY);
for (int iY = leftY; iY <= rightY; iY++) {
    for (int iX = leftX; iX <= rightX; iX++) {
```

```
            line[iX] = 0X000000FF; // Red color
        }
        line = line + windowBuffer.stride;
    }
}
...
```

Finish drawing operations with `ANativeWindow_unlockAndPost()` and pend call
to `pendANativeWindow_lock()`. These must always be called in pairs:

```
...
    // Finshed drawing.
    ANativeWindow_unlockAndPost(mApplication->window);
    return STATUS_OK;
}
```

7. Create a new component `jni/Ship.hpp` that represents our spaceship.

We will handle initialization only for now, using `initialize()`.

`Ship` is created with the factory method `registerShip()`.

The `GraphicsManager` and the ship `GraphicsElement` are needed to initialize
the ship properly.

```
#ifndef _PACKT_SHIP_HPP_
#define _PACKT_SHIP_HPP_

#include "GraphicsManager.hpp"

class Ship {
public:
    Ship(android_app* pApplication,
        GraphicsManager& pGraphicsManager);

    void registerShip(GraphicsElement* pGraphics);

    void initialize();

private:
    GraphicsManager& mGraphicsManager;

    GraphicsElement* mGraphics;
};
#endif
```

8. Implement `jni/Ship.cpp`. The important part is `initialize()`, which positions the ship on the lower quarter of the screen, as shown in the following code:

```
#include "Log.hpp"
#include "Ship.hpp"
#include "Types.hpp"

static const float INITAL_X = 0.5f;
static const float INITAL_Y = 0.25f;

Ship::Ship(android_app* pApplication,
        GraphicsManager& pGraphicsManager) :
  mGraphicsManager(pGraphicsManager),
  mGraphics(NULL) {
}

void Ship::registerShip(GraphicsElement* pGraphics) {
    mGraphics = pGraphics;
}

void Ship::initialize() {
    mGraphics->location.x = INITAL_X
            * mGraphicsManager.getRenderWidth();
    mGraphics->location.y = INITAL_Y
            * mGraphicsManager.getRenderHeight();
}
```

9. Append the newly created manager and component to `jni/DroidBlaster.hpp`:

```
...
#include "ActivityHandler.hpp"
#include "EventLoop.hpp"
#include "GraphicsManager.hpp"
#include "Ship.hpp"
#include "Types.hpp"

class DroidBlaster : public ActivityHandler {
    ...
private:
    ...

    GraphicsManager mGraphicsManager;
    EventLoop mEventLoop;

    Ship mShip;
};
#endif
```

10. Finally, update the `jni/DroidBlaster.cpp` constructor:

```
...
static const int32_t SHIP_SIZE = 64;

DroidBlaster::DroidBlaster(android_app* pApplication):
    mGraphicsManager(pApplication),
    mEventLoop(pApplication, *this),

    mShip(pApplication, mGraphicsManager) {
    Log::info("Creating DroidBlaster");

    GraphicsElement* shipGraphics = mGraphicsManager.registerElement(
            SHIP_SIZE, SHIP_SIZE);
    mShip.registerShip(shipGraphics);
}
...
```

11. Initialize `GraphicsManager` and the `Ship` component in `onActivate()`:

```
...
status DroidBlaster::onActivate() {
    Log::info("Activating DroidBlaster");

    if (mGraphicsManager.start() != STATUS_OK) return
    STATUS_KO;

    mShip.initialize();

    return STATUS_OK;
}
...
```

12. Finally, update the manager in `onStep()`:

```
...
status DroidBlaster::onStep() {
    return mGraphicsManager.update();
}
```

What just happened?

Compile and run `DroidBlaster`. The result should be a simple red square representing our spaceship in the first quarter of the screen, as follows:

Graphical feedback is provided through the `ANativeWindow` API, which gives native access to the display window. It allows manipulating its surface like a bitmap. Similarly, accessing the window surface requires locking and unlocking both before and after processing.

The `AnativeWindow` API is defined in `android/native_window.h` and `android/native_window_jni.h`. It provides the following:

`ANativeWindow_setBuffersGeometry()` initializes the Pixel format (or Depth format) and size of the window buffer. The possible Pixel formats are:

- `WINDOW_FORMAT_RGBA_8888` for 32-bit colors per pixel, 8 bits for each of the Red, Green, Blue, and Alpha (for transparency) channels.

- `WINDOW_FORMAT_RGBX_8888` is the same as the previous one, except that the Alpha channel is ignored.

- `WINDOW_FORMAT_RGB_565` for 16-bit colors per pixel (5 bits for Red and Blue, and 6 for the Green channel).

If the supplied dimension is 0, the window size is used. If it is non-zero, then the window buffer is scaled to match window dimensions when displayed onscreen:

```
int32_t ANativeWindow_setBuffersGeometry(ANativeWindow* window, int32_t
width, int32_t height, int32_t format);
```

◆ `ANativeWindow_lock()` must be called before performing any drawing operations:

```
int32_t ANativeWindow_lock(ANativeWindow* window, ANativeWindow_Buffer*
outBuffer,
        ARect* inOutDirtyBounds);
```

◆ `ANativeWindow_unlockAndPost()` releases the window after drawing operations are done and sends it to the display. It must be called in a pair with `ANativeWindow_lock()`:

```
int32_t ANativeWindow_unlockAndPost(ANativeWindow* window);
```

◆ `ANativeWindow_acquire()` gets a reference, in the Java way, on the specified window to prevent potential deletion. This might be necessary if you do not have fine control on the surface life cycle:

```
void ANativeWindow_acquire(ANativeWindow* window);
```

◆ `ANativeWindow_fromSurface()` associates the window with the given Java `android.view.Surface`. This method automatically acquires a reference to the given surface. It must be released with `ANativeWindow_release()` to avoid memory leaks:

```
ANativeWindow* ANativeWindow_fromSurface(JNIEnv* env, jobject surface);
```

◆ `ANativeWindow_release()` removes an acquired reference to allow freeing window resources:

```
void ANativeWindow_release(ANativeWindow* window);
```

◆ The following methods return the width, height (in pixels), and the format of the window surface. The returned value is negative incase an error occurs. Note that these methods are tricky to use because their behavior is a bit inconsistent. Prior to Android 4, it is preferable to lock the surface once to get reliable information (which is already provided by `ANativeWindow_lock()`):

```
int32_t ANativeWindow_getWidth(ANativeWindow* window);
int32_t ANativeWindow_getHeight(ANativeWindow* window);
int32_t ANativeWindow_getFormat(ANativeWindow* window);
```

We now know how to draw. However, how do we animate what is drawn? A key is needed in order to do this: *time*.

Measuring time natively

Those who talk about graphics also need to talk about timing. Indeed, Android devices have different capabilities, and animations should be adapted to their speed. To help us in this task, Android gives access to time primitives, thanks to its good support of Posix APIs.

To experiment with these capabilities, we will use a timer to move asteroids onscreen according to time.

 The resulting project is provided with this book under the name `DroidBlaster_Part4`.

Time for action – animating graphics with a timer

Let's animate the game.

1. Create `jni/TimeManager.hpp` with the `time.h` manager and define the following methods:

   - `reset()` to initialize the manager.
   - `update()` to measure game step duration.
   - `elapsed()` and `elapsedTotal()` to get game step duration and game duration. They are going to allow the adaptation of the application behavior to the device speed.
   - `now()` is a utility method to recompute the current time.

   Define the following member variables:

   - `mFirstTime` and `mLastTime` to save a time checkpoint in order to compute `elapsed()` and `elapsedTotal()`
   - `mElapsed` and `mElapsedTotal` to save computed time measures

   ```
   #ifndef _PACKT_TIMEMANAGER_HPP_
   #define _PACKT_TIMEMANAGER_HPP_

   #include "Types.hpp"

   #include <ctime>

   class TimeManager {
   ```

```
        public:
            TimeManager();

            void reset();
            void update();

            double now();
            float elapsed() { return mElapsed; };
            float elapsedTotal() { return mElapsedTotal; };

        private:
            double mFirstTime;
            double mLastTime;
            float mElapsed;
            float mElapsedTotal;
        };
        #endif
```

2. Implement `jni/TimeManager.cpp`. When reset, `TimeManager` saves the current time computed by the `now()` method.

```
#include "Log.hpp"
#include "TimeManager.hpp"

#include <cstdlib>
#include <time.h>

TimeManager::TimeManager():
    mFirstTime(0.0f),
    mLastTime(0.0f),
    mElapsed(0.0f),
    mElapsedTotal(0.0f) {
    srand(time(NULL));
}

void TimeManager::reset() {
    Log::info("Resetting TimeManager.");
    mElapsed = 0.0f;
    mFirstTime = now();
    mLastTime = mFirstTime;
}
...
```

3. Implement `update()` which checks:

- ❏ elapsed time since last frame in `mElapsed`
- ❏ elapsed time since the very first frame in `mElapsedTotal`

 Note that it is important to work with double types when handling the current time to avoid losing accuracy. Then, the resulting delay can be converted back to float for the elapsed time, since the time difference between the two frames is quite low.

```
. . .
void TimeManager::update() {
    double currentTime = now();
    mElapsed = (currentTime - mLastTime);
    mElapsedTotal = (currentTime - mFirstTime);
    mLastTime = currentTime;
}
. . .
```

4. Compute the current time in the `now()` method. Use the Posix primitive `clock_gettime()` to retrieve the current time. A monotonic clock is essential to ensure that the time always goes forward and is not subject to system changes (for example, if the user travels around the world):

```
. . .
double TimeManager::now() {
    timespec timeVal;
    clock_gettime(CLOCK_MONOTONIC, &timeVal);
    return timeVal.tv_sec + (timeVal.tv_nsec * 1.0e-9);
}
```

5. Create a new file, `jni/PhysicsManager.hpp`. Define a structure `PhysicsBody` to hold asteroid location, dimensions, and velocity:

```
#ifndef PACKT_PHYSICSMANAGER_HPP
#define PACKT_PHYSICSMANAGER_HPP

#include "GraphicsManager.hpp"
#include "TimeManager.hpp"
#include "Types.hpp"

struct PhysicsBody {
    PhysicsBody(Location* pLocation, int32_t pWidth, int32_t pHeight):
        location(pLocation),
```

```
        width(pWidth), height(pHeight),
        velocityX(0.0f), velocityY(0.0f) {
    }

    Location* location;
    int32_t width; int32_t height;
    float velocityX; float velocityY;
};
...
```

6. Define a basic PhysicsManager. We need a reference to TimeManager to adapt bodies of movements to time.

Define a method update() to move asteroids during each game step. The PhysicsManager stores the asteroids to update in mPhysicsBodies and mPhysicsBodyCount:

```
...
class PhysicsManager {
public:
    PhysicsManager(TimeManager& pTimeManager,
            GraphicsManager& pGraphicsManager);
    ~PhysicsManager();

    PhysicsBody* loadBody(Location& pLocation, int32_t pWidth,
            int32_t pHeight);
    void update();

private:
    TimeManager& mTimeManager;
    GraphicsManager& mGraphicsManager;

    PhysicsBody* mPhysicsBodies[1024]; int32_t
    mPhysicsBodyCount;
};
#endif
```

7. Implement jni/PhysicsManager.cpp, starting with the constructor, destructor, and registration methods:

```
#include "PhysicsManager.hpp"
#include "Log.hpp"

PhysicsManager::PhysicsManager(TimeManager& pTimeManager,
        GraphicsManager& pGraphicsManager) :
  mTimeManager(pTimeManager), mGraphicsManager(pGraphicsManager),
```

```
    mPhysicsBodies(), mPhysicsBodyCount(0) {
        Log::info("Creating PhysicsManager.");
    }

    PhysicsManager::~PhysicsManager() {
        Log::info("Destroying PhysicsManager.");
        for (int32_t i = 0; i < mPhysicsBodyCount; ++i) {
            delete mPhysicsBodies[i];
        }
    }

    PhysicsBody* PhysicsManager::loadBody(Location& pLocation,
            int32_t pSizeX, int32_t pSizeY) {
        PhysicsBody* body = new PhysicsBody(&pLocation, pSizeX, pSizeY);
        mPhysicsBodies[mPhysicsBodyCount++] = body;
        return body;
    }
    ...
```

8. Move asteroids in `update()` according to their velocity. The computation is performed according to the amount of time between the two game steps:

```
    ...
    void PhysicsManager::update() {
        float timeStep = mTimeManager.elapsed();
        for (int32_t i = 0; i < mPhysicsBodyCount; ++i) {
            PhysicsBody* body = mPhysicsBodies[i];
            body->location->x += (timeStep * body->velocityX);
            body->location->y += (timeStep * body->velocityY);
        }
    }
```

9. Create the `jni/Asteroid.hpp` component with the following methods:

- `initialize()` to set up asteroids with random properties when the game starts

- `update()` to detect asteroids that get out of game boundaries

- `spawn()` is used by both `initialize()` and `update()` to set up one individual asteroid

We also need the following members:

- `mBodies` and `mBodyCount` to store the list of asteroids to be managed

❑ A few integer members to store game boundaries

```
#ifndef _PACKT_ASTEROID_HPP_
#define _PACKT_ASTEROID_HPP_

#include "GraphicsManager.hpp"
#include "PhysicsManager.hpp"
#include "TimeManager.hpp"
#include "Types.hpp"

class Asteroid {
public:
    Asteroid(android_app* pApplication,
        TimeManager& pTimeManager, GraphicsManager&
        pGraphicsManager,
        PhysicsManager& pPhysicsManager);

    void registerAsteroid(Location& pLocation, int32_t pSizeX,
            int32_t pSizeY);

    void initialize();
    void update();

private:
    void spawn(PhysicsBody* pBody);

    TimeManager& mTimeManager;
    GraphicsManager& mGraphicsManager;
    PhysicsManager& mPhysicsManager;

    PhysicsBody* mBodies[1024]; int32_t mBodyCount;
    float mMinBound;
    float mUpperBound; float mLowerBound;
    float mLeftBound; float mRightBound;
};
#endif
```

10. Write the `jni/Asteroid.cpp` implementation. Start with a few constants, as well as the constructor and registration method, as follows:

```
#include "Asteroid.hpp"
#include "Log.hpp"

static const float BOUNDS_MARGIN = 128;
```

```
static const float MIN_VELOCITY = 150.0f, VELOCITY_RANGE = 600.0f;

Asteroid::Asteroid(android_app* pApplication,
        TimeManager& pTimeManager, GraphicsManager&
        pGraphicsManager,
        PhysicsManager& pPhysicsManager) :
    mTimeManager(pTimeManager),
    mGraphicsManager(pGraphicsManager),
    mPhysicsManager(pPhysicsManager),
    mBodies(), mBodyCount(0),
    mMinBound(0.0f),
    mUpperBound(0.0f), mLowerBound(0.0f),
    mLeftBound(0.0f), mRightBound(0.0f) {
}

void Asteroid::registerAsteroid(Location& pLocation,
        int32_t pSizeX, int32_t pSizeY) {
    mBodies[mBodyCount++] = mPhysicsManager.loadBody(pLocation,
            pSizeX, pSizeY);
}
...
```

11. Set up boundaries in `initialize()`. Asteroids are generated above the top of screen (in `mMinBound`, the maximum boundary `mUpperBound` is twice the height of the screen). They move from the top to the bottom of the screen. Other boundaries correspond to screen edges padded with a margin (representing twice the size of an asteroid).

Then, initialize all asteroids using `spawn()`:

```
...
void Asteroid::initialize() {
    mMinBound = mGraphicsManager.getRenderHeight();
    mUpperBound = mMinBound * 2;
    mLowerBound = -BOUNDS_MARGIN;
    mLeftBound = -BOUNDS_MARGIN;
    mRightBound = (mGraphicsManager.getRenderWidth() +
    BOUNDS_MARGIN);

    for (int32_t i = 0; i < mBodyCount; ++i) {
        spawn(mBodies[i]);
    }
}
...
```

12. During each game step, check the asteroids that get out of bounds and reinitialize them:

```
...
void Asteroid::update() {
    for (int32_t i = 0; i < mBodyCount; ++i) {
        PhysicsBody* body = mBodies[i];
        if ((body->location->x < mLeftBound)
         || (body->location->x > mRightBound)
         || (body->location->y < mLowerBound)
         || (body->location->y > mUpperBound)) {
            spawn(body);
        }
    }
}
...
```

13. Finally, initialize each asteroid in `spawn()`, with velocity and location being generated randomly:

```
...
void Asteroid::spawn(PhysicsBody* pBody) {
    float velocity = -(RAND(VELOCITY_RANGE) + MIN_VELOCITY);
    float posX = RAND(mGraphicsManager.getRenderWidth());
    float posY = RAND(mGraphicsManager.getRenderHeight())
                    + mGraphicsManager.getRenderHeight();

    pBody->velocityX = 0.0f;
    pBody->velocityY = velocity;
    pBody->location->x = posX;
    pBody->location->y = posY;
}
```

14. Add the newly created managers and components to `jni/DroidBlaster.hpp`:

```
#ifndef _PACKT_DROIDBLASTER_HPP_
#define _PACKT_DROIDBLASTER_HPP_

#include "ActivityHandler.hpp"
#include "Asteroid.hpp"
#include "EventLoop.hpp"
#include "GraphicsManager.hpp"
#include "PhysicsManager.hpp"
#include "Ship.hpp"
```

```
#include "TimeManager.hpp"
#include "Types.hpp"

class DroidBlaster : public ActivityHandler {
    ...
private:
    TimeManager     mTimeManager;
    GraphicsManager mGraphicsManager;
    PhysicsManager  mPhysicsManager;
    EventLoop mEventLoop;

    Asteroid mAsteroids;
    Ship mShip;
};
#endif
```

15. Register asteroids with `GraphicsManager` and `PhysicsManager` in the `jni/DroidBlaster.cpp` constructor:

```
...
static const int32_t SHIP_SIZE = 64;
static const int32_t ASTEROID_COUNT = 16;
static const int32_t ASTEROID_SIZE = 64;

DroidBlaster::DroidBlaster(android_app* pApplication):
    mTimeManager(),
    mGraphicsManager(pApplication),
    mPhysicsManager(mTimeManager, mGraphicsManager),
    mEventLoop(pApplication, *this),

    mAsteroids(pApplication, mTimeManager, mGraphicsManager,
            mPhysicsManager),
    mShip(pApplication, mGraphicsManager) {
    Log::info("Creating DroidBlaster");

    GraphicsElement* shipGraphics = mGraphicsManager.registerElement(
            SHIP_SIZE, SHIP_SIZE);
    mShip.registerShip(shipGraphics);

    for (int32_t i = 0; i < ASTEROID_COUNT; ++i) {
```

```
            GraphicsElement* asteroidGraphics =
                    mGraphicsManager.registerElement(ASTEROID_SIZE,
                                            ASTEROID_SIZE);
            mAsteroids.registerAsteroid(
                    asteroidGraphics->location, ASTEROID_SIZE,
                    ASTEROID_SIZE);
        }
    }
    ...
```

16. Initialize the newly added classes in `onActivate()` properly:

```
    ...
    status DroidBlaster::onActivate() {
        Log::info("Activating DroidBlaster");

        if (mGraphicsManager.start() != STATUS_OK) return STATUS_KO;

        mAsteroids.initialize();
        mShip.initialize();

        mTimeManager.reset();
        return STATUS_OK;
    }
    ...
    Finally, update managers and components for each game step:
    ...
    status DroidBlaster::onStep() {
        mTimeManager.update();
        mPhysicsManager.update();

        mAsteroids.update();

        return mGraphicsManager.update();
    }
    ...
```

What just happened?

Compile and run the application. This time it should be a bit more animated! Red squares representing asteroids cross the screen at a constant rhythm. The `TimeManger` helps with setting the pace.

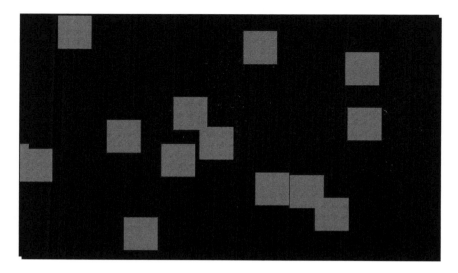

Timers are essential to display animations and movement at the correct speed. They can be implemented with the POSIX method `clock_gettime()`, which retrieves time with a high precision, theoretically to the nanosecond.

In this tutorial, we used the `CLOCK_MONOTONIC` flag to set up the timer. A monotonic clock gives the elapsed clock time from an arbitrary starting point in the past. It is unaffected by potential system date change, and thus cannot go back in the past like other options. The downside with `CLOCK_MONOTONIC` is that it is system-specific and it is not guaranteed to be supported. Hopefully Android supports it, but care should be taken when porting Android code to other platforms. Another point specific to Android to be aware of is that monotonic clocks stop when the system is suspended.

An alternative, that is less precise and affected by changes in the system time (which may or may not be desirable), is `gettimeofday()`, which is also provided in `ctime`. The usage is similar but the precision is in microseconds instead of nanoseconds. The following could be a usage example that could replace the current `now()` implementation in `TimeManager`:

```
double TimeManager::now() {
    timeval lTimeVal;
    gettimeofday(&lTimeVal, NULL);
    return (lTimeVal.tv_sec * 1000.0) + (lTimeVal.tv_usec / 1000.0);
}
```

For more information, have a look at the Man-pages at `http://man7.org/linux/man-pages/man2/clock_gettime.2.html`.

Summary

The Android NDK allows us to write fully native applications without a line of Java code. `NativeActivity` provides a skeleton to implement an event loop that processes application events. Associated with the Posix time management API, the NDK provides the required base to build complex multimedia applications or games.

In summary, we created `NativeActivity` that polls activity events to start or stop native code accordingly. We accessed the display window natively, like a bitmap, to display raw graphics. Finally, we retrieved time to make the application adapt to device speed using a monotonic clock.

The basic framework initiated here will form the base of the 2D/3D game that we will develop throughout this book. However, although the flat design is in fashion nowadays, we need something a bit fancier than red squares!

In the next chapter, we will discover how to render advanced graphics with OpenGL ES 2 for Android.

6

Rendering Graphics with OpenGL ES

Let's face the fact that one of the main interests of Android NDK is to write multimedia applications and games. Indeed, these programs consume lots of resources and need responsiveness. That is why one of the first available APIs (and almost the only one until recently) in Android NDK is an API for graphics: the **Open Graphics Library for Embedded Systems** *(abbreviated as* **OpenGL ES***).*

OpenGL is a standard API created by Silicon Graphics and is now managed by the Khronos Group (see http://www.khronos.org/*). OpenGL provides a common interface for all standard* **GPU**s *(***Graphics Processing Unit** *like your graphics card, and so on) on desktops. OpenGL ES is a derivative API available on many embedded platforms, such as Android or iOS. It is your best hope to write portable and efficient graphics code. OpenGL can render both 2D and 3D graphics.*

There are three main releases of OpenGL ES currently supported by Android:

◆ OpenGL ES 1.0 and 1.1 are supported on all Android devices (except 1.1, which is supported on a few very old devices). It offers an old school graphic API with a **fixed pipeline** (that is, a fixed set of configurable operations to transform and render geometry). Specification is not completely implemented, but most features are available. This could still be a good choice for simple 2D or 3D graphics or to port legacy OpenGL code.

- ◆ OpenGL ES 2 is supported on almost all phones nowadays, even older ones, starting from API Level 8. It replaces the fixed pipeline with a modern programmable pipeline with **Vertex** and **Fragment Shaders**. It is a bit more complex but also more powerful. It is a good choice for the more complex 2D or 3D games, while still maintaining a very good compatibility. Note that OpenGL ES 1.X is frequently emulated by an OpenGL 2 implementation behind the scenes.

- ◆ OpenGL ES 3.0 is available on modern devices starting from API Level 18, and OpenGL ES 3.1 is available starting from API Level 21 (not all devices at these API level may support it though). They bring a set of new improvements to GLES 2 (**Texture Compression** as a standard feature, **Occlusion Queries, Instanced Rendering**, and others for 3.0, **Compute Shaders, Indirect Draw** commands, and others for 3.1) and a better compatibility with the desktop version of OpenGL. It is backward compatible with OpenGL ES 2.

This chapter teaches you how to create some basic 2D graphics using OpenGL ES 2. More specifically, you are going to discover how to:

- ◆ Initialize OpenGL ES
- ◆ Load a texture from a PNG file packaged in the assets
- ◆ Draw sprites using vertex and fragment shaders
- ◆ Render a particle effect
- ◆ Adapt graphics to various resolutions

With OpenGL ES, and graphics in general, being a wide subject, this chapter covers only the basics to being with.

Initializing OpenGL ES

The first step to create awesome 2D and 3D graphics is to initialize OpenGL ES. Although not terribly complex, this task requires some boilerplate code to bind a rendering context to an Android window. These pieces are glued together with the help of the **Embedded-System Graphics Library** (**EGL**), a companion API of OpenGL ES.

For this first section, we are going to replace the raw drawing system implemented in the previous chapter with OpenGL ES. A black to white fading effect will demonstrate that the EGL initialization works properly.

 The resulting project is provided with this book under the name `DroidBlaster_Part5`.

Time for action – initializing OpenGL ES

Let's rewrite our `GraphicsManager` to initialize an OpenGL ES context:

1. Modify `jni/GraphicsManager.hpp` by performing the following:

   ❑ Include `EGL/egl.h` to bind OpenGL ES to the Android platform and `GLES2/gl2.h` to render graphics

   ❑ Add a method `stop()` to unbind the OpenGL rendering context and free graphics resources when you're leaving the activity

   ❑ Define `EGLDisplay`, `EGLSurface`, and `EGLContext` member variables, which represent handles to system resources, as shown here:

```
...
#include "Types.hpp"

#include <android_native_app_glue.h>
#include <GLES2/gl2.h>
#include <EGL/egl.h>
...

class GraphicsManager {
public:
    ...
    status start();
    void stop();
    status update();

private:
    ...
    int32_t mRenderWidth; int32_t mRenderHeight;
    EGLDisplay mDisplay; EGLSurface mSurface; EGLContext mContext;

    GraphicsElement* mElements[1024]; int32_t mElementCount;
};
#endif
```

2. Reimplement `jni/GraphicsManager.cpp` by replacing the previous code based on Android raw graphics API with OpenGL-based code. Start by adding new members to the constructor initialization list:

```
#include "GraphicsManager.hpp"
#include "Log.hpp"

GraphicsManager::GraphicsManager(android_app* pApplication) :
    mApplication(pApplication),
    mRenderWidth(0), mRenderHeight(0),
    mDisplay(EGL_NO_DISPLAY), mSurface(EGL_NO_CONTEXT),
    mContext(EGL_NO_SURFACE),
    mElements(), mElementCount(0) {
    Log::info("Creating GraphicsManager.");
}
...
```

3. The hard work must be done in the method `start()`:

    ❑ First, declare some variables. Note how EGL defines its own types and re-declares primitive types `EGLint` and `EGLBoolean` to favor platform independence.

    ❑ Then, define the needed OpenGL configuration in constant attribute lists. Here, we want OpenGL ES 2 and a 16 bit surface (5 bits for red, 6 bits for green, and 5 bits for blue). We could also choose a 32 bit surface for better color fidelity (but less performance on some devices). The attribute lists are terminated by `EGL_NONE` sentinel:

```
...
status GraphicsManager::start() {
    Log::info("Starting GraphicsManager.");
    EGLint format, numConfigs, errorResult; GLenum status;
    EGLConfig config;
    // Defines display requirements. 16bits mode here.
    const EGLint DISPLAY_ATTRIBS[] = {
        EGL_RENDERABLE_TYPE, EGL_OPENGL_ES2_BIT,
        EGL_BLUE_SIZE, 5, EGL_GREEN_SIZE, 6, EGL_RED_SIZE, 5,
        EGL_SURFACE_TYPE, EGL_WINDOW_BIT,
        EGL_NONE
    };
    // Request an OpenGL ES 2 context.
    const EGLint CONTEXT_ATTRIBS[] = {
        EGL_CONTEXT_CLIENT_VERSION, 2, EGL_NONE
    };
    ...
```

4. Connect to the default **display**, that is, the Android main window, with
`eglGetDisplay()` and `eglInitialize()`. Then, find an appropriate **framebuffer**
(An OpenGL term referring to the rendering surface, and possibly additional buffers,
such as **Z-buffer** or **Stencil** buffer) configuration with `eglChooseConfig()` as the
display. Configurations are selected according to the requested attributes:

```
. . .
    mDisplay = eglGetDisplay(EGL_DEFAULT_DISPLAY);
    if (mDisplay == EGL_NO_DISPLAY) goto ERROR;
    if (!eglInitialize(mDisplay, NULL, NULL)) goto ERROR;

    if(!eglChooseConfig(mDisplay, DISPLAY_ATTRIBS, &config, 1,
        &numConfigs) || (numConfigs <= 0)) goto ERROR;
. . .
```

5. Reconfigure the Android window with the selected configuration (retrieved with
`eglGetConfigAttrib()`). This operation is Android-specific and performed with
the Android `ANativeWindow` API.

After that, create the display surface and the OpenGL context using the display and
configuration selected previously. A context contains all data related to OpenGL
state (enabled settings, disabled settings, and so on):

```
. . .
    if (!eglGetConfigAttrib(mDisplay, config,
        EGL_NATIVE_VISUAL_ID, &format)) goto ERROR;
    ANativeWindow_setBuffersGeometry(mApplication->window, 0, 0,
        format);

    mSurface = eglCreateWindowSurface(mDisplay, config,
        mApplication->window, NULL);
    if (mSurface == EGL_NO_SURFACE) goto ERROR;
    mContext = eglCreateContext(mDisplay, config, NULL,
        CONTEXT_ATTRIBS);
    if (mContext == EGL_NO_CONTEXT) goto ERROR;
. . .
```

6. Activate the created rendering context with `eglMakeCurrent()`. Finally,
define the display viewport according to the surface attributes retrieved with
`eglQuerySurface()`. The Z-buffer is not needed and can be disabled:

```
. . .
    if (!eglMakeCurrent(mDisplay, mSurface, mSurface, mContext)
    || !eglQuerySurface(mDisplay, mSurface, EGL_WIDTH, &mRenderWidth)
```

```
        || !eglQuerySurface(mDisplay, mSurface, EGL_HEIGHT, &mRenderHeight)
        || (mRenderWidth <= 0) || (mRenderHeight <= 0)) goto ERROR;

        glViewport(0, 0, mRenderWidth, mRenderHeight);
        glDisable(GL_DEPTH_TEST);
        return STATUS_OK;

ERROR:
        Log::error("Error while starting GraphicsManager");
        stop();
        return STATUS_KO;
    }
    ...
```

7. When the application stops running, unbind the application from the Android window and release the EGL resources:

```
    ...
    void GraphicsManager::stop() {
        Log::info("Stopping GraphicsManager.");

        // Destroys OpenGL context.
        if (mDisplay != EGL_NO_DISPLAY) {
            eglMakeCurrent(mDisplay, EGL_NO_SURFACE, EGL_NO_SURFACE,
                        EGL_NO_CONTEXT);
            if (mContext != EGL_NO_CONTEXT) {
                eglDestroyContext(mDisplay, mContext);
                mContext = EGL_NO_CONTEXT;
            }
            if (mSurface != EGL_NO_SURFACE) {
                eglDestroySurface(mDisplay, mSurface);
                mSurface = EGL_NO_SURFACE;
            }
            eglTerminate(mDisplay);
            mDisplay = EGL_NO_DISPLAY;
        }
    }
    ...
```

What just happened?

We have initialized and connected both OpenGL ES and the Android native window system together with EGL. Thanks to this API, we have queried a display configuration that matches our expectations and creates a framebuffer to render our scene on. EGL is a standard API specified by the Khronos group (like OpenGL). Platforms often implement their own variant (haphazardly, EAGL on iOS and so on) so that the display window initialization remains OS-specific. Thus, portability is quite limited in practice.

This initialization process results in the creation of an OpenGL context, which is the first step to enable the OpenGL graphics pipeline. Special care should be taken with OpenGL contexts, which are frequently lost on Android: when you're leaving or going back to the home screen, when a call is received, when devices go to sleep, when you're switching to another application, and so on. As a lost context becomes unusable, it is important to release graphics resources as soon as possible.

The OpenGL ES specification supports the creation of multiple contexts for one display surface. This allows dividing rendering operations among threads or rendering to several windows. However, it is not well supported on Android hardware and should be avoided.

OpenGL ES is now initialized but nothing will show up unless we start rendering some graphics on the display screen.

Time for action – clearing and swapping buffers

Let's clear the display buffers with a color fading from black to white:

1. While still being in `jni/GraphicsManager.cpp`, refresh the screen during each update step with `eglSwapBuffers()`.

   To have a visual feedback, change the display background color gradually with the help of `glClearColor()` before erasing the Framebuffer with `glClear()`:

   ```
   ...
   status GraphicsManager::update() {
       static float clearColor = 0.0f;
       clearColor += 0.001f;
       glClearColor(clearColor, clearColor, clearColor, 1.0f);
       glClear(GL_COLOR_BUFFER_BIT);

       if (eglSwapBuffers(mDisplay, mSurface) != EGL_TRUE) {
           Log::error("Error %d swapping buffers.", eglGetError());
   ```

```
            return STATUS_KO;
        } else {
            return STATUS_OK;
        }
    }
```

2. Update the `Android.mk` file to link the EGL and GLESv2 libraries:

```
LOCAL_PATH := $(call my-dir)

include $(CLEAR_VARS)

LS_CPP=$(subst $(1)/,,$(wildcard $(1)/*.cpp))
LOCAL_MODULE := droidblaster
LOCAL_SRC_FILES := $(call LS_CPP,$(LOCAL_PATH))
LOCAL_LDLIBS := -landroid -llog -lEGL -lGLESv2
LOCAL_STATIC_LIBRARIES := android_native_app_glue

include $(BUILD_SHARED_LIBRARY)

$(call import-module,android/native_app_glue)
```

What just happened?

Launch the application. If everything works fine, your device screen will progressively fade from black to white. Instead of clearing the display with a raw `memset()`, or setting pixels one by one as seen in the previous chapter, we invoke efficient OpenGL ES drawing primitives. Note that the effect appears only the first time the application starts because the clear color is stored in a static variable. To make it appear again, kill the application and relaunch it.

Rendering a scene requires clearing the framebuffer and swapping the display buffer. The latter operation is triggered when `eglSwapBuffers()` is invoked. Swapping on Android is synchronized with the screen refresh rate to avoid image **Tearing**; this is a **VSync**. The refresh rate is variable depending on the device. A common value is 60 Hz but some devices have different refresh rates.

Internally, rendering is performed on a back buffer which is swapped with the front buffer shown to the user. The front buffer becomes the back buffer and vice versa (the pointers are switched). This technique is more commonly referred to as **page flipping**. According to the driver implementation, the swapping chain can be extended with a third buffer. In this situation, we talk about **Triple Buffering**.

Our OpenGL pipeline is now properly initialized and able to display graphics on the screen. However, you may still find this concept of "pipeline" a bit nebulous. Let's see what is hidden behind it.

An insight into the OpenGL pipeline

We talk about pipeline because the graphics data goes through a series of steps in which it is transformed. The following diagram shows a simplified representation of the OpenGL ES 2 pipeline:

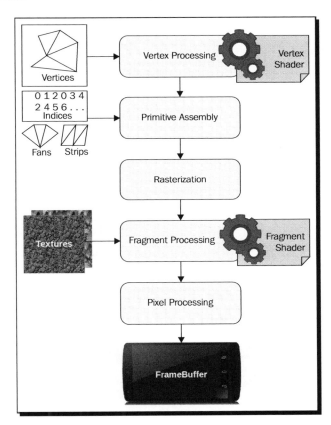

◆ **Vertex Processing**: An input mesh of vertices, given as a **vertex buffer object** or a **vertex array**, is transformed vertex by vertex in a vertex shader. The vertex shader can, for example, move or rotate single vertices, project them onto the screen, adapt texture coordinates, compute lighting, and so on. It generates an output vertex that can be processed further in the pipe.

◆ **Primitive Assembly**: Individual vertices are connected together into triangles, points, lines, and so on. More connection information is specified by the client code when the draw call is sent. It can take the form of an index buffer (each index points to a vertex through its rank) or a predefined rule, such as stripping or fanning. Transformations such as **back face culling** or **clipping** are done at this stage.

◆ **Rasterization**: Primitives are interpolated into fragments, which is a term covering all the data associated with one pixel to render (such as color, normals, and so on). One fragment is related to one pixel. These fragments feed the fragment shader.

◆ **Fragment Processing**: The fragment shader is a program which processes each fragment to compute the pixel to display. This is the stage where texture mapping, using the coordinates computed by the vertex shader and interpolated by the rasterizer, is applied. Different shading algorithms can be computed to render specific effects (for example, **Toon shading**).

◆ **Pixel Processing**: The fragment shader outputs pixels which have to be merged in the existing framebuffer (the rendering surface), where some pixels may be already drawn. Transparency effects or blending is applied at this stage.

The vertex and fragment shaders are programmable in the **GL Shading Language** (**GLSL**). They are available only in OpenGL ES 2 and 3. OpenGL ES 1 provides a fixed function pipeline with a predefined set of possible transformations.

This is only a brief overview of all the processing done by the OpenGL rendering pipeline. To find more information about it, have a look at the OpenGL.org wiki at `http://www.opengl.org/wiki/Rendering_Pipeline_Overview`.

Loading textures using the Asset manager

I guess you need something more consistent than just changing the screen color! But before showing awesome graphics in our application, we need to load some external resources.

In this second part, we are going to load a texture into OpenGL ES thanks to the Android Asset manager, an API provided since NDK R5. It allows programmers to access any resources stored in the `assets` folder in their project. Assets stored there are then packaged into the final APK archive during application compilation. Asset resources are considered as raw binary files that your application needs to interpret and access using their filename relative to the `assets` folder (a file `assets/mydir/myfile` can be accessed with `mydir/myfile` path). Files are available in the read-only mode and might be compressed.

If you have already written some Java Android application, then you know that Android also provides resources accessible through compile-time generated IDs inside the res project folder. This is not directly available on the Android NDK. Unless you are ready to use a JNI bridge, assets are the only way to package resources in your APK.

We are now going to load a texture encoded in one of the most popular picture formats used nowadays, the **Portable Network Graphics (PNG)**. For this, we are going to integrate **libpng** in a NDK module.

 The resulting project is provided with this book under the name
DroidBlaster_Part6.

Time for action – reading assets with the Asset manager

Let's create a class to read the Android asset files:

1. Create jni/Resource.hpp to encapsulate the access to asset files. We are going to use the AAsset API defined in android/asset_manager.hpp (which is already included in android_native_app_glue.h).

   Declare the three main operations: open(), close(), and read(). We also need to retrieve the resource's path in getPath().

   The Android Asset management API entry point is an AAsetManager opaque structure. We can access asset files, represented by a second opaque structure AAsset, from it:

```
#ifndef _PACKT_RESOURCE_HPP_
#define _PACKT_RESOURCE_HPP_

#include "Types.hpp"

#include <android_native_app_glue.h>

class Resource {
public:
    Resource(android_app* pApplication, const char* pPath);

    const char* getPath() { return mPath; };

    status open();
```

```
        void close();
        status read(void* pBuffer, size_t pCount);

        bool operator==(const Resource& pOther);

private:
    const char* mPath;
    AAssetManager* mAssetManager;
    AAsset* mAsset;
};

#endif
```

2. Implement the class `Resource` in `jni/Resource.cpp`.

The Asset manager is provided by the **Native App Glue** module in its `android_app->activity` structure:

```
#include "Resource.hpp"

#include <sys/stat.h>

Resource::Resource(android_app* pApplication, const char*
pPath):
    mPath(pPath),
    mAssetManager(pApplication->activity->assetManager),
    mAsset(NULL) {
}
...
```

3. The Asset manager opens assets with `AassetManager_open()`. This is the sole responsibility of this method, apart from listing folders. We use the default open mode `AASSET_MODE_UNKNOWN` (more about this soon):

```
...
status Resource::open() {
    mAsset = AAssetManager_open(mAssetManager, mPath,
                                AASSET_MODE_UNKNOWN);
    return (mAsset != NULL) ? STATUS_OK : STATUS_KO;
}
...
```

4. Like files in classic applications, an opened asset must be closed when finished with
`AAsset_close()` so that any resource allocated by the system is released:

```
...
void Resource::close() {
    if (mAsset != NULL) {
        AAsset_close(mAsset);
        mAsset = NULL;
    }
}
...
```

5. Finally, the code operates on asset files with `AAsset_read()` to read data. This is
quite similar to what you can find with the standard Posix file API. Here, we try to
read the `pCount` data in a memory buffer and retrieve the amount of data that was
effectively read (in case we reach the end of the asset):

```
...
status Resource::read(void* pBuffer, size_t pCount) {
    int32_t readCount = AAsset_read(mAsset, pBuffer, pCount);
    return (readCount == pCount) ? STATUS_OK : STATUS_KO;
}

bool Resource::operator==(const Resource& pOther) {
    return !strcmp(mPath, pOther.mPath);
}
```

What just happened?

We have seen how to call the Android Asset API to read a file stored in the `assets` directory.
Android assets are read-only and should be used to hold static assets only. The Android Asset
API is defined in the `android/assert_manager.h` including file.

More about the Asset Manager API

The Android Asset manager provides a small set of method to access directories:

◆ `AAssetManager_openDir()` gives the possibility to explore an asset directory.
Use it in conjunction with `AAssetDir_getNextFileName()` and `AAssetDir_
rewind()`. An opened directory must be closed with `AAssetDir_close()`:

```
AAssetDir* AAssetManager_openDir(AAssetManager* mgr,
                                 const char* dirName);
```

- ◆ `AAssetDir_getNextFileName()` lists all the files available in the specified asset directory. One filename is returned each time you call it, or `NULL` is returned when all files have been listed:

```
const char* AAssetDir_getNextFileName(AAssetDir* assetDir);
```

- ◆ `AAssetDir_rewind()` gives the possibility to restart the file iteration process with `AAssetDir_getNextFileName()` from the beginning of the process:

```
void AAssetDir_rewind(AAssetDir* assetDir);
```

- ◆ `AAssetDir_close()` frees all the resources allocated when the directory has been opened. This method must be called in pair with `AAssetManager_openDir()`:

```
void AAssetDir_close(AAssetDir* assetDir);
```

Files can be opened with an API similar to the POSIX file API:

- ◆ `AAssetManager_open()` opens an asset file to read its content, retrieve its content as a buffer, or access its file descriptor. An opened asset must be closed with `AAsset_close()`:

```
AAsset* AAssetManager_open(AAssetManager* mgr,
                          const char* filename, int mode);
```

- ◆ `AAsset_read()` attempts to read the requested number of bytes in the provided buffer. The number of bytes actually read is returned or a negative value is returned in case an error occurs:

```
int AAsset_read(AAsset* asset, void* buf, size_t count);
```

- ◆ `AAsset_seek()` moves directly to the specified offset in the file, ignoring the previous data:

```
off_t AAsset_seek(AAsset* asset, off_t offset, int whence);
```

- ◆ `AAsset_close()` closes the asset and frees all the resources allocated when the file has been opened. This method must be called in pair with `AAssetManager_open()`:

```
void AAsset_close(AAsset* asset);
```

- ◆ `AAsset_getBuffer()` returns a pointer to a memory buffer containing the whole asset content or `NULL` if a problem occurs. The buffer might be memory mapped. Beware, as Android compresses some assets (depending on their extension) so that the buffer might not be directly readable:

```
const void* AAsset_getBuffer(AAsset* asset);
```

- `AAsset_getLength()` gives the total asset size in bytes. This method might be useful to preallocate a buffer of the right size before reading an asset:

  `off_t AAsset_getLength(AAsset* asset);`

- `Aasset_getRemainingLength()` is similar to `AAsset_getLength()` except that it does take into account the bytes already read:

  `off_t AAsset_getRemainingLength(AAsset* asset);`

- `AAsset_openFileDescriptor()` returns a raw Unix file descriptor. This is used in OpenSL to read a music file:

  `int AAsset_openFileDescriptor(AAsset* asset, off_t* outStart, off_t* outLength);`

- `AAsset_isAllocated()` indicates if the buffer returned by the asset is memory mapped:

  `int AAsset_isAllocated(AAsset* asset);`

We will see more about these methods in the subsequent chapters.

The modes available to open asset files are:

- `AASSET_MODE_BUFFER`: This helps to perform fast small reads
- `AASSET_MODE_RANDOM`: This helps to read chunks of data forward and backward
- `AASSET_MODE_STREAMING`: This helps to read data sequentially with occasional forward seeks
- `AASSET_MODE_UNKNOWN`: This helps to keep the system default settings

Most of the time `AASSET_MODE_UNKNOWN` will be the way to go.

Installing, large APK can be problematic even when they are deployed on an SD card (see the `installLocation` option in the Android manifest). Thus, a good strategy to deal with tons of megabytes of assets is to keep only the essential ones in your APK. Download the remaining files to the SD card at runtime or package them within a second APK.

Now that we have the PNG asset files to read, let's load them using `libpng`.

Time for action – compiling and embedding libpng module

Let's load an OpenGL texture from a PNG file in DroidBlaster.

1. Go to the website `http://www.libpng.org/pub/png/libpng.html` and download the `libpng` source package (which is Version 1.6.10 in this book).

 The original `libpng` 1.6.10 archive is provided with this book in the `Libraries/libpng` folder.

Create a folder named `libpng` inside `$ANDROID_NDK/sources/`. Move all files from the `libpng` package into this.

Copy the file `libpng/scripts/pnglibconf.h.prebuilt` into the root folder `libpng` with other source files. Rename it as `pnglibconf.h`.

 The folder `$ANDROID_NDK/sources` is a special folder considered as a module folder by default. It contains reusable libraries. See *Chapter 9, Porting Existing Libraries to Android*, for more information.

2. Write the `$ANDROID_NDK/sources/libpng/Android.mk` file with the content given in the following code:

```
LOCAL_PATH:= $(call my-dir)

include $(CLEAR_VARS)

LS_C=$(subst $(1)/,,$(wildcard $(1)/*.c))

LOCAL_MODULE := png
LOCAL_SRC_FILES := \
    $(filter-out example.c pngtest.c,$(call LS_C,$(LOCAL_PATH)))
LOCAL_EXPORT_C_INCLUDES := $(LOCAL_PATH)
LOCAL_EXPORT_LDLIBS := -lz

include $(BUILD_STATIC_LIBRARY)
```

3. Now, open `jni/Android.mk` in the `DroidBlaster` directory.

Link and import `libpng` with the help of the `LOCAL_STATIC_LIBRARIES` and `import-module` directives. This is similar to what we have done with the Native App Glue module:

```
LOCAL_PATH := $(call my-dir)

include $(CLEAR_VARS)

LS_CPP=$(subst $(1)/,,$(wildcard $(1)/*.cpp))
LOCAL_MODULE := droidblaster
LOCAL_SRC_FILES := $(call LS_CPP,$(LOCAL_PATH))
LOCAL_LDLIBS := -landroid -llog -lEGL -lGLESv2
LOCAL_STATIC_LIBRARIES := android_native_app_glue png

include $(BUILD_SHARED_LIBRARY)

$(call import-module,android/native_app_glue)
$(call import-module,libpng)
```

What just happened?

In the previous chapter, we embedded the existing Native App Glue module to create a fully native application. This time we have created our first native reusable module to integrate `libpng`. Ensure that it works by compiling `DroidBlaster`. If you look at the **Console** view of the `libpng` source files, it should get compiled for each target platform. Note that NDK provides incremental compilation and will not recompile the already compiled sources:

```
[x86] Compile        : android_native_app_glue <= android_native_app_glue.c
[x86] StaticLibrary  : libandroid_native_app_glue.a
[x86] Compile        : png <= png.c
[x86] Compile        : png <= pngerror.c
[x86] Compile        : png <= pngget.c
[x86] Compile        : png <= pngmem.c
[x86] Compile        : png <= pngpread.c
[x86] Compile        : png <= pngread.c
[x86] Compile        : png <= pngrio.c
[x86] Compile        : png <= pngrtran.c
[x86] Compile        : png <= pngrutil.c
[x86] Compile        : png <= pngset.c
```

A native library module (here, `libpng`) is defined in a Makefile located at the root of its own directory. It is then referenced from another Makefile module, typically the application module (here `Droidblaster`).

Here, the `libpng` library Makefile selects all the C files with the help of a custom macro `LS_C`. This macro is invoked from the `LOCAL_SRC_FILES` directive. We exclude `example.c` and `pngtest.c`, which are just test files, using the standard "Make" function `filter-out()`.

All the prerequisites include files that are made available to client modules with the directive `LOCAL_EXPORT_C_INCLUDES`, which refers to the source directory `LOCAL_PATH` here. The prerequisite libraries like `libzip` (option `-lz`) are also provided to the client modules using the `LOCAL_EXPORT_LDLIBS` directive this time. All directives containing the `_EXPORT_` term exports directives that are appended to the client module's own directives.

For more information about Makefiles, directives, and standard functions, have a look at *Chapter 9, Porting Existing Libraries to Android*.

Time for action – loading a PNG image

Now that `libpng` is compiled, let's read a real PNG file with it:

1. Edit `jni/GraphicsManager.hpp` and include the `Resource` header file.

    Create a new structure named `TextureProperties` containing:

    - A resource representing the texture asset
    - An OpenGL texture identifier (which is a kind of handle)
    - A width and a height

    ```
    . . .
    #include "Resource.hpp"
    #include "Types.hpp"
    . . .

    struct TextureProperties {
        Resource* textureResource;
        GLuint texture;
        int32_t width;
        int32_t height;
    };
    . . .
    ```

2. Append a method `loadTexture()` to the `GraphicsManager` to read a PNG and load it into an OpenGL texture.

    Textures are saved in an `mTextures` array to cache and finalize them.

    ```
    . . .
    class GraphicsManager {
    ```

```
public:
    ...
    status start();
    void stop();
    status update();

    TextureProperties* loadTexture(Resource& pResource);

private:
    ...
    int32_t mRenderWidth; int32_t mRenderHeight;
    EGLDisplay mDisplay; EGLSurface mSurface; EGLContext mContext;

    TextureProperties mTextures[32]; int32_t mTextureCount;
    GraphicsElement* mElements[1024]; int32_t mElementCount;
};
#endif
```

3. Edit `jni/GraphicsManager.cpp` to include a new header named `png.h` and update the constructor initialization list:

```
#include "GraphicsManager.hpp"
#include "Log.hpp"

#include <png.h>

GraphicsManager::GraphicsManager(android_app* pApplication) :
    mApplication(pApplication),
    mRenderWidth(0), mRenderHeight(0),
    mDisplay(EGL_NO_DISPLAY), mSurface(EGL_NO_CONTEXT),
    mContext(EGL_NO_SURFACE),
    mTextures(), mTextureCount(0),
    mElements(), mElementCount(0) {
    Log::info("Creating GraphicsManager.");
}
...
```

4. Free the texture-related resources when `GraphicsManager` stops using `glDeleteTetxures()`. This function can delete several textures at once, which explains why this method expects an ordinal and an array. But we will not use this possibility here:

```
...
void GraphicsManager::stop() {
    Log::info("Stopping GraphicsManager.");
```

```
    for (int32_t i = 0; i < mTextureCount; ++i) {
        glDeleteTextures(1, &mTextures[i].texture);
    }
    mTextureCount = 0;

    // Destroys OpenGL context.
    if (mDisplay != EGL_NO_DISPLAY) {
        ...
    }
}
...
```

5. To be fully independent from the data source, `libpng` provides a mechanism to integrate custom-read operations. This takes the form of a callback and reads the requested quantity of data into a buffer provided by `libpng`.

Implement this callback in conjunction with the Android Asset API to access the read data from application assets. The asset file is read through a `Resource` instance given by `png_get_io_ptr()` as an untyped pointer. This pointer is going to be provided by us while setting up the callback function (using `png_set_read_fn()`). We will see how this is done in the next steps:

```
...
void callback_readPng(png_structp pStruct,
    png_bytep pData, png_size_t pSize) {
    Resource* resource = ((Resource*) png_get_io_ptr(pStruct));
    if (resource->read(pData, pSize) != STATUS_OK) {
        resource->close();
    }
}
...
```

6. Implement `loadTexture()`. First, look for the `texture` in the cache. Textures are expensive in terms of memory and performance and should be managed with care (like all OpenGL resources in general):

```
...
TextureProperties* GraphicsManager::loadTexture(Resource&
pResource) {
    for (int32_t i = 0; i < mTextureCount; ++i) {
        if (pResource == *mTextures[i].textureResource) {
            Log::info("Found %s in cache", pResource.getPath());
            return &mTextures[i];
        }
    }
...
```

7. If you could not find the texture in the cache, let's read it. Define a few variables needed to read the PNG file first.

Then, open the image using the `AAsset` API and check the image signature (the first 8 bytes of the file) to ensure that the file is a PNG (note that it might still be corrupted):

```
...
    Log::info("Loading texture %s", pResource.getPath());
    TextureProperties* textureProperties; GLuint texture; GLint format;
    png_byte header[8];
    png_structp pngPtr = NULL; png_infop infoPtr = NULL;
    png_byte* image = NULL; png_bytep* rowPtrs = NULL;
    png_int_32 rowSize; bool transparency;

    if (pResource.open() != STATUS_OK) goto ERROR;
    Log::info("Checking signature.");
    if (pResource.read(header, sizeof(header)) != STATUS_OK)
        goto ERROR;
    if (png_sig_cmp(header, 0, 8) != 0) goto ERROR;
...
```

8. Allocate all the structures necessary to read a PNG image. After that, prepare reading operations by passing our `callback_readPng()`, implemented earlier in this tutorial, to `libpng`, along with our `Resource` reader. `Resource` pointer is the one retrieved in the callback with `png_get_io_ptr()`.

Also, set up error management with `setjmp()`. This mechanism allows jumping in code like a `goto` but through the call stack. If an error occurs, the control flow comes back at the point where `setjmp()` has been called first but enters the `if` block instead (here `goto ERROR`). This is the moment where we can provide the following script:

```
...
    Log::info("Creating required structures.");
    pngPtr = png_create_read_struct(PNG_LIBPNG_VER_STRING,
        NULL, NULL, NULL);
    if (!pngPtr) goto ERROR;
    infoPtr = png_create_info_struct(pngPtr);
    if (!infoPtr) goto ERROR;

    // Prepares reading operation by setting-up a read callback.
    png_set_read_fn(pngPtr, &pResource, callback_readPng);
    // Set-up error management. If an error occurs while reading,
    // code will come back here and jump
    if (setjmp(png_jmpbuf(pngPtr))) goto ERROR;
...
```

9. Ignore the first 8 bytes from the signature, which have already been read, for file signatures with `png_set_sig_bytes()` and `png_read_info()`:

Start reading the PNG file header with `png_get_IHDR()`:

```
...
    // Ignores first 8 bytes already read.
    png_set_sig_bytes(pngPtr, 8);
    // Retrieves PNG info and updates PNG struct accordingly.
    png_read_info(pngPtr, infoPtr);
    png_int_32 depth, colorType;
    png_uint_32 width, height;
    png_get_IHDR(pngPtr, infoPtr, &width, &height,
        &depth, &colorType, NULL, NULL, NULL);
...
```

10. The PNG files can be encoded in several formats: RGB, RGBA, 256 colors with a palette, grayscale, and so on. R, G, and B color channels can be encoded up to 16 bits. Hopefully, `libpng` provides transformation functions to decode unusual formats and transforms them into more classical RGB and luminance formats (with 8 bits per channel, with or without an alpha channel).

Select the right transformation using `png_set` functions. Transformations are validated with `png_read_update_info()`.

At the same time, select the corresponding OpenGL texture format:

```
...
    // Creates a full alpha channel if transparency is encoded as
    // an array of palette entries or a single transparent color.
    transparency = false;
    if (png_get_valid(pngPtr, infoPtr, PNG_INFO_tRNS)) {
        png_set_tRNS_to_alpha(pngPtr);
        transparency = true;
    }
    // Expands PNG with less than 8bits per channel to 8bits.
    if (depth < 8) {
        png_set_packing (pngPtr);
    // Shrinks PNG with 16bits per color channel down to 8bits.
    } else if (depth == 16) {
        png_set_strip_16(pngPtr);
    }
    // Indicates that image needs conversion to RGBA if needed.
    switch (colorType) {
    case PNG_COLOR_TYPE_PALETTE:
        png_set_palette_to_rgb(pngPtr);
```

```
            format = transparency ? GL_RGBA : GL_RGB;
            break;
        case PNG_COLOR_TYPE_RGB:
            format = transparency ? GL_RGBA : GL_RGB;
            break;
        case PNG_COLOR_TYPE_RGBA:
            format = GL_RGBA;
            break;
        case PNG_COLOR_TYPE_GRAY:
            png_set_expand_gray_1_2_4_to_8(pngPtr);
            format = transparency ? GL_LUMINANCE_ALPHA:GL_LUMINANCE;
            break;
        case PNG_COLOR_TYPE_GA:
            png_set_expand_gray_1_2_4_to_8(pngPtr);
            format = GL_LUMINANCE_ALPHA;
            break;
    }
    // Validates all transformations.
    png_read_update_info(pngPtr, infoPtr);
...
```

11. Allocate the necessary temporary buffer to hold image data and a second one with the address of each output image row for libpng. Note that the row order is inverted because OpenGL uses a different coordinate system (the first pixel is at bottom-left) than PNG (first pixel at top-left).

```
...
    // Get row size in bytes.
    rowSize = png_get_rowbytes(pngPtr, infoPtr);
    if (rowSize <= 0) goto ERROR;
    // Ceates the image buffer that will be sent to OpenGL.
    image = new png_byte[rowSize * height];
    if (!image) goto ERROR;
    // Pointers to each row of the image buffer. Row order is
    // inverted because different coordinate systems are used by
    // OpenGL (1st pixel is at bottom left) and PNGs (top-left).
    rowPtrs = new png_bytep[height];
    if (!rowPtrs) goto ERROR;
    for (int32_t i = 0; i < height; ++i) {
        rowPtrs[height - (i + 1)] = image + i * rowSize;
    }
...
```

12. Then, start reading the image content with `png_read_image()`.

Finally, when it's finished, release all temporary resources:

```
. . .
    // Reads image content.
    png_read_image(pngPtr, rowPtrs);
    // Frees memory and resources.
    pResource.close();
    png_destroy_read_struct(&pngPtr, &infoPtr, NULL);
    delete[] rowPtrs;
```

13. Finally, when it's finished, release all temporary resources:

```
. . .
ERROR:
    Log::error("Error loading texture into OpenGL.");
    pResource.close();
    delete[] rowPtrs; delete[] image;
    if (pngPtr != NULL) {
        png_infop* infoPtrP = infoPtr != NULL ? &infoPtr: NULL;
        png_destroy_read_struct(&pngPtr, infoPtrP, NULL);
    }
    return NULL;
}
```

What just happened?

Combining our native library module `libpng` with the Asset manager API gives us the power to load PNG files packaged in the assets directory. PNG is a relatively simple image format that is rather easy to integrate. In addition, it supports compression, which is good to limit the size of your APKs. Please note that once loaded, the PNG image buffer is uncompressed and can consume a lot of memory. So, release them as soon as you can. For detailed information about the PNG format, see `http://www.w3.org/TR/PNG/`.

Now that our PNG image is loaded, we can generate an OpenGL texture from it.

Time for action – generating an OpenGL texture

The `image` buffer filled by `libpng` now contains raw texture data. The next step is to generate a texture from it:

1. Let's continue our previous method `which is` `GraphicsManager::loadTexture()`.

Generate a new texture identifier with `glGenTextures()`.

Indicate that we are working on a texture with `glBindTexture()`.

Configure texture parameters with `glTexParameteri()` to specify the way a texture is filtered and wrapped. Use `GL_NEAREST`, as smoothing is not essential for a 2D game without zoom effects. Texture repetition is also not necessary and can be prevented with `GL_CLAMP_TO_EDGE`:

```
. . .
    png_destroy_read_struct(&pngPtr, &infoPtr, NULL);
    delete[] rowPtrs;

    GLenum errorResult;
    glGenTextures(1, &texture);
    glBindTexture(GL_TEXTURE_2D, texture);
    // Set-up texture properties.
    glTexParameteri(GL_TEXTURE_2D, GL_TEXTURE_MIN_FILTER,
        GL_NEAREST);
    glTexParameteri(GL_TEXTURE_2D, GL_TEXTURE_MAG_FILTER,
        GL_NEAREST);
    glTexParameteri(GL_TEXTURE_2D, GL_TEXTURE_WRAP_S,
        GL_CLAMP_TO_EDGE);
    glTexParameteri(GL_TEXTURE_2D, GL_TEXTURE_WRAP_T,
        GL_CLAMP_TO_EDGE);
. . .
```

2. Push the image data into OpenGL texture with `glTexImage2D()`.

This unbinds the texture to put OpenGL pipeline back in its previous state. This is not strictly necessary, but it helps to avoid configuration mistakes in future draw calls (that is, drawing with an unwanted texture).

Finally, do not forget to free the temporary image buffer.

You can check that the texture has been created properly with `glGetError()`:

```
. . .
    // Loads image data into OpenGL.
    glTexImage2D(GL_TEXTURE_2D, 0, format, width, height, 0, format,
                GL_UNSIGNED_BYTE, image);
    // Finished working with the texture.
    glBindTexture(GL_TEXTURE_2D, 0);
    delete[] image;
    if (glGetError() != GL_NO_ERROR) goto ERROR;
    Log::info("Texture size: %d x %d", width, height);
. . .
```

3. Finally, cache the `texture` before returning it:

```
...
    // Caches the loaded texture.
    textureProperties = &mTextures[mTextureCount++];
    textureProperties->texture = texture;
    textureProperties->textureResource = &pResource;
    textureProperties->width = width;
    textureProperties->height = height;
    return textureProperties;

ERROR:
    ...
}
...
```

4. In `jni/DroidBlaster.hpp`, include the `Resource` header and define two resources, of which one is for the ship and another is for the asteroids:

```
...
#include "PhysicsManager.hpp"
#include "Resource.hpp"
#include "Ship.hpp"
#include "TimeManager.hpp"
#include "Types.hpp"

class DroidBlaster : public ActivityHandler {
    ...
private:
    ...
    EventLoop mEventLoop;

    Resource mAsteroidTexture;
    Resource mShipTexture;

    Asteroid mAsteroids;
    Ship mShip;
};
#endif
```

5. Open `jni/DroidBlaster.cpp` and initialize the `texture` resources in the constructor.

```
...
DroidBlaster::DroidBlaster(android_app* pApplication):
    mTimeManager(),
    mGraphicsManager(pApplication),
```

```
        mPhysicsManager(mTimeManager, mGraphicsManager),
        mEventLoop(pApplication, *this),

        mAsteroidTexture(pApplication, "droidblaster/asteroid.png"),
        mShipTexture(pApplication, "droidblaster/ship.png"),

        mAsteroids(pApplication, mTimeManager, mGraphicsManager,
                mPhysicsManager),
        mShip(pApplication, mGraphicsManager) {
        ...
    }
    ...
```

6. To ensure that the code is working, load textures in `onActivate()`. The textures can be loaded only after OpenGL is initialized by `GraphicsManager`:

```
...
status DroidBlaster::onActivate() {
    Log::info("Activating DroidBlaster");

    if (mGraphicsManager.start() != STATUS_OK) return STATUS_KO;
    mGraphicsManager.loadTexture(mAsteroidTexture);
    mGraphicsManager.loadTexture(mShipTexture);

    mAsteroids.initialize();
    mShip.initialize();

    mTimeManager.reset();
    return STATUS_OK;
}
...
```

Before running `DroidBlaster`, add `asteroid.png` and `ship.png` into the `droidblaster/assets` directory (create it if it's necessary).

> The PNG files are provided with this book in the `DroidBlaster_Part6/assets` directory.

What just happened?

Run the application and you should not see much difference. Indeed, we have loaded two PNG textures, but we are not actually rendering them. However, if you check the logs, you should see traces showing that the textures are properly loaded and retrieved from the cache, as shown in the following screenshot:

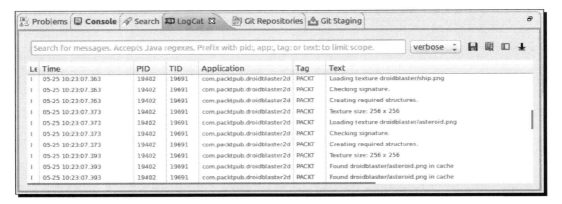

Textures in OpenGL are objects (in the OpenGL way) which are in the form of an array of memory allocated on the **Graphical Processing Unit (GPU)** to store specific data. Storing graphics data in the GPU memory provides faster memory access than if it was stored in the main memory, which is a bit like a cache on a CPU. This efficiency comes at a price: texture loading is costly and must be performed as much as possible during startup.

 The pixels of a texture are named **Texels**. Texel is the contraction of **"Texture Pixel"**. Textures, and thus Texels, are projected on 3D objects during scene rendering.

More about textures

An important requirement to remember while dealing with textures is their dimensions; OpenGL textures must have a power of two dimensions (for example, 128 or 256 pixels). Other dimensions will fail on most devices. These dimensions ease a technique called **MIPmapping (Multum In Parvo (MIP)**, which mean much in little). MIPmaps are smaller versions of the same texture (see the following figure) applied selectively depending on the rendered object distance. They increase performance and reduce aliasing artifacts.

The texture configuration is set with `glTexParameteri()`. They need to be specified at the texture creation time only. The following two main kinds of parameters can be applied:

◆ **Texture Filtering** with `GL_TEXTURE_MAG_FILTER` and `GL_TEXTURE_MIN_FILTER`.

These parameters control the way texture magnification and minification are performed, that is, the processing applied when texture is respectively smaller or bigger than the rasterized primitive. Two values are possible in this, as shown in the next figure.

◆ `GL_LINEAR` interpolates textures drawn onscreen based on the closest texel colors (also known as Bilinear filtering). This calculation results in a smooth effect. `GL_NEAREST` displays the closest texel color without any interpolation. This value gives slightly better performance than `GL_LINEAR`.

GL_LINEAR   GL_NEAREST

There exist variants that can be used in conjunction with MIPmaps to indicate how to apply minification; some of these variants are `GL_NEAREST_MIPMAP_NEAREST`, `GL_LINEAR_MIPMAP_NEAREST`, `GL_NEAREST_MIPMAP_LINEAR` and `GL_LINEAR_MIPMAP_LINEAR` (this one is better known as **Trilinear filtering**).

◆ **Texture Wrapping** with GL_TEXTURE_WRAP_S and GL_TEXTURE_WRAP_T.

These parameters control the way textures are repeated when texture coordinates go outside the range [0.0, 1.0]. S represents the X axis and T, the Y axis. Their different naming is used to avoid any confusion with position coordinates. They are often referred to as U and V. The following figure shows some of the possible values and their effect:

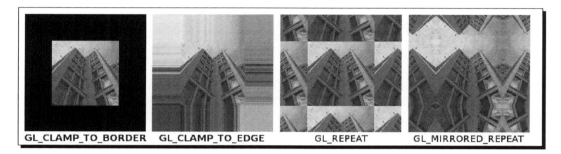

GL_CLAMP_TO_BORDER   GL_CLAMP_TO_EDGE   GL_REPEAT   GL_MIRRORED_REPEAT

A few good practices to remember while dealing with textures are:

◆ Switching textures is an expensive operation, so avoid OpenGL pipeline state changes as much as possible (binding a new texture and changing an option with glEnable() are examples of state changes).

◆ Textures are probably the most memory and bandwidth consuming resources. Consider using **compressed** texture formats to greatly improve performances. Sadly, texture compression algorithms are rather tied to the hardware.

◆ Create big textures to pack, as much data as you can, even from multiple objects. This is known as **Texture Atlas**. For example, if you look at the ship and asteroid texture, you will find that several sprite images are packed in them (we could even pack more):

This introduction to textures gives a slight overview of what OpenGL ES can achieve. For more information about texturing, have a look at the OpenGL.org wiki at `http://www.opengl.org/wiki/Texture`.

Drawing 2D sprites

2D games are based on **sprites**, which are pieces of images composited onscreen. They can represent an object, a character, a static, or an animated element. Sprites can be displayed with a transparency effect using the alpha channel of an image. Typically, an image will contain several frames for a sprite, each frame representing a different animation step or different objects.

> If you need a powerful multiplatform image editor, consider using **GNU Image Manipulation Program (GIMP)**. This program is available on Windows, Linux, and Mac OS X, and is a powerful and open source. You can download it from `http://www.gimp.org/`.

Several techniques exist to draw sprites using OpenGL. One of these is called **Sprite Batch**. This is one of the most efficient ways to create 2D games with OpenGL ES 2. It is based on a vertex array (stored in main memory) that is regenerated during each frame with all the sprites to render. Rendering is performed with the help of a simple vertex shader that projects 2D coordinates onto the screen and a fragment shader that outputs the raw sprite texture color.

We are now going to implement a sprite batch to render the ship and multiple asteroids onscreen in `DroidBlaster`.

> The resulting project is provided with this book under the name `DroidBlaster_Part7`.

Time for action – initializing OpenGL ES

Let's now see how to implement a sprite batch in DroidBlaster:

1. Modify `jni/GraphicsManager.hpp`. Create the class `GraphicsComponent`, which defines a common interface for all rendering techniques starting with sprite batches. Define a few new methods such as:

    □ `getProjectionMatrix()` which provides an OpenGL matrix to project 2D graphics on screen

- ❑ loadShaderProgram() to load a vertex and fragment shader and link them together into an OpenGL program
- ❑ registerComponent() which records a list of GraphicsComponent to initialize and render

Create the RenderVertex private structure representing the structure of an individual sprite vertex.

Also, declare a few new member variables such as:

- ❑ mProjectionMatrix to store an orthographic projection (as opposed to a perspective projection used in 3D games).
- ❑ mShaders, mShaderCount, mComponents, and mComponentCount to keep trace of all resources.

Finally, get rid of all the GraphicsElement stuff used in the previous chapter to render raw graphics, as shown in the following code:

```
...
class GraphicsComponent {
public:
    virtual status load() = 0;
    virtual void draw() = 0;
};
...
```

2. Then, define a few new methods in GraphicsManager:

- ❑ getProjectionMatrix() which provides an OpenGL matrix to project 2D graphics on screen
- ❑ loadShaderProgram() to load a vertex and fragment shader and link them together into an OpenGL program
- ❑ registerComponent() which records a list of GraphicsComponent to initialize and render

Create the RenderVertex private structure representing the structure of an individual sprite vertex.

Also, declare a few new member variables such as:

- ❑ mProjectionMatrix to store an orthographic projection (as opposed to a perspective projection used in 3D games)
- ❑ mShaders, mShaderCount, mComponents, and mComponentCount to keep trace of all resources.

Finally, get rid of all the `GraphicsElement` stuff used in the previous chapter to render raw graphics:

```
...
class GraphicsManager {
public:
    GraphicsManager(android_app* pApplication);
    ~GraphicsManager();

    int32_t getRenderWidth() { return mRenderWidth; }
    int32_t getRenderHeight() { return mRenderHeight; }
    GLfloat* getProjectionMatrix() { return mProjectionMatrix[0]; }

    void registerComponent(GraphicsComponent* pComponent);

    status start();
    void stop();
    status update();

    TextureProperties* loadTexture(Resource& pResource);
    GLuint loadShader(const char* pVertexShader,
            const char* pFragmentShader);

private:
    struct RenderVertex {
        GLfloat x, y, u, v;
    };

    android_app* mApplication;

    int32_t mRenderWidth; int32_t mRenderHeight;
    EGLDisplay mDisplay; EGLSurface mSurface; EGLContext mContext;
    GLfloat mProjectionMatrix[4][4];

    TextureProperties mTextures[32]; int32_t mTextureCount;
    GLuint mShaders[32]; int32_t mShaderCount;

    GraphicsComponent* mComponents[32]; int32_t mComponentCount;
};
#endif
```

3. Open `jni/GraphicsManager.cpp`.

Update the constructor initialization list and the destructor. Again, get rid of everything related to `GraphicsElement`.

Also implement `registerComponent()` in place of `registerElement()`:

```
. . .
GraphicsManager::GraphicsManager(android_app* pApplication) :
    mApplication(pApplication),
    mRenderWidth(0), mRenderHeight(0),
    mDisplay(EGL_NO_DISPLAY), mSurface(EGL_NO_CONTEXT),
    mContext(EGL_NO_SURFACE),
    mProjectionMatrix(),
    mTextures(), mTextureCount(0),
    mShaders(), mShaderCount(0),
    mComponents(), mComponentCount(0) {
    Log::info("Creating GraphicsManager.");
}

GraphicsManager::~GraphicsManager() {
    Log::info("Destroying GraphicsManager.");
}

void GraphicsManager::registerComponent(GraphicsComponent* pComponent)
{
    mComponents[mComponentCount++] = pComponent;
}
. . .
```

4. Amend `onStart()` to initialize the **Orthographic** projection matrix array with display dimensions (we will see how to compute matrices more easily using GLM in *Chapter 9, Porting Existing Libraries to Android*) and load components.

 A projection matrix is a mathematical way to project 3D objects composing a scene into a 2D plane, which is the screen. In orthographic projection, a projection is perpendicular to the display surface. That means that an object has exactly the same size whether it is close or far away from the point of view. Orthographic projection is appropriate for 2D games. **Perspective** projection, in which objects look smaller the farther they are, is rather used for 3D games.

For more information, have a look at `http://en.wikipedia.org/wiki/Graphical_projection`.

```
. . .
status GraphicsManager::start() {
    . . .
    glViewport(0, 0, mRenderWidth, mRenderHeight);
```

```
    glDisable(GL_DEPTH_TEST);

    // Prepares the projection matrix with viewport dimesions.
    memset(mProjectionMatrix[0], 0, sizeof(mProjectionMatrix));
    mProjectionMatrix[0][0] =  2.0f / GLfloat(mRenderWidth);
    mProjectionMatrix[1][1] =  2.0f / GLfloat(mRenderHeight);
    mProjectionMatrix[2][2] = -1.0f; mProjectionMatrix[3][0] = -1.0f;
    mProjectionMatrix[3][1] = -1.0f; mProjectionMatrix[3][2] =  0.0f;
    mProjectionMatrix[3][3] =  1.0f;

    // Loads graphics components.
    for (int32_t i = 0; i < mComponentCount; ++i) {
        if (mComponents[i]->load() != STATUS_OK) {
            return STATUS_KO;
        }
    }
    return STATUS_OK;
    ...
}
...
```

5. Free any resources loaded with `loadShaderProgram()` in `stop()`.

```
...
void GraphicsManager::stop() {
    Log::info("Stopping GraphicsManager.");
    for (int32_t i = 0; i < mTextureCount; ++i) {
        glDeleteTextures(1, &mTextures[i].texture);
    }
    mTextureCount = 0;

    for (int32_t i = 0; i < mShaderCount; ++i) {
        glDeleteProgram(mShaders[i]);
    }
    mShaderCount = 0;

    // Destroys OpenGL context.
    ...
}
...
```

6. Render any registered components in `update()` after the display is cleared but before it is refreshed:

```
...
status GraphicsManager::update() {
    glClear(GL_COLOR_BUFFER_BIT);

    for (int32_t i = 0; i < mComponentCount; ++i) {
        mComponents[i]->draw();
    }

    if (eglSwapBuffers(mDisplay, mSurface) != EGL_TRUE) {
        ...
}
...
```

7. Create the new method `loadShader()`. Its role is to compile and load the given shaders passed as a human-readable GLSL program. To do so:

- ❑ Generate a new vertex shader with `glCreateShader()`.

- ❑ Upload the vertex shader source into OpenGL with `glShaderSource()`.

- ❑ Compile the shader with `glCompileShader()` and check the compilation status with `glGetShaderiv()`. The compilation errors can be read with `glGetShaderInfoLog()`.

Repeat the operation for the given fragment shader:

```
...
GLuint GraphicsManager::loadShader(const char* pVertexShader,
        const char* pFragmentShader) {
    GLint result; char log[256];
    GLuint vertexShader, fragmentShader, shaderProgram;

    // Builds the vertex shader.
    vertexShader = glCreateShader(GL_VERTEX_SHADER);
    glShaderSource(vertexShader, 1, &pVertexShader, NULL);
    glCompileShader(vertexShader);
    glGetShaderiv(vertexShader, GL_COMPILE_STATUS, &result);
    if (result == GL_FALSE) {
        glGetShaderInfoLog(vertexShader, sizeof(log), 0, log);
        Log::error("Vertex shader error: %s", log);
        goto ERROR;
    }

    // Builds the fragment shader.
```

```
fragmentShader = glCreateShader(GL_FRAGMENT_SHADER);
glShaderSource(fragmentShader, 1, &pFragmentShader, NULL);
glCompileShader(fragmentShader);
glGetShaderiv(fragmentShader, GL_COMPILE_STATUS, &result);
if (result == GL_FALSE) {
    glGetShaderInfoLog(fragmentShader, sizeof(log), 0, log);
    Log::error("Fragment shader error: %s", log);
    goto ERROR;
}
. . .
```

8. Once compiled, link the compiled vertex and fragment shaders together. To do so:

   ❑ Create a program object with `glCreateProgram()`.

   ❑ Specify the shaders to use `glAttachShader()`.

   ❑ Link them together with `glLinkProgram()` to create the final program. Shader consistencies and compatibility with the hardware is checked at that point. The result can be checked with `glGetProgramiv()`.

   ❑ Finally, get rid of the shaders as they are useless once linked in a program.

```
. . .
    shaderProgram = glCreateProgram();
    glAttachShader(shaderProgram, vertexShader);
    glAttachShader(shaderProgram, fragmentShader);
    glLinkProgram(shaderProgram);
    glGetProgramiv(shaderProgram, GL_LINK_STATUS, &result);
    glDeleteShader(vertexShader);
    glDeleteShader(fragmentShader);
    if (result == GL_FALSE) {
        glGetProgramInfoLog(shaderProgram, sizeof(log), 0, log);
        Log::error("Shader program error: %s", log);
        goto ERROR;
    }

    mShaders[mShaderCount++] = shaderProgram;
    return shaderProgram;

ERROR:
    Log::error("Error loading shader.");
    if (vertexShader > 0) glDeleteShader(vertexShader);
    if (fragmentShader > 0) glDeleteShader(fragmentShader);
    return 0;
}
. . .
```

9. Create `jni/Sprite.hpp`, which defines a class with all the necessary data to animate and draw a single sprite.

Create a `Vertex` structure which defines the content of a sprite vertex. We need a 2D position and texture coordinates which delimit the sprite picture.

Then, define a few methods:

- □ Sprite animation can be updated and retrieved with `setAnimation()` and `animationEnded()`. Location is publicly available for simplicity purposes.

- □ Give privileged access to a component that we are going to define later, named `SpriteBatch`. It can `load()` and `draw()` sprites.

```cpp
#ifndef _PACKT_GRAPHICSSPRITE_HPP_
#define _PACKT_GRAPHICSSPRITE_HPP_

#include "GraphicsManager.hpp"
#include "Resource.hpp"
#include "Types.hpp"

#include <GLES2/gl2.h>

class SpriteBatch;

class Sprite {
    friend class SpriteBatch;
public
    struct Vertex {
        GLfloat x, y, u, v;
    };

    Sprite(GraphicsManager& pGraphicsManager,
        Resource& pTextureResource, int32_t pHeight, int32_t pWidth);

    void setAnimation(int32_t pStartFrame, int32_t pFrameCount,
        float pSpeed, bool pLoop);
    bool animationEnded() { return mAnimFrame > (mAnimFrameCount-1); }

    Location location;

protected:
    status load(GraphicsManager& pGraphicsManager);
    void draw(Vertex pVertex[4], float pTimeStep);
...
```

10. Finally, define a few properties:

❏ A texture containing the sprite sheet and its corresponding resource

❏ **Sprite frame data:** `mWidth` and `mHeight`, horizontal, vertical, and total number of frames in `mFrameXCount`, `mFrameYCount`, and `mFrameCount`

❏ **Animation data:** first and total number of frames of an animation in `mAnimStartFrame` and `mAnimFrameCount`, animation speed in `mAnimSpeed`, the currently shown frame in `mAnimFrame`, and a looping indicator in `mAnimLoop`:

```
...
private:
    Resource& mTextureResource;
    GLuint mTexture;
    // Frame.
    int32_t mSheetHeight, mSheetWidth;
    int32_t mSpriteHeight, mSpriteWidth;
    int32_t mFrameXCount, mFrameYCount, mFrameCount;
    // Animation.
    int32_t mAnimStartFrame, mAnimFrameCount;
    float mAnimSpeed, mAnimFrame;
    bool mAnimLoop;
};
#endif
```

11. Write the `jni/Sprite.cpp` constructor and initialize the members to default values:

```
#include "Sprite.hpp"
#include "Log.hpp"

Sprite::Sprite(GraphicsManager& pGraphicsManager,
        Resource& pTextureResource,
    int32_t pHeight, int32_t pWidth) :
    location(),
    mTextureResource(pTextureResource), mTexture(0),
    mSheetWidth(0), mSheetHeight(0),
    mSpriteHeight(pHeight), mSpriteWidth(pWidth),
    mFrameCount(0), mFrameXCount(0), mFrameYCount(0),
    mAnimStartFrame(0), mAnimFrameCount(1),
    mAnimSpeed(0), mAnimFrame(0), mAnimLoop(false)
{}
...
```

12. Frame information (horizontal, vertical, and total number of frames) needs to be recomputed in `load()` as texture dimensions are known only at load time:

```
...
status Sprite::load(GraphicsManager& pGraphicsManager) {
    TextureProperties* textureProperties =
            pGraphicsManager.loadTexture(mTextureResource);
    if (textureProperties == NULL) return STATUS_KO;
    mTexture = textureProperties->texture;
    mSheetWidth = textureProperties->width;
    mSheetHeight = textureProperties->height;

    mFrameXCount = mSheetWidth / mSpriteWidth;
    mFrameYCount = mSheetHeight / mSpriteHeight;
    mFrameCount = (mSheetHeight / mSpriteHeight)
                * (mSheetWidth / mSpriteWidth);
    return STATUS_OK;
}
...
```

13. An animation starts from a given   in the sprite sheet and ends after a certain amount of frames, whose number changes according to speed. An animation can loop to restart from the beginning when it is over:

```
...
void Sprite::setAnimation(int32_t pStartFrame,
    int32_t pFrameCount, float pSpeed, bool pLoop) {
    mAnimStartFrame = pStartFrame;
    mAnimFrame = 0.0f, mAnimSpeed = pSpeed, mAnimLoop = pLoop;
    mAnimFrameCount = pFrameCount;
}
...
```

14. In `draw()`, first update the frame to draw according to the sprite animation and the time spent since the last frame. What we need is the indices of the frame in the spritesheet:

```
...
void Sprite::draw(Vertex pVertices[4], float pTimeStep) {
    int32_t currentFrame, currentFrameX, currentFrameY;
    // Updates animation in loop mode.
    mAnimFrame += pTimeStep * mAnimSpeed;
    if (mAnimLoop) {
        currentFrame = (mAnimStartFrame +
                        int32_t(mAnimFrame) % mAnimFrameCount);
    } else {
        // Updates animation in one-shot mode.
```

```
        if (animationEnded()) {
            currentFrame = mAnimStartFrame + (mAnimFrameCount-1);
        } else {
            currentFrame = mAnimStartFrame + int32_t(mAnimFrame);
        }
    }
    // Computes frame X and Y indexes from its id.
    currentFrameX = currentFrame % mFrameXCount;
    // currentFrameY is converted from OpenGL coordinates
    // to top-left coordinates.
    currentFrameY = mFrameYCount - 1
                    - (currentFrame / mFrameXCount);
...
```

15. A sprite is composed of four vertices drawn in an output array, pVertices. Each
of these vertices is composed of a sprite position (posX1, posY1, posX2, posY2)
and texture coordinates (u1, u2, v1, v2). Compute and generate these vertices
dynamically in the memory buffer, pVertices, provided in the parameter. This
memory buffer will be given later to OpenGL to render the sprite:

```
...
    // Draws selected frame.
    GLfloat posX1 = location.x - float(mSpriteWidth / 2);
    GLfloat posY1 = location.y - float(mSpriteHeight / 2);
    GLfloat posX2 = posX1 + mSpriteWidth;
    GLfloat posY2 = posY1 + mSpriteHeight;
    GLfloat u1 = GLfloat(currentFrameX * mSpriteWidth)
                / GLfloat(mSheetWidth);
    GLfloat u2 = GLfloat((currentFrameX + 1) * mSpriteWidth)
                / GLfloat(mSheetWidth);
    GLfloat v1 = GLfloat(currentFrameY * mSpriteHeight)
                / GLfloat(mSheetHeight);
    GLfloat v2 = GLfloat((currentFrameY + 1) * mSpriteHeight)
                / GLfloat(mSheetHeight);

    pVertices[0].x = posX1; pVertices[0].y = posY1;
    pVertices[0].u = u1;    pVertices[0].v = v1;
    pVertices[1].x = posX1; pVertices[1].y = posY2;
    pVertices[1].u = u1;    pVertices[1].v = v2;
    pVertices[2].x = posX2; pVertices[2].y = posY1;
    pVertices[2].u = u2;    pVertices[2].v = v1;
    pVertices[3].x = posX2; pVertices[3].y = posY2;
    pVertices[3].u = u2;    pVertices[3].v = v2;
}
```

16. Specify `jni/SpriteBatch.hpp` with methods such as:

- ❑ `registerSprite()` to add a new sprite to draw
- ❑ `load()` to initialize all the registered sprites
- ❑ `draw()` to effectively render all the registered sprites

We are going to need member variables:

- ❑ A set of sprites to draw in `mSprites` and `mSpriteCount`
- ❑ `mVertices`, `mVertexCount`, `mIndexes`, and `mIndexCount`, which define a vertex and an index buffer
- ❑ A shader program identified by `mShaderProgram`

The vertex and fragment shader parameters are:

- ❑ `aPosition`, which is one of the sprite corner positions.
- ❑ `aTexture`, which is the sprite corner texture coordinate. It defines the sprite to display in the sprite sheet.
- ❑ `uProjection`, is the orthographic projection matrix.
- ❑ `uTexture`, contains the sprite picture.

```
#ifndef _PACKT_GRAPHICSSPRITEBATCH_HPP_
#define _PACKT_GRAPHICSSPRITEBATCH_HPP_

#include "GraphicsManager.hpp"
#include "Sprite.hpp"
#include "TimeManager.hpp"
#include "Types.hpp"

#include <GLES2/gl2.h>

class SpriteBatch : public GraphicsComponent {
public:
    SpriteBatch(TimeManager& pTimeManager,
            GraphicsManager& pGraphicsManager);
    ~SpriteBatch();

    Sprite* registerSprite(Resource& pTextureResource,
        int32_t pHeight, int32_t pWidth);

    status load();
```

```
                void draw();

        private:
            TimeManager& mTimeManager;
            GraphicsManager& mGraphicsManager;

            Sprite* mSprites[1024]; int32_t mSpriteCount;
            Sprite::Vertex mVertices[1024]; int32_t mVertexCount;
            GLushort mIndexes[1024]; int32_t mIndexCount;
            GLuint mShaderProgram;
            GLuint aPosition; GLuint aTexture;
            GLuint uProjection; GLuint uTexture;
        };
        #endif
```

17. Implement the `jni/SpriteBach.cpp` constructor to initialize the default values. The component must register with `GraphicsManager` to be loaded and rendered.

In the destructor, the allocated sprites must be freed when the component is destroyed.

```
#include "SpriteBatch.hpp"
#include "Log.hpp"

#include <GLES2/gl2.h>

SpriteBatch::SpriteBatch(TimeManager& pTimeManager,
        GraphicsManager& pGraphicsManager) :
    mTimeManager(pTimeManager),
    mGraphicsManager(pGraphicsManager),
    mSprites(), mSpriteCount(0),
    mVertices(), mVertexCount(0),
    mIndexes(), mIndexCount(0),
    mShaderProgram(0),
    aPosition(-1), aTexture(-1), uProjection(-1), uTexture(-1)
{
    mGraphicsManager.registerComponent(this);
}


SpriteBatch::~SpriteBatch() {
    for (int32_t i = 0; i < mSpriteCount; ++i) {
        delete mSprites[i];
    }
}
...
```

18. The index buffer is rather static. We can precompute its content when a sprite is registered. Each index points to a vertex in the vertex buffer (0 representing the very first vertex, 1 the 2nd, and so on). As a sprite is represented by 2 triangles of 3 vertices (to form a quad), we need 6 indexes per sprite:

```
...
Sprite* SpriteBatch::registerSprite(Resource& pTextureResource,
        int32_t pHeight, int32_t pWidth) {
    int32_t spriteCount = mSpriteCount;
    int32_t index = spriteCount * 4; // Points to 1st vertex.

    // Precomputes the index buffer.
    GLushort* indexes = (&mIndexes[0]) + spriteCount * 6;
    mIndexes[mIndexCount++] = index+0;
    mIndexes[mIndexCount++] = index+1;
    mIndexes[mIndexCount++] = index+2;
    mIndexes[mIndexCount++] = index+2;
    mIndexes[mIndexCount++] = index+1;
    mIndexes[mIndexCount++] = index+3;

    // Appends a new sprite to the sprite array.
    mSprites[mSpriteCount] = new Sprite(mGraphicsManager,
            pTextureResource, pHeight, pWidth);
    return mSprites[mSpriteCount++];
}
...
```

19. Write the GLSL vertex and fragment shaders as constant strings.

The shader code is written inside a `main()` function similar to what can be coded in C. As any normal computer program, shaders require variables to process data: attributes (per-vertex data like the position), uniforms (global parameters per draw call), and varying (values interpolated per fragment like the texture coordinates).

Here, texture coordinates are passed to the fragment shader in `vTexture`. The vertex position is transformed from a 2D vector to a 4D vector into a predefined GLSL variable `gl_Position`. The fragment shader retrieves interpolated texture coordinates in `vTexture`. This information is used as an index in the predefined function `texture2D()` to access the texture color. Color is saved in the predefined output variable `gl_FragColor`, which represents the final pixel:

```
...
static const char* VERTEX_SHADER =
    "attribute vec4 aPosition;\n"
    "attribute vec2 aTexture;\n"
    "varying vec2 vTexture;\n"
```

```
"uniform mat4 uProjection;\n"
"void main() {\n"
"    vTexture = aTexture;\n"
"    gl_Position = uProjection * aPosition;\n"
"}";

static const char* FRAGMENT_SHADER =
    "precision mediump float;\n"
    "varying vec2 vTexture;\n"
    "uniform sampler2D u_texture;\n"
    "void main() {\n"
    " gl_FragColor = texture2D(u_texture, vTexture);\n"
    "}";
...
```

20. Load the shader program and retrieve the shader attributes and uniform identifiers in `load()`. Then, initialize sprites, as shown in the following code:

```
...
status SpriteBatch::load() {
    GLint result; int32_t spriteCount;

    mShaderProgram = mGraphicsManager.loadShader(VERTEX_SHADER,
            FRAGMENT_SHADER);
    if (mShaderProgram == 0) return STATUS_KO;
    aPosition = glGetAttribLocation(mShaderProgram, "aPosition");
    aTexture = glGetAttribLocation(mShaderProgram, "aTexture");
    uProjection = glGetUniformLocation(mShaderProgram,"uProjection");
    uTexture = glGetUniformLocation(mShaderProgram, "u_texture");

    // Loads sprites.
    for (int32_t i = 0; i < mSpriteCount; ++i) {
        if (mSprites[i]->load(mGraphicsManager)
                != STATUS_OK) goto ERROR;
    }
    return STATUS_OK;

ERROR:
    Log::error("Error loading sprite batch");
    return STATUS_KO;
}
...
```

21. Write `draw()`, which executes the OpenGL sprite rendering logic.

First, select the sprite shader and pass its parameters: the matrix and the texture uniforms:

```
...
void SpriteBatch::draw() {
    glUseProgram(mShaderProgram);
    glUniformMatrix4fv(uProjection, 1, GL_FALSE,
            mGraphicsManager.getProjectionMatrix());
    glUniform1i(uTexture, 0);
...
```

Then, indicate to OpenGL how the position and UV coordinates are stored in the vertex buffer with `glEnableVertexAttribArray()` and `glVertexAttribPointer()`. These calls basically describe the `mVertices` structure. Note how vertex data is linked to shader attributes:

```
...
    glEnableVertexAttribArray(aPosition);
    glVertexAttribPointer(aPosition, // Attribute Index
                    2, // Size in bytes (x and y)
                    GL_FLOAT, // Data type
                    GL_FALSE, // Normalized
                    sizeof(Sprite::Vertex),// Stride
                    &(mVertices[0].x)); // Location
    glEnableVertexAttribArray(aTexture);
    glVertexAttribPointer(aTexture, // Attribute Index
                    2, // Size in bytes (u and v)
                    GL_FLOAT, // Data type
                    GL_FALSE, // Normalized
                    sizeof(Sprite::Vertex), // Stride
                    &(mVertices[0].u)); // Location
...
```

Activate transparency using a blending function to draw sprites over the background, or other sprites:

```
...
    glEnable(GL_BLEND);
    glBlendFunc(GL_SRC_ALPHA, GL_ONE_MINUS_SRC_ALPHA);
...
```

 For more information about the blending modes provided by OpenGL, have a look at `https://www.opengl.org/wiki/Blending`.

22. We can now start the rendering loop to render all sprites in a batch.

The first outer loop basically iterates over textures. Indeed, the pipeline state changes in OpenGL are costly. Methods like `glBindTexture()` should be called as little as possible to guarantee performance:

```
...
    const int32_t vertexPerSprite = 4;
    const int32_t indexPerSprite = 6;
    float timeStep = mTimeManager.elapsed();
    int32_t spriteCount = mSpriteCount;
    int32_t currentSprite = 0, firstSprite = 0;
    while (bool canDraw = (currentSprite < spriteCount)) {
        // Switches texture.
        Sprite* sprite = mSprites[currentSprite];
        GLuint currentTexture = sprite->mTexture;
        glActiveTexture(GL_TEXTURE0);
        glBindTexture(GL_TEXTURE_2D, sprite->mTexture);
...
```

The inner loop generates vertices for all sprites with the same texture:

```
...
        // Generate sprite vertices for current textures.
        do {
            sprite = mSprites[currentSprite];
            if (sprite->mTexture == currentTexture) {
                Sprite::Vertex* vertices =
                        (&mVertices[currentSprite * 4]);
                sprite->draw(vertices, timeStep);
            } else {
                break;
            }
        } while (canDraw = (++currentSprite < spriteCount));
...
```

23. Each time the texture changes, render the bunch of sprites with `glDrawElements()`. The vertex buffer specified earlier is combined with the index buffer given here to render the right sprites with the right texture. At this point, draw calls are sent to OpenGL, which executes the shader program:

```
...
        glDrawElements(GL_TRIANGLES,
                // Number of indexes
                (currentSprite - firstSprite) * indexPerSprite,
                GL_UNSIGNED_SHORT, // Indexes data type
```

```
                        // First index
                        &mIndexes[firstSprite * indexPerSprite]);

            firstSprite = currentSprite;
        }
    ...
```

When all sprites are rendered, restore the OpenGL state:

```
    ...
    glUseProgram(0);
    glDisableVertexAttribArray(aPosition);
    glDisableVertexAttribArray(aTexture);
    glDisable(GL_BLEND);
}
```

24. Update `jni/Ship.hpp` with the new sprite system. You can remove the previous `GraphicsElement` stuff:

```
#include "GraphicsManager.hpp"
#include "Sprite.hpp"

class Ship {
public:
    ...
    void registerShip(Sprite* pGraphics);
    ...
private:
    GraphicsManager& mGraphicsManager;
    Sprite* mGraphics;
};
#endif
```

The file `jni/Ship.cpp` does not change much apart from the `Sprite` type:

```
...
void Ship::registerShip(Sprite* pGraphics) {
    mGraphics = pGraphics;
}
...
```

Include the new `SpriteBatch` component in `jni/DroidBlaster.hpp`:

```
...
#include "Resource.hpp"
#include "Ship.hpp"
#include "SpriteBatch.hpp"
```

```
#include "TimeManager.hpp"
#include "Types.hpp"

class DroidBlaster : public ActivityHandler {
    ...
private:
    ...
    Asteroid mAsteroids;
    Ship mShip;
    SpriteBatch mSpriteBatch;
};
#endif
```

25. In `jni/DroidBlaster.cpp`, define some new constants with animation properties.

Then, use the `SpriteBatch` component to register the ship and asteroids graphics.

Remove the previous stuff related to `GraphicsElement` again:

```
...
static const int32_t SHIP_SIZE = 64;
static const int32_t SHIP_FRAME_1 = 0;
static const int32_t SHIP_FRAME_COUNT = 8;
static const float SHIP_ANIM_SPEED = 8.0f;

static const int32_t ASTEROID_COUNT = 16;
static const int32_t ASTEROID_SIZE = 64;
static const int32_t ASTEROID_FRAME_1 = 0;
static const int32_t ASTEROID_FRAME_COUNT = 16;
static const float ASTEROID_MIN_ANIM_SPEED = 8.0f;
static const float ASTEROID_ANIM_SPEED_RANGE = 16.0f;

DroidBlaster::DroidBlaster(android_app* pApplication) :
    ...
    mAsteroids(pApplication, mTimeManager, mGraphicsManager,
            mPhysicsManager),
    mShip(pApplication, mGraphicsManager),
    mSpriteBatch(mTimeManager, mGraphicsManager) {
    Log::info("Creating DroidBlaster");

    Sprite* shipGraphics = mSpriteBatch.registerSprite(mShipTexture,
            SHIP_SIZE, SHIP_SIZE);
    shipGraphics->setAnimation(SHIP_FRAME_1, SHIP_FRAME_COUNT,
            SHIP_ANIM_SPEED, true);
```

```
        mShip.registerShip(shipGraphics);

        // Creates asteroids.
        for (int32_t i = 0; i < ASTEROID_COUNT; ++i) {
            Sprite* asteroidGraphics = mSpriteBatch.registerSprite(
                    mAsteroidTexture, ASTEROID_SIZE,
    ASTEROID_SIZE);
            float animSpeed = ASTEROID_MIN_ANIM_SPEED
                                + RAND(ASTEROID_ANIM_SPEED_RANGE);
            asteroidGraphics->setAnimation(ASTEROID_FRAME_1,
                    ASTEROID_FRAME_COUNT, animSpeed, true);
            mAsteroids.registerAsteroid(
                    asteroidGraphics->location, ASTEROID_SIZE,
                    ASTEROID_SIZE);
        }
    }
    ...
```

26. We do not need to load textures manually in `onActivate()` anymore. Sprites will handle this for us.

Finally, release the graphic resources in `onDeactivate()`:

```
...
status DroidBlaster::onActivate() {
    Log::info("Activating DroidBlaster");

    if (mGraphicsManager.start() != STATUS_OK) return STATUS_KO;

    // Initializes game objects.
    mAsteroids.initialize();
    mShip.initialize();

    mTimeManager.reset();
    return STATUS_OK;
}

void DroidBlaster::onDeactivate() {
    Log::info("Deactivating DroidBlaster");
    mGraphicsManager.stop();
}
...
```

What just happened?

Launch DroidBlaster. You should now see an animated ship surrounded by frightening rotating asteroids:

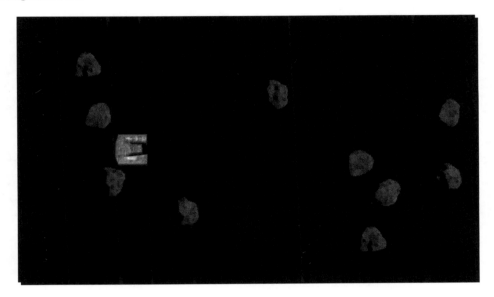

In this part, we have seen how to draw a sprite efficiently with the help of the Sprite Batch technique. Indeed, a common cause of bad performance in OpenGL programs lies in state changes. Changing the OpenGL device state (for example, binding a new buffer or texture, changing an option with `glEnable()`, and so on) is a costly operation and should be avoided as much as possible. Thus, a good practice to maximize OpenGL performance is to order draw calls and change only the needed states.

 One of the best OpenGL ES documentation is available from the Apple developer site at `https://developer.apple.com/library/IOS/documentation/3DDrawing/Conceptual/OpenGLES_ProgrammingGuide/`.

But first, let's see more about the way OpenGL stores vertices in memory and the basics of OpenGL ES shaders.

Vertex Arrays versus Vertex Buffer Object

Vertex Arrays (**VA**) and **Vertex Buffer Objects** (**VBO**) are the two main ways to manage vertices in OpenGL ES. Like with textures, multiple VAs/VBOs can be bound simultaneously to one vertex shader.

There are two main ways to manage vertices in OpenGL ES:

◆ In main memory (that is, in RAM), we talk about Vertex Arrays (abbreviated VA). Vertex arrays are transmitted from the CPU to the GPU for each draw call. As a consequence, they are slower to render, but also much easier to update. Thus, they are appropriate when a mesh of vertices is changing frequently. This explains the decision to use a vertex array to implement sprite batches; each sprite is updated each time a new frame is rendered (position, as well as texture coordinates, to switch to a new frame).

◆ In driver memory (generally in GPU memory or **VRAM**), we talk about **Vertex Buffers Objects**. Vertex buffers are faster to draw but more expensive to update. Thus, they are often used to render static data that never changes. You can still transform it with vertex shaders, which we are going to see in the next part. Note that some hints can be provided to the driver during initialization (GL_DYNAMIC_DRAW) to allow fast updates but at the price of more complex buffer management (that is, multiple buffering).

After transformation, the vertices are connected together during the primitive assembly stage. They can be assembled in the following ways:

◆ As lists 3 by 3 (which can lead to vertex duplication), in fans, in strips, and so on; in which case, we use glDrawArrays().

◆ Using an index buffers which specifies 3 by 3, where vertices are connected together. Index buffers are often the best way to achieve better performance. Indices need to be sorted to favor caching. Indices are drawn with their associated VBO or VA using glDrawElements().

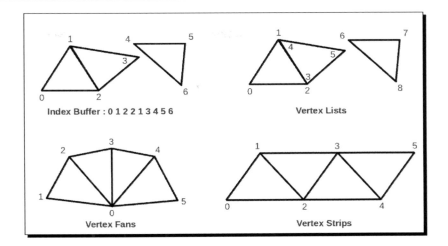

Some good practices to remember when you're dealing with vertices are:

◆   Pack as many vertices in each buffer as you can, even from multiple meshes. Indeed, switching from one set of vertices to another, either a VA or a VBO, is slow.

◆   Avoid updating static vertex buffers at runtime.

◆   Make vertex structure the size of a power of 2 (in bytes) to favor data alignment. It is often preferred to pad data rather than to transmit unaligned data because of the way GPU processes it.

For more information about vertex management, have a look at the OpenGL.org wiki at `http://www.opengl.org/wiki/Vertex_Specification` and `http://www.opengl.org/wiki/Vertex_Specification_Best_Practices`.

Rendering particle effects

DroidBlaster needs a background to make it more pleasant-looking. As the action is located in space, what about a falling star to give an impression of speed?

Such an effect can be simulated in several ways. One possible choice consists of showing a particle effect, where each particle corresponds to a star. OpenGL provides such a feature through **Point Sprites**. A point sprite is a special kind of element that requires only one vertex to draw a sprite. Combined with a whole vertex buffer, many sprites can be drawn at the same time efficiently.

Point sprites are usable with vertex and fragment shaders. To be even more efficient, we can use their power to process particle movement directly inside the shaders. Thus, we will not need to regenerate the vertex buffer each time a particle changes, like we have to do with sprite batches.

 The resulting project is provided with this book under the name `DroidBlaster_Part8`.

Time for action – rendering a star field

Let's now see how to apply this particle effect in `DroidBlaster`:

1. In `jni/GraphicsManager.hpp`, define a new method to load a vertex buffer. Add an array to store vertex buffer resources:

```
...
class GraphicsManager {
public:
    ...
    GLuint loadShader(const char* pVertexShader,
            const char* pFragmentShader);
    GLuint loadVertexBuffer(const void* pVertexBuffer,
            int32_t pVertexBufferSize);

private:
    ...
    GLuint mShaders[32]; int32_t mShaderCount;
    GLuint mVertexBuffers[32]; int32_t mVertexBufferCount;

    GraphicsComponent* mComponents[32]; int32_t
mComponentCount;
};
#endif
```

2. In `jni/GraphicsManager.cpp`, update the constructor initialization list and free vertex buffer resources in `stop()`:

```
...
GraphicsManager::GraphicsManager(android_app* pApplication) :
    ...
    mTextures(), mTextureCount(0),
    mShaders(), mShaderCount(0),
    mVertexBuffers(), mVertexBufferCount(0),
```

```
        mComponents(), mComponentCount(0) {
        Log::info("Creating GraphicsManager.");
    }

    ...

    void GraphicsManager::stop() {
        Log::info("Stopping GraphicsManager.");
        ...

        for (int32_t i = 0; i < mVertexBufferCount; ++i) {
            glDeleteBuffers(1, &mVertexBuffers[i]);
        }
        mVertexBufferCount = 0;

        // Destroys OpenGL context.
        ...
    }
    ...
```

3. Create the new method `loadVertexBuffer()` to upload the data from the given memory location into an OpenGL vertex buffer. As opposed to the SpriteBatch example, which uses a dynamic vertex buffer in computer memory, the following vertex buffer is static and located in GPU memory. This makes it faster but quite inflexible too. To do so:

   ❑ Generate a buffer identifier with `glGenBuffers()`.

   ❑ Indicate that we are working on a vertex buffer with `glBindBuffer()`.

   ❑ Push the vertex data from the given memory location into OpenGL vertex buffer with `glBufferData()`.

   ❑ Unbind the vertex buffer to put OpenGL back in its previous state. This is not strictly necessary, like for textures, but it helps avoiding configuration mistakes in future draw calls.

   ❑ You can check that the vertex buffer has been created properly with `glGetError()`:

```
        ...
        GLuint GraphicsManager::loadVertexBuffer(const void* pVertexBuffer,
                int32_t pVertexBufferSize) {
            GLuint vertexBuffer;
            // Upload specified memory buffer into OpenGL.
            glGenBuffers(1, &vertexBuffer);
            glBindBuffer(GL_ARRAY_BUFFER, vertexBuffer);
```

```
                glBufferData(GL_ARRAY_BUFFER, pVertexBufferSize, pVertexBuffer,
                        GL_STATIC_DRAW);
                // Unbinds the buffer.
                glBindBuffer(GL_ARRAY_BUFFER, 0);
                if (glGetError() != GL_NO_ERROR) goto ERROR;

                mVertexBuffers[mVertexBufferCount++] = vertexBuffer;
                return vertexBuffer;

        ERROR:
            Log::error("Error loading vertex buffer.");
            if (vertexBuffer > 0) glDeleteBuffers(1, &vertexBuffer);
            return 0;
        }
        ...
```

4. Define the new `StarField` component in `jni/StarField.hpp`.

    Override the `GraphicsComponent` methods, as done previously.

    Define a specific `Vertex` structure with 3 coordinates `x`, `y`, and `z`.

    A star field is characterized by the number of stars in `mStarCount` and a texture that represents a single one in `mTextureResource`.

    We will need some OpenGL resources: a vertex buffer, a texture, and a shader program with its variables:

    ❑ `aPosition`, which is the star position.

    ❑ `uProjection`, which is the orthographic projection matrix.

    ❑ `uTime`, which is the total elapsed time given by `TimeManager`. This is necessary to simulate the movement of stars.

    ❑ `uHeight`, which is the height of the display. The stars are going to be recycled when they reach the screen boundaries.

    ❑ `uTexture`, which contains the star picture.

    ```
    #ifndef _PACKT_STARFIELD_HPP_
    #define _PACKT_STARFIELD_HPP_

    #include "GraphicsManager.hpp"
    #include "TimeManager.hpp"
    #include "Types.hpp"

    #include <GLES2/gl2.h>

    class StarField : public GraphicsComponent {
    ```

```
    public:
        StarField(android_app* pApplication, TimeManager& pTimeManager,
                GraphicsManager& pGraphicsManager, int32_t pStarCount,
                Resource& pTextureResource);

        status load();
        void draw();

    private:
        struct Vertex {
            GLfloat x, y, z;
        };

        TimeManager& mTimeManager;
        GraphicsManager& mGraphicsManager;

        int32_t mStarCount;
        Resource& mTextureResource;

        GLuint mVertexBuffer; GLuint mTexture; GLuint mShaderProgram;
        GLuint aPosition; GLuint uProjection;
        GLuint uTime; GLuint uHeight; GLuint uTexture;
    };
    #endif
```

5. Create `jni/StarField.cpp` and implement its constructor:

```
#include "Log.hpp"
#include "StarField.hpp"

StarField::StarField(android_app* pApplication,
    TimeManager& pTimeManager, GraphicsManager& pGraphicsManager,
    int32_t pStarCount, Resource& pTextureResource):
        mTimeManager(pTimeManager),
        mGraphicsManager(pGraphicsManager),
        mStarCount(pStarCount),
        mTextureResource(pTextureResource),
        mVertexBuffer(0), mTexture(-1), mShaderProgram(0),
        aPosition(-1),
        uProjection(-1), uHeight(-1), uTime(-1), uTexture(-1) {
    mGraphicsManager.registerComponent(this);
}
...
```

6. The star field logic is mostly implemented in the vertex shader. Each star, represented by a single vertex, is moved from top to bottom according to time, speed (which is constant), and star distance. The farther it is (distance being determined by the z vertex component), the slower it scrolls.

The GLSL function mod, which stands for modulo, resets the star position when it has reached the bottom of the screen. The final star position is saved in the predefined variable gl_Position.

The star size on screen is also a function of its distance. The size is saved in the predefined variable gl_PointSize in pixel units:

```
. . .
static const char* VERTEX_SHADER =
    "attribute vec4 aPosition;\n"
    "uniform mat4 uProjection;\n"
    "uniform float uHeight;\n"
    "uniform float uTime;\n"
    "void main() {\n"
    "    const float speed = -800.0;\n"
    "    const float size = 8.0;\n"
    "    vec4 position = aPosition;\n"
    "    position.x = aPosition.x;\n"
    "    position.y = mod(aPosition.y + (uTime * speed * aPosition.z),"
    "                                   uHeight);\n"
    "    position.z = 0.0;\n"
    "    gl_Position =  uProjection * position;\n"
    "    gl_PointSize = aPosition.z * size;"
    "}";
. . .
```

The fragment shader is much simpler and only draws the star texture onscreen:

```
. . .
static const char* FRAGMENT_SHADER =
    "precision mediump float;\n"
    "uniform sampler2D uTexture;\n"
    "void main() {\n"
    "  gl_FragColor = texture2D(uTexture, gl_PointCoord);\n"
    "}";
. . .
```

7. In the `load()` function, generate the vertex buffer with the help of the
`loadVertexBuffer()` method implemented in `GraphicsManager`. Each star
is represented by a single vertex. The position on screen and depth are generated
randomly. Depth is determined on a [0.0, 1.0] scale. Once this is done, release the
temporary memory buffer holding the star field data:

```
...
status StarField::load() {
    Log::info("Loading star field.");
    TextureProperties* textureProperties;

    // Allocates a temporary buffer and populate it with point data:
    // 1 vertices composed of 3 floats (X/Y/Z) per point.
    Vertex* vertexBuffer = new Vertex[mStarCount];
    for (int32_t i = 0; i < mStarCount; ++i) {
        vertexBuffer[i].x = RAND(mGraphicsManager.getRenderWidth());
        vertexBuffer[i].y = RAND(mGraphicsManager.getRenderHeight());
        vertexBuffer[i].z = RAND(1.0f);
    }
    // Loads the vertex buffer into OpenGL.
    mVertexBuffer = mGraphicsManager.loadVertexBuffer(
        (uint8_t*) vertexBuffer, mStarCount * sizeof(Vertex));
    delete[] vertexBuffer;
    if (mVertexBuffer == 0) goto ERROR;
...
```

8. Then, load the `star` texture and generate the program from the shaders defined
above. Retrieve their attribute and uniform identifiers:

```
...
    // Loads the texture.
    textureProperties =
            mGraphicsManager.loadTexture(mTextureResource);
    if (textureProperties == NULL) goto ERROR;
    mTexture = textureProperties->texture;

    // Creates and retrieves shader attributes and uniforms.
    mShaderProgram = mGraphicsManager.loadShader(VERTEX_SHADER,
            FRAGMENT_SHADER);
    if (mShaderProgram == 0) goto ERROR;
    aPosition = glGetAttribLocation(mShaderProgram, "aPosition");
    uProjection = glGetUniformLocation(mShaderProgram,"uProjection");
    uHeight = glGetUniformLocation(mShaderProgram, "uHeight");
```

```
            uTime = glGetUniformLocation(mShaderProgram, "uTime");
            uTexture = glGetUniformLocation(mShaderProgram, "uTexture");

            return STATUS_OK;

    ERROR:
            Log::error("Error loading starfield");
            return STATUS_KO;
    }
    ...
```

9. Finally, render the `star` field by sending the static vertex buffer, the texture, and the shader program together in one draw call. To do so:

- Disable blending, that is, the management of transparency. Indeed, the star "particles" are small, sparse, and drawn over a black background.

- Select the vertex buffer first with `glBindBuffer()`. This call is necessary when a static vertex buffer has been generated at load time.

- Indicate how vertex data is structured with `glVertexAttribPointer()`, and to which shader attributes it relates with `glEnableVertexAttribArray()`. Note that the last parameter of `glVertexAttribPointer()` is not a pointer to a buffer this time but an index within the vertex buffer. Indeed, the vertex buffer is static, and in GPU memory, so we do not know its address.

- Select the texture to draw with `glActiveTexture()` and `glBindTexture()`.

- Select the shader program with `glUseProgram()`.

- Bind the program parameters with `glUniform` function variants.

- Finally, send the draw call to OpenGL with `glDrawArrays()`.

You can then restore the OpenGL pipeline state:

```
...
void StarField::draw() {
    glDisable(GL_BLEND);

    // Selects the vertex buffer and indicates how data is stored.
    glBindBuffer(GL_ARRAY_BUFFER, mVertexBuffer);
    glEnableVertexAttribArray(aPosition);
    glVertexAttribPointer(aPosition, // Attribute Index
                    3, // Number of components
```

```
                              GL_FLOAT, // Data type
                              GL_FALSE, // Normalized
                              3 * sizeof(GLfloat), // Stride
                              (GLvoid*) 0); // First vertex

        // Selects the texture.
        glActiveTexture(GL_TEXTURE0);
        glBindTexture(GL_TEXTURE_2D, mTexture);

        // Selects the shader and passes parameters.
        glUseProgram(mShaderProgram);
        glUniformMatrix4fv(uProjection, 1, GL_FALSE,
                mGraphicsManager.getProjectionMatrix());
        glUniform1f(uHeight, mGraphicsManager.getRenderHeight());
        glUniform1f(uTime, mTimeManager.elapsedTotal());
        glUniform1i(uTexture, 0);

        // Renders the star field.
        glDrawArrays(GL_POINTS, 0, mStarCount);

        // Restores device state.
        glBindBuffer(GL_ARRAY_BUFFER, 0);
        glUseProgram(0);
    }
```

10. In `jni/DroidBlaster.hpp`, define the new `StarField` component along with a new texture resource:

```
...
#include "Ship.hpp"
#include "SpriteBatch.hpp"
#include "StarField.hpp"
#include "TimeManager.hpp"
#include "Types.hpp"

class DroidBlaster : public ActivityHandler {
    ...
private:
    ...
    Resource mAsteroidTexture;
    Resource mShipTexture;
    Resource mStarTexture;

    Asteroid mAsteroids;
```

```
        Ship mShip;
        StarField mStarField;
        SpriteBatch mSpriteBatch;
    };
    #endif
```

11. Instantiate it in the `jni/DroidBlaster.cpp` constructor with 50 stars:

```
    ...

    static const int32_t STAR_COUNT = 50;

    DroidBlaster::DroidBlaster(android_app* pApplication):
        mTimeManager(),
        mGraphicsManager(pApplication),
        mPhysicsManager(mTimeManager, mGraphicsManager),
        mEventLoop(pApplication, *this),

        mAsteroidTexture(pApplication, "droidblaster/asteroid.png"),
        mShipTexture(pApplication, "droidblaster/ship.png"),
        mStarTexture(pApplication, "droidblaster/star.png"),

        mAsteroids(pApplication, mTimeManager, mGraphicsManager,
                mPhysicsManager),
        mShip(pApplication, mGraphicsManager),
        mStarField(pApplication, mTimeManager, mGraphicsManager,
                STAR_COUNT, mStarTexture),
        mSpriteBatch(mTimeManager, mGraphicsManager) {
        Log::info("Creating DroidBlaster");
        ...
    }
```

Before running `DroidBlaster`, add `droidblaster/star.png` into the assets directory. These files are provided with this book in the `DroidBlaster_Part8/assets` directory.

What just happened?

Run `DroidBlaster`. The star field should look as shown in the following screenshot, when scrolling through the screen at a random pace:

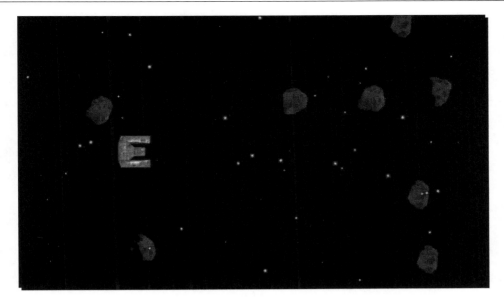

All of these stars are rendered as point sprites, where each point represents a quad determined by:

- **A position on screen**: The position represents the center of the point sprite
- **A point size**: The size defines implicitly the point sprite quad

Point sprites are an interesting way to create particle effects, but, they have a few drawbacks, which are:

- Their possible size is more or less limited depending on the hardware capabilities. You can find the maximum size by querying GL_ALIASED_POINT_SIZE_RANGE with glGetFloatv(); look at the following example for this:

```
float pointSizeRange[2];
glGetFloatv(GL_ALIASED_POINT_SIZE_RANGE, pointSizeRange);
```

- If you draw bigger point sprites, you will notice that the particles are clipped (that is, masked) at their center and the whole sprite boundaries don't get out of screen.

Thus, depending on your needs, it might be more appropriate to use classic vertices.

Talking about vertices, you may have noticed that we have not created a vertex array but a vertex buffer object. Indeed, point sprites are evaluated completely in the vertex shader. This optimization allows us to use a static geometry (`glBufferData()` with the hint `GL_STATIC_DRAW`) which can be managed efficiently by the driver. Note that vertex buffer objects can also be marked as being subject to updates using the hint `GL_DYNAMIC_DRAW` (which means buffer will change frequently) or `GL_STREAM_DRAW` (which means buffer will be used once and thrown). The process of creating a VBO is similar to the process of creating any other kind of object in OpenGL, and involves generating a new identifier, selecting it, and finally uploading data in driver memory. If you understand this process, you understand the way OpenGL works.

Programming shaders with GLSL

Shaders are written in GLSL, a (relatively) high-level programming language which allows defining functions (with in, out, and inout parameters), conditionals, loops, variables, arrays, structures, arithmetic operators, and so on. It abstracts as much as possible hardware specificities. GLSL allows the following kind of variables to be used:

attributes	These contain per-vertex data, such as vertex position or texture coordinates. Only one vertex is processed each time the shader executes.
const	It represents compile-time constants or read-only function parameters.
uniforms	These are a kind of global parameter that can be changed per primitive (that is, per draw call). It has the same value for a whole mesh. An example of this could be a model-view matrix (for a vertex shader) or a texture (for a fragment shader).
varying	These are per-pixel interpolated values computed according to the vertex shader output. They are an output parameter in vertex shaders and an input parameter in fragment shaders. In OpenGL ES 3, the "varying" parameters have a new syntax: `out` in a vertex shader and `in` in a pixel shader.

The main types of parameters allowed to declare such variables are shown in the following table:

void	This is for function result only.
bool	This is a boolean value.
float	This is a floating point value.
int	This is a signed integer value.
vec2, vec3, vec4	This is a floating point vector. Vectors exist for other types such as `bvec` for booleans or `ivec` for signed integer.
mat2, mat3, mat4	These are 2x2, 3x3, and 4x4 floating point matrices.
sampler2D	This gives access to 2D texture texels.

Note that the GLSL specification provides some predefined variables, such as the ones shown in the following table:

highp vec4 gl_Position	Vertex shader Output	This is the transformed vertex position.
mediump float gl_PointSize	Vertex shader Output	This is the size of a point sprite in pixels (more about this will be discussed in the next part).
mediump vec4 gl_FragCoord	Fragment shader Input	These are the coordinates of the fragment within framebuffer.
mediump vec4 gl_FragColor	Fragment shader Output	This is the color to display for the fragment.

Numerous functions, mostly arithmetic, are also provided, such as `sin()`, `cos()`, `tan()`, `radians()`, `degrees()`, `mod()`, `abs()`, `floor()`, `ceil()`, `dot()`, `cross()`, `normalize()`, `texture2D()`, and so on.

These are some of the best practices to remember while dealing with shaders:

- Do not compile or link shaders at runtime.
- Beware of different hardware that has different capabilities and, more specifically, a limited number of variables allowed.
- Find a good trade-off between performance and accuracy while defining precision specifiers (for example, `highp`, `medium`, or `lowp`). Do not hesitate to redefine them to get consistent behavior. Note that a `float` precision specifier should be defined in the GLES fragment shaders.
- Avoid conditional branches as much as possible.

For more information, have a look at OpenGL.org wiki at `http://www.opengl.org/wiki/OpenGL_Shading_Language`, `http://www.opengl.org/wiki/Vertex_Shader` and `http://www.opengl.org/wiki/Fragment_Shader`.

Beware, as the content of these pages is applicable to OpenGL but not necessarily to GLES.

Adapting graphics to various resolutions

A complex subject to handle while writing a game is the Android screen size fragmentation. Low-end phones have resolutions of a few hundred pixels, whereas some high-end devices provide resolutions of more than two thousand.

There exist several ways to handle various screen sizes. We can adapt graphic resources, use black bands around the screen, or apply and adapt responsive designs to games.

Another simple solution consists of rendering the game scene off-screen with a fixed size. The off-screen framebuffer is then copied onto the screen and scaled to an appropriate size. This *one size fits all* technique does not provide the best quality and might be a bit slow on low-end devices (especially if they have a lower resolution than the off-screen framebuffer). However, it is quite simple to apply.

 The resulting project is provided with this book under the name `DroidBlaster_Part9`.

Time for action – adapting resolution with off-screen rendering

Let's render the game scene off-screen:

1. Change `jni/GraphicsManager.hpp`, followed by these steps:

    ❑ Define new getter methods for the screen width and height with their corresponding member variables

    ❑ Create a new function `initializeRenderBuffer()`, which creates an off-screen buffer to render the scene:

```
...
class GraphicsManager {
public:
    ...
    int32_t getRenderWidth() { return mRenderWidth; }s
    int32_t getRenderHeight() { return mRenderHeight; }
    int32_t getScreenWidth() { return mScreenWidth; }
    int32_t getScreenHeight() { return mScreenHeight; }
    GLfloat* getProjectionMatrix() { return mProjectionMatrix[0]; }

    ...
```

2. While still being in the same file, follow these steps:

- ❑ Declare a new `RenderVertex` structure with four components - x, y, u, and v

- ❑ Define the OpenGL resources necessary for the framebuffer, namely, the texture, the vertex buffer, the shader program, and its variables:

```
...
private:
    status initializeRenderBuffer();

    struct RenderVertex {
        GLfloat x, y, u, v;
    };

    android_app* mApplication;

    int32_t mRenderWidth; int32_t mRenderHeight;
    int32_t mScreenWidth; int32_t mScreenHeight;
    EGLDisplay mDisplay; EGLSurface mSurface; EGLContext mContext;
    GLfloat mProjectionMatrix[4][4];
    ...

    // Rendering resources.
    GLint mScreenFrameBuffer;
    GLuint mRenderFrameBuffer; GLuint mRenderVertexBuffer;
    GLuint mRenderTexture; GLuint mRenderShaderProgram;
    GLuint aPosition; GLuint aTexture;
    GLuint uProjection; GLuint uTexture;
};
#endif
```

3. Update the `jni/GraphicsManager.cpp` constructor initialization list to initialize default values:

```
#include "GraphicsManager.hpp"
#include "Log.hpp"

#include <png.h>

GraphicsManager::GraphicsManager(android_app* pApplication) :
    ...
    mComponents(), mComponentCount(0),
    mScreenFrameBuffer(0),
    mRenderFrameBuffer(0), mRenderVertexBuffer(0),
```

```
        mRenderTexture(0), mRenderShaderProgram(0),
        aPosition(0), aTexture(0),
        uProjection(0), uTexture(0) {
        Log::info("Creating GraphicsManager.");
}
...
```

4. Change `start()` method to save the display surface width and height respectively in `mScreenWidth` and `mScreenHeight`.

Then, call `initializeRenderBuffer()`:

```
...
status GraphicsManager::start() {
    ...
    Log::info("Initializing the display.");
    mSurface = eglCreateWindowSurface(mDisplay, config,
        mApplication->window, NULL);
    if (mSurface == EGL_NO_SURFACE) goto ERROR;
    mContext = eglCreateContext(mDisplay, config, NULL,
        CONTEXT_ATTRIBS);
    if (mContext == EGL_NO_CONTEXT) goto ERROR;

    if (!eglMakeCurrent(mDisplay, mSurface, mSurface, mContext)
    || !eglQuerySurface(mDisplay, mSurface, EGL_WIDTH, &mScreenWidth)
    || !eglQuerySurface(mDisplay, mSurface, EGL_HEIGHT, &mScreenHeight)
    || (mScreenWidth <= 0) || (mScreenHeight <= 0)) goto ERROR;

    // Defines and initializes offscreen surface.
    if (initializeRenderBuffer() != STATUS_OK) goto ERROR;

    glViewport(0, 0, mRenderWidth, mRenderHeight);
    glDisable(GL_DEPTH_TEST);
    ...
}
...
```

5. Define a vertex and fragment shader for off-screen rendering. This is similar to what we have seen until now:

```
...
static const char* VERTEX_SHADER =
    "attribute vec2 aPosition;\n"
    "attribute vec2 aTexture;\n"
```

```
"varying vec2 vTexture;\n"
"void main() {\n"
"    vTexture = aTexture;\n"
"    gl_Position = vec4(aPosition, 1.0, 1.0 );\n"
"}";

static const char* FRAGMENT_SHADER =
    "precision mediump float;"
    "uniform sampler2D uTexture;\n"
    "varying vec2 vTexture;\n"
    "void main() {\n"
    " gl_FragColor = texture2D(uTexture, vTexture);\n"
    "}\n";
...
```

6. In `initializeRenderBuffer()`, create a predefined array of a vertex that is going to be loaded into OpenGL. It represents a single quad with a full texture rendered on it.

   Compute the new render height based on a fixed target width of 600 pixels.

   Retrieve the current screen framebuffer from the location where the final scene is rendered using `glGetIntegerv()` and the special value `GL_FRAMEBUFFER_BINDING`:

```
...
const int32_t DEFAULT_RENDER_WIDTH = 600;

status GraphicsManager::initializeRenderBuffer() {
    Log::info("Loading offscreen buffer");
    const RenderVertex vertices[] = {
        { -1.0f, -1.0f, 0.0f, 0.0f },
        { -1.0f,  1.0f, 0.0f, 1.0f },
        {  1.0f, -1.0f, 1.0f, 0.0f },
        {  1.0f,  1.0f, 1.0f, 1.0f }
    };

    float screenRatio = float(mScreenHeight) / float(mScreenWidth);
    mRenderWidth = DEFAULT_RENDER_WIDTH;
    mRenderHeight = float(mRenderWidth) * screenRatio;
    glGetIntegerv(GL_FRAMEBUFFER_BINDING, &mScreenFrameBuffer);
...
```

7. Create a texture for off-screen rendering, like we have seen previously. In `glTexImage2D()`, pass a `NULL` value as the last parameter to create only the surface without initializing its content:

```
...
    glGenTextures(1, &mRenderTexture);
    glBindTexture(GL_TEXTURE_2D, mRenderTexture);
    glTexParameteri(GL_TEXTURE_2D, GL_TEXTURE_MAG_FILTER, GL_LINEAR);
    glTexParameteri(GL_TEXTURE_2D, GL_TEXTURE_MIN_FILTER, GL_LINEAR);
    glTexParameteri(GL_TEXTURE_2D, GL_TEXTURE_WRAP_S,
            GL_CLAMP_TO_EDGE);
    glTexParameteri(GL_TEXTURE_2D, GL_TEXTURE_WRAP_T,
            GL_CLAMP_TO_EDGE);
    glTexImage2D(GL_TEXTURE_2D, 0, GL_RGB, mRenderWidth,
            mRenderHeight, 0, GL_RGB, GL_UNSIGNED_SHORT_5_6_5, NULL);
...
```

8. Then, create an off-screen framebuffer with `glGenFramebuffers()`.

Attach the previous texture to it with `glBindFramebuffer()`.

Terminate by restoring the device state:

```
...
    glGenFramebuffers(1, &mRenderFrameBuffer);
    glBindFramebuffer(GL_FRAMEBUFFER, mRenderFrameBuffer);
    glFramebufferTexture2D(GL_FRAMEBUFFER, GL_COLOR_ATTACHMENT0,
            GL_TEXTURE_2D, mRenderTexture, 0);
    glBindTexture(GL_TEXTURE_2D, 0);
    glBindFramebuffer(GL_FRAMEBUFFER, 0);
...
```

9. Create the shader program used to render texture to screen and retrieve its attributes and uniforms:

```
...
    mRenderVertexBuffer = loadVertexBuffer(vertices,
            sizeof(vertices));
    if (mRenderVertexBuffer == 0) goto ERROR;

    mRenderShaderProgram = loadShader(VERTEX_SHADER, FRAGMENT_SHADER);
    if (mRenderShaderProgram == 0) goto ERROR;
    aPosition = glGetAttribLocation(mRenderShaderProgram,"aPosition");
    aTexture = glGetAttribLocation(mRenderShaderProgram, "aTexture");
```

```
    uTexture = glGetUniformLocation(mRenderShaderProgram,"uTexture");

    return STATUS_OK;

ERROR:
    Log::error("Error while loading offscreen buffer");
    return STATUS_KO;
}
...
```

10. Do not forget to release allocated resources in `stop()` when the activity finishes:

```
...
void GraphicsManager::stop() {
    ...

    if (mRenderFrameBuffer != 0) {
        glDeleteFramebuffers(1, &mRenderFrameBuffer);
        mRenderFrameBuffer = 0;
    }
    if (mRenderTexture != 0) {
        glDeleteTextures(1, &mRenderTexture);
        mRenderTexture = 0;
    }

    // Destroys OpenGL context.
    ...
}
...
```

11. Finally, use the new off-screen framebuffer to render the scene. To do so, you need to:

Select the framebuffer with `glBindFramebuffer()`.

Specify the rendering viewport, which has to match the off-screen framebuffer dimensions, as shown here:

```
...
status GraphicsManager::update() {
    glBindFramebuffer(GL_FRAMEBUFFER, mRenderFrameBuffer);
    glViewport(0, 0, mRenderWidth, mRenderHeight);
    glClear(GL_COLOR_BUFFER_BIT);

    // Render graphic components.
    for (int32_t i = 0; i < mComponentCount; ++i) {
        mComponents[i]->draw();
    }
...
```

12. Once it's rendered, restore the normal screen framebuffer and the correct viewport dimensions.

Then, select as a source the following parameters:

- The off-screen texture which is attached to the off-screen framebuffer
- The shader program, which does basically nothing apart from projecting vertices and scaling texture, on the screen framebuffer
- The vertex buffer, which contains a single quad with texture coordinates, as shown in the following code:

```
    . . .
        glBindFramebuffer(GL_FRAMEBUFFER, mScreenFrameBuffer);
        glClear(GL_COLOR_BUFFER_BIT);
        glViewport(0, 0, mScreenWidth, mScreenHeight);

        glActiveTexture(GL_TEXTURE0);
        glBindTexture(GL_TEXTURE_2D, mRenderTexture);
        glUseProgram(mRenderShaderProgram);
        glUniform1i(uTexture, 0);

        // Indicates to OpenGL how position and uv coordinates are stored.
        glBindBuffer(GL_ARRAY_BUFFER, mRenderVertexBuffer);
        glEnableVertexAttribArray(aPosition);
        glVertexAttribPointer(aPosition, // Attribute Index
                        2, // Number of components (x and y)
                        GL_FLOAT, // Data type
                        GL_FALSE, // Normalized
                        sizeof(RenderVertex), // Stride
                        (GLvoid*) 0); // Offset
        glEnableVertexAttribArray(aTexture);
        glVertexAttribPointer(aTexture, // Attribute Index
                        2, // Number of components (u and v)
                        GL_FLOAT, // Data type
                        GL_FALSE, // Normalized
                        sizeof(RenderVertex), // Stride
                        (GLvoid*) (sizeof(GLfloat) * 2)); // Offset
    . . .
```

13. Terminate by rendering the off-screen buffer into the screen.

You can then restore the device state again, like this:

```
    . . .
        glDrawArrays(GL_TRIANGLE_STRIP, 0, 4);
```

```
glBindBuffer(GL_ARRAY_BUFFER, 0);

// Shows the result to the user.
if (eglSwapBuffers(mDisplay, mSurface) != EGL_TRUE) {
    ...
}
...
```

What just happened?

Launch the application on several devices. Every device should display a proportionally similar scene. Indeed, graphics are now rendered to an off-screen framebuffer attached to a texture. The result is then scaled according to the target screen resolution to provide the same experience across different devices. This simple and cheap solution comes with a price, which is that the low-end devices might suffer depending on the chosen fixed resolution, whereas high-end devices will look blurry.

Handling various screen resolutions is one thing. Managing their various aspect ratios is another. Several solutions exist for this problem, such as using black stripes, stretching the screen, or defining a minimum and maximum displayable area with only the first one containing important information.

More generally, the rendering of a scene off-screen is often referred to as **Render to Texture**. This technique is commonly used to implement shadows, reflection, or postprocessing effects. Mastering this technique is a key in implementing high quality games.

Summary

OpenGL, and graphics in general, is a complex and highly technical API. One book is not enough to cover it entirely, but drawing 2D graphics with textures and buffer objects opens the door to much more advanced stuff!

In more detail, you have learned how to initialize an OpenGL ES context and bind it to an Android window. Then, you have seen how to turn libpng into a module and load a texture from a PNG asset. We have used this texture and then combined it with vertex buffers and shaders to render sprites and particles. Finally, we have found a solution to the Android resolution fragmentation issue with a simple off-screen and scaling rendering technique.

OpenGL ES is a complex API that requires an in-depth understanding to get the best performance and quality. This is even true with OpenGL ES 3, which we have not covered here, that is available since Android KitKat. Do not hesitate to have a look at:

◆ The Openg ES and GLSL specification at `http://www.khronos.org/registry/gles/`

◆ The Android Developer website at `http://developer.android.com/guide/topics/graphics/opengl.html`

With the knowledge acquired here, the road to OpenGL ES 2 or 3 is at a perfectly walkable distance! So now, let's discover how to reach the fourth dimension, the musical one, with OpenSL ES in our next chapter.

7

Playing Sound with OpenSL ES

Multimedia is not only about graphics, it is also about sound and music. Applications in this domain are among the most popular in the Android market. Indeed, music has always been a strong engine for mobile device sales and music lovers are a target of choice. This is why an OS like Android could probably not go far without some musical talent! Open Sound Library for Embedded Systems, more frequently called OpenSL ES, is the pendant of OpenGL for sound. Although rather low-levewl, it is a first-class API for all sound-related tasks, either input or output.

When talking about sound on Android, we should distinguish Java from the native world. Indeed, both sides feature completely different APIs: **MediaPlayer**, **SoundPool**, **AudioTrack**, and **JetPlayer** on one hand, and **OpenSL ES** on the other hand:

- ◆ MediaPlayer is more high level and easy to use. It handles not only music but also video. It is the way to go when a simple file playback is sufficient.

- ◆ SoundPool and AudioTrack are more low level and closer to low latency when playing sound. AudioTrack is the most flexible but also complex to use. It allows sound buffer modifications on the fly (by hand!).

- ◆ JetPlayer is more dedicated to the playback of MIDI files. This API can be interesting for dynamic musing synthesis in a multimedia application or game (see the JetBoy example provided with Android SDK).

- ◆ OpenSL ES aims at offering a cross-platform API to manage audio on embedded systems; in other words, the OpenGL ES for audio. Like GLES, its specification is led by the Khronos group. On Android, OpenSL ES is in fact implemented on top of the AudioTrack API.

OpenSL ES was first released on Android 2.3 Gingerbread and was not available in previous releases (Android 2.2 and lower). While there is a profusion of APIs in Java, OpenSL ES is the only one provided on the native side and is exclusively available on it.

However, OpenSL ES is still immature. The OpenSL specification is still incompletely supported and several limitations shall be expected. In addition, the OpenSL specification is implemented in its version 1.0.1 on Android, although version 1.1 is already out. Thus, some breaking changes can be expected in the future since the OpenSL ES implementation is still evolving.

3D Audio features are available through OpenSL ES only for devices whose system is compiled with the appropriate profile. Indeed, the current OpenSL ES specification provides three different profiles, Game, Music, and Phone for different types of devices. At the time this book is written, none of these profiles are supported.

However, OpenSL ES has qualities. First, it may be easier to integrate in the architecture of a native application, since it is itself written in C/C++. It does not have to carry a garbage collector on its back. Native code is not interpreted and can be optimized in-depth through assembly code. These are some of the many reasons to consider it.

This chapter is an introduction to the musical capabilities of OpenSL ES on the Android NDK. We are about to discover how to do the following:

- Initialize OpenSL ES on Android
- Play background music
- Play sounds with a sound buffer queue
- Record sounds and play them

Audio and, more specifically, real-time audio is a highly technical subject. This chapter covers the basics to embed sound and music in your own applications.

Initializing OpenSL ES

OpenSL will not be very useful if we do not initialize it first. As usual, this step requires some boilerplate code. The verbosity of OpenSL does not improve the situation. Let's start this chapter by creating a new SoundManager to wrap OpenSL ES-related logic.

 The resulting project is provided with this book under the name DroidBlaster_Part10.

Time for action – creating OpenSL ES engine and output

Let's create a new manager dedicated to sounds:

1. Create a new file `jni/SoundManager.hpp`.

First, include the OpenSL ES standard header `SLES/OpenSLES.h`. The two latter define objects and methods and are specifically created for Android. Then, create the `SoundManager` class to do the following:

- ❑ Initialize OpenSL ES with the `start()` method
- ❑ Stop the sound and release OpenSL ES with the `stop()` method

There are two main kinds of pseudo-object structures (that is, containing function pointers applied on the structure itself, such as a C++ object with this) in OpenSL ES:

- ❑ **Objects**: These are represented by `SLObjectItf`, which provides a few common methods to get allocated resources and object interfaces. This could be roughly compared to an object in Java.

- ❑ **Interfaces**: These give access to object features. There can be several interfaces for an object. Depending on the host device, some interfaces may or may not be available. These are very roughly comparable to interfaces in Java.

In `SoundManager`, declare two `SLObjectItf` instances, one for the OpenSL ES engine and an other for the speakers. Engines are available through a `SLEngineItf` interface:

```
#ifndef _PACKT_SoundManager_HPP_
#define _PACKT_SoundManager_HPP_

#include "Types.hpp"

#include <android_native_app_glue.h>
#include <SLES/OpenSLES.h>

class SoundManager {
public:
    SoundManager(android_app* pApplication);

    status start();
```

```
            void stop();

    private:
        android_app* mApplication;

        SLObjectItf mEngineObj; SLEngineItf mEngine;
        SLObjectItf mOutputMixObj;
    };
    #endif
```

2. Implement `SoundManager` in `jni/SoundManager.cpp` with its constructor:

```
#include "Log.hpp"
#include "Resource.hpp"
#include "SoundManager.hpp"

SoundManager::SoundManager(android_app* pApplication) :
    mApplication(pApplication),
    mEngineObj(NULL), mEngine(NULL),
    mOutputMixObj(NULL) {
    Log::info("Creating SoundManager.");
}
...
```

3. Write the method `start()`, which is going to create an OpenSL Engine object and an `Output Mix` object. We need three variables per object to initialize:

- The number of interfaces to support for each object (`engineMixIIDCount` and `outputMixIIDCount`).

- An array of all the interfaces objects should support (`engineMixIIDs` and `outputMixIIDs`), for example `SL_IID_ENGINE` for the engine.

- An array of Boolean values to indicate whether the interface is required or optional for the program (`engineMixReqs` and `outputMixReqs`).

```
    ...
    status SoundManager::start() {
        Log::info("Starting SoundManager.");
        SLresult result;
        const SLuint32      engineMixIIDCount = 1;
        const SLInterfaceID engineMixIIDs[]   = {SL_IID_ENGINE};
        const SLboolean     engineMixReqs[]   = {SL_BOOLEAN_TRUE};
        const SLuint32      outputMixIIDCount = 0;
        const SLInterfaceID outputMixIIDs[]   = {};
        const SLboolean     outputMixReqs[]   = {};
    ...
```

4. Continue the method `start()`:

- Initialize the OpenSL ES engine object (that is, the basic type `SLObjectItf`) with the `slCreateEngine()` method. When we create an OpenSL ES object, the specific interfaces we are going to use have to be indicated. Here, we request the `SL_IID_ENGINE` interface, which allows creating other OpenSL ES objects. The engine is the central object of the OpenSL ES API.

- Then, invoke `Realize()` on the engine object. Any OpenSL ES object needs to be *realized* to allocate the required internal resources before use.

- Finally, retrieve `SLEngineItf`-specific interface.

- The engine interface gives us the possibility to instantiate an audio output mix with the `CreateOutputMix()` method. The audio output mix defined here delivers sound to the default speakers. It is autonomous (the played sound is sent automatically to the speaker), so there is no need to request any specific interface here.

```
...
// Creates OpenSL ES engine and dumps its capabilities.
result = slCreateEngine(&mEngineObj, 0, NULL,
    engineMixIIDCount, engineMixIIDs, engineMixReqs);
if (result != SL_RESULT_SUCCESS) goto ERROR;
result = (*mEngineObj)->Realize(mEngineObj,SL_BOOLEAN_FALSE);
if (result != SL_RESULT_SUCCESS) goto ERROR;
result = (*mEngineObj)->GetInterface(mEngineObj, SL_IID_ENGINE,
    &mEngine);
if (result != SL_RESULT_SUCCESS) goto ERROR;

// Creates audio output.
result = (*mEngine)->CreateOutputMix(mEngine, &mOutputMixObj,
    outputMixIIDCount, outputMixIIDs, outputMixReqs);
result = (*mOutputMixObj)->Realize(mOutputMixObj,
    SL_BOOLEAN_FALSE);

return STATUS_OK;

ERROR:
    Log::error("Error while starting SoundManager");
    stop();
    return STATUS_KO;
}
...
```

5. Write the `stop()` method to destroy what has been created in `start()`:

```
...
void SoundManager::stop() {
    Log::info("Stopping SoundManager.");

    if (mOutputMixObj != NULL) {
        (*mOutputMixObj)->Destroy(mOutputMixObj);
        mOutputMixObj = NULL;
    }
    if (mEngineObj != NULL) {
        (*mEngineObj)->Destroy(mEngineObj);
        mEngineObj = NULL; mEngine = NULL;
    }
}
```

6. Edit `jni/DroidBlaster.hpp` and embed our new `SoundManager`:

```
...
#include "Resource.hpp"
#include "Ship.hpp"
#include "SoundManager.hpp"
#include "SpriteBatch.hpp"
#include "StarField.hpp"
...

class DroidBlaster : public ActivityHandler {
    ...
private:
    TimeManager     mTimeManager;
    GraphicsManager mGraphicsManager;
    PhysicsManager  mPhysicsManager;
    SoundManager     mSoundManager;
    EventLoop mEventLoop;

    ...
};
#endif
```

7. Create, start, and stop the sound service in `jni/DroidBlaster.cpp`:

```
...
DroidBlaster::DroidBlaster(android_app* pApplication):
    mTimeManager(),
    mGraphicsManager(pApplication),
    mPhysicsManager(mTimeManager, mGraphicsManager),
```

```
        mSoundManager(pApplication),
        mEventLoop(pApplication, *this),
        ...
        mShip(pApplication, mTimeManager, mGraphicsManager) {
        ...
    }

    ...

    status DroidBlaster::onActivate() {
        Log::info("Activating DroidBlaster");

        if (mGraphicsManager.start() != STATUS_OK) return STATUS_KO;
        if (mSoundManager.start() != STATUS_OK) return STATUS_KO;

        mAsteroids.initialize();
        ...
    }

    void DroidBlaster::onDeactivate() {
        Log::info("Deactivating DroidBlaster");
        mGraphicsManager.stop();
        mSoundManager.stop();
    }
```

8. Finally, link to `libOpenSLES.so` in the `jni/Android.mk` file:

```
...
LS_CPP=$(subst $(1)/,,$(wildcard $(1)/*.cpp))
LOCAL_MODULE := droidblaster
LOCAL_SRC_FILES := $(call LS_CPP,$(LOCAL_PATH))
LOCAL_LDLIBS := -landroid -llog -lEGL -lGLESv2 -lOpenSLES
LOCAL_STATIC_LIBRARIES := android_native_app_glue png
...
```

What just happened?

Run the application and check that no error is logged. We initialized the OpenSL ES library, which gives us access to efficient sound handling primitives directly from the native code. The current code does not perform anything apart from initialization. No sound comes out of the speakers yet.

The entry point to OpenSL ES here is `SLEngineItf`, which is mainly an OpenSL ES object factory. It can create a channel to an output device (a speaker or anything else), as well as sound players or recorders (and even more!), as we will see later in this chapter.

The `SLOutputMixItf` is the object representing the audio output. Generally, this will be the device speaker or headset. Although the OpenSL ES specification allows enumerating the available output (and also input) devices, NDK implementation is not mature enough to obtain or select a proper one (`SLAudioIODeviceCapabilitiesItf`, the official interface to obtain such information). So, when dealing with output and input device selection (only input device for recorders needs to be specified currently), it is preferable to stick to default values, `SL_DEFAULTDEVICEID_AUDIOINPUT` and `SL_DEFAULTDEVICEID_AUDIOOUTPUT` defined in `SLES/OpenSLES.h`.

The current Android NDK implementation allows only one engine per application (this should not be an issue) and, at most, 32 created objects. Beware, however, that the creation of any object can fail, as this is dependent on the available system resources.

More on OpenSL ES philosophy

OpenSL ES is different from its graphics compatriot GLES, partly because it does not have a long history to carry. It is constructed on (more or less) an object-oriented principle based on objects and interfaces. The following definitions come from the official specification:

- An **object** is an abstraction of a set of resources, assigned for a well-defined set of tasks, and the state of these resources. An object has a type determined on its creation. The object type determines the set of tasks that an object can perform. This can be considered similar to a class in C++.

- An **interface** is an abstraction of a set of related features that a certain object provides. An interface includes a set of methods, which are functions of the interface. An interface also has a type, which determines the exact set of methods of the interface. We can define the interface itself as a combination of its type and the object to which it is related.

- An **interface ID** identifies an interface type. This identifier is used within the source code to refer to the interface type.

An OpenSL ES object is set up in a few steps as follows:

1. Instantiating it through a build method (which usually belongs to the engine).

2. Realizing it to allocate the necessary resources.

3. Retrieving object interfaces. A basic object only has a very limited set of operations (`Realize()`, `Resume()`, `Destroy()`, and so on). Interfaces give access to real object features and describes what operations can be performed on an object, for example, a `Play` interface to play or pause a sound.

Any interfaces can be requested but only the one supported by the object is going to be successfully retrieved. You cannot retrieve the record interface for an audio player because it returns (sometimes annoyingly!) `SL_RESULT_FEATURE_UNSUPPORTED` (error code 12). In technical terms, an OpenSL ES interface is a structure containing function pointers (initialized by the OpenSL ES implementation) with a self-parameter to simulate C++ objects and `this`, for example:

```
struct SLObjectItf_ {
    SLresult (*Realize) (SLObjectItf self, SLboolean async);
    SLresult (*Resume) ( SLObjectItf self, SLboolean async);
    ...
}
```

Here, `Realize()`, `Resume()`, and so on are object methods that can be applied on an `SLObjectItf` object. The approach is identical for interfaces.

For more detailed information on what OpenSL ES can provide, refer to the specification on the Khronos website `http://www.khronos.org/opensles`, as well as the OpenSL ES documentation in the Android NDK docs directory. Android implementation does not fully respect the specification, at least for now. So, do not be disappointed when discovering that only a limited subset of the specification (especially sample codes) works on Android.

Playing music files

OpenSL ES is initialized, but the only thing coming out of speakers is silence! So what about finding a nice piece of **Background Music (BGM)** and playing it natively with Android NDK? OpenSL ES provides the necessary stuff to read music files such as MP3 files.

 The resulting project is provided with this book under the name `DroidBlaster_Part11`.

Time for action – playing background music

Let's open and play an MP3 music file with OpenSL ES:

1. MP3 files are opened by OpenSL using a POSIX file descriptor pointing to the chosen file. Improve `jni/ResourceManager.cpp` created in the previous chapters by defining a new structure `ResourceDescriptor` and appending a new method `descriptor()`:

   ```
   ...
   struct ResourceDescriptor {
       int32_t mDescriptor;
   ```

```
        off_t mStart;
        off_t mLength;
};

class Resource {
public:
    ...
    status open();
    void close();
    status read(void* pBuffer, size_t pCount);

    ResourceDescriptor descriptor();

    bool operator==(const Resource& pOther);

private:
    ...
};
#endif
```

2. Implement `jni/ResourceManager.cpp`. Of course, makes use of the asset manager API to open the descriptor and fill a `ResourceDescriptor` structure:

```
...
ResourceDescriptor Resource::descriptor() {
    ResourceDescriptor lDescriptor = { -1, 0, 0 };
    AAsset* lAsset = AAssetManager_open(mAssetManager, mPath,
                                        AASSET_MODE_UNKNOWN);
    if (lAsset != NULL) {
        lDescriptor.mDescriptor = AAsset_openFileDescriptor(
            lAsset, &lDescriptor.mStart, &lDescriptor.mLength);
        AAsset_close(lAsset);
    }
    return lDescriptor;
}
...
```

3. Go back to `jni/SoundManager.hpp` and define two methods `playBGM()` and `stopBGM()` to play/stop a background MP3 file.

Declare an OpenSL ES object for the music player, along with the following interfaces:

❑   `SLPlayItf` plays and stops music files

❑   SLSeekItf **controls position and looping**

```
...
#include <android_native_app_glue.h>
#include <SLES/OpenSLES.h>
#include <SLES/OpenSLES_Android.h>

class SoundManager {
public:
    ...
    status start();
    void stop();

    status playBGM(Resource& pResource);
    void stopBGM();

private:
    ...
    SLObjectItf mEngineObj; SLEngineItf mEngine;
    SLObjectItf mOutputMixObj;

    SLObjectItf mBGMPlayerObj; SLPlayItf mBGMPlayer;
    SLSeekItf mBGMPlayerSeek;
};
#endif
```

4. Start implementing jni/SoundManager.cpp.

Include Resource.hpp to get access to asset file descriptors.

Initialize new members in the constructor and update stop() to stop the background music automatically (or some users are not going to be happy!):

```
#include "Log.hpp"
#include "Resource.hpp"
#include "SoundManager.hpp"

SoundManager::SoundManager(android_app* pApplication) :
    mApplication(pApplication),
    mEngineObj(NULL), mEngine(NULL),
    mOutputMixObj(NULL),
    mBGMPlayerObj(NULL), mBGMPlayer(NULL), mBGMPlayerSeek(NULL) {
```

```
            Log::info("Creating SoundManager.");
    }

    ...

    void SoundManager::stop() {
        Log::info("Stopping SoundManager.");
        stopBGM();

        if (mOutputMixObj != NULL) {
            (*mOutputMixObj)->Destroy(mOutputMixObj);
            mOutputMixObj = NULL;
        }
        if (mEngineObj != NULL) {
            (*mEngineObj)->Destroy(mEngineObj);
            mEngineObj = NULL; mEngine = NULL;
        }
    }
    ...
```

5. Implement `playBGM()` to enrich the manager with playback features.

First, describe our audio setup through two main structures, `SLDataSource` and `SLDataSink`. The first describes the audio input channel and the second, the audio output channel.

Here, we configure the data source as a MIME source so that the file type gets detected automatically from the file descriptor. The file descriptor is, of course, opened with a call to `ResourceManager::descriptor()`.

The data sink (that is, the destination channel) is configured with the `OutputMix` object created in the first part of this chapter while initializing the OpenSL ES engine (and refers to the default audio output, that is, speakers or headset):

```
    ...
    status SoundManager::playBGM(Resource& pResource) {
        SLresult result;
        Log::info("Opening BGM %s", pResource.getPath());

        ResourceDescriptor descriptor = pResource.descriptor();
        if (descriptor.mDescriptor < 0) {
            Log::info("Could not open BGM file");
            return STATUS_KO;
        }

        SLDataLocator_AndroidFD dataLocatorIn;
        dataLocatorIn.locatorType = SL_DATALOCATOR_ANDROIDFD;
```

```
dataLocatorIn.fd         = descriptor.mDescriptor;
dataLocatorIn.offset     = descriptor.mStart;
dataLocatorIn.length     = descriptor.mLength;

SLDataFormat_MIME dataFormat;
dataFormat.formatType    = SL_DATAFORMAT_MIME;
dataFormat.mimeType      = NULL;
dataFormat.containerType = SL_CONTAINERTYPE_UNSPECIFIED;

SLDataSource dataSource;
dataSource.pLocator = &dataLocatorIn;
dataSource.pFormat  = &dataFormat;

SLDataLocator_OutputMix dataLocatorOut;
dataLocatorOut.locatorType = SL_DATALOCATOR_OUTPUTMIX;
dataLocatorOut.outputMix   = mOutputMixObj;

SLDataSink dataSink;
dataSink.pLocator = &dataLocatorOut;
dataSink.pFormat  = NULL;
...
```

6. Then, create the OpenSL ES audio player. As always, with OpenSL ES objects, instantiate it through the engine first and then realize it. Two interfaces, SL_IID_PLAY and SL_IID_SEEK, are imperatively required:

```
...
const SLuint32 bgmPlayerIIDCount = 2;
const SLInterfaceID bgmPlayerIIDs[] =
    { SL_IID_PLAY, SL_IID_SEEK };
const SLboolean bgmPlayerReqs[] =
    { SL_BOOLEAN_TRUE, SL_BOOLEAN_TRUE };

result = (*mEngine)->CreateAudioPlayer(mEngine,
    &mBGMPlayerObj, &dataSource, &dataSink,
    bgmPlayerIIDCount, bgmPlayerIIDs, bgmPlayerReqs);
if (result != SL_RESULT_SUCCESS) goto ERROR;
result = (*mBGMPlayerObj)->Realize(mBGMPlayerObj,
    SL_BOOLEAN_FALSE);
if (result != SL_RESULT_SUCCESS) goto ERROR;

result = (*mBGMPlayerObj)->GetInterface(mBGMPlayerObj,
    SL_IID_PLAY, &mBGMPlayer);
```

```
        if (result != SL_RESULT_SUCCESS) goto ERROR;
        result = (*mBGMPlayerObj)->GetInterface(mBGMPlayerObj,
            SL_IID_SEEK, &mBGMPlayerSeek);
        if (result != SL_RESULT_SUCCESS) goto ERROR;
    ...
```

7. Finally, using the `play` and `seek` interfaces, switch the playback in loop mode (that is, the music keeps playing) from the track's beginning (that is, 0 milliseconds) until its end (`SL_TIME_UNKNOWN`), and then start playing (`SetPlayState()` with `SL_PLAYSTATE_PLAYING`).

```
    ...
    result = (*mBGMPlayerSeek)->SetLoop(mBGMPlayerSeek,
        SL_BOOLEAN_TRUE, 0, SL_TIME_UNKNOWN);
    if (result != SL_RESULT_SUCCESS) goto ERROR;
    result = (*mBGMPlayer)->SetPlayState(mBGMPlayer,
        SL_PLAYSTATE_PLAYING);
    if (result != SL_RESULT_SUCCESS) goto ERROR;

    return STATUS_OK;

ERROR:
    Log::error("Error playing BGM");
    return STATUS_KO;
}
...
```

8. Terminate with the last method `stopBGM()` to stop and destroy the player:

```
...
void SoundManager::stopBGM() {
    if (mBGMPlayer != NULL) {
        SLuint32 bgmPlayerState;
        (*mBGMPlayerObj)->GetState(mBGMPlayerObj,
            &bgmPlayerState);
        if (bgmPlayerState == SL_OBJECT_STATE_REALIZED) {
            (*mBGMPlayer)->SetPlayState(mBGMPlayer,
                SL_PLAYSTATE_PAUSED);

            (*mBGMPlayerObj)->Destroy(mBGMPlayerObj);
            mBGMPlayerObj = NULL;
            mBGMPlayer = NULL; mBGMPlayerSeek = NULL;
        }
    }
}
```

9. Add a resource pointing to the music file in `jni/DroidBlaster.hpp`:

```
...
class DroidBlaster : public ActivityHandler {
    ...
private:
    ...
    Resource mAsteroidTexture;
    Resource mShipTexture;
    Resource mStarTexture;
    Resource mBGM;
    ...
};
#endif
```

10. Finally, in `jni/DroidBlaster.cpp`, start playing the music right after SoundManager is started:

```
...
DroidBlaster::DroidBlaster(android_app* pApplication):
    ...
    mAsteroidTexture(pApplication, "droidblaster/asteroid.png"),
    mShipTexture(pApplication, "droidblaster/ship.png"),
    mStarTexture(pApplication, "droidblaster/star.png"),
    mBGM(pApplication, "droidblaster/bgm.mp3"),
    ...
    mSpriteBatch(mTimeManager, mGraphicsManager) {
    ...
}
...
status DroidBlaster::onActivate() {
    Log::info("Activating DroidBlaster");

    if (mGraphicsManager.start() != STATUS_OK) return STATUS_KO;
    if (mSoundManager.start() != STATUS_OK) return STATUS_KO;
    mSoundManager.playBGM(mBGM);

    mAsteroids.initialize();
    mShip.initialize();

    mTimeManager.reset();
    return STATUS_OK;
}
...
```

Copy an MP3 file into the `droidblaster`'s `assets` directory and name it `bgm.mp3`.

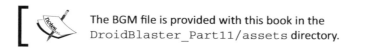

> The BGM file is provided with this book in the `DroidBlaster_Part11/assets` directory.

What just happened?

We discovered how to play a music clip from an MP3 file. Playback loops until the game is terminated. When using a MIME data source, the file type is auto-detected. Several formats are currently supported in Gingerbread, including Wave PCM, Wave alaw, Wave ulaw, MP3, Ogg Vorbis, and so on. The MIDI playback is currently not supported. Have a look at `$ANDROID_NDK/docs/opensles/index.html` for more information.

The way the sample code is presented here is typical of how OpenSL ES works. The OpenSL ES engine object, which is basically an object factory, creates an `AudioPlayer`. In its raw state, this object cannot do much. First, it needs to be realized to allocate the necessary resources. However, that is not enough. It needs to retrieve the right interfaces, like the `SL_IID_PLAY` interface to change the audio player state to playing/stopped. Then, the OpenSL API can be effectively used.

That is quite some work, taking into account result verification (as any call is susceptible to fail), which kind of clutters the code. Getting inside this API can take a little bit more time than usual, but once understood, these concepts become rather easy to deal with.

You may be surprised to see that `startBGM()` and `stopBGM()` recreates and destroys the audio player respectively. The reason is that there is currently no way to change an MIME data source without completely recreating the OpenSL ES `AudioPlayer` object. So, although this technique is fine to play a long clip, it is not suitable to play a short sound dynamically.

Playing sounds

The technique presented to play BGM from a MIME source is very practical but, sadly, not flexible enough. Recreating an `AudioPlayer` object is not necessary and accessing asset files each time is not good in terms of efficiency.

So, when it comes to playing sounds quickly in response to an event and generating them dynamically, we need to use a sound buffer queue. Each sound is preloaded or generated in a memory buffer, and placed into a queue when the playback is requested. No need to access a file at runtime!

A sound buffer, in the current OpenSL ES Android implementation, can contain PCM data. **Pulse Code Modulation (PCM)** is a data format dedicated to the representation of digital sounds. It is the format used in CD and in some Wave files. A PCM can be Mono (the same sound on all speakers) or Stereo (different sounds for left and right speakers if available).

PCM is not compressed and is not efficient in terms of storage (just compare a musical CD with a data CD full of MP3). However, this format is lossless and offers the best quality. Quality depends on the sampling rate: analog sounds are represented digitally as a series of measure (that is, `sample`) of the sound signal.

A sound sample at 44100 Hz (that is 44100 measures per second) has better quality but also takes place more than a sound sampled at 16000 Hz. Also, each measure can be represented with a more or less fine degree of precision (the encoding). On current Android implementation:

◆ Sounds can use 8000 Hz, 11025 Hz, 12000 Hz, 16000 Hz, 22050 Hz, 24000 Hz, 32000 Hz, 44100 Hz, or 48000 Hz sampling,

◆ Samples can be encoded on 8-bit unsigned or 16-bit signed (finer precision) in **little-endian** or **big-endian**.

In the following step-by-step tutorial, we will use a raw PCM file encoded over 16-bit in little-endian.

The resulting project is provided with this book under the name `DroidBlaster_Part12`.

Time for action – creating and playing a sound buffer queue

Let's use OpenSL ES to play an explosion sound stored in a memory buffer:

1. Update `jni/Resource.hpp` again to add a new method `getLength()`, which provides the size in bytes of an `asset` file:

```
...
class Resource {
public:
    ...

    ResourceDescriptor descriptor();
    off_t getLength();
    ...
};

#endif
```

2. Implement this method in `jni/Resource.cpp`:

```
...
off_t Resource::getLength() {
    return AAsset_getLength(mAsset);
}
...
```

3. Create `jni/Sound.hpp` to manage a sound buffer.

Define a method `load()` to load a PCM file and `unload()` to release it.

Also, define the appropriate getters. Hold the raw sound data in a buffer along with its size. The sound is loaded from a `Resource`:

```
#ifndef _PACKT_SOUND_HPP_
#define _PACKT_SOUND_HPP_

class SoundManager;

#include "Resource.hpp"
#include "Types.hpp"

class Sound {
public:
    Sound(android_app* pApplication, Resource* pResource);

    const char* getPath();
    uint8_t* getBuffer() { return mBuffer; };
    off_t getLength() { return mLength; };

    status load();
    status unload();

private:
    friend class SoundManager;

    Resource* mResource;
    uint8_t* mBuffer; off_t mLength;
};
#endif
```

4. Sound loading implementation done in `jni/Sound.cpp` is quite simple; it creates a buffer with the same size as the PCM file and loads all the raw file content in it:

```cpp
#include "Log.hpp"
#include "Sound.hpp"

#include <SLES/OpenSLES.h>
#include <SLES/OpenSLES_Android.h>

Sound::Sound(android_app* pApplication, Resource* pResource) :
    mResource(pResource),
    mBuffer(NULL), mLength(0)
{}

const char* Sound::getPath() {
    return mResource->getPath();
}

status Sound::load() {
    Log::info("Loading sound %s", mResource->getPath());
    status result;

    // Opens sound file.
    if (mResource->open() != STATUS_OK) {
        goto ERROR;
    }

    // Reads sound file.
    mLength = mResource->getLength();
    mBuffer = new uint8_t[mLength];
    result = mResource->read(mBuffer, mLength);
    mResource->close();
    return STATUS_OK;

ERROR:
    Log::error("Error while reading PCM sound.");
    return STATUS_KO;
}

status Sound::unload() {
    delete[] mBuffer;
    mBuffer = NULL; mLength = 0;

    return STATUS_OK;
}
```

5. Create `jni/SoundQueue.hpp` to encapsulate the creation of a player object and its queue. Create three methods to:

- ❏ Initialize the `queue` when the application starts to allocate OpenSL resources
- ❏ Finalize the `queue` to release OpenSL resources
- ❏ Play a sound buffer of a predefined length

A sound queue can be manipulated through the `SLPlayItf` and `SLBufferQueueItf` interfaces:

```
#ifndef _PACKT_SOUNDQUEUE_HPP_
#define _PACKT_SOUNDQUEUE_HPP_

#include "Sound.hpp"

#include <SLES/OpenSLES.h>
#include <SLES/OpenSLES_Android.h>

class SoundQueue {
public:
    SoundQueue();

    status initialize(SLEngineItf pEngine, SLObjectItf pOutputMixObj);
    void finalize();
    void playSound(Sound* pSound);

private:
    SLObjectItf mPlayerObj; SLPlayItf mPlayer;
    SLBufferQueueItf mPlayerQueue;
};
#endif
```

6. Implement `jni/SoundQueue.cpp`:

```
#include "Log.hpp"
#include "SoundQueue.hpp"

SoundQueue::SoundQueue() :
    mPlayerObj(NULL), mPlayer(NULL),
    mPlayerQueue() {
}
...
```

7. Write `initialize()`, beginning with `SLDataSource` and `SLDataSink` to describe the input and output channel. Use a `SLDataFormat_PCM` data format (instead of `SLDataFormat_MIME`), which includes sampling, encoding, and endianness information. Sounds need to be mono (that is, only one sound channel for both left and right speakers when available). The queue is created with the Android-specific extension `SLDataLocator_AndroidSimpleBufferQueue()`:

```
...
status SoundQueue::initialize(SLEngineItf pEngine,
        SLObjectItf pOutputMixObj) {
    Log::info("Starting sound player.");
    SLresult result;

    // Set-up sound audio source.
    SLDataLocator_AndroidSimpleBufferQueue dataLocatorIn;
    dataLocatorIn.locatorType =
        SL_DATALOCATOR_ANDROIDSIMPLEBUFFERQUEUE;
    // At most one buffer in the queue.
    dataLocatorIn.numBuffers = 1;

    SLDataFormat_PCM dataFormat;
    dataFormat.formatType = SL_DATAFORMAT_PCM;
    dataFormat.numChannels = 1; // Mono sound.
    dataFormat.samplesPerSec = SL_SAMPLINGRATE_44_1;
    dataFormat.bitsPerSample = SL_PCMSAMPLEFORMAT_FIXED_16;
    dataFormat.containerSize = SL_PCMSAMPLEFORMAT_FIXED_16;
    dataFormat.channelMask = SL_SPEAKER_FRONT_CENTER;
    dataFormat.endianness = SL_BYTEORDER_LITTLEENDIAN;

    SLDataSource dataSource;
    dataSource.pLocator = &dataLocatorIn;
    dataSource.pFormat = &dataFormat;

    SLDataLocator_OutputMix dataLocatorOut;
    dataLocatorOut.locatorType = SL_DATALOCATOR_OUTPUTMIX;
    dataLocatorOut.outputMix = pOutputMixObj;

    SLDataSink dataSink;
    dataSink.pLocator = &dataLocatorOut;
    dataSink.pFormat = NULL;
...
```

8. Then, create and realize the sound player. We are going to need its `SL_IID_PLAY` and `SL_IID_BUFFERQUEUE` interface, available thanks to the data locator configured in the previous step:

```
...
    const SLuint32 soundPlayerIIDCount = 2;
    const SLInterfaceID soundPlayerIIDs[] =
        { SL_IID_PLAY, SL_IID_BUFFERQUEUE };
    const SLboolean soundPlayerReqs[] =
        { SL_BOOLEAN_TRUE, SL_BOOLEAN_TRUE };

    result = (*pEngine)->CreateAudioPlayer(pEngine, &mPlayerObj,
        &dataSource, &dataSink, soundPlayerIIDCount,
        soundPlayerIIDs, soundPlayerReqs);
    if (result != SL_RESULT_SUCCESS) goto ERROR;
    result = (*mPlayerObj)->Realize(mPlayerObj, SL_BOOLEAN_FALSE);
    if (result != SL_RESULT_SUCCESS) goto ERROR;

    result = (*mPlayerObj)->GetInterface(mPlayerObj, SL_IID_PLAY,
        &mPlayer);
    if (result != SL_RESULT_SUCCESS) goto ERROR;
    result = (*mPlayerObj)->GetInterface(mPlayerObj,
        SL_IID_BUFFERQUEUE, &mPlayerQueue);
    if (result != SL_RESULT_SUCCESS) goto ERROR;
...
```

9. Finally, start the queue by setting it in the playing state. This does not actually mean that a sound is played. The queue is empty so that would not be possible. However, if a sound gets enqueued, it is automatically played:

```
...
    result = (*mPlayer)->SetPlayState(mPlayer,
        SL_PLAYSTATE_PLAYING);
    if (result != SL_RESULT_SUCCESS) goto ERROR;
    return STATUS_OK;

ERROR:
    Log::error("Error while starting SoundQueue");
    return STATUS_KO;
}
...
```

10. OpenSL ES objects need to be released when we no longer need them:

```
...
void SoundQueue::finalize() {
    Log::info("Stopping SoundQueue.");

    if (mPlayerObj != NULL) {
        (*mPlayerObj)->Destroy(mPlayerObj);
        mPlayerObj = NULL; mPlayer = NULL; mPlayerQueue = NULL;
    }
}
...
```

11. Finally, write `playSound()`, which first stops any sound being played and then enqueue the new sound buffer to be played. This is the simplest strategy to play a sound immediately:

```
...
void SoundQueue::playSound(Sound* pSound) {
    SLresult result;
    SLuint32 playerState;
    (*mPlayerObj)->GetState(mPlayerObj, &playerState);
    if (playerState == SL_OBJECT_STATE_REALIZED) {
        int16_t* buffer = (int16_t*) pSound->getBuffer();
        off_t length = pSound->getLength();

        // Removes any sound from the queue.
        result = (*mPlayerQueue)->Clear(mPlayerQueue);
        if (result != SL_RESULT_SUCCESS) goto ERROR;
        // Plays the new sound.
        result = (*mPlayerQueue)->Enqueue(mPlayerQueue, buffer,
                                          length);
        if (result != SL_RESULT_SUCCESS) goto ERROR;
    }
    return;

ERROR:
    Log::error("Error trying to play sound");
}
```

12. Open `jni/SoundManager.hpp` and include the newly created headers.
Create two new methods:

- ❑ `registerSound()` to load and manage a new sound buffer
- ❑ `playSound()` to send a sound buffer to the sound play queue

Define a `SoundQueue` array so that up to four sounds may be played
simultaneously.

Sound buffers are stored in a fixed-size C++ array:

```
...
#include "Sound.hpp"
#include "SoundQueue.hpp"
#include "Types.hpp"
...

class SoundManager {
public:
    SoundManager(android_app* pApplication);
    ~SoundManager();

    ...

    Sound* registerSound(Resource& pResource);
    void playSound(Sound* pSound);

private:
    ...
    static const int32_t QUEUE_COUNT = 4;
    SoundQueue mSoundQueues[QUEUE_COUNT]; int32_t mCurrentQueue;
    Sound* mSounds[32]; int32_t mSoundCount;
};
#endif
```

13. Update the constructor in `jni/SoundManager.cpp` and create a new destructor to
release resources:

```
...
SoundManager::SoundManager(android_app* pApplication) :
    mApplication(pApplication),
    mEngineObj(NULL), mEngine(NULL),
    mOutputMixObj(NULL),
    mBGMPlayerObj(NULL), mBGMPlayer(NULL), mBGMPlayerSeek(NULL),
```

```
        mSoundQueues(), mCurrentQueue(0),
        mSounds(), mSoundCount(0) {
    Log::info("Creating SoundManager.");
}

SoundManager::~SoundManager() {
    Log::info("Destroying SoundManager.");
    for (int32_t i = 0; i < mSoundCount; ++i) {
        delete mSounds[i];
    }
    mSoundCount = 0;
}
...
```

14. Update `start()` to initialize the `SoundQueue` instances. Then, load sound resources registered with `registerSound()`:

```
...
status SoundManager::start() {
    ...
    result = (*mEngine)->CreateOutputMix(mEngine, &mOutputMixObj,
        outputMixIIDCount, outputMixIIDs, outputMixReqs);
    result = (*mOutputMixObj)->Realize(mOutputMixObj,
        SL_BOOLEAN_FALSE);

    Log::info("Starting sound player.");
    for (int32_t i= 0; i < QUEUE_COUNT; ++i) {
        if (mSoundQueues[i].initialize(mEngine, mOutputMixObj)
                != STATUS_OK) goto ERROR;
    }

    for (int32_t i = 0; i < mSoundCount; ++i) {
        if (mSounds[i]->load() != STATUS_OK) goto ERROR;
    }
    return STATUS_OK;

ERROR:
    ...
}
...
```

15. Finalize the `SoundQueue` instances when the application stops to release OpenSL ES resources. Also, release the sound buffers:

```
...
void SoundManager::stop() {
    Log::info("Stopping SoundManager.");
    stopBGM();

    for (int32_t i= 0; i < QUEUE_COUNT; ++i) {
        mSoundQueues[i].finalize();
    }

    // Destroys audio output and engine.
    ...

    for (int32_t i = 0; i < mSoundCount; ++i) {
        mSounds[i]->unload();
    }
}
...
```

16. Save and cache the sounds in `registerSound()`:

```
...
Sound* SoundManager::registerSound(Resource& pResource) {
    for (int32_t i = 0; i < mSoundCount; ++i) {
        if (strcmp(pResource.getPath(), mSounds[i]->getPath()) == 0) {
            return mSounds[i];
        }
    }

    Sound* sound = new Sound(mApplication, &pResource);
    mSounds[mSoundCount++] = sound;
    return sound;
}
...
```

17. Finally, write `playSound()`, which sends the buffer to play to a `SoundQueue`. Use a simple round-robin strategy to play several sounds simultaneously. Send each new sound to play next in the queue (which is more likely to be available). Obviously, this playing strategy is suboptimal for sounds of various lengths:

```
...
void SoundManager::playSound(Sound* pSound) {
    int32_t currentQueue = ++mCurrentQueue;
    SoundQueue& soundQueue = mSoundQueues[currentQueue % QUEUE_COUNT];
    soundQueue.playSound(pSound);
}
```

18. We will play a sound when the DroidBlaster ship collides with an asteroid. Since the collision is not yet managed (see *Chapter 10, Intensive Computing with RenderScript* for collision handling with **Box2D**), we will simply play a sound when the ship is initialized.

To do so, in `jni/Ship.hpp`, retrieve a reference to `SoundManager` in the constructor and a collision sound buffer to play in `registerShip()`:

```
...
#include "GraphicsManager.hpp"
#include "Sprite.hpp"
#include "SoundManager.hpp"
#include "Sound.hpp"

class Ship {
public:
    Ship(android_app* pApplication,
            GraphicsManager& pGraphicsManager,
            SoundManager& pSoundManager);

    void registerShip(Sprite* pGraphics, Sound* pCollisionSound);

    void initialize();

private:
    GraphicsManager& mGraphicsManager;
    SoundManager& mSoundManager;

    Sprite* mGraphics;
    Sound* mCollisionSound;
};
#endif
```

19. Then, in `jni/Ship.cpp`, after having stored all the necessary references, play the sound when the ship is initialized:

```
...
Ship::Ship(android_app* pApplication,
        GraphicsManager& pGraphicsManager,
        SoundManager& pSoundManager) :
    mGraphicsManager(pGraphicsManager),
    mGraphics(NULL),
    mSoundManager(pSoundManager),
```

```
            mCollisionSound(NULL) {
    }


    void Ship::registerShip(Sprite* pGraphics, Sound* pCollisionSound) {
        mGraphics = pGraphics;
        mCollisionSound = pCollisionSound;
    }


    void Ship::initialize() {
        mGraphics->location.x = INITAL_X
                * mGraphicsManager.getRenderWidth();
        mGraphics->location.y = INITAL_Y
                * mGraphicsManager.getRenderHeight();
        mSoundManager.playSound(mCollisionSound);
    }
```

20. In jni/DroidBlaster.hpp, define a reference to a file, which contains a collision sound:

```
    ...
    class DroidBlaster : public ActivityHandler {
        ...

    private:
        ...
        Resource mAsteroidTexture;
        Resource mShipTexture;
        Resource mStarTexture;
        Resource mBGM;
        Resource mCollisionSound;


        ...
    };
    #endif
```

21. Finally, in jni/DroidBlaster.cpp, register the new sound and pass it to the Ship class:

```
    #include "DroidBlaster.hpp"
    #include "Sound.hpp"
    #include "Log.hpp"
    ...
    DroidBlaster::DroidBlaster(android_app* pApplication):
        ...
        mAsteroidTexture(pApplication, "droidblaster/asteroid.png"),
        mShipTexture(pApplication, "droidblaster/ship.png"),
```

```
        mStarTexture(pApplication, "droidblaster/star.png"),
        mBGM(pApplication, "droidblaster/bgm.mp3"),
        mCollisionSound(pApplication, "droidblaster/collision.pcm"),


        mAsteroids(pApplication, mTimeManager, mGraphicsManager,
                mPhysicsManager),
        mShip(pApplication, mGraphicsManager, mSoundManager),
        mStarField(pApplication, mTimeManager, mGraphicsManager,
                STAR_COUNT, mStarTexture),
        mSpriteBatch(mTimeManager, mGraphicsManager) {
        Log::info("Creating DroidBlaster");

        Sprite* shipGraphics = mSpriteBatch.registerSprite(mShipTexture,
                SHIP_SIZE, SHIP_SIZE);
        shipGraphics->setAnimation(SHIP_FRAME_1, SHIP_FRAME_COUNT,
                SHIP_ANIM_SPEED, true);
        Sound* collisionSound =
                mSoundManager.registerSound(mCollisionSound);
        mShip.registerShip(shipGraphics, collisionSound);
        ...
    }
    ...
```

What just happened?

We discovered how to preload sounds in a buffer and play them as needed. What differentiates the sound playing technique from the BGM one seen earlier is the use of a buffer queue. A buffer queue is exactly what its name reveals: a **First In, First Out (FIFO)** collection of sound buffers played one after the other. Buffers are enqueued for playback when all the previous buffers are played.

Buffers can be recycled. This technique is essential in combination with streaming files: two or more buffers are filled and sent to the queue. When the first buffer has finished playing, the second one starts while the first buffer is filled with new data. As soon as possible, the first buffer is enqueued before the queue gets empty. This process repeats forever until the playback is over. In addition, buffers are raw data and can thus be processed or filtered on the fly.

In the present tutorial, because `DroidBlaster` does not need to play more than one sound at once and no form of streaming is necessary, the buffer queue size is simply set to one buffer (step 7, `dataLocatorIn.numBuffers = 1;`). In addition, we want new sounds to pre-empt older ones, which explains why the queue is systematically cleared. Your OpenSL ES architecture should, of course, be adapted to your needs. If it becomes necessary to play several sounds simultaneously, several audio players (and therefore buffer queues) should be created.

Sound buffers are stored in the PCM format, which does not self-describe its internal format. Sampling, encoding, and other format information needs to be selected in the application code. Although this is fine for most of them, a solution, if that is not flexible enough, can be to load a Wave file, which contains all the necessary header information.

 A great open source tool to filter and sequence sounds is **Audacity**. It allows altering the sampling rate and modifying channels (Mono/Stereo). Audacity is able to export as well as import sound as raw PCM data.

Using callbacks to detect sound queue events

It is possible to detect when a sound has finished playing using callbacks. A callback can be set up by calling the `RegisterCallback()` method on a queue (but other types of objects can also register callbacks). For example, the callback can receive this, that is, a `SoundManager` self-reference, to allow processing with any contextual information if needed. Although this is facultative, an event mask is set up to ensure that the callback is called only when the `SL_PLAYEVENT_HEADATEND` (player has finished playing the buffer) event is triggered. A few others play events are available in `OpenSLES.h`:

```
...
void callback_sound(SLBufferQueueItf pBufferQueue, void
*pContext) {
    // Context can be casted back to the original type.
    SoundService& lService = *(SoundService*) pContext;
    ...
    Log::info("Ended playing sound.");
}
...
status SoundService::start() {
    ...
    result = (*mEngine)->CreateOutputMix(mEngine, &mOutputMixObj,
        outputMixIIDCount, outputMixIIDs, outputMixReqs);
```

```
    result = (*mOutputMixObj)->Realize(mOutputMixObj,
        SL_BOOLEAN_FALSE);

    // Registers a callback called when sound is finished.
    result = (*mPlayerQueue)->RegisterCallback(mPlayerQueue,
        callback_sound, this);
    if (result != SL_RESULT_SUCCESS) goto ERROR;
    result = (*mPlayer)->SetCallbackEventsMask(mPlayer,
                                    SL_PLAYEVENT_HEADATEND);
    if (result != SL_RESULT_SUCCESS) goto ERROR;

    Log::info("Starting sound player.");
    ...
}
...
```

Now, when a buffer finishes playing, a message is logged. Operations such as, enqueuing a new buffer (to handle streaming for example) can be performed.

Low latency on Android

Callbacks are like system interruptions or application events, their processing must be short and fast. If advanced processing is necessary, it should not be performed inside the callback but on another thread- native threads being perfect candidates.

Indeed, callbacks are emitted on a system thread, different than the one requesting OpenSL ES services (that is, the `NativeActivity` native thread in our case). Of course, with threads, arises the problem of thread-safety when accessing your own variables from the callback. Although protecting code with mutexes is tempting, they are not the best way to deal with real-time audio. Their effect on scheduling (**inversion of priority** issues for example) can cause glitches during playback.

So, prefer using thread-safe techniques, like a lock-free queue to communicate with callbacks. Lock-free techniques can be implemented using GCC built-in atomic functions such as `__sync_fetch_and_add()` (which does not require any include file). For more information about atomic operations with the Android NDK, have a look at, `${ANDROID_NDK}/docs/ANDROID-ATOMICS.html`.

Although proper lock-free code is essential to achieve low-latency on Android, another important point to consider is that not all Android platforms and devices are suited for it! Indeed, low latency support came quite late in Android, starting from OS Version 4.1/4.2. If you are in the need for low latency, you can check its support with the following piece of Java code:

```
import android.content.pm.PackageManager;
...
PackageManager pm = getContext().getPackageManager();
boolean claimsFeature = pm.hasSystemFeature(PackageManager.FEATURE_AUDIO_
LOW_LATENCY);
```

However, beware! Many devices, even with the latest system versions, cannot achieve low latencies because of driver issues.

Once you know that the target platform supports low-latency, take care of using the proper sampling rate and buffer size. Indeed, the Android audio system provides a "fast path", which does not apply any resampling, when using the optimal configuration. To do so, from API level 17 or higher, use `android.media.AudioManager.getProperty()` from the Java side:

```
import android.media.AudioManager;
...
AudioManager am = (AudioManager) getSystemService(Context.AUDIO_SERVICE);
String sampleRateStr =
        am.getProperty(AudioManager.PROPERTY_OUTPUT_SAMPLE_RATE);
int sampleRate = !TextUtils.isEmpty(sampleRateStr) ?
                            Integer.parseInt(sampleRateStr) : -1;
String framesPerBufferStr =
        am.getProperty(AudioManager.PROPERTY_OUTPUT_FRAMES_PER_BUFFER);
int framesPerBuffer = !TextUtils.isEmpty(framesPerBufferStr) ?
                            Integer.parseInt(framesPerBufferStr) : -1;
```

For more information on this subject, have a look at the *High Performance Audio* talk at `https://developers.google.com/events/io/sessions/325993827`.

Recording sounds

Android devices are all about interactions. Interactions can come not only from touches and sensors, but also from audio input. Most Android devices provide a microphone to record sound and allow an application such as the Android desktop search to offer vocal features to record queries.

If the sound input is available, OpenSL ES gives native access to the sound recorder. It collaborates with a buffer queue to take data from the input device and fill an output sound buffer from it. The setup is pretty similar to what has been done with `AudioPlayer`, except that data source and data sink are permuted.

Have a go hero – recording and playing a sound

To discover how recording works, record a sound when an application starts and play it when it has finished recording. Turning `SoundManager` into a recorder can be done in four steps:

1. Using status `startSoundRecorder()` to initialize the sound recorder. Invoke it right after `startSoundPlayer()`.

2. With void `recordSound()`, start recording a sound buffer with device micro. Invoke this method at instances such as when the application is activated in `onActivate()` after the background music playback starts.

3. A new callback static `void callback_recorder(SLAndroidSimpleBufferQ ueueItf, void*)` to be notified of the record queue events. You have to register this callback so that it is triggered when a recorder event happens. Here, we are interested in buffer full events, that is, when the sound recording is finished.

4. `void playRecordedSound()` to play a sound once recorded. Play it at instances such as when the sound has finished being recorded in `callback_recorder()`. This is not technically correct because of potential race conditions but is fine for an illustration.

> The resulting project is provided with this book under the name `DroidBlaster_PartRecorder`.

Before going any further, recording requires a specific Android permission and, of course, an appropriate Android device (you would not like an application to record your secret conversations behind your back!). This authorization has to be requested in the Android manifest:

```xml
<?xml version="1.0" encoding="utf-8"?>
<manifest xmlns:android="http://schemas.android.com/apk/res/android"
    package="com.packtpub.droidblaster2d" android:versionCode="1"
    android:versionName="1.0">
    ...
    <uses-permission android:name="android.permission.RECORD_AUDIO"/>
</manifest>
```

Creating and releasing the recorder

Sounds are recorded with a recorder object created from the OpenSL ES engine, as usual. The recorder offers two interesting interfaces:

- `SLRecordItf`: This interface is used to start and stop recording. The identifier is `SL_IID_RECORD`.

- `SLAndroidSImpleBufferQueueItf`: This manages a sound queue for the recorder. This is an Android extension provided by NDK because the current OpenSL ES 1.0.1 specification does not support recording to a queue. The identifier is `SL_IID_ANDROIDSIMPLEBUFFERQUEUE`:

```
const SLuint32 soundRecorderIIDCount = 2;
const SLInterfaceID soundRecorderIIDs[] =
        { SL_IID_RECORD, SL_IID_ANDROIDSIMPLEBUFFERQUEUE };
const SLboolean soundRecorderReqs[] =
        { SL_BOOLEAN_TRUE, SL_BOOLEAN_TRUE };
SLObjectItf mRecorderObj;
(*mEngine)->CreateAudioRecorder(mEngine, &mRecorderObj,
        &dataSource, &dataSink,
        soundRecorderIIDCount, soundRecorderIIDs,
soundRecorderReqs);
```

To create the recorder, you will need to declare your audio source and sink, similar to the following one. The data source is not a sound but a default recorder device (such as a microphone). On the other hand, the data sink (that is, the output channel) is not a speaker but a sound buffer in the PCM format (with the requested sampling, encoding, and endianness). The Android extension `SLDataLocator_AndroidSimpleBufferQueue` must be used to work with a recorder since the standard OpenSL buffer queues will not:

```
SLDataLocator_AndroidSimpleBufferQueue dataLocatorOut;
dataLocatorOut.locatorType =
    SL_DATALOCATOR_ANDROIDSIMPLEBUFFERQUEUE;
dataLocatorOut.numBuffers = 1;

SLDataFormat_PCM dataFormat;
dataFormat.formatType = SL_DATAFORMAT_PCM;
dataFormat.numChannels = 1;
dataFormat.samplesPerSec = SL_SAMPLINGRATE_44_1;
dataFormat.bitsPerSample = SL_PCMSAMPLEFORMAT_FIXED_16;
dataFormat.containerSize = SL_PCMSAMPLEFORMAT_FIXED_16;
dataFormat.channelMask = SL_SPEAKER_FRONT_CENTER;
dataFormat.endianness = SL_BYTEORDER_LITTLEENDIAN;

SLDataSink dataSink;
```

```
dataSink.pLocator = &dataLocatorOut;
dataSink.pFormat  = &dataFormat;

SLDataLocator_IODevice dataLocatorIn;
dataLocatorIn.locatorType = SL_DATALOCATOR_IODEVICE;
dataLocatorIn.deviceType = SL_IODEVICE_AUDIOINPUT;
dataLocatorIn.deviceID = SL_DEFAULTDEVICEID_AUDIOINPUT;
dataLocatorIn.device = NULL;

SLDataSource dataSource;
dataSource.pLocator = &dataLocatorIn;
dataSource.pFormat  = NULL;
```

When an application ends, do not forget to release the recorder object as all other OpenSL objects.

Recording a sound

To record a sound, you need to create a sound buffer with an appropriate size according to the duration of your recording. You can adapt the Sound class to allow the creation of an empty buffer with a given size. The size depends on the sampling rate. For example, for a record of 2 seconds with a sampling rate of 44100 Hz and 16-bit quality, the sound buffer size would look like the following:

```
recordSize   = 2 * 44100 * sizeof(int16_t);
recordBuffer = new int16_t[mRecordSize];
```

In recordSound(), first stop the recorder, thanks to SLRecordItf, to ensure it is not already recording. Then, clear the queue to ensure your record buffer is used immediately. Finally, you can enqueue a new buffer and start recording:

```
(*mRecorder)->SetRecordState(mRecorder, SL_RECORDSTATE_STOPPED);
(*mRecorderQueue)->Clear(mRecorderQueue);
(*mRecorderQueue)->Enqueue(mRecorderQueue, recordBuffer,
    recordSize * sizeof(int16_t));
(*mRecorder)->SetRecordState(mRecorder, SL_RECORDSTATE_RECORDING);
```

 It is perfectly possible to enqueue new sound buffers so that any current recording is processed to its end. This allows creating a continuous chain of recording or, in other words, streaming the recording. The sound being enqueued will be processed only once the previous is filled.

Recording a callback

You eventually need to know when your sound buffer has finished recording. To do so, register a callback triggered when a recorder event happens (for example, a buffer has been filled). An event mask should be set to ensure that callback is called only when a buffer has been filled (SL_RECORDEVENT_BUFFER_FULL). A few others are available in OpenSLES.h, but not all are supported (SL_RECORDEVENT_HEADATLIMIT, and so on):

```
(*mRecorderQueue)->RegisterCallback(mRecorderQueue,
                                    callback_recorder, this);
(*mRecorder)->SetCallbackEventMask(mRecorder,
                                   SL_RECORDEVENT_BUFFER_FULL);
```

Finally, when callback_recorder() is triggered, stop recording and play the recorded buffer with playRecordedSound(). The recorded buffer needs to be enqueued in the audio player's queue for playback, as we did in the previous section. You can use a specific SoundQueue to play the sound for simplicity purposes.

Summary

In summary, we saw in this chapter how to initialize OpenSL ES on Android. The engine object is the main entry point to manage all OpenSL objects. Objects in OpenSL follow a specific lifecycle of creation, realization, and destruction. Then, we saw how to play background music from an encoded file and in-memory sounds with a sound buffer queue. Finally, we discovered how to record and then play a sound in a way that is thread-safe and non-blocking.

Do you prefer OpenSL ES over Java APIs? If all you need is a nice high-level API, Java APIs may suit your requirements better. If you need finer playback or recording control, there is no significant difference between low-level Java APIs and OpenSL ES. In this case, the choice should be architectural. If your code is mainly Java, you should probably go with Java.

If you need to reuse an existing sound-related library, optimize the performance, or perform intense computations, such as sound filtering on the fly, OpenSL ES is probably the right choice. OpenSL ES is also the way to go to low-latency, although Android is not quite there yet (fragmentations, device-specific issues, and so on). At the least, this verbose API is probably the one that is going to give the best performance. There is no garbage collector overhead and aggressive optimization is favored in the native code.

Whatever choice you make, know that the Android NDK has a lot more to offer. After dealing with *Chapter 6*, *Rendering Graphics with OpenGL ES* and *Chapter 7*, *Playing Sound with OpenSL ES*, the next chapter will take care of handling input natively: keyboard, touches, and sensors.

Handling Input Devices and Sensors

8

Android is all about interaction. Admittedly, that means feedback, through graphics, audio, vibrations, and so on. But there is no interaction without input! The success of today's smartphones takes its root in their multiple and modern input possibilities: touchscreens, keyboard, mouse, GPS, accelerometer, light detector, sound recorder, and so on. Handling and combining them properly is a key to enrich your application and to make it successful.

Although Android handles many input peripherals, the Android NDK has long been very limited in its support (not to say the very least), until the release of R5! We can now access it directly through a native API. Examples of available devices are:

- ◆ Keyboard, either physical (with a slide-out keyboard) or virtual (which appears on screen)
- ◆ Directional pad (up, down, left, right, and action buttons), often abbreviated as D-Pad.
- ◆ Trackball, optical ones included
- ◆ Touchscreen, which has made modern smart-phones successful
- ◆ Mouse or Track Pad (since NDK R5, but available on Honeycomb devices only)

We can also access hardware sensors, which are as follows:

- ◆ Accelerometer, which measures the linear acceleration applied to a device.

- ◆ Gyroscope, which measures the angular velocity. It is often combined with the magnetometer to compute orientation accurately and quickly. Gyroscope has been introduced recently and is not available on most devices yet.

- ◆ Magnetometer, which gives the ambient magnetic field and consequently the cardinal direction.

- ◆ Light sensor, for example, to automatically adapt to screen luminosity.

- ◆ Proximity sensor, for example, to detect ear distance during a call.

In addition to hardware sensors, "software sensors" have been introduced with Gingerbread. These sensors are derived from the hardware sensor's data:

- ◆ Gravity sensor, to measure the gravity direction and magnitude

- ◆ Linear acceleration sensor, which measures device "movement" excluding gravity

- ◆ Rotation vector, which indicates device orientation in space

The gravity sensor and the linear acceleration sensor are derived from the accelerometer. On the other hand, rotation vector is derived from the magnetometer and the accelerometer. Because these sensors are generally computed over time, they usually incur a slight delay in getting up-to-date values.

To familiarize ourselves more deeply with input devices and sensors, this chapter teaches how to:

- ◆ Handle screen touches

- ◆ Detect keyboard, D-Pad, and trackball events

- ◆ Turn the accelerometer sensor into a joypad

Interacting with touch events

The most emblematic innovation of today's smart phones is the touchscreen, which has replaced the now antique mice. A touchscreen detects, as its name suggests, touches made with fingers or styluses on a device's surface. Depending on the quality of the screen, several touches (also referred to as cursors in Android) can be handled, de-multiplying interaction possibilities.

So let's start this chapter by handling touch events in DroidBlaster. To keep the example simple, we will only handle a single "touch". The goal is to move the ship in the direction of touch. The farther the touch, the faster the ship goes. Beyond a predefined range TOUCH_ MAX_RANGE, the ship's speed reaches its speed limit, as shown in the following figure:

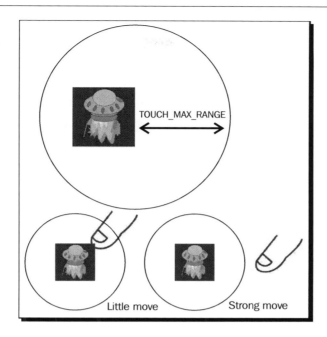

 The resulting project is provided with this book under the name
`DroidBlaster_Part13`.

Time for action – handling touch events

Let's intercept touch events in `DroidBlaster`:

1. In the same way that we created `ActivityHandler` to process application events
   in *Chapter 5, Writing a Fully Native Application*, create `jni/InputHandler.`
   `hpp` to process input events. The input API is declared in `android/input.h`.
   Create `onTouchEvent()` to handle touch events. These events are packaged in
   an `AInputEvent` structure. Other input peripherals will be described later in this
   chapter:

```
#ifndef _PACKT_INPUTHANDLER_HPP_
#define _PACKT_INPUTHANDLER_HPP_

#include <android/input.h>

class InputHandler {
```

```
public:
    virtual ~InputHandler() {};

    virtual bool onTouchEvent(AInputEvent* pEvent) = 0;
};
#endif
```

2. Modify the `jni/EventLoop.hpp` header file to include and handle an `InputHandler` instance.

   In a similar way, to activity events, define an internal method `processInputEvent()`, which is triggered by a static callback `callback_input()`:

```
...
#include "ActivityHandler.hpp"
#include "InputHandler.hpp"

#include <android_native_app_glue.h>

class EventLoop {
public:
EventLoop(android_app* pApplication,
            ActivityHandler& pActivityHandler,
            InputHandler& pInputHandler);
    ...
private:
    ...
    void processAppEvent(int32_t pCommand);
    int32_t processInputEvent(AInputEvent* pEvent);

    static void callback_appEvent(android_app* pApplication,
            int32_t pCommand);
    static int32_t callback_input(android_app* pApplication,
            AInputEvent* pEvent);

    ...
    ActivityHandler& mActivityHandler;
    InputHandler& mInputHandler;
};
#endif
```

3. We need to process input events in the `jni/EventLoop.cpp` source file and notify the associated `InputHandler`.

First, connect the Android input queue to `callback_input()`. The `EventLoop` itself (that is, `this`) is passed anonymously through the `userData` member of the `android_app` structure. That way, callback is able to delegate input processing back to our own object, that is, to `processInputEvent()`:

```
...
EventLoop::EventLoop(android_app* pApplication,
    ActivityHandler& pActivityHandler, InputHandler& pInputHandler):
        mApplication(pApplication),
        mActivityHandler(pActivityHandler),
        mEnabled(false), mQuit(false),
        mInputHandler(pInputHandler) {
    mApplication->userData = this;
    mApplication->onAppCmd = callback_appEvent;
    mApplication->onInputEvent = callback_input;
}

...

int32_t EventLoop::callback_input(android_app* pApplication,
                                  AInputEvent* pEvent) {
    EventLoop& eventLoop = *(EventLoop*) pApplication->userData;
    return eventLoop.processInputEvent(pEvent);
}
...
```

4. Touchscreen events are of the type `MotionEvent` (as opposed to key events). They can be discriminated according to their source (`AINPUT_SOURCE_TOUCHSCREEN`) thanks to the Android native input API (here, `AinputEvent_getSource()`):

Note how `callback_input()` and by extension `processInputEvent()` return an integer value (which is intrinsically a Boolean value). This value indicates that an input event (for example, a pressed button) has been processed by the application and does not need to be processed further by the system. For example, 1 is returned when the back button is pressed to stop event processing and prevent the activity from getting terminated.

```
...
int32_t EventLoop::processInputEvent(AInputEvent* pEvent) {
    if (!mEnabled) return 0;

    int32_t eventType = AInputEvent_getType(pEvent);
    switch (eventType) {
```

```
case AINPUT_EVENT_TYPE_MOTION:
    switch (AInputEvent_getSource(pEvent)) {
    case AINPUT_SOURCE_TOUCHSCREEN:
        return mInputHandler.onTouchEvent(pEvent);
        break;
    }
    break;
}
return 0;
}
```

5. Create `jni/InputManager.hpp` to handle touch events and implement our new `InputHandler` interface.

Define the methods as follows:

- ❏ `start()` to perform the necessary initialization.

- ❏ `onTouchEvent()` to update the manager state when a new event is triggered.

- ❏ `getDirectionX()` and `getDirectionY()` to indicate the ship direction.

- ❏ `setRefPoint()` refers to the ship position. Indeed, the direction is defined as the vector between the touch point and the ship location (that is, the reference point).

Also, declare the necessary members and more specifically `mScaleFactor`, which contains the proper ratio to convert the input event from screen coordinates to game coordinates (remember that we use a fixed size).

```
#ifndef _PACKT_INPUTMANAGER_HPP_
#define _PACKT_INPUTMANAGER_HPP_

#include "GraphicsManager.hpp"
#include "InputHandler.hpp"
#include "Types.hpp"

#include <android_native_app_glue.h>

class InputManager : public InputHandler {
public:
    InputManager(android_app* pApplication,
            GraphicsManager& pGraphicsManager);

    float getDirectionX() { return mDirectionX; };
```

```
    float getDirectionY() { return mDirectionY; };
    void setRefPoint(Location* pRefPoint) { mRefPoint = pRefPoint; };

    void start();

protected:
    bool onTouchEvent(AInputEvent* pEvent);

private:
    android_app* mApplication;
    GraphicsManager& mGraphicsManager;

    // Input values.
    float mScaleFactor;
    float mDirectionX, mDirectionY;
    // Reference point to evaluate touch distance.
    Location* mRefPoint;
};
#endif
```

6. Create `jni/InputManager.cpp`, starting with the constructor:

```
#include "InputManager.hpp"
#include "Log.hpp"

#include <android_native_app_glue.h>
#include <cmath>

InputManager::InputManager(android_app* pApplication,
        GraphicsManager& pGraphicsManager) :
    mApplication(pApplication), mGraphicsManager(pGraphicsManager),
    mDirectionX(0.0f), mDirectionY(0.0f),
    mRefPoint(NULL) {
}
...
```

7. Write the `start()` method to clear members and compute the scale factor. The scale factor is necessary because, as seen in *Chapter 6, Rendering Graphics with OpenGL ES*, we need to convert screen coordinates provided in input events (which depends on the device) into game coordinates:

```
...
void InputManager::start() {
    Log::info("Starting InputManager.");
    mDirectionX = 0.0f, mDirectionY = 0.0f;
```

```
        mScaleFactor = float(mGraphicsManager.getRenderWidth())
                        / float(mGraphicsManager.getScreenWidth());
}
...
```

8. The effective event processing comes in `onTouchEvent()`. Horizontal and vertical directions are computed according to the distance between the reference point and the touch point. This distance is restricted by `TOUCH_MAX_RANGE` to an arbitrary range of 65 units. Thus, a ship's maximum speed is reached when the reference-to-touch point distance is beyond `TOUCH_MAX_RANGE` pixels.

Touch coordinates are retrieved thanks to `AMotionEvent_getX()` and `AMotionEvent_getY()` when you move your finger. The direction vector is reset to 0 when no more touch is detected:

```
...
bool InputManager::onTouchEvent(AInputEvent* pEvent) {
    static const float TOUCH_MAX_RANGE = 65.0f; // In game units.

    if (mRefPoint != NULL) {
        if (AMotionEvent_getAction(pEvent)
                    == AMOTION_EVENT_ACTION_MOVE) {
            float x = AMotionEvent_getX(pEvent, 0) * mScaleFactor;
            float y = (float(mGraphicsManager.getScreenHeight())
                    - AMotionEvent_getY(pEvent, 0)) * mScaleFactor;
            // Needs a conversion to proper coordinates
            // (origin at bottom/left). Only moveY needs it.
            float moveX = x - mRefPoint->x;
            float moveY = y - mRefPoint->y;
            float moveRange = sqrt((moveX * moveX) + (moveY * moveY));

            if (moveRange > TOUCH_MAX_RANGE) {
                float cropFactor = TOUCH_MAX_RANGE / moveRange;
                moveX *= cropFactor; moveY *= cropFactor;
            }

            mDirectionX = moveX / TOUCH_MAX_RANGE;
            mDirectionY  = moveY / TOUCH_MAX_RANGE;
        } else {
            mDirectionX = 0.0f; mDirectionY = 0.0f;
        }
    }
    return true;
}
```

9. Create a simple component `jni/MoveableBody.hpp`, whose role is to move `PhysicsBody` according to input events:

```
#ifndef _PACKT_MOVEABLEBODY_HPP_
#define _PACKT_MOVEABLEBODY_HPP_

#include "InputManager.hpp"
#include "PhysicsManager.hpp"
#include "Types.hpp"

class MoveableBody {
public:
    MoveableBody(android_app* pApplication,
        InputManager& pInputManager, PhysicsManager& pPhysicsManager);

    PhysicsBody* registerMoveableBody(Location& pLocation,
            int32_t pSizeX, int32_t pSizeY);

    void initialize();
    void update();

private:
    PhysicsManager& mPhysicsManager;
    InputManager& mInputManager;

    PhysicsBody* mBody;
};
#endif
```

10. Implement this component in `jni/MoveableBody.cpp`.

`InputManager` and the body are bound in `registerMoveableBody()`:

```
#include "Log.hpp"
#include "MoveableBody.hpp"

MoveableBody::MoveableBody(android_app* pApplication,
        InputManager& pInputManager, PhysicsManager&
pPhysicsManager) :
    mInputManager(pInputManager),
    mPhysicsManager(pPhysicsManager),
    mBody(NULL) {
}

PhysicsBody* MoveableBody::registerMoveableBody(Location& pLocation,
int32_t pSizeX, int32_t pSizeY) {
    mBody = mPhysicsManager.loadBody(pLocation, pSizeX, pSizeY);
```

```
        mInputManager.setRefPoint(&pLocation);
        return mBody;
    }
    ...
```

11. Initially, the body has no velocity.

Then, each time it is updated, the velocity mirrors the current input state. This velocity is taken in input by `PhysicsManager` created in *Chapter 5, Writing a Fully Native Application*, to update the entity's position:

```
...
void MoveableBody::initialize() {
    mBody->velocityX = 0.0f;
    mBody->velocityY = 0.0f;
}

void MoveableBody::update() {
    static const float MOVE_SPEED = 320.0f;
    mBody->velocityX = mInputManager.getDirectionX() * MOVE_SPEED;
    mBody->velocityY = mInputManager.getDirectionY() * MOVE_SPEED;
}
```

Reference the new `InputManager` and `MoveableComponent` in `jni/DroidBlaster.hpp`:

```
...
#include "EventLoop.hpp"
#include "GraphicsManager.hpp"
#include "InputManager.hpp"
#include "MoveableBody.hpp"
#include "PhysicsManager.hpp"
#include "Resource.hpp"
...

class DroidBlaster : public ActivityHandler {
    ...
private:
    TimeManager      mTimeManager;
    GraphicsManager  mGraphicsManager;
    PhysicsManager   mPhysicsManager;
    SoundManager     mSoundManager;
    InputManager     mInputManager;
    EventLoop mEventLoop;
    ...
    Asteroid mAsteroids;
    Ship mShip;
```

```
    StarField mStarField;
    SpriteBatch mSpriteBatch;
    MoveableBody mMoveableBody;
};
#endif
```

12. Finally, adapt the `jni/DroidBlaster.cpp` constructor to instantiate `InputManager` and `MoveableComponent`.

Append `InputManager` to `EventLoop`, which dispatches input events, at construction time.

The spaceship is the entity being moved. So, pass a reference to its location to the `MoveableBody` component:

```
...
DroidBlaster::DroidBlaster(android_app* pApplication):
    mTimeManager(),
    mGraphicsManager(pApplication),
    mPhysicsManager(mTimeManager, mGraphicsManager),
    mSoundManager(pApplication),
    mInputManager(pApplication, mGraphicsManager),
    mEventLoop(pApplication, *this, mInputManager),
    ...
    mAsteroids(pApplication, mTimeManager, mGraphicsManager,
    mPhysicsManager),
    mShip(pApplication, mGraphicsManager, mSoundManager),
    mStarField(pApplication, mTimeManager, mGraphicsManager,
            STAR_COUNT, mStarTexture),
    mSpriteBatch(mTimeManager, mGraphicsManager),
    mMoveableBody(pApplication, mInputManager, mPhysicsManager) {
    ...
    Sprite* shipGraphics = mSpriteBatch.registerSprite(mShipTexture,
            SHIP_SIZE, SHIP_SIZE);
    shipGraphics->setAnimation(SHIP_FRAME_1, SHIP_FRAME_COUNT,
            SHIP_ANIM_SPEED, true);
    Sound* collisionSound =
            mSoundManager.registerSound(mCollisionSound);
    mMoveableBody.registerMoveableBody(shipGraphics->location,
            SHIP_SIZE, SHIP_SIZE);
    mShip.registerShip(shipGraphics, collisionSound);

    // Creates asteroids.
    ...
}
...
```

13. Initialize and update `MoveableBody` and `InputManager` in the corresponding methods:

```
...
status DroidBlaster::onActivate() {
    Log::info("Activating DroidBlaster");
    if (mGraphicsManager.start() != STATUS_OK) return STATUS_KO;
    if (mSoundManager.start() != STATUS_OK) return STATUS_KO;
    mInputManager.start();

    mSoundManager.playBGM(mBGM);

    mAsteroids.initialize();
    mShip.initialize();
    mMoveableBody.initialize();

    mTimeManager.reset();
    return STATUS_OK;
}

...

status DroidBlaster::onStep() {
    mTimeManager.update();
    mPhysicsManager.update();

    mAsteroids.update();
    mMoveableBody.update();

    return mGraphicsManager.update();
}
...
```

What just happened?

We created a simple example of an input system, based on touch events. The ship flies toward the touch point at a speed dependent on the touch distance. The touch event coordinates are absolute. Their origin is in the upper-left corner of the screen, on the opposite of OpenGL, which is on the lower-left corner. If screen rotation is permitted by an application, then the screen origin remains on the upper-left corner from the user's point of view, whether the device is in portrait or landscape mode.

To implement this new feature, we connected our event loop to the input event queue provided by the `native_app_glue` module. This queue is internally represented as a UNIX pipe, like the activity event queue. Touchscreen events are embedded in an `AInputEvent` structure, which stores other kinds of input events. Input events are handled with the `AInputEvent` and `AMotionEvent` API declared in `android/input.h`. The `AInputEvent` API is necessary to discriminate input event types using `AInputEvent_getType()` and `AInputEvent_getSource()` methods. The `AMotionEvent` API provides methods to handle touch events only.

The touch API is rather rich. Many details can be requested as shown in the following table (non-exhaustively):

Method	Description
`AMotionEvent_getAction()`	To detect whether a finger makes contact with the screen, leaving it, or moving over the surface.
	The result is an integer value composed of the event type (on byte 1, for example, `AMOTION_EVENT_ACTION_DOWN`) and a pointer index (on byte 2, to know which finger the event refers to).
`AMotionEvent_getX()` `AMotionEvent_getY()`	To retrieve touch coordinates on screen, expressed in pixels as a float (sub-pixel values are possible).
`AMotionEvent_getDownTime()` `AMotionEvent_getEventTime()`	To retrieve how much time a finger has been sliding over the screen and when the event was generated in nanoseconds.
`AMotionEvent_getPressure()` `AMotionEvent_getSize()`	To detect the pressure intensity and zone. Values usually range between `0.0` and `1.0` (but may exceed it). Size and pressure are generally closely related. The behavior can vary greatly and be noisy, depending on hardware.

Method	Description
AMotionEvent_getHistorySize() AMotionEvent_getHistoricalX() AMotionEvent_getHistoricalY()	Touch events of type AMOTION_EVENT_ACTION_MOVE can be grouped together for efficiency purposes. These methods give access to these *historical points* that occurred between previous and current events.

Have a look at android/input.h for an exhaustive list of methods.

If you look more deeply at the AMotionEvent API, you will notice that some events have a second parameter pointer_index, which ranges between 0 and the number of active pointers. Indeed, most touchscreens today are multi-touch! Two or more fingers on a screen (if hardware supports it) are translated in Android by two or more pointers. To manipulate them, look at the following table:

Method	Description
AMotionEvent_getPointerCount()	To know how many fingers touch the screen.
AMotionEvent_getPointerId()	To get a pointer unique identifier from a pointer index. This is the only way to track a particular pointer (that is, *finger*) over time, as its index may change when fingers touch or leave the screen.

If you followed the story of the (*now prehistoric!*) Nexus One, then you know that it came out with a hardware defect. Pointers were often getting mixed up, two of them exchanging one of their coordinates. So always be prepared to handle hardware specificities or hardware that behaves incorrectly!

Detecting keyboard, D-Pad, and Trackball events

The most common input device among all is the keyboard. This is true for Android too. An Android keyboard can be physical: in the device front face (like traditional Blackberries) or on a slide-out screen. However, a keyboard is more commonly virtual, that is, emulated on the screen at the cost of a large portion of space taken. In addition to the keyboard itself, every Android device must include a few physical or emulated buttons such as **Menu**, **Home**, and **Tasks**.

A much less common type of input device is the Directional-Pad. A D-Pad is a set of physical buttons to move up, down, left, or right and a specific action/confirmation button. Although they often disappear from recent phones and tablets, D-Pads remain one of the most convenient ways to move across text or UI widgets. D-Pads are often replaced by trackballs. Trackballs behave similarly to a mouse (the one with a ball inside) that would be upside down. Some trackballs are analogical, but others (for example, optical ones) behave as a D-Pad (that is, all or nothing).

To see how they work, let's use these peripherals to move our space ship in `DroidBlaster`. The Android NDK now allows handling all these input peripherals on the native side. So, let's try them!

 The resulting project is provided with this book under the name `DroidBlaster_Part14`.

Time for action – handling keyboard, D-Pad, and trackball events natively

Let's extend our new Input system with more event types:

1. Open `jni/InputHandler.hpp` and add the keyboard and trackball event handlers:

```
#ifndef _PACKT_INPUTHANDLER_HPP_
#define _PACKT_INPUTHANDLER_HPP_

#include <android/input.h>

class InputHandler {
```

```
public:
    virtual ~InputHandler() {};

    virtual bool onTouchEvent(AInputEvent* pEvent) = 0;
    virtual bool onKeyboardEvent(AInputEvent* pEvent) = 0;
    virtual bool onTrackballEvent(AInputEvent* pEvent) = 0;
};
#endif
```

2. Update the method `processInputEvent()` inside the existing file `jni/EventLoop.cpp` to redirect the keyboard and trackball events to `InputHandler`.

Trackballs and touch events are assimilated to motion events and can be discriminated according to their source. On the opposite side, key events are discriminated according to their type. Indeed, there exists two dedicated APIs for `MotionEvents` (the same for trackballs and touch events) and for `KeyEvents` (identical for keyboard, D-Pad, and so on):

```
...
int32_t EventLoop::processInputEvent(AInputEvent* pEvent) {
    if (!mEnabled) return 0;

    int32_t eventType = AInputEvent_getType(pEvent);
    switch (eventType) {
    case AINPUT_EVENT_TYPE_MOTION:
        switch (AInputEvent_getSource(pEvent)) {
        case AINPUT_SOURCE_TOUCHSCREEN:
            return mInputHandler.onTouchEvent(pEvent);
            break;

        case AINPUT_SOURCE_TRACKBALL:
            return mInputHandler.onTrackballEvent(pEvent);
            break;
        }
        break;

    case AINPUT_EVENT_TYPE_KEY:
        return mInputHandler.onKeyboardEvent(pEvent);
        break;
    }
    return 0;
}
...
```

3. Modify the `jni/InputManager.hpp` file to override these new methods:

```
...
class InputManager : public InputHandler {
    ...
protected:
    bool onTouchEvent(AInputEvent* pEvent);
    bool onKeyboardEvent(AInputEvent* pEvent);
    bool onTrackballEvent(AInputEvent* pEvent);

    ...
};
#endif
```

4. In `jni/InputManager.cpp`, process the keyboard events in `onKeyboardEvent()` using:

- ☐ `AKeyEvent_getAction()` to get the event type (that is, pressed or not).
- ☐ `AKeyEvent_getKeyCode()` to get the button identity.

In the following code, when left, right, up, or down buttons are pressed, `InputManager` calculates the direction and saves it into `mDirectionX` and `mDirectionY`. The movement starts when the button is down and stops when it is up.

Return `true` when the key has been consumed and `false` when it has not. Indeed, if a user has pressed, for example, the back button (`AKEYCODE_BACK`) or volume buttons (`AKEYCODE_VOLUME_UP`, `AKEYCODE_VOLUME_DOWN`), then we let the system react appropriately for us:

```
...
bool InputManager::onKeyboardEvent(AInputEvent* pEvent) {
    static const float ORTHOGONAL_MOVE = 1.0f;

    if (AKeyEvent_getAction(pEvent) == AKEY_EVENT_ACTION_DOWN) {
        switch (AKeyEvent_getKeyCode(pEvent)) {
        case AKEYCODE_DPAD_LEFT:
            mDirectionX = -ORTHOGONAL_MOVE;
            return true;
        case AKEYCODE_DPAD_RIGHT:
            mDirectionX = ORTHOGONAL_MOVE;
            return true;
        case AKEYCODE_DPAD_DOWN:
            mDirectionY = -ORTHOGONAL_MOVE;
            return true;
        case AKEYCODE_DPAD_UP:
            mDirectionY = ORTHOGONAL_MOVE;
```

```
                           return true;
                   }
           } else {
               switch (AKeyEvent_getKeyCode(pEvent)) {
               case AKEYCODE_DPAD_LEFT:
               case AKEYCODE_DPAD_RIGHT:
                   mDirectionX = 0.0f;
                   return true;
               case AKEYCODE_DPAD_DOWN:
               case AKEYCODE_DPAD_UP:
                   mDirectionY = 0.0f;
                   return true;
               }
           }
           return false;
   }
   ...
```

5. Similarly, process trackball events in a new method `onTrackballEvent()`. Retrieve the trackball magnitude with `AMotionEvent_getX()` and `AMotionEvent_getY()`. Because some trackballs do not offer a gradated magnitude, the movements are quantified with plain constants. The possible noise is ignored with an arbitrary trigger threshold:

```
...
bool InputManager::onTrackballEvent(AInputEvent* pEvent) {
    static const float ORTHOGONAL_MOVE = 1.0f;
    static const float DIAGONAL_MOVE   = 0.707f;
    static const float THRESHOLD       = (1/100.0f);

     if (AMotionEvent_getAction(pEvent) == AMOTION_EVENT_ACTION_MOVE) {
         float directionX = AMotionEvent_getX(pEvent, 0);
         float directionY = AMotionEvent_getY(pEvent, 0);
         float horizontal, vertical;

         if (directionX < -THRESHOLD) {
             if (directionY < -THRESHOLD) {
                 horizontal = -DIAGONAL_MOVE;
                 vertical   = DIAGONAL_MOVE;
             } else if (directionY > THRESHOLD) {
                 horizontal = -DIAGONAL_MOVE;
                 vertical   = -DIAGONAL_MOVE;
```

```
        } else {
            horizontal = -ORTHOGONAL_MOVE;
            vertical   = 0.0f;
        }
    } else if (directionX > THRESHOLD) {
        if (directionY < -THRESHOLD) {
            horizontal = DIAGONAL_MOVE;
            vertical   = DIAGONAL_MOVE;
        } else if (directionY > THRESHOLD) {
            horizontal = DIAGONAL_MOVE;
            vertical   = -DIAGONAL_MOVE;
        } else {
            horizontal = ORTHOGONAL_MOVE;
            vertical   = 0.0f;
        }
    } else if (directionY < -THRESHOLD) {
        horizontal = 0.0f;
        vertical   = ORTHOGONAL_MOVE;
    } else if (directionY > THRESHOLD) {
        horizontal = 0.0f;
        vertical   = -ORTHOGONAL_MOVE;
    }
```

. . .

6. When using a trackball that way, the ship moves until a "counter-movement" (for example, requesting to go to the right when going left) or action button is pressed (the last else section):

```
    . . .
    // Ends movement if there is a counter movement.
    if ((horizontal < 0.0f) && (mDirectionX > 0.0f)) {
        mDirectionX = 0.0f;
    } else if ((horizontal > 0.0f) && (mDirectionX < 0.0f)) {
        mDirectionX = 0.0f;
    } else {
        mDirectionX = horizontal;
    }

    if ((vertical < 0.0f) && (mDirectionY > 0.0f)) {
        mDirectionY = 0.0f;
    } else if ((vertical > 0.0f) && (mDirectionY < 0.0f)) {
        mDirectionY = 0.0f;
```

```
            } else {
                mDirectionY = vertical;
            }
        } else {
            mDirectionX = 0.0f; mDirectionY = 0.0f;
        }
        return true;
    }
```

What just happened?

We extended our input system to handle the keyboard, D-Pad, and trackball events. D-Pad can be considered as a keyboard extension and is processed the same way. Indeed, D-Pad and keyboard events are transported in the same structure (AInputEvent) and handled by the same API (prefixed with AKeyEvent).

The following table lists the main key event methods:

Method	Description
AKeyEvent_getAction()	Indicates whether the button is down (AKEY_EVENT_ACTION_DOWN) or released (AKEY_EVENT_ACTION_UP). Note that multiple key actions can be emitted in batch (AKEY_EVENT_ACTION_MULTIPLE).
AKeyEvent_getKeyCode()	To retrieve the actual button being pressed (defined in android/keycodes.h), for example, AKEYCODE_DPAD_LEFT for the left button.
AKeyEvent_getFlags()	Key events can be associated with one or more flags that give various kinds of information on the event, such as AKEY_EVENT_LONG_PRESS, AKEY_EVENT_FLAG_SOFT_KEYBOARD for the event originated from an emulated keyboard.
AKeyEvent_getScanCode()	Is similar to a key code except that this is the raw key ID, dependent and different from device to device.
AKeyEvent_getMetaState()	Meta states are flags that indicate whether some modifier keys, such as Alt or Shift, are pressed simultaneously (for example, AMETA_SHIFT_ON, AMETA_NONE, and so on).
AKeyEvent_getRepeatCount()	Indicates how many times the button event occurred, usually when you leave the button down.
AKeyEvent_getDownTime()	To know when a button was pressed.

Although some of them (especially optical ones) behave like a D-Pad, trackballs do not use the same API. Actually, trackballs are handled through the `AMotionEvent` API (such as touch events). Of course, some information provided for touch events is not always available on trackballs. The most important functions to look at are as follows:

`AMotionEvent_getAction()`	To know whether an event represents a move action (as opposed to a press action).

`AMotionEvent_getX()`
 	
`AMotionEvent_getY()`
	To get trackball movement.

`AKeyEvent_getDownTime()`	To know whether the trackball is pressed (such as the D-Pad action button). Currently, most trackballs use an all-or-nothing pressure to indicate the press event.

A tricky point to keep in mind when dealing with trackballs is that no event is generated to indicate that the trackball is not moving. Moreover, trackball events are generated as a "burst", which makes it harder to detect when the movement is finished. There is no easy way to handle this, except using a manual timer and checking regularly that no event has happened for a sufficient amount of time.

Never expect peripherals to behave exactly the same on all phones. Trackballs are a very good example; they can either indicate a direction like an analogical pad or a straight direction like a D-Pad (for example, optical trackballs). There is currently no way to differentiate device characteristics from the available APIs. The only solutions are to either calibrate the device or configure it at runtime or save a kind of device database.

Probing device sensors

Handling input devices is essential to any application, but probing sensors is important for the smartest one! The most spread sensor among Android game applications is the accelerometer.

An accelerometer, as its name suggests, measures the linear acceleration applied to a device. When moving a device up, down, left, or right, the accelerometer gets excited and indicates an acceleration vector in 3D space. Vector is expressed in relation to the screen's default orientation. The coordinate system is relative to the device's natural orientation:

- ◆ X axis points to the right
- ◆ Y points up
- ◆ Z points from back to front

Axes become inverted if the device is rotated (for example, Y points left if the device is rotated 90 degrees clockwise).

A very interesting feature of accelerometers is that they undergo a constant acceleration: gravity, around 9.8m/s2 on earth. For example, when lying flat on a table, acceleration vector indicates -9.8 on the Z-axis. When straight, it indicates the same value on Y axis. So assuming the device position is fixed, device orientation on two axes in space can be deduced from the gravity acceleration vector. A magnetometer is still required to get full device orientation in 3D space.

> Remember that accelerometers work with linear acceleration. They allow detecting the translation when the device is not rotating and partial orientation when the device is fixed. However, both movements cannot be combined without a magnetometer and/or gyroscope.

So we can use the device orientation deduced from the accelerometer to compute a direction. Let's now see how to apply this process in DroidBlaster.

> The resulting project is provided with this book under the name DroidBlaster_Part15.

Time for action – handling accelerometer events

Let's handle accelerometer events in DroidBlaster:

1. Open jni/InputHandler.hpp and add a new method onAccelerometerEvent(). Include the android/sensor.h official header for sensors:

    ```
    #ifndef _PACKT_INPUTHANDLER_HPP_
    #define _PACKT_INPUTHANDLER_HPP_

    #include <android/input.h>
    #include <android/sensor.h>

    class InputHandler {
    public:
        virtual ~InputHandler() {};

        virtual bool onTouchEvent(AInputEvent* pEvent) = 0;
        virtual bool onKeyboardEvent(AInputEvent* pEvent) = 0;
    ```

```
        virtual bool onTrackballEvent(AInputEvent* pEvent) = 0;
        virtual bool onAccelerometerEvent(ASensorEvent* pEvent) = 0;
    };
    #endif
```

2. Create new methods in `jni/EventLoop.hpp`:

- ❑ `activateAccelerometer()` and `deactivateAccelerometer()` to enable/disable the accelerometer sensor when the activity starts and stops.

- ❑ `processSensorEvent()` retrieves and dispatches sensor events.

- ❑ The callback `callback_input()` static method is bound to the Looper.

Also, define the following members:

- ❑ `mSensorManager`, of type `ASensorManager`, is the main "object" to interact with sensors.

- ❑ `mSensorEventQueue` is `ASensorEventQueue`, which is a structure defined by the Sensor API to retrieve occurring events.

- ❑ `mSensorPollSource` is `android_poll_source` defined in the Native Glue. This structure describes how to bind the native thread Looper to the sensor callback.

- ❑ `mAccelerometer`, declared as an `ASensor` structure, represents the sensor used:

```
#ifndef _PACKT_EVENTLOOP_HPP_
#define _PACKT_EVENTLOOP_HPP_

#include "ActivityHandler.hpp"
#include "InputHandler.hpp"

#include <android_native_app_glue.h>

class EventLoop {
    ...
private:
    void activate();
    void deactivate();
    void activateAccelerometer();
    void deactivateAccelerometer();

    void processAppEvent(int32_t pCommand);
    int32_t processInputEvent(AInputEvent* pEvent);
```

```cpp
        void processSensorEvent();

        static void callback_appEvent(android_app* pApplication,
                int32_t pCommand);
        static int32_t callback_input(android_app* pApplication,
                AInputEvent* pEvent);
        static void callback_sensor(android_app* pApplication,
                android_poll_source* pSource);


        ...
        InputHandler& mInputHandler;

        ASensorManager* mSensorManager;
        ASensorEventQueue* mSensorEventQueue;
        android_poll_source mSensorPollSource;
        const ASensor* mAccelerometer;
    };
    #endif
```

3. Update constructor initialization list in `jni/EventLoop.cpp`:

```cpp
#include "EventLoop.hpp"
#include "Log.hpp"

EventLoop::EventLoop(android_app* pApplication,
    ActivityHandler& pActivityHandler, InputHandler& pInputHandler):
        mApplication(pApplication),
        mActivityHandler(pActivityHandler),
        mEnabled(false), mQuit(false),
        mInputHandler(pInputHandler),
        mSensorPollSource(), mSensorManager(NULL),
        mSensorEventQueue(NULL), mAccelerometer(NULL) {
    mApplication->userData = this;
    mApplication->onAppCmd = callback_appEvent;
    mApplication->onInputEvent = callback_input;
}
...
```

4. Create the sensor event queue, through which all `sensor` events are notified.

Bind it to `callback_sensor()`. Note here that we use the `LOOPER_ID_USER` constant provided by the Native App Glue to attach a user-defined queue.

Then, call `activateAccelerometer()` to initialize the accelerometer sensor:

```cpp
...
void EventLoop::activate() {
    if ((!mEnabled) && (mApplication->window != NULL)) {
        mSensorPollSource.id = LOOPER_ID_USER;
```

```
        mSensorPollSource.app = mApplication;
        mSensorPollSource.process = callback_sensor;
        mSensorManager = ASensorManager_getInstance();
        if (mSensorManager != NULL) {
            mSensorEventQueue = ASensorManager_createEventQueue(
                    mSensorManager, mApplication->looper,
                    LOOPER_ID_USER, NULL, &mSensorPollSource);
            if (mSensorEventQueue == NULL) goto ERROR;
        }
        activateAccelerometer();

        mQuit = false; mEnabled = true;
        if (mActivityHandler.onActivate() != STATUS_OK) {
            goto ERROR;
        }
    }
    return;

ERROR:
    mQuit = true;
    deactivate();
    ANativeActivity_finish(mApplication->activity);
}
...
```

5. When an activity is disabled or terminated, disable the running accelerometer to avoid consuming battery needlessly.

   Then, destroy the sensor event queue:

```
...
void EventLoop::deactivate() {
    if (mEnabled) {
        deactivateAccelerometer();
        if (mSensorEventQueue != NULL) {
            ASensorManager_destroyEventQueue(mSensorManager,
                    mSensorEventQueue);
            mSensorEventQueue = NULL;
        }
        mSensorManager = NULL;

        mActivityHandler.onDeactivate();
        mEnabled = false;
    }
}
...
```

6. `callback_sensor()` is triggered when event loop is polled. It dispatches events to `processSensorEvent()` on the `EventLoop` instance. We only care about `ASENSOR_TYPE_ACCELEROMETER` events:

```
...
void EventLoop::callback_sensor(android_app* pApplication,
    android_poll_source* pSource) {
    EventLoop& eventLoop = *(EventLoop*) pApplication->userData;
    eventLoop.processSensorEvent();
}

void EventLoop::processSensorEvent() {
    ASensorEvent event;
    if (!mEnabled) return;

    while (ASensorEventQueue_getEvents(mSensorEventQueue,
            &event, 1) > 0) {
        switch (event.type) {
        case ASENSOR_TYPE_ACCELEROMETER:
            mInputHandler.onAccelerometerEvent(&event);
            break;
        }
    }
}
...
```

7. Activate the sensor in `activateAccelerometer()` in three main steps:

- ❑ Get a sensor of a specific type with `AsensorManager_getDefaultSensor()`.

- ❑ Then, enable it with `ASensorEventQueue_enableSensor()` so that the sensor event queue gets filled with related events.

- ❑ Set the desired event rate with `ASensorEventQueue_setEventRate()`. For a game, we typically want measures close to real time. The minimum delay can be queried with `ASensor_getMinDelay()` (setting it to a lower value might result in a failure).

Obviously, we should perform this setup only when the sensor event queue is ready:

```
...
void EventLoop::activateAccelerometer() {
    mAccelerometer = ASensorManager_getDefaultSensor(
            mSensorManager, ASENSOR_TYPE_ACCELEROMETER);
    if (mAccelerometer != NULL) {
        if (ASensorEventQueue_enableSensor(
                mSensorEventQueue, mAccelerometer) < 0) {
```

```
            Log::error("Could not enable accelerometer");
            return;
        }

        int32_t minDelay = ASensor_getMinDelay(mAccelerometer);
        if (ASensorEventQueue_setEventRate(mSensorEventQueue,
                mAccelerometer, minDelay) < 0) {
            Log::error("Could not set accelerometer rate");
        }
    } else {
        Log::error("No accelerometer found");
    }
}
...
```

8. Sensor deactivation is easier and only requires a call to the method
`AsensorEventQueue_disableSensor()`:

```
...
void EventLoop::deactivateAccelerometer() {
    if (mAccelerometer != NULL) {
        if (ASensorEventQueue_disableSensor(mSensorEventQueue,
                mAccelerometer) < 0) {
            Log::error("Error while deactivating sensor.");
        }
        mAccelerometer = NULL;
    }
}
```

What just happened?

We created an event queue to listen to sensor events. Events are wrapped in an
`ASensorEvent` structure, defined in `android/sensor.h`. This structure provides
the following:

- Sensor event origin, that is, which sensor produced this event.

- Sensor event occurrence time.

- Sensor output value. This value is stored in a union structure, that is, you
  can use either one of the inside structures (here, we are interested in the
  `acceleration` vector).

```
typedef struct ASensorEvent {
    int32_t version;
    int32_t sensor;
    int32_t type;
```

```
        int32_t reserved0;
        int64_t timestamp;
        union {
            float             data[16];
            ASensorVector     vector;
            ASensorVector     acceleration;
            ASensorVector     magnetic;
            float             temperature;
            float             distance;
            float             light;
            float             pressure;
        };
        int32_t reserved1[4];
    } ASensorEvent;
```

The same `ASensorEvent` structure is used for any Android sensor. In the case of the accelerometer, we retrieve a vector with three coordinates x, y, and z, one for each axis:

```
typedef struct ASensorVector {
    union {
        float v[3];
        struct {
            float x;
            float y;
            float z;
        };
        struct {
            float azimuth;
            float pitch;
            float roll;
        };
    };
    int8_t status;
    uint8_t reserved[3];
} ASensorVector;
```

In our example, the accelerometer is set up with the lowest event rate possible, which may vary between devices. It is important to note that the sensor event rate has a direct impact on battery saving! So, use a rate that is sufficient for your application. The `ASensor` API offers some methods to query the available sensors and their capabilities, such as `ASensor_getName()`, `ASensor_getVendor()`, `ASensor_getMinDelay()`, and so on.

Now that we can retrieve sensor events, let's use them to compute a ship's direction.

Time for action – turning an Android device into a Joypad

Let's find the device orientation and properly determine the direction.

1. Write a new file jni/Configuration.hpp to help us get device information, and more specifically device rotation (defined as screen_rot).

Declare findRotation() to discover the device orientation with the help of JNI:

```
#ifndef _PACKT_CONFIGURATION_HPP_
#define _PACKT_CONFIGURATION_HPP_

#include "Types.hpp"

#include <android_native_app_glue.h>
#include <jni.h>

typedef int32_t screen_rot;

const screen_rot ROTATION_0   = 0;
const screen_rot ROTATION_90  = 1;
const screen_rot ROTATION_180 = 2;
const screen_rot ROTATION_270 = 3;

class Configuration {
public:
    Configuration(android_app* pApplication);

    screen_rot getRotation() { return mRotation; };

private:
    void findRotation(JNIEnv* pEnv);

    android_app* mApplication;
    screen_rot mRotation;
};
#endif
```

2. Retrieve configuration details in `jni/Configuration.cpp`.

First, in the constructor, use the `AConfiguration` API to dump configuration properties, such as the current language, country, screen size, screen orientation. This information may be interesting, but is not sufficient to properly analyze accelerometer events:

```cpp
#include "Configuration.hpp"
#include "Log.hpp"

#include <stdlib.h>

Configuration::Configuration(android_app* pApplication) :
    mApplication(pApplication),
    mRotation(0) {
    AConfiguration* configuration = AConfiguration_new();
    if (configuration == NULL) return;

    int32_t result;
    char i18NBuffer[] = "__";
    static const char* orientation[] = {
        "Unknown", "Portrait", "Landscape", "Square"
    };
    static const char* screenSize[] = {
        "Unknown", "Small", "Normal", "Large", "X-Large"
    };
    static const char* screenLong[] = {
        "Unknown", "No", "Yes"
    };

    // Dumps current configuration.
    AConfiguration_fromAssetManager(configuration,
        mApplication->activity->assetManager);
    result = AConfiguration_getSdkVersion(configuration);
    Log::info("SDK Version : %d", result);
    AConfiguration_getLanguage(configuration, i18NBuffer);
    Log::info("Language    : %s", i18NBuffer);
    AConfiguration_getCountry(configuration, i18NBuffer);
    Log::info("Country     : %s", i18NBuffer);
    result = AConfiguration_getOrientation(configuration);
    Log::info("Orientation : %s (%d)", orientation[result], result);
    result = AConfiguration_getDensity(configuration);
    Log::info("Density     : %d dpi", result);
    result = AConfiguration_getScreenSize(configuration);
```

```
Log::info("Screen Size : %s (%d)", screenSize[result], result);
result = AConfiguration_getScreenLong(configuration);
Log::info("Long Screen : %s (%d)", screenLong[result], result);
AConfiguration_delete(configuration);
```
. . .

Then, attach the current native thread to the Android VM.

 If you have carefully read *Chapter 4, Calling Java Back from Native Code*, you know that this step is necessary to get access to the JNIEnv object (which is thread-specific). The JavaVM itself can be retrieved from the android_app structure.

3. After that, call findRotation() to retrieve the current device rotation.

Finally, we can detach the thread from Dalvik as we will not use JNI any more. Remember that an attached thread should always be detached before terminating the application:

. . .

```
    JavaVM* javaVM = mApplication->activity->vm;
    JavaVMAttachArgs javaVMAttachArgs;
    javaVMAttachArgs.version = JNI_VERSION_1_6;
    javaVMAttachArgs.name = "NativeThread";
    javaVMAttachArgs.group = NULL;
    JNIEnv* env;
    if (javaVM->AttachCurrentThread(&env,
                    &javaVMAttachArgs) != JNI_OK) {
        Log::error("JNI error while attaching the VM");
        return;
    }
    // Finds screen rotation and get-rid of JNI.
    findRotation(env);
    mApplication->activity->vm->DetachCurrentThread();
}
```
. . .

4. Implement findRotation(), which basically executes the following Java code through JNI:

```
WindowManager mgr = (InputMethodManager)
myActivity.getSystemService(Context.WINDOW_SERVICE);
int rotation = mgr.getDefaultDisplay().getRotation();
```

Obviously, this is slightly more complex to write in JNI.

- ❏ First, retrieve JNI classes, then methods, and finally, fields
- ❏ Then, perform the JNI calls
- ❏ Finally, release the allocated JNI references

The following code has been voluntarily simplified to avoid extra checks (that is, `FindClass()` and `GetMethodID()` return value and exception checks for each method call):

```
...
void Configuration::findRotation(JNIEnv* pEnv) {
    jobject WINDOW_SERVICE, windowManager, display;
    jclass ClassActivity, ClassContext;
    jclass ClassWindowManager, ClassDisplay;
    jmethodID MethodGetSystemService;
    jmethodID MethodGetDefaultDisplay;
    jmethodID MethodGetRotation;
    jfieldID FieldWINDOW_SERVICE;

    jobject activity = mApplication->activity->clazz;

    // Classes.
    ClassActivity = pEnv->GetObjectClass(activity);
    ClassContext = pEnv->FindClass("android/content/Context");
    ClassWindowManager = pEnv->FindClass(
        "android/view/WindowManager");
    ClassDisplay = pEnv->FindClass("android/view/Display");

    // Methods.
    MethodGetSystemService = pEnv->GetMethodID(ClassActivity,
        "getSystemService",
        "(Ljava/lang/String;)Ljava/lang/Object;");
    MethodGetDefaultDisplay = pEnv->GetMethodID(
        ClassWindowManager, "getDefaultDisplay",
        "()Landroid/view/Display;");
    MethodGetRotation = pEnv->GetMethodID(ClassDisplay,
        "getRotation", "()I");

    // Fields.
    FieldWINDOW_SERVICE = pEnv->GetStaticFieldID(
      ClassContext, "WINDOW_SERVICE", "Ljava/lang/String;");

    // Retrieves Context.WINDOW_SERVICE.
```

```
WINDOW_SERVICE = pEnv->GetStaticObjectField(ClassContext,
    FieldWINDOW_SERVICE);
// Runs getSystemService(WINDOW_SERVICE).
windowManager = pEnv->CallObjectMethod(activity,
    MethodGetSystemService, WINDOW_SERVICE);
// Runs getDefaultDisplay().getRotation().
display = pEnv->CallObjectMethod(windowManager,
    MethodGetDefaultDisplay);
mRotation = pEnv->CallIntMethod(display, MethodGetRotation);

pEnv->DeleteLocalRef(ClassActivity);
pEnv->DeleteLocalRef(ClassContext);
pEnv->DeleteLocalRef(ClassWindowManager);
pEnv->DeleteLocalRef(ClassDisplay);
}
```

5. Manage the new accelerometer sensor in `jni/InputManager.hpp`.

Accelerometer axes are transformed in `toScreenCoord()`.

This transformation implies that we keep track of device rotation:

```
...
#include "Configuration.hpp"
#include "GraphicsManager.hpp"
#include "InputHandler.hpp"
...
class InputManager : public InputHandler {
    ...
protected:
    bool onTouchEvent(AInputEvent* pEvent);
    bool onKeyboardEvent(AInputEvent* pEvent);
    bool onTrackballEvent(AInputEvent* pEvent);
    bool onAccelerometerEvent(ASensorEvent* pEvent);
    void toScreenCoord(screen_rot pRotation,
            ASensorVector* pCanonical, ASensorVector* pScreen);

private:
    ...
    float mScaleFactor;
    float mDirectionX, mDirectionY;
     // Reference point to evaluate touch distance.
     Location* mRefPoint;
    screen_rot mRotation;
};
#endif
```

6. In `jni/InputManager.hpp`, read the current screen rotation settings with the help of the new `Configuration` class. Since `DroidBlaster` forces portrait mode, we can store rotation once and for all:

```
...
InputManager::InputManager(android_app* pApplication,
        GraphicsManager& pGraphicsManager) :
        mApplication(pApplication), mGraphicsManager(pGraphicsManager),
        mDirectionX(0.0f), mDirectionY(0.0f),
        mRefPoint(NULL) {
    Configuration configuration(pApplication);
    mRotation = configuration.getRotation();
}
...
```

7. Let's compute a direction from the accelerometer sensor values.

First, convert accelerometer values from canonical to screen coordinates to handle portrait and landscape devices.

Then, compute a direction from the captured accelerometer values. In the following code, the `X` and `Z` axis express the roll and pitch, respectively. Check for both axes whether the device is in a neutral orientation (that is, `CENTER_X` and `CENTER_Z`) or is sloping (`MIN_X`, `MIN_Z`, `MAX_X`, and `MAX_Z`). Note that Z values need to be inverted for our needs:

```
...
bool InputManager::onAccelerometerEvent(ASensorEvent* pEvent) {
    static const float GRAVITY =  ASENSOR_STANDARD_GRAVITY / 2.0f;
    static const float MIN_X = -1.0f; static const float MAX_X = 1.0f;
    static const float MIN_Z =  0.0f; static const float MAX_Z = 2.0f;
    static const float CENTER_X = (MAX_X + MIN_X) / 2.0f;
    static const float CENTER_Z = (MAX_Z + MIN_Z) / 2.0f;

    // Converts from canonical to screen coordinates.
    ASensorVector vector;
    toScreenCoord(mRotation, &pEvent->vector, &vector);

    // Roll tilt.
    float rawHorizontal = pEvent->vector.x / GRAVITY;
    if (rawHorizontal > MAX_X) {
        rawHorizontal = MAX_X;
    } else if (rawHorizontal < MIN_X) {
        rawHorizontal = MIN_X;
    }
```

```
    mDirectionX = CENTER_X - rawHorizontal;

    // Pitch tilt. Final value needs to be inverted.
    float rawVertical = pEvent->vector.z / GRAVITY;
    if (rawVertical > MAX_Z) {
        rawVertical = MAX_Z;
    } else if (rawVertical < MIN_Z) {
        rawVertical = MIN_Z;
    }
    mDirectionY = rawVertical - CENTER_Z;
    return true;
}
...
```

8. In the `toScreenCoord()` helper, swap or invert accelerometer axes depending on screen rotation, so that X and Z axes point toward the same direction, whatever device you use when playing `DroidBlaster` in portrait mode:

```
...
void InputManager::toScreenCoord(screen_rot pRotation,
    ASensorVector* pCanonical, ASensorVector* pScreen) {
    struct AxisSwap {
        int8_t negX; int8_t negY;
        int8_t xSrc; int8_t ySrc;
    };
    static const AxisSwap axisSwaps[] = {
        {  1, -1,  0,  1},  // ROTATION_0
        { -1, -1,  1,  0},  // ROTATION_90
        { -1,  1,  0,  1},  // ROTATION_180
        {  1,  1,  1,  0}}; // ROTATION_270
    const AxisSwap& swap = axisSwaps[pRotation];

    pScreen->v[0] = swap.negX * pCanonical->v[swap.xSrc];
    pScreen->v[1] = swap.negY * pCanonical->v[swap.ySrc];
    pScreen->v[2] = pCanonical->v[2];
}
```

What just happened?

The accelerometer is now a Joypad! Android devices can be naturally portrait-oriented (mainly smartphones and smaller tablets) or landscape-oriented (mainly tablets). This has an impact on applications, which receive accelerometer events. Axes are not aligned the same way between these types of devices and depending on the way they are rotated.

Indeed, the screen can be oriented in four different ways: 0, 90, 180, and 270 degrees. 0 degree is the device's natural orientation. Accelerometer X axis always points right, Y points up, and Z points towards the front. On a phone, Y points up in portrait mode, whereas on most tables, Y points up in landscape mode. When the device is oriented at 90 degrees, the axes orientation obviously changes (X points up, and so on). This situation may also happen with a tablet (where 0 degree corresponds to landscape mode) that is used in portrait mode.

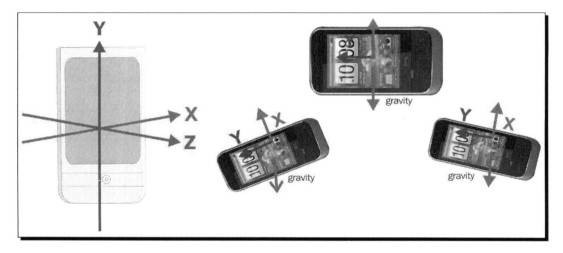

There is sadly no way to get device rotation relative to a screen's natural orientation with native APIs. Thus, we need to rely on JNI to get accurate device rotation. Then, we can easily deduce a direction vector from this like done in `onAccelerometerEvent()`.

More on sensors

Each Android sensor has a unique identifier, defined in `android/sensor.h`. These identifiers are the same across all Android devices:

- `ASENSOR_TYPE_ACCELEROMETER`
- `ASENSOR_TYPE_MAGNETIC_FIELD`
- `ASENSOR_TYPE_GYRISCOPE`
- `ASENSOR_TYPE_LIGHT`
- `ASENSOR_TYPE_PROXIMITY`

Additional sensors may exist and be available, even if they are not named in the `android/sensor.h` header. On Gingerbread, we have the same case with:

- Gravity sensor (identifier 9)
- Linear acceleration sensor (identifier 10)
- Rotation vector (identifier 11).

The rotation vector sensor, successor of the now deprecated orientation vector, is essential in the `Augmented Reality` application. It gives you device orientation in 3D space. Combined with the GPS, it allows locating any object through the eye of your device. The rotation sensor provides a data vector, which can be translated to an OpenGL view matrix, thanks to the `android.hardware.SensorManager` class (see its source code). That way, you can directly materialize device orientation into screen content, linking together real and virtual life.

Summary

In this chapter, we covered multiple ways to interact with Android from native code. More precisely, we discovered how to attach an input queue to the `Native App Glue` event loop. Then, we handled touch events and processed key events from keyboards and D-Pads or motion events from trackballs. Finally, we turned the accelerometer into a Joypad.

Because of Android fragmentation, expect specificities in an input device's behavior and be prepared to tweak your code. We have already been far in the capabilities of Android NDK in terms of application structure, graphics, sound, input, and sensors. However, reinventing the wheel is not a solution!

In the next chapter, we will unleash the real power of the NDK by porting existing C/C++ libraries to Android.

9

Porting Existing Libraries to Android

There are two main reasons why one would be interested in the Android NDK: first, for performance, and, second, for portability. In the previous chapters, we saw how to access the main native Android APIs from native code for efficiency purposes. In this chapter, we will bring the whole C/C++ ecosystem to Android, well, at least discovering the path, as decades of C/C++ development would be difficult to fit the limited memory of mobile devices anyway! Indeed, C and C++ are still some of the most widely used programming languages nowadays.

*In previous NDK releases, portability was limited due to the partial support of C++, especially **Exceptions** and **Run-Time Type** Information (**RTTI**, a basic C++ reflection mechanism to get data types at runtime such as* instanceof *in Java). Any library requiring them could not be ported without modifying their code or installing a custom NDK (the **Crystax NDK**, rebuilt by the community from official sources, and available at* http://www.crystax.net/*). Hopefully, many of these restrictions have been lifted since (except wide character support).*

Although not necessarily difficult, porting an existing library is not a trivial process. A few APIs might be missed (despite good POSIX support), some #define directives have to be tweaked, some dependencies have to be ported, as well as dependencies of dependencies. Some libraries will be easy to port, while some other will involve more effort.

In this chapter, in order to port existing code to Android, we are going to learn how to do the following code:

- Activate the **Standard Template Library (STL)**
- Port the **Box2D** physics engine
- Prebuild and use the **Boost** framework
- Discover more in-depth how to write NDK module **Makefiles**

By the end of this chapter, you should understand the native building process and know how to use Makefiles appropriately.

Activating the Standard Template Library

The Standard Template Library is a normalized library of containers, iterators, algorithms, and helper classes to ease most common programming operations, such as dynamic arrays, associative arrays, strings, sorting, and so on. This library gained recognition among developers over the years and is widely spread. Developing in C++ without the STL is like coding with one hand behind your back!

In this first part, let's embed GNU STL in DroidBlaster to ease collection management.

 Resulting project is provided with this book under the name `DroidBlaster_Part16`.

Time for action – activating GNU STL in DroidBlaster

Let's activate and make use of the STL in DroidBlaster. Edit the `jni/Application.mk` file beside `jni/Android.mk` and write the following content. That's it! Your application is now STL-enabled, thanks to this single line:

```
APP_ABI := armeabi armeabi-v7a x86
APP_STL := gnustl_static
```

What just happened?

In only a single line of code, we have activated GNU STL in the `Application.mk` file! This STL implementation, selected through the `APP_STL` variable, replaces the default NDK C/C++ runtime. The following three STL implementations are currently supported:

- **GNU STL** (more commonly **libstdc++**), the official GCC STL: This is often the preferred choice when using the STL on an NDK project. Exceptions and RTTI are supported.

♦ **STLport** (a multiplatform STL): This implementation is not actively maintained and lacks some features. Choose it as a last resort. Exceptions and RTTI are supported.

♦ **Libc++**: This is part of LLVM (the technology behind the Clang compiler) and aims to provide a functional C++ 11 runtime. Note that this library is now becoming the default STL on OS-X and may gain popularity in the future. Exceptions and RTTI are supported. Libc++ support is still incomplete and experimental. Libc++ is often chosen in conjunction with the Clang compiler (read more about this in the *Mastering module Makefiles* section).

Android also provides two other C++ runtimes:

♦ **System**: This is the default NDK runtime when no STL implementation is activated. Its code name is **Bionic** and it provides a minimalist set of headers (cstdint, cstdio, cstring, and so on). Bionic does not provide STL features, as well as exceptions and **run-time type information** (**RTTI**). For more details about its limitations, have a look at $ANDROID_NDK/docs/system/libc/OVERVIEW.html.

♦ **Gabi**: This is similar to the System runtime, except that it supports exceptions and RTTI.

We will see in the part dedicated to **Boost** in this chapter how to enable exceptions and RTTI during compilation.

Each runtime is linkable either statically or dynamically (at the notable exception of the default system C/C++ runtime). Dynamically loaded runtimes are posts fixed with _shared, and statically loaded ones with _static. The full list of runtime identifiers you can pass to APP_STL is as follows:

♦ system

♦ gabi++_static and gabi++_shared

♦ stlport_static and stlport_shared

♦ gnustl_static and gnustl_shared

♦ c++_static and c++_shared

Remember that shared libraries need to be loaded manually at runtime. If you forget to load a shared library, an error is raised at runtime as soon as dependent libraries modules are loaded. As the compiler cannot predict in advance which functions are going to be called, libraries are loaded entirely in memory, even if most of their contents remain unused.

On the other hand, static libraries are in fact loaded with dependent libraries. Indeed, static libraries do not really exist as such at runtime. Their content is copied into dependent libraries at compile time when they are linked. Since the linker knows precisely which part of the library gets called from the embedding module, it can strip its code and keep only what is needed.

 Stripping is the process of discarding unnecessary symbols from binaries. This helps reducing (potentially a lot!) binary size after linkage. This can be somewhat compared to the Proguard shrinking post processing in Java.

However, linking results in binary code duplication if a static library is included more than once. Such a situation can potentially lead to a waste of memory or, more worryingly, issues related to, for example, global variable duplication. However, static C++ constructors in shared libraries are called only once.

 Remember that you should avoid using static libraries that are included more than once in a project unless you know what you are doing.

Another point to consider is that Java applications can load shared libraries only, which can themselves be linked against either shared or static libraries. For example, the main library of `NativeActivity` is a shared library, specified through the `android.app.lib_name` manifest property. Shared libraries referenced from another library must be loaded manually before. The NDK does not do it itself.

Shared libraries can be loaded easily, using `System.loadLibrary()` in a JNI applications, but `NativeActivity` are "transparent" activities. So, if you decide to use shared libraries, the only solution is to write your own Java activity, inheriting from `NativeActivity` and invoking the appropriate `loadLibrary()` directives. For instance, below is what DroidBlaster activity would look like, if we were using `gnustl_shared` instead:

```java
package com.packtpub.DroidBlaster

import android.app.NativeActivity

public class MyNativeActivity extends NativeActivity {
    static {
        System.loadLibrary("gnustl_shared");
        System.loadLibrary("DroidBlaster");
    }
}
```

If you prefer to load your native library directly from native code, you can use the system call `dlopen()`, which is also provided by the NDK.

Now that the STL is enabled, let's employ it in DroidBlaster.

Time for action – read files with STL stream

Let's use the STL to read resources from the SD card instead of the application asset directory, as shown in the following steps:

1. Obviously, enabling the STL is useless if we do not actively use it in our code. Let's take advantage of this opportunity to switch from asset files to external files (on a `sdcard` or internal memory).

Open the existing file, `jni/Resource.hpp`, and do the following:

- ❑ Include the `fstream` and `string` STL headers.
- ❑ Use a `std::string` object for the file name and replace the Asset management members with an `std::ifstream` object (that is, an input file stream).
- ❑ Change the `getPath()` method to return a C string from the new `string` member.
- ❑ Remove the `descriptor()` method and the `ResourceDescriptor` class (descriptors work with the Asset API only), as shown in the following:

```
#ifndef _PACKT_RESOURCE_HPP_
#define _PACKT_RESOURCE_HPP_

#include "Types.hpp"

#include <android_native_app_glue.h>
#include <fstream>
#include <string>

...
class Resource {
public:
    Resource(android_app* pApplication, const char* pPath);

    const char* getPath() { return mPath.c_str(); };

    status open();
```

```
        void close();
        status read(void* pBuffer, size_t pCount);

        off_t getLength();

        bool operator==(const Resource& pOther);

    private:
        std::string mPath;
        std::ifstream mInputStream;
    };
    #endif
```

2. Open the corresponding implementation file `jni/Resource.cpp`. Replace the previous implementation, based on the asset management API with STL streams and strings. Files will be opened in binary mode, as follows:

```
#include "Resource.hpp"

#include <sys/stat.h>

Resource::Resource(android_app* pApplication, const char* pPath) :
    mPath(std::string("/sdcard/") + pPath),
    mInputStream(){
}

status Resource::open() {
    mInputStream.open(mPath.c_str(), std::ios::in | std::ios::binary);
    return mInputStream ? STATUS_OK : STATUS_KO;
}

void Resource::close() {
    mInputStream.close();
}

status Resource::read(void* pBuffer, size_t pCount) {
    mInputStream.read((char*)pBuffer, pCount);
    return (!mInputStream.fail()) ? STATUS_OK : STATUS_KO;
}
...
```

3. To read the file length, we can use the `stat()` POSIX primitive from the `sys/stat.h` header:

```
...
off_t Resource::getLength() {
    struct stat filestatus;
```

```
        if (stat(mPath.c_str(), &filestatus) >= 0) {
            return filestatus.st_size;
        } else {
            return -1;
        }
    }
...
```

4. Finally, we can use STL string comparison operator to compare two Resource objects:

```
...
bool Resource::operator==(const Resource& pOther) {
    return mPath == pOther.mPath;
}
```

5. These changes to the reading system should be almost transparent, except for the BGM, whose content was played through an asset file descriptor.

Now, we need to provide a real file. So, in jni/SoundService.cpp, change the data source by replacing the SLDataLocator_AndroidFD structure with SLDataLocation_URI, as shown in the following:

```
#include "Log.hpp"
#include "Resource.hpp"
#include "SoundService.hpp"

#include <string>
...
status SoundManager::playBGM(Resource& pResource) {
    SLresult result;
    Log::info("Opening BGM %s", pResource.getPath());

    // Set-up BGM audio source.
    SLDataLocator_URI dataLocatorIn;
    std::string path = pResource.getPath();
    dataLocatorIn.locatorType = SL_DATALOCATOR_URI;
    dataLocatorIn.URI = (SLchar*) path.c_str();

    SLDataFormat_MIME dataFormat;
    dataFormat.formatType    = SL_DATAFORMAT_MIME;
    ...
}
...
```

6. In the `AndroidManifest.xml` file, add the permission to read SD card files as follows:

```
<?xml version="1.0" encoding="utf-8"?>
<manifest xmlns:android="http://schemas.android.com/apk/res/android"
    package="com.packtpub.droidblaster2d" android:versionCode="1"
    android:versionName="1.0">

    <uses-permission
        android:name="android.permission.READ_EXTERNAL_STORAGE" />

    ...
</manifest>
```

Copy all asset resources from the asset directory to your device SD card (or internal memory, depending on your device) in `/sdcard/droidblaster`.

What just happened?

We have seen how to access binary files located on the SD card with STL streams. We have also switched the OpenSL ES player from a file descriptor to a file name locator. The file name itself is created here from an STL string. STL strings are a real benefit as they allow us to get rid of complex C string manipulation primitives.

> Almost all Android devices can store files in an additional storage location mounted in directory `/sdcard`. ""Almost"" is the important word here. Since the first Android G1, the meaning of ""sdcard"" has changed. Some recent devices have an external storage that is in fact internal (for example, flash memory on some tablets), and some others have a second storage location at their disposal (although in most cases, the second storage is mounted inside `/sdcard`). Moreover, the `/sdcard` path itself is not engraved into the marble. So, to detect safely the additional storage location, the only solution is to rely on JNI by calling `android.os.Environment.getExternalStorageDirectory()`. You can also check that storage is available with `getExternalStorageState()`. Note that the word ""External"" in API method name is here for historical reasons only. Also, the permission `WRITE_EXTERNAL_STORAGE` in manifest is required.

The STL provides much more features than Files and Strings. The most popular among them are probably STL containers. Let's see some usage examples in DroidBlaster.

Time for action – using STL containers

Let's now replace raw arrays with standard STL containers by following these steps:

1. Open the `jni/GraphicsManager.hpp` header and include the headers:

- ❑ `Vector`, which defines an STL container encapsulating C arrays (with a few more interesting features such as dynamic resizing)

- ❑ `Map`, which encapsulates the equivalent of a Java HashMap (that is, an associative array)

Then, remove the `textureResource` member in the `TextureProperties` structure. Use a `map` container instead of a raw array for `mTextures` (prefixed with the `std` namespace). The first parameter is the key type and the second the value type.

Finally, replace all the other raw arrays with a `vector`, as shown in the following:

```
...
#include <android_native_app_glue.h>
#include <GLES2/gl2.h>
#include <EGL/egl.h>

#include <map>
#include <vector>
...
struct TextureProperties {
    GLuint texture;
    int32_t width;
    int32_t height;
};

class GraphicsManager {
    ...
    // Graphics resources.
    std::map<Resource*, TextureProperties> mTextures;
    std::vector<GLuint> mShaders;
    std::vector<GLuint> mVertexBuffers;

    std::vector<GraphicsComponent*> mComponents;

    // Rendering resources.
    ...
};
#endif
```

2. Edit `jni/GraphicsManager.cpp` and initialize the new STL containers in the constructor initialization list as follows:

```
#include "GraphicsManager.hpp"
#include "Log.hpp"

#include <png.h>

GraphicsManager::GraphicsManager(android_app* pApplication) :
    ...
    mProjectionMatrix(),
    mTextures(), mShaders(), mVertexBuffers(), mComponents(),
    mScreenFrameBuffer(0),
    mRenderFrameBuffer(0), mRenderVertexBuffer(0),
    ... {
    Log::info("Creating GraphicsManager.");
}
...
```

3. Use the `vector::push_back()` method to insert components into the `mComponents` list when they get registered, as shown in the following:

```
...
void GraphicsManager::registerComponent(GraphicsComponent* pComponent)
{
    mComponents.push_back(pComponent);
}
...
```

4. In `start()`, we can iterate through the vector using an iterator to initialize each registered component, as shown in the following:

```
...
status GraphicsManager::start() {
    ...
    mProjectionMatrix[3][3] =  1.0f;

    // Loads graphics components.
    for (std::vector<GraphicsComponent*>::iterator
            componentIt = mComponents.begin();
            componentIt < mComponents.end(); ++componentIt) {
        if ((*componentIt)->load() != STATUS_OK) return STATUS_KO;
    }
    return STATUS_OK;
    ...
}
...
```

5. In `stop()`, we can iterate through the map (with second representing entry's value) and vector collections to release each allocated OpenGL resource this time, as shown in the following:

```
...
void GraphicsManager::stop() {
    Log::info("Stopping GraphicsManager.");
    // Releases textures.
    std::map<Resource*, TextureProperties>::iterator textureIt;
    for (textureIt = mTextures.begin(); textureIt != mTextures.end();
            ++textureIt) {
        glDeleteTextures(1, &textureIt->second.texture);
    }

    // Releases shaders.
    std::vector<GLuint>::iterator shaderIt;
    for (shaderIt = mShaders.begin(); shaderIt < mShaders.end();
            ++shaderIt) {
        glDeleteProgram(*shaderIt);
    }
    mShaders.clear();

    // Releases vertex buffers.
    std::vector<GLuint>::iterator vertexBufferIt;
    for (vertexBufferIt = mVertexBuffers.begin();
            vertexBufferIt < mVertexBuffers.end(); ++vertexBufferIt) {
        glDeleteBuffers(1, &(*vertexBufferIt));
    }
    mVertexBuffers.clear();

    ...
}
...
```

6. Also iterate over components stored to render them in `update()`, as shown in the following:

```
...
status GraphicsManager::update() {
    // Uses the offscreen FBO for scene rendering.
    glBindFramebuffer(GL_FRAMEBUFFER, mRenderFrameBuffer);
    glViewport(0, 0, mRenderWidth, mRenderHeight);
    glClear(GL_COLOR_BUFFER_BIT);

    // Render graphic components.
    std::vector<GraphicsComponent*>::iterator componentIt;
```

```
    for (componentIt = mComponents.begin();
            componentIt < mComponents.end(); ++componentIt) {
        (*componentIt)->draw();
    }

    // The FBO is rendered and scaled into the screen.
    glBindFramebuffer(GL_FRAMEBUFFER, mScreenFrameBuffer);
    ...
}
...
```

7. Since textures are expensive resources, use the map to check if a texture has already been loaded before loading and caching a new instance, as shown in the following:

```
...
TextureProperties* GraphicsManager::loadTexture(Resource& pResource) {
    // Looks for the texture in cache first.
    std::map<Resource*, TextureProperties>::iterator textureIt =

mTextures.find(&pResource);
    if (textureIt != mTextures.end()) {
        return &textureIt->second;
    }

    Log::info("Loading texture %s", pResource.getPath());
    ...
    Log::info("Texture size: %d x %d", width, height);

    // Caches the loaded texture.
    textureProperties = &mTextures[&pResource];
    textureProperties->texture = texture;
    textureProperties->width = width;
    textureProperties->height = height;
    return textureProperties;
    ...
}
...
```

8. Use the defined vector objects to save shaders and vertex buffers. Use push_ back() again to add an element to the vector, as shown in the following:

```
...
GLuint GraphicsManager::loadShader(const char* pVertexShader,
        const char* pFragmentShader) {
    ...
    if (result == GL_FALSE) {
        glGetProgramInfoLog(shaderProgram, sizeof(log), 0, log);
```

```
            Log::error("Shader program error: %s", log);
            goto ERROR;
        }

    mShaders.push_back(shaderProgram);
    return shaderProgram;

        ...
    }

GLuint GraphicsManager::loadVertexBuffer(const void* pVertexBuffer,
        int32_t pVertexBufferSize) {
        ...
    if (glGetError() != GL_NO_ERROR) goto ERROR;

    mVertexBuffers.push_back(vertexBuffer);
    return vertexBuffer;
        ...
    }
```

9. Now, open jni/SpriteBatch.hpp.

   Here again, include and use vector objects instead of raw arrays:

```
...
#ifndef _PACKT_GRAPHICSSPRITEBATCH_HPP_
#define _PACKT_GRAPHICSSPRITEBATCH_HPP_

#include "GraphicsManager.hpp"
#include "Sprite.hpp"
#include "TimeManager.hpp"
#include "Types.hpp"

#include <GLES2/gl2.h>
#include <vector>

class SpriteBatch : public GraphicsComponent {
    ...
    TimeManager& mTimeManager;
    GraphicsManager& mGraphicsManager;

    std::vector<Sprite*> mSprites;
    std::vector<Sprite::Vertex> mVertices;
    std::vector<GLushort> mIndexes;
    GLuint mShaderProgram;
```

```
        GLuint aPosition; GLuint aTexture;
        GLuint uProjection; GLuint uTexture;
};
#endif
```

10. In `jni/SpriteBatch.cpp`, replace the usage of raw arrays with vectors, as shown in the following:

```
...
SpriteBatch::SpriteBatch(TimeManager& pTimeManager,
        GraphicsManager& pGraphicsManager) :
    mTimeManager(pTimeManager),
    mGraphicsManager(pGraphicsManager),
    mSprites(), mVertices(), mIndexes(),
    mShaderProgram(0),
    aPosition(-1), aTexture(-1), uProjection(-1), uTexture(-1)
{
    mGraphicsManager.registerComponent(this);
}


SpriteBatch::~SpriteBatch() {
    std::vector<Sprite*>::iterator spriteIt;
    for (spriteIt = mSprites.begin(); spriteIt < mSprites.end();
            ++spriteIt) {
        delete (*spriteIt);
    }
}


Sprite* SpriteBatch::registerSprite(Resource& pTextureResource,
        int32_t pHeight, int32_t pWidth) {
    int32_t spriteCount = mSprites.size();
    int32_t index = spriteCount * 4; // Points to 1st vertex.

    // Precomputes the index buffer.
    mIndexes.push_back(index+0); mIndexes.push_back(index+1);
    mIndexes.push_back(index+2); mIndexes.push_back(index+2);
    mIndexes.push_back(index+1); mIndexes.push_back(index+3);
    for (int i = 0; i < 4; ++i) {
        mVertices.push_back(Sprite::Vertex());
    }

    // Appends a new sprite to the sprite array.
    mSprites.push_back(new Sprite(mGraphicsManager,
            pTextureResource, pHeight, pWidth));
    return mSprites.back();
}
...
```

11. During the loading and drawing process, loop over the `vector`. You can use an `iterator` (here in `load()`), as shown in the following:

```
...
status SpriteBatch::load() {
    ...
    uTexture = glGetUniformLocation(mShaderProgram, "u_texture");

    // Loads sprites.
    std::vector<Sprite*>::iterator spriteIt;
    for (spriteIt = mSprites.begin(); spriteIt < mSprites.end();
            ++spriteIt) {
        if ((*spriteIt)->load(mGraphicsManager)
                != STATUS_OK) goto ERROR;
    }
    return STATUS_OK;

ERROR:
    Log::error("Error loading sprite batch");
    return STATUS_KO;
}

void SpriteBatch::draw() {
    ...
    // Renders all sprites in batch.
    const int32_t vertexPerSprite = 4;
    const int32_t indexPerSprite = 6;
    float timeStep = mTimeManager.elapsed();
    int32_t spriteCount = mSprites.size();
    int32_t currentSprite = 0, firstSprite = 0;
    while (bool canDraw = (currentSprite < spriteCount)) {
        Sprite* sprite = mSprites[currentSprite];
        ...
    }
    ...
}
```

12. Finally, declare a `std::vector` in `jni/Asteroid.hpp` as follows:

```
#ifndef _PACKT_ASTEROID_HPP_
#define _PACKT_ASTEROID_HPP_

#include "GraphicsManager.hpp"
#include "PhysicsManager.hpp"
```

```
#include "TimeManager.hpp"
#include "Types.hpp"

#include <vector>

class Asteroid {
public:
    ...
    PhysicsManager& mPhysicsManager;

    std::vector<PhysicsBody*> mBodies;
    float mMinBound;
    float mUpperBound; float mLowerBound;
    float mLeftBound; float mRightBound;
};
#endif
```

13. Use the vector to insert and iterate over bodies in jni/Asteroid.cpp, as shown in the following code:

```
#include "Asteroid.hpp"
#include "Log.hpp"

static const float BOUNDS_MARGIN = 128;
static const float MIN_VELOCITY = 150.0f, VELOCITY_RANGE = 600.0f;

Asteroid::Asteroid(android_app* pApplication,
        TimeManager& pTimeManager, GraphicsManager& pGraphicsManager,
        PhysicsManager& pPhysicsManager) :
    mTimeManager(pTimeManager),
    mGraphicsManager(pGraphicsManager),
    mPhysicsManager(pPhysicsManager),
    mBodies(),
    mMinBound(0.0f),
    mUpperBound(0.0f), mLowerBound(0.0f),
    mLeftBound(0.0f), mRightBound(0.0f) {
}

void Asteroid::registerAsteroid(Location& pLocation,
        int32_t pSizeX, int32_t pSizeY) {
    mBodies.push_back(mPhysicsManager.loadBody(pLocation,
            pSizeX, pSizeY));
```

```
        }

    void Asteroid::initialize() {
        mMinBound = mGraphicsManager.getRenderHeight();
        mUpperBound = mMinBound * 2;
        mLowerBound = -BOUNDS_MARGIN;
        mLeftBound = -BOUNDS_MARGIN;
        mRightBound = (mGraphicsManager.getRenderWidth() + BOUNDS_MARGIN);

        std::vector<PhysicsBody*>::iterator bodyIt;
        for (bodyIt = mBodies.begin(); bodyIt < mBodies.end(); ++bodyIt) {
            spawn(*bodyIt);
        }
    }

    void Asteroid::update() {
        std::vector<PhysicsBody*>::iterator bodyIt;
        for (bodyIt = mBodies.begin(); bodyIt < mBodies.end(); ++bodyIt) {
            PhysicsBody* body = *bodyIt;
            if ((body->location->x < mLeftBound)
             || (body->location->x > mRightBound)
             || (body->location->y < mLowerBound)
             || (body->location->y > mUpperBound)) {
                spawn(body);
            }
        }
    }
    ...
```

What just happened?

There has been a use of STL containers throughout the application to replace raw C arrays. For example, we have managed a set of Asteroid game objects inside an STL container vector instead of a raw C array. We have also replaced the texture cache using an STL map container. STL containers have many advantages, such as automatically handling memory management (array resizing operations and so on), to alleviate our burden.

STL is definitely a huge improvement that avoids repetitive and error-prone code. Many open source libraries require it and it can now be ported without much trouble. More documentation about it can be found at http://www.cplusplus.com/reference/stl and on SGI's website (publisher of the first STL) at http://www.sgi.com/tech/stl.

When developing for performance, standard STL containers are not always the best choice, especially in terms of memory management and allocation. Indeed, STL is an all-purpose library, written for common cases. Alternative libraries might be considered for performance-critical code. A few examples are as follows:

◆ **EASTL**: This is an STL replacement developed by Electronic Arts with gaming in mind. An extract is available in the repository at `https://github.com/paulhodge/EASTL`. A must-read paper detailing EASTL technical details can be found on the Open Standards website at `http://www.open-std.org/jtc1/sc22/wg21/docs/papers/2007/n2271.html`.

◆ **Bitsquid Foundation library**: This is another STL replacement targeting games and can be found at `https://bitbucket.org/bitsquid/foundation/`.

◆ **RDESTL**: This is an open source subset of the STL, based on the EASTL technical paper, which was published several years before EASTL code release. The code repository can be found at `http://code.google.com/p/rdestl/`.

◆ **Google SparseHash**: This is for a high performance associative array library (note that RDESTL is also quite good at that).

This is far from exhaustive. Just define your exact needs to make the most appropriate choice.

 STL is still the best choice for most applications or libraries. Before going away from it, profile your source code and make sure it is really necessary.

Porting Box2D to Android

With the STL in our basket, we are ready to port almost any library to Android. Actually, many third-party libraries are already ported and many more are coming. However, when nothing is available, you have to rely on our own skills.

To see how to handle this situation, we are now going to port Box2D with the NDK. Box2D is a highly popular physics simulation engine initiated by Erin Catto in 2006. Many 2D games, either amateur or professional like Angry Birds, embed this powerful open source library. It is available in several languages, including Java, though its primary language is C++.

Box2D is an answer to the complex subject, that is, physics simulation. Maths, numerical integration, software optimization, and so on are some of the multiple techniques applied to simulate rigid body movements and collisions in a 2D environment. Bodies are the essential element of Box2D and are characterized by the following:

◆ A geometrical **shape** (polygons, circles, and so on)

◆ Physics properties (such as **density, friction, restitution**, and so on)

◆ Movement **constraints** and **joints** (to link bodies together and restrict their movement)

All these bodies are orchestrated inside a *World* that steps simulation according to time.

So, now that you know the very basics of Box2D, let's port and integrate it in DroidBlaster to simulate collisions.

 Resulting project is provided with this book under the name `DroidBlaster_Part17`.

Time for action – compiling Box2D on Android

First, let's port Box2D on the Android NDK following these steps:

Box2D 2.3.1 archive is provided with this book in directory `Libraries/box2d`.

1. Unzip Box2D source archive (2.3.1 in this book) into `${ANDROID_NDK}/sources/` (beware directory must be named `box2d`).

   Create and open an `Android.mk` file in the root of the `box2d` directory.

   First, save the current directory inside the `LOCAL_PATH` variable. This step is always necessary because an NDK build system may switch to another directory at any time during compilation.

2. After this, list all Box2D source files to compile, as shown in the following. We are interested in source file name only, which can be found in `${ANDROID_NDK}/sources/box2d/Box2D/Box2D`. Use the `LS_CPP` helper function to avoid copying each filename.

```
LOCAL_PATH:= $(call my-dir)

LS_CPP=$(subst $(1)/,,$(wildcard $(1)/$(2)/*.cpp))

BOX2D_CPP:= $(call LS_CPP,$(LOCAL_PATH),Box2D/Collision) \
            $(call LS_CPP,$(LOCAL_PATH),Box2D/Collision/Shapes) \
            $(call LS_CPP,$(LOCAL_PATH),Box2D/Common) \
            $(call LS_CPP,$(LOCAL_PATH),Box2D/Dynamics) \
            $(call LS_CPP,$(LOCAL_PATH),Box2D/Dynamics/Contacts) \
            $(call LS_CPP,$(LOCAL_PATH),Box2D/Dynamics/Joints) \
            $(call LS_CPP,$(LOCAL_PATH),Box2D/Rope)

...
```

3. Then, write the Box2D module definition for a static library. First, call the $(CLEAR_VARS) script. This script has to be included before any module definition to remove any potential change made by other modules, and to avoid any unwanted side effects. Then, define the following settings:

- Module name in LOCAL_MODULE: The module name is suffixed with _static to avoid a name collision with the shared version we are going to define right after.

- Module source files in LOCAL_SRC_FILES (using BOX2D_CPP defined previously).

- Header file directory exported to client modules in LOCAL_EXPORT_C_INCLUDES.

- Header file used internally for module compilation in LOCAL_C_INCLUDES. Here, the headers used for Box2D compilation and the headers needed for the client module are the same (and are often the same in other libraries). So, reuse LOCAL_EXPORT_C_INCLUDES, as defined previously, in the following way:

```
...
include $(CLEAR_VARS)

LOCAL_MODULE:= box2d_static
LOCAL_SRC_FILES:= $(BOX2D_CPP)
LOCAL_EXPORT_C_INCLUDES := $(LOCAL_PATH)
LOCAL_C_INCLUDES := $(LOCAL_EXPORT_C_INCLUDES)
...
```

Finally, request Box2D module compilation as a static library as follows:

```
...
include $(BUILD_STATIC_LIBRARY)
...
```

Optionally, the same process can be repeated to build a shared version of the same library by selecting a different module name and invoking $(BUILD_SHARED_LIBRARY) instead, as shown in the following:

```
...
include $(CLEAR_VARS)

LOCAL_MODULE:= box2d_shared
LOCAL_SRC_FILES:= $(BOX2D_CPP)
LOCAL_EXPORT_C_INCLUDES := $(LOCAL_PATH)
LOCAL_C_INCLUDES := $(LOCAL_EXPORT_C_INCLUDES)

include $(BUILD_SHARED_LIBRARY)
```

The Android.mk archive is provided in the Libraries/ box2d directory.

4. Open DroidBlaster Android.mk and link against box2d_static by appending it to LOCAL_STATIC_LIBRARIES. Indicate which Android.mk module file to include with the import-module directive. Remember that modules are found, thanks to the NDK_MODULE_PATH variable, which points by default to ${ANDROID_NDK}/ sources, as shown in the following:

```
LOCAL_PATH := $(call my-dir)

include $(CLEAR_VARS)

LS_CPP=$(subst $(1)/,,$(wildcard $(1)/*.cpp))
LOCAL_MODULE      := droidblaster
LOCAL_SRC_FILES := $(call LS_CPP,$(LOCAL_PATH))
LOCAL_LDLIBS      := -landroid -llog -lEGL -lGLESv1_CM -lOpenSLES

LOCAL_STATIC_LIBRARIES:=android_native_app_glue png \
                        box2d_static

include $(BUILD_SHARED_LIBRARY)


$(call import-module,android/native_app_glue)
$(call import-module,libpng)
$(call import-module,box2d)
```

Optionally, activate include file resolution in Eclipse if you see warnings about Box2D including files. To do so, in Eclipse **Project properties**, navigate to **the C/C++ General/ Paths and Symbols** section and then the **Includes** tab, and add the Box2d directory ${env_ var:ANDROID_NDK}/sources/box2d.

What just happened?

Launch the DroidBlaster compilation. Box2D is compiled without errors. We have ported our second open source library (after libpng) to Android thanks to the NDK! We can finally reuse one of the many wheels already created by the community! Porting a native library to Android involves mainly writing an Android.mk module makefile to describe source files, dependencies, compilation flags, and so on, as we have done until now for our main module DroidBlaster.

We have seen some of the most essential variables to use in a module, and they are as follows:

- ◆ LOCAL_MODULE: This declares a unique module name where the final library name depends on its value
- ◆ LOCAL_SRC_FILES: This lists all the files to compile relative to the module's root
- ◆ LOCAL_C_INCLUDES: This defines include file directories
- ◆ LOCAL_EXPORT_C_INCLUDES: This defines include file directories but for including modules this time

The order to build Box2D module build is given by one of the following directives:

- ◆ BUILD_STATIC_LIBRARY: This compiles the module as a static library
- ◆ BUILD_SHARED_LIBRARY: This also compiles the module but as a shared library this time

A module can be compiled as a static or shared library in the same way as the STL. Compilation is performed dynamically (that is, on-demand) each time a client application imports the module or changes its compilation settings. Hopefully, the NDK is able to compile sources incrementally.

To create a module for a header only library, such as parts of Boost or GLM (a library for OpenGL ES matrix calculations), define a module without LOCAL_SRC_FILES defined. Only LOCAL_MODULE and LOCAL_EXPORT_C_INCLUDES are necessary.

From the client Android.mk perspective (that is the DroidBlaster makefile in our case), the NDK import-module directive triggers, roughly speaking, include sub-module Android.mk files. Without it, the NDK will not be able to discover dependent modules, compile them, and include their headers. All the modules, the main module as well as the sub-modules, are produced in <PROJECT_DIR>/libs, and intermediate binary files are in <PROJECT_DIR>/obj for the main application module.

The import-module directive should be located at the end of the file to avoid altering module definition.

The following are the three ways to link against "sub-module" libraries in the main `Android.mk` Makefile:

◆ Static libraries must be listed in the `LOCAL_STATIC_LIBRARIES` variable (as we have done for Box2D)

◆ Shared libraries need to be listed in the `LOCAL_SHARED_LIBRARIES` variable

◆ Shared system libraries should be listed in `LOCAL_LDLIBS` (as we have done for OpenGL ES, for example)

For more information about Makefiles, see the *Mastering module Makefiles* section.

Writing a Makefile is an important part of the porting process. However, it is not always sufficient. Porting a library can be slightly more involved, depending on its originating platforms. For example, a piece code already ported to iOS is often easier to port to Android. In more complex cases, it may become necessary to patch code to make it behave properly on Android. When you are condemned to such a hard and non-trivial task, which is honestly quite frequent, always consider the following:

◆ Make sure required libraries exist, and port them first if not.

◆ Look for the main configuration header file if one is provided with your library (as this is often the case). It is a good place to tweak enabled or disabled features, remove unwanted dependencies, or define new Macros.

◆ Give attention to system-related macros (that is, `#ifdef _LINUX ...`), which are one of the first places to look for changes to make in the code. Generally, one will need to define macros, such as `_ANDROID_`, and insert them where appropriate.

◆ Comment non-essential code to check if the library can compile and if its core features can possibly work. Indeed, do not bother fixing everything if you are unsure yet whether it will work.

Hopefully, Box2D was not tight to a specific platform, as it relies mainly on pure C/C++ computation and not on external APIs. In such cases, porting code becomes much easier. Now that Box2D is compiled, let's run it in our own code.

Time for action – running Box2D physics engine

Let's rewrite the DroidBlaster physics engine with Box2D with the following steps:

1. Open the `jni/PhysicsManager.hpp` header and insert the Box2D `include` file.

Define a constant `PHYSICS_SCALE` to convert the body position from physics to game coordinates. Indeed, Box2D uses its own scale for a better precision.

Then, replace `PhysicsBody` with a new structure, `PhysicsCollision`, that will indicate which bodies entered in collision, as shown in the following:

```
#ifndef PACKT_PHYSICSMANAGER_HPP
#define PACKT_PHYSICSMANAGER_HPP

#include "GraphicsManager.hpp"
#include "TimeManager.hpp"
#include "Types.hpp"

#include <Box2D/Box2D.h>
#include <vector>

#define PHYSICS_SCALE 32.0f

struct PhysicsCollision {
    bool collide;

    PhysicsCollision():
        collide(false)
    {}
};
...
```

2. Then, make `PhysicsManager` inherit from `b2ContactListener`. A contact listener gets notified about new collisions each time the simulation is updated. Our `PhysicsManager` inherits one of its method's named `BeginContact()`, used to react to collisions.

We will need three more methods, which are as follows:

- ❑ `loadBody()` to create a new entity within the physics engine
- ❑ `loadTarget()` to create an entity that moves toward a target (our spaceship)
- ❑ `start()` to initialize the engine when the game starts

Also, define member variables, which are as follows:

- ❑ `mWorld` represents the whole Box2D simulation which contains all the bodies we are going to create
- ❑ `mBodies` is the list of all the physics entities we have registered
- ❑ `mLocations` contains a copy of the `b2Body` position in game coordinates (instead of physics coordinates which have a different scale)

❑ mBoundsBodyObj defines the boundaries in which our space ship will be able to move

```
. . .
class PhysicsManager : private b2ContactListener {
public:
    PhysicsManager(TimeManager& pTimeManager,
            GraphicsManager& pGraphicsManager);
    ~PhysicsManager();

    b2Body* loadBody(Location& pLocation, uint16 pCategory,
        uint16 pMask, int32_t pSizeX, int32_t pSizeY,
        float pRestitution);
    b2MouseJoint* loadTarget(b2Body* pBodyObj);
    void start();
    void update();

private:
    PhysicsManager(const PhysicsManager&);
    void operator=(const PhysicsManager&);

    void BeginContact(b2Contact* pContact);

    TimeManager& mTimeManager;
    GraphicsManager& mGraphicsManager;

    b2World mWorld;
    std::vector<b2Body*> mBodies;
    std::vector<Location*> mLocations;
    b2Body* mBoundsBodyObj;
};
#endif
```

3. Implement jni/PhysicsManager.cpp.

Iteration constants determine the simulation accuracy. Here, Box2D is going to handle mainly collisions and simple movements. So, fixing velocity and position iterations to 6 and 2, respectively, is sufficient (more about their meaning a bit later).

Initialize the new PhysicsManager members and let it listen to collision events with SetContactListener() on the mWorld object, as shown in the following:

```
#include "PhysicsManager.hpp"
#include "Log.hpp"

static const int32_t VELOCITY_ITER = 6;
```

```
static const int32_t POSITION_ITER = 2;

PhysicsManager::PhysicsManager(TimeManager& pTimeManager,
        GraphicsManager& pGraphicsManager) :
    mTimeManager(pTimeManager), mGraphicsManager(pGraphicsManager),
    mWorld(b2Vec2_zero), mBodies(),
    mLocations(),
    mBoundsBodyObj(NULL) {
    Log::info("Creating PhysicsManager.");
    mWorld.SetContactListener(this);
}

PhysicsManager::~PhysicsManager() {
    std::vector<b2Body*>::iterator bodyIt;
    for (bodyIt = mBodies.begin(); bodyIt < mBodies.end(); ++bodyIt) {
        delete (PhysicsCollision*) (*bodyIt)->GetUserData();
    }
}
...
```

4. Initialize Box2D world boundaries when the game starts. These boundaries match the display window size converted into *physics system coordinates*. Indeed, the physics system uses its own predefined scale to preserve float-point value accuracy. We need four edges to define these boundaries, as shown in the following:

```
...
void PhysicsManager::start() {
    if (mBoundsBodyObj == NULL) {
        b2BodyDef boundsBodyDef;
        b2ChainShape boundsShapeDef;
        float renderWidth = mGraphicsManager.getRenderWidth()
                            / PHYSICS_SCALE;
        float renderHeight = mGraphicsManager.getRenderHeight()
                            / PHYSICS_SCALE;
        b2Vec2 boundaries[4];
        boundaries[0].Set(0.0f, 0.0f);
        boundaries[1].Set(renderWidth, 0.0f);
        boundaries[2].Set(renderWidth, renderHeight);
        boundaries[3].Set(0.0f, renderHeight);
        boundsShapeDef.CreateLoop(boundaries, 4);

        mBoundsBodyObj = mWorld.CreateBody(&boundsBodyDef);
        mBoundsBodyObj->CreateFixture(&boundsShapeDef, 0);
    }
}
```

5. Initialize and register asteroid or ship physics bodies in `loadBody()`.

The body definition describes a dynamic body (as opposed to static), awake (that is, actively simulated by Box2D), and which cannot rotate (a property especially important for polygon shapes, meaning that it is always pointing upward).

Also note how we save a `PhysicsCollision` self-reference in the `userData` field, in order to access it later inside Box2D callbacks.

Define the body shape, which we approximate to a circle. Note that Box2D requires a half dimension, from the object's center to its borders, as shown in the following code snippet:

```
b2Body* PhysicsManager::loadBody(Location& pLocation,
        uint16 pCategory, uint16 pMask, int32_t pSizeX, int32_t pSizeY,
        float pRestitution) {
    PhysicsCollision* userData = new PhysicsCollision();

    b2BodyDef mBodyDef;
    b2Body* mBodyObj;
    b2CircleShape mShapeDef; b2FixtureDef mFixtureDef;

    mBodyDef.type = b2_dynamicBody;
    mBodyDef.userData = userData;
    mBodyDef.awake = true;
    mBodyDef.fixedRotation = true;

    mShapeDef.m_p = b2Vec2_zero;
    int32_t diameter = (pSizeX + pSizeY) / 2;
    mShapeDef.m_radius = diameter / (2.0f * PHYSICS_SCALE);
    ...
```

6. Body fixture is the "glue" that ties together body definition, shape, and physical properties. We also use it to set the body's category and mask, and to filter collisions between objects (for instance, asteroids can collide with the ship but not between themselves in DroidBlaster). One bit represents one category.

Finally, effectively instantiate your `body` inside the Box2D physical world, as shown in the following code:

```
    ...
    mFixtureDef.shape = &mShapeDef;
    mFixtureDef.density = 1.0f;
    mFixtureDef.friction = 0.0f;
    mFixtureDef.restitution = pRestitution;
    mFixtureDef.filter.categoryBits = pCategory;
```

```
        mFixtureDef.filter.maskBits = pMask;
        mFixtureDef.userData = userData;

        mBodyObj = mWorld.CreateBody(&mBodyDef);
        mBodyObj->CreateFixture(&mFixtureDef);
        mBodyObj->SetUserData(userData);
        mLocations.push_back(&pLocation);
        mBodies.push_back(mBodyObj);
        return mBodyObj;
    }
    ...
```

7. Implement the `loadTarget()` method that creates a Box2D mouse joint to simulate spaceship movements. Such a `Joint` defines an empty target toward which the body (here specified in parameter) moves, like a kind of elastic. The settings used here (`maxForce`, `dampingRatio`, and `frequencyHz`) control how the ship reacts and can be determined by tweaking them, as shown in the following code:

```
    ...
    b2MouseJoint* PhysicsManager::loadTarget(b2Body* pBody) {
        b2BodyDef emptyBodyDef;
        b2Body* emptyBody = mWorld.CreateBody(&emptyBodyDef);

        b2MouseJointDef mouseJointDef;
        mouseJointDef.bodyA = emptyBody;
        mouseJointDef.bodyB = pBody;
        mouseJointDef.target = b2Vec2(0.0f, 0.0f);
        mouseJointDef.maxForce = 50.0f * pBody->GetMass();
        mouseJointDef.dampingRatio = 0.15f;
        mouseJointDef.frequencyHz = 3.5f;

        return (b2MouseJoint*) mWorld.CreateJoint(&mouseJointDef);
    }
    ...
```

8. Write the `update()` method.

- First, clear any collision flag buffered in `BeginContact()` during previous iteration.

- Then, perform simulation by calling `Step()`. The time period specifies how much time must be simulated. Iterations constants determine simulation accuracy.

❑ Finally, loop over all of the physics bodies to extract their coordinates, convert them from Box2D to game coordinates, and store the result into our own `Location` object, as shown in the following code:

```
...
void PhysicsManager::update() {
    // Clears collision flags.
    int32_t size = mBodies.size();
    for (int32_t i = 0; i < size; ++i) {
        PhysicsCollision* physicsCollision =
                ((PhysicsCollision*) mBodies[i]->GetUserData());
        physicsCollision->collide = false;
    }
    // Updates simulation.
    float timeStep = mTimeManager.elapsed();
    mWorld.Step(timeStep, VELOCITY_ITER, POSITION_ITER);

    // Caches the new state.
    for (int32_t i = 0; i < size; ++i) {
        const b2Vec2& position = mBodies[i]->GetPosition();
        mLocations[i]->x = position.x * PHYSICS_SCALE;
        mLocations[i]->y = position.y * PHYSICS_SCALE;
    }
}
...
```

9. Finish with the `BeginContact()` method inherited by `b2ContactListener`. This callback notifies new collisions between bodies, two at a time (named A and B). Event information is stored in a `b2contact` structure, which contains various properties, such as friction, restitution, and the two bodies, involved through their fixture. These fixtures contain in themselves a reference to our own `PhysicsCollision`. We can use the following link to switch the `PhysicsCollision` collision flag when Box2D detects one contact:

```
...
void PhysicsManager::BeginContact(b2Contact* pContact) {
    void* userDataA = pContact->GetFixtureA()->GetUserData();
    void* userDataB = pContact->GetFixtureB()->GetUserData();
    if (userDataA != NULL && userDataB != NULL) {
        ((PhysicsCollision*)userDataA)->collide = true;
        ((PhysicsCollision*)userDataB)->collide = true;
    }
}
```

10. In `jni/Asteroid.hpp`, replace the usage of `PhysicsBody` with Box2D `b2Body` structure, as shown in the following code:

```
...
class Asteroid {
    ...
private:
    void spawn(b2Body* pBody);

    TimeManager& mTimeManager;
    GraphicsManager& mGraphicsManager;
    PhysicsManager& mPhysicsManager;

    std::vector<b2Body*> mBodies;
    float mMinBound;
    float mUpperBound; float mLowerBound;
    float mLeftBound; float mRightBound;
};
#endif
```

11. In `jni/Asteroid.cpp`, scale constants and boundaries to the physics coordinate system:

```
#include "Asteroid.hpp"
#include "Log.hpp"

static const float BOUNDS_MARGIN = 128 / PHYSICS_SCALE;
static const float MIN_VELOCITY = 150.0f / PHYSICS_SCALE;
static const float VELOCITY_RANGE = 600.0f / PHYSICS_SCALE;

...
void Asteroid::initialize() {
    mMinBound = mGraphicsManager.getRenderHeight() / PHYSICS_SCALE;
    mUpperBound = mMinBound * 2;
    mLowerBound = -BOUNDS_MARGIN;
    mLeftBound = -BOUNDS_MARGIN;
    mRightBound = (mGraphicsManager.getRenderWidth() / PHYSICS_SCALE)
                    + BOUNDS_MARGIN;

    std::vector<b2Body*>::iterator bodyIt;
    for (bodyIt = mBodies.begin(); bodyIt < mBodies.end(); ++bodyIt) {
        spawn(*bodyIt);
    }
}
...
```

12. Then, update the way an asteroid body is registered. Register physics properties with a category and mask. Here, asteroids are declared as belonging to category 1 (0X1 in hexadecimal notation), and only bodies in group 2 (0X2 in hexadecimal) are considered when evaluating collisions:

```
. . .
void Asteroid::registerAsteroid(Location& pLocation,
        int32_t pSizeX, int32_t pSizeY) {
    mBodies.push_back(mPhysicsManager.loadBody(pLocation,
            0X1, 0x2, pSizeX, pSizeY, 2.0f));
}
. . .
```

Replace and update the remaining code to accommodate the use of the new b2Body structure instead of the PhysicsBody one:

```
. . .
void Asteroid::update() {
    std::vector<b2Body*>::iterator bodyIt;
    for (bodyIt = mBodies.begin(); bodyIt < mBodies.end(); ++bodyIt) {
        b2Body* body = *bodyIt;
        if ((body->GetPosition().x < mLeftBound)
          || (body->GetPosition().x > mRightBound)
          || (body->GetPosition().y < mLowerBound)
          || (body->GetPosition().y > mUpperBound)) {
            spawn(body);
        }
    }
}
. . .
```

13. Finally, also update spawn() code to initialize the PhysicsBody, as shown in the following code:

```
. . .
void Asteroid::spawn(b2Body* pBody) {
    float velocity = -(RAND(VELOCITY_RANGE) + MIN_VELOCITY);
    float posX = mLeftBound + RAND(mRightBound - mLeftBound);
    float posY = mMinBound + RAND(mUpperBound - mMinBound);
    pBody->SetTransform(b2Vec2(posX, posY), 0.0f);
    pBody->SetLinearVelocity(b2Vec2(0.0f, velocity));
}
```

14. Open `jni/Ship.hpp` to turn it into a Box2D body.

Add a new `b2Body` parameter to the `registerShip()` method.

Then, define the following two additional methods:

- `update()`, which contains some new game logic to destroy the ship when it collides with asteroids
- `isDestroyed()` to indicate if the ship has been destroyed

Declare the following necessary variables:

- `mBody` to manage the ship representation in Box2D
- `mDestroyed` and `mLives` for the game logic

```
...
#include "GraphicsManager.hpp"
#include "PhysicsManager.hpp"
#include "SoundManager.hpp"
...

class Ship {
public:
    Ship(android_app* pApplication,
            GraphicsManager& pGraphicsManager,
            SoundManager& pSoundManager);

    void registerShip(Sprite* pGraphics, Sound* pCollisionSound,
            b2Body* pBody);

    void initialize();
    void update();

    bool isDestroyed() { return mDestroyed; }

private:
    GraphicsManager& mGraphicsManager;
    SoundManager& mSoundManager;
    Sprite* mGraphics;
    Sound* mCollisionSound;
    b2Body* mBody;
    bool mDestroyed; int32_t mLives;
};
#endif
```

15. Declare a few new constants in `jni/Ship.cpp`.

Then, initialize the new member variables properly. Note that you don't need to play the collision sound anymore in `initialize()`:

```cpp
#include "Log.hpp"
#include "Ship.hpp"

static const float INITAL_X = 0.5f;
static const float INITAL_Y = 0.25f;
static const int32_t DEFAULT_LIVES = 10;

static const int32_t SHIP_DESTROY_FRAME_1 = 8;
static const int32_t SHIP_DESTROY_FRAME_COUNT = 9;
static const float SHIP_DESTROY_ANIM_SPEED = 12.0f;

Ship::Ship(android_app* pApplication,
        GraphicsManager& pGraphicsManager,
        SoundManager& pSoundManager) :
  mGraphicsManager(pGraphicsManager),
  mGraphics(NULL),
  mSoundManager(pSoundManager),
  mCollisionSound(NULL),
  mBody(NULL),
  mDestroyed(false), mLives(0) {
}

void Ship::registerShip(Sprite* pGraphics, Sound* pCollisionSound,
                        b2Body* pBody) {
    mGraphics = pGraphics;
    mCollisionSound = pCollisionSound;
    mBody = pBody;
}

void Ship::initialize() {
    mDestroyed = false;
    mLives = DEFAULT_LIVES;

    b2Vec2 position(
        mGraphicsManager.getRenderWidth() * INITAL_X / PHYSICS_SCALE,
        mGraphicsManager.getRenderHeight() * INITAL_Y / PHYSICS_SCALE);
    mBody->SetTransform(position, 0.0f);
    mBody->SetActive(true);
}
...
```

16. In `update()`, check if the ship body has collided with an asteroid. To do so, check the `PhysicsCollision` structure stored in the ship `b2Body` custom user data. Remember that its content is set in the `PhysicsManager::BeginContact()` method

When the ship collides, we can decrease its life and play a collision sound.

If it has no more life, we can start playing a destruction animation. The body should be inactive when this happens to avoid further collision with asteroids.

When ship is fully destroyed, we can save its state so that the game loop can act appropriately, as shown in the following code:

```
...
void Ship::update() {
    if (mLives >= 0) {
        if (((PhysicsCollision*) mBody->GetUserData())->collide) {
            mSoundManager.playSound(mCollisionSound);
            --mLives;
            if (mLives < 0) {
                Log::info("Ship has been destroyed");
                mGraphics->setAnimation(SHIP_DESTROY_FRAME_1,
                    SHIP_DESTROY_FRAME_COUNT, SHIP_DESTROY_ANIM_SPEED,
                    false);
                mBody->SetActive(false);
            } else {
                Log::info("Ship collided");
            }
        }
    }
    // Destroyed.
    else {
        if (mGraphics->animationEnded()) {
            mDestroyed = true;
        }
    }
}
```

17. Update the `jni/MoveableBody.hpp` component so that it returns a `b2Body` structure in `registerMoveableBody()`.

Add the following two new members:

❑ `mBody` for the physical body

❑ `mTarget` for the mouse joint:

```cpp
#ifndef _PACKT_MOVEABLEBODY_HPP_
#define _PACKT_MOVEABLEBODY_HPP_

#include "InputManager.hpp"
#include "PhysicsManager.hpp"
#include "Types.hpp"

class MoveableBody {
public:
    MoveableBody(android_app* pApplication,
        InputManager& pInputManager, PhysicsManager& pPhysicsManager);

    b2Body* registerMoveableBody(Location& pLocation,
            int32_t pSizeX, int32_t pSizeY);

    void initialize();
    void update();

private:
    PhysicsManager& mPhysicsManager;
    InputManager& mInputManager;

    b2Body* mBody;
    b2MouseJoint* mTarget;
};
#endif
```

18. Adapt `jni/MoveableBody.cpp` constants to the new scale and initialize new members in the constructor:

```cpp
#include "Log.hpp"
#include "MoveableBody.hpp"

static const float MOVE_SPEED = 10.0f / PHYSICS_SCALE;

MoveableBody::MoveableBody(android_app* pApplication,
        InputManager& pInputManager, PhysicsManager& pPhysicsManager) :
  mInputManager(pInputManager),
  mPhysicsManager(pPhysicsManager),
  mBody(NULL), mTarget(NULL) {
}

b2Body* MoveableBody::registerMoveableBody(Location& pLocation,
        int32_t pSizeX, int32_t pSizeY) {
    mBody = mPhysicsManager.loadBody(pLocation, 0x2, 0x1, pSizeX,
            pSizeY, 0.0f);
```

```
        mTarget = mPhysicsManager.loadTarget(mBody);
        mInputManager.setRefPoint(&pLocation);
        return mBody;
    }
    ...
```

19. Then, set up and update the `physicsbody` so that it follows the ship's target. The target moves according to user input, as shown in the following code:

```
    ...
    void MoveableBody::initialize() {
        mBody->SetLinearVelocity(b2Vec2(0.0f, 0.0f));
    }

    void MoveableBody::update() {
        b2Vec2 target = mBody->GetPosition() + b2Vec2(
            mInputManager.getDirectionX() * MOVE_SPEED,
            mInputManager.getDirectionY() * MOVE_SPEED);
        mTarget->SetTarget(target);
    }
```

20. Finally, edit `jni/DroidBlaster.cpp` and change the ship registration code to accommodate the new changes, as shown in the following code:

```
    ...

    DroidBlaster::DroidBlaster(android_app* pApplication):
        ... {
        Log::info("Creating DroidBlaster");

        Sprite* shipGraphics = mSpriteBatch.registerSprite(mShipTexture,
                SHIP_SIZE, SHIP_SIZE);
        shipGraphics->setAnimation(SHIP_FRAME_1, SHIP_FRAME_COUNT,
                SHIP_ANIM_SPEED, true);
        Sound* collisionSound =
                mSoundManager.registerSound(mCollisionSound);
        b2Body* shipBody = mMoveableBody.registerMoveableBody(
                shipGraphics->location, SHIP_SIZE, SHIP_SIZE);
        mShip.registerShip(shipGraphics, collisionSound, shipBody);

        // Creates asteroids.
        ...
    }
    ...
```

21. Don't forget to start the `PhysicsManager` in `onActivate()`, as shown in the following code:

```
...
status DroidBlaster::onActivate() {
    Log::info("Activating DroidBlaster");
    // Starts managers.
    if (mGraphicsManager.start() != STATUS_OK) return STATUS_KO;
    if (mSoundManager.start() != STATUS_OK) return STATUS_KO;
    mInputManager.start();
    mPhysicsManager.start();

    ...
}
...
```

22. Terminate by updating and checking ship state in `onStep()`. When it is destroyed, exit the game loop as follows:

```
...
status DroidBlaster::onStep() {
    mTimeManager.update();
    mPhysicsManager.update();

    // Updates modules.
    mAsteroids.update();
    mMoveableBody.update();
    mShip.update();

    if (mShip.isDestroyed()) return STATUS_EXIT;
    return mGraphicsManager.update();
}
...
```

What just happened?

We have created a physical simulation using the Box2D physics engine. More specifically, we have seen how to do the following:

◆ Create a Box2D world to describe the physical simulation

◆ Define a physical representation of entities (ships and asteroids)

◆ Step a simulation

◆ Filter and detect collisions between entities

◆ Extract simulation state (that is, coordinates) to feed the graphical representation

Box2D uses its own allocators to optimize memory management. So, to create and destroy Box2D objects, one needs to systematically use the provided factory methods (`CreateX()`, `DestroyX()`). Most of the time, Box2D will manage memory automatically for you. When an object is destroyed, all related *child objects* get destroyed (for instance, the bodies are destroyed when the world is destroyed). But, if you need to get rid of your objects earlier, and thus manually, always destroy the bodies.

Box2D is a complex piece of code and is quite hard to tune properly. Let's dive a bit deeper into the way its world is described and how to handle collision.

Diving into the Box2D world

The central point of access in Box2D is the `b2World` object, which stores a collection of physical bodies to simulate. A Box2D body is composed of the following:

◆ `b2BodyDef`: This defines the body type (`b2_staticBody`, `b2_dynamicBody`, and so on) and initial properties, such as its position, angle (in radians), and so on.

◆ `b2Shape`: This is used for collision detection and to derive body mass from its density. It can be a `b2PolygonShape`, `b2CircleShape`, and so on.

◆ `b2FixtureDef`: This links together a body shape, a body definition, and its physical properties, such as density.

◆ `b2Body`: This is a body instance in the world (that is, one per game object). It is created from a body definition, a shape, and a fixture.

Bodies are characterized by a few physical properties, which are as follows:

◆ **Shape**: This represents a circle in DroidBlaster, although a polygon or box could also be used.

◆ **Density**: This is expressed in kg/m2 to compute body mass depending on its shape and size. Value should be greater or equal to `0.0`. A bowling ball has a bigger density than a soccer ball.

◆ **Friction**: This indicates how much a body slides on another (for example, a car on a road or on an icy path). Values are typically in the range `0.0` to `1.0`, where `0.0` implies no friction and `1.0` implies strong friction.

◆ **Restitution**: This indicates how much a body reacts to a collision, for example, a bouncing ball. Value `0.0` means no restitution and `1.0` means full restitution.

When running, bodies are subject to the following:

- **Forces**: This makes bodies move linearly.

- **Torques**: This represents rotational force applied on a body.

- **Damping**: This is similar to friction, although it does not only occur when a body is in contact with another. Consider it as the effect of drag slowing down a body.

Box2D is tuned for worlds containing objects at a scale from `0.1` to `10` (unit in meters). When used outside this range, again, numerical approximation can make simulation inaccurate. Thus, it is very necessary to scale coordinates from the Box2D referential, where objects should to be kept in the (rough) range [`0.1`, `10`], and to the game, or directly to the graphics referential. This is why we have defined `SCALE_FACTOR` to scale coordinate transformation.

More on collision detection

Several ways of detecting and handling collisions exist in Box2D. The most basic one consists of checking all contacts stored in the world or in a body after they are updated. However, this can result in missed contacts that happen surreptitiously during Box2D internal iterations.

A better way we have seen to detect contacts is the `b2ContactListener`, which can be registered on the world object. The following four callbacks can be overridden:

- `BeginContact (b2Contact)`: This detects when two bodies enter in collision.

- `EndContact(b2Contact)`: This is a counterpart of `BeginContact()`, which indicates when bodies are not in collision any more. A call to `BeginContact()` is always followed by a matching `EndContact()`.

- `PreSolve (b2Contact, b2Manifold)`: This is called after a collision is detected but before collision resolution, that is, before impulse resulting from the collision is computed. The `b2Manifold` structure holds information about contact points, normals, and so on in a single place.

- `PostSolve(b2Contact, b2ContactImpulse)`: This is called after actual impulse (that is, physical reaction) has been computed by Box2D.

The first two callbacks are interesting to trigger game logic (for example, entity destruction). The last two are interesting to alter physics simulation (more specifically to ignore some collisions by *disabling* a contact) while it is being computed, or to get more accurate details about it. For instance, use `PreSolve()` to create a one-sided platform to which an entity collides only when it falls from above (not when it jumps from below). Use `PostSolve()` to detect collision strength and calculate damages accordingly.

The `PreSolve()` and `PostSolve()` methods can be called several times between `BeginContact()` and `EndContact()`, which can be called themselves from zero to several times during one world update. A contact can begin during one simulation step and terminate after several steps. In that case, event-solving callbacks occur continuously during "in-between" steps. As many collisions can occur while stepping simulation. Thus, callbacks can be called a lot of times and should be as efficient as possible.

When analyzing collisions inside the `BeginContact()` callback, we buffered a collision flag. This is necessary because Box2D reuses the `b2Contact` parameter passed when a callback is triggered. In addition, as these callbacks are called while simulation is computed, physics bodies cannot be destroyed at that instant, only after simulation stepping is over. Thus, it is highly advised to copy any information gathered there for `postprocessing` (for example, to destroy entities).

Collision modes and filtering

I would like to point out that Box2D offers a so-called `bullet` mode that can be activated on a body definition using corresponding Boolean member:

```
mBodyDef.bullet = true;
```

The bullet mode is necessary for fast moving objects like bullets! By default, Box2D uses **Discrete Collision Detection**, which considers bodies at their final position for collision detection, missing any body located between initial and final positions. However, for a fast moving body, the whole path followed should be considered. This is more formally called **Continuous Collision Detection (CCD)**. Obviously, CCD is expensive and should be used with parsimony. Please refer to the following figure:

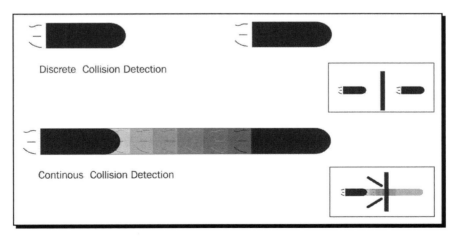

We sometimes want to detect when bodies overlap without generating collisions (like a car reaching the finish line): this is called a sensor. A sensor can be easily set by setting the isSensor Boolean member to true in the fixture as follows:

```
mFixtureDef.isSensor = true;
```

A sensor can be queried with a listener through BeginContact() and EndContact() or by using the IsTouching() shortcut on a b2Contact class.

Another important aspect of collision is not colliding or, more precisely, filtering collisions. A kind of filtering can be performed in PreSolve() by disabling contacts. This is the most flexible and powerful solution, but also the most complex.

But, as we have seen it, filtering can be performed in a more simple way by using a categories and masks technique. Each body is assigned one or more category (each being represented by one bit in a short integer, the categoryBits member) and a mask describing categories of the body they can collide with (each filtered category being represented by a bit set to 0, the maskBits member), as shown in the following figure:

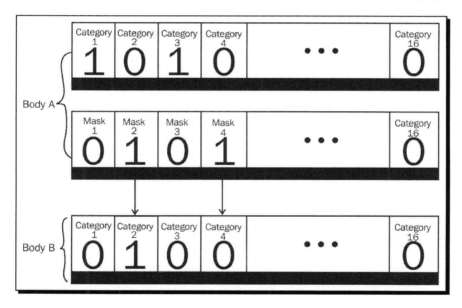

In the preceding figure, Body A is in categories 1 and 3, and collides with bodies in categories 2 and 4, which is the case for this poor Body B, unless its mask filters collision with Body A categories (that is, 1 and 3). In other words, both bodies A and B must agree to collide!

Box2D also has a notion of collision groups. A body has a collision group set to any of the following:

- **Positive integer**: This means others bodies with the same collision group value can collide

- **Negative integer**: This means others bodies with the same collision group value are filtered

Using collision groups could have also been a solution to avoid collision between asteroids in DroidBlaster, although it is less flexible than categories and masks. Note that groups are filtered before categories.

A more flexible solution than category and group filters is the b2ContactFilter class. This class has a ShouldCollide(b2Fixture, b2Fixture) method that you can customize to perform your own filtering. Actually, category/group filtering are themselves implemented that way.

Going further with Box2D

This short introduction to Box2D gives you only an overview of what Box2D is capable of! The following non-exhaustive list has been left in the shadow:

- Joints to link two bodies together

- **Raycasting** to query a physics world (for example, which location is a gun pointing toward)

- Contact properties: normals, impulses, manifolds, and so on

 Box2D has now a little brother called **LiquidFun**, which is used to simulate fluids. You can download and see it in action at http://google.github.io/liquidfun/.

Box2D has a really nice documentation with useful information that can be found at http://www.box2d.org/manual.html. Moreover, Box2D is packaged with a test bed directory (in Box2D/Testbed/Tests) featuring many use cases. Have a look at them to get a better understanding of its capabilities. Because physics simulations can sometimes be rather tricky, I also encourage you to visit Box2D forum, which is quite active, at http://www.box2d.org/forum/.

Prebuilding Boost on Android

If STL is the most common framework among C++ programs, Boost probably comes second. A real Swiss army knife! This toolkit contains a profusion of utilities to handle most common needs, and even more.

Most Boost features are provided as header-only code, which means that we do not need to compile it. Including headers is enough of an advantage to use it. This is the case of the most popular features of Boost: **Smart Pointers**, a reference-counting pointer class that handles memory allocation and de-allocation automatically. They avoid most memory leaks and pointer misuse for almost free.

However, a few parts of Boost require compilation first, such as the threading or the unit test library. We are now going to see how to build them with the Android NDK and compile a unit test executable.

 Resulting project is provided with this book under the name `DroidBlaster_Part18`.

Time for action – prebuilding Boost static library

Let's prebuild Boost for Android as a static library with the following steps:

1. Download Boost from `http://www.boost.org/` (Version 1.55.0, in this book). Unzip the archive into `${ANDROID_NDK}/sources`. Name the directory `boost`.

Open a command line window and go to the `boost` directory. Launch `bootstrap.bat` on Windows or `./bootstrap.sh` on Linux and Mac OS X to build **b2**. This program, previously named **BJam**, is a custom building tool similar to **Make**.

 Boost 1.55.0 archive is provided with this book in the `Libraries/boost` directory.

Change the NDK build command in DroidBlaster to generate verbose compilation logs. To do so, in Eclipse **Project properties**, navigate to the **C/C++ Build** section. There, you should see the following build command: `ndk-build NDK_DEBUG=1`. Change it to `build NDK_DEBUG=0 V=1` to compile in release mode with verbose logs.

2. Rebuild DroidBlaster (you might need to clean your project first). If you look, for example, at the following compilation extract, you should see some logs similar to the extract below. This log, although barely readable, gives all the information about the commands run to build DroidBlaster.

- ❏ The toolchain used to build DroidBlaster (`arm-linux-androideabi-4.6`)
- ❏ The system on which DroidBlaster is built (`linux-x86_64`)
- ❏ The compiler executable (`arm-linux-androideabi-g++`)
- ❏ The archiver executable (`arm-linux-androideabi-ar`)
- ❏ Also all the compilation flags passed to them (here for ARM processors)

We can use the following as an inspiration source to determine `Boost` compilation flags (in this flag soup!):

```
. . .
/opt/android-ndk/toolchains/arm-linux-androideabi-4.6/prebuilt/
linux-x86_64/bin/arm-linux-androideabi-g++ -MMD -MP -MF ./obj/
local/armeabi/objs/DroidBlaster/Asteroid.o.d -fpic -ffunction-
sections -funwind-tables -fstack-protector -no-canonical-prefixes
-march=armv5te -mtune=xscale -msoft-float -fno-exceptions -fno-rtti
-mthumb -Os -g -DNDEBUG -fomit-frame-pointer -fno-strict-aliasing
-finline-limit=64 -I/opt/android-ndk/sources/android/native_app_glue
-I/opt/android-ndk/sources/libpng -I/opt/android-ndk/sources/box2d
-I/opt/android-ndk/sources/cxx-stl/gnu-libstdc++/4.6/include -I/opt/
android-ndk/sources/cxx-stl/gnu-libstdc++/4.6/libs/armeabi/include -I/
opt/android-ndk/sources/cxx-stl/gnu-libstdc++/4.6/include/backward
-Ijni -DANDROID  -Wa,--noexecstack -Wformat -Werror=format-security
-I/opt/android-ndk/platforms/android-16/arch-arm/usr/include -c  jni/
Asteroid.cpp -o ./obj/local/armeabi/objs/DroidBlaster/Asteroid.o

. . .
/opt/android-ndk/toolchains/arm-linux-androideabi-4.6/prebuilt/
linux-x86_64/bin/arm-linux-androideabi-ar crsD ./obj/local/armeabi/
libandroid_native_app_glue.a ./obj/local/armeabi/objs/android_native_
app_glue/android_native_app_glue.o
. . .
```

3. In the `boost` directory, open the `tools/build/v2/user-config.jam` file. This file, like its name suggests, is a configuration file that can be set up to customize `Boost` compilation. Initial content contains only comments and can be erased. Start including the following content:

```
import feature ;
import os ;

if [ os.name ] = CYGWIN || [ os.name ] = NT {
    androidPlatform = windows ;
```

```
} else if [ os.name ] = LINUX {
    if [ os.platform ] = X86_64 {
        androidPlatform = linux-x86_64 ;
    } else {
        androidPlatform = linux-x86 ;
    }
} else if [ os.name ] = MACOSX {
    androidPlatform = darwin-x86 ;
}
...
```

4. Compilation is performed statically. **BZip** is deactivated because it is unavailable, by default, on Android (we could however compile it separately):

```
...
modules.poke : NO_BZIP2 : 1 ;
...
```

5. Retrieve the `android_ndk` environment variable which points to the NDK location on disk.

Declare what we could call a "configuration" `android4.6_armeabi`.

Then, reconfigure Boost to use the NDK ARM GCC toolchain (`g++`, `ar`, and `ranlib`) in static mode, the archiver being in charge of creating the static library. We can use the information found in the log in step 2 to fill their respective paths.

The `sysroot` directive indicates which Android API release to compile and link against. The specified directory, located in the NDK, contains `include` files and libraries specific to this release, as shown in the following code:

```
...
android_ndk = [ os.environ ANDROID_NDK ] ;
using gcc : android4.6_armeabi :
    $(android_ndk)/toolchains/arm-linux-androideabi-4.6/
prebuilt/$(androidPlatform)/bin/arm-linux-androideabi-g++ :
    <archiver>$(android_ndk)/toolchains/arm-linux-androideabi-4.6/
prebuilt/$(androidPlatform)/bin/arm-linux-androideabi-ar
    <ranlib>$(android_ndk)/toolchains/arm-linux-androideabi-4.6/
prebuilt/$(androidPlatform)/bin/arm-linux-androideabi-ranlib
    <compileflags>--sysroot=$(android_ndk)/platforms/android-16/arch-
arm
    <compileflags>-I$(android_ndk)/sources/cxx-stl/gnu-libstdc++/4.6/
include
    <compileflags>-I$(android_ndk)/sources/cxx-stl/gnu-libstdc++/4.6/
libs/armeabi/include
...
```

6. Boost needs exceptions and RTTI. Enable them with the `-fexceptions` and `-frtti` flags, as shown in the following code:

...

```
<compileflags>-fexceptions
<compileflags>-frtti
```

...

7. A few options have to be defined to tweak `Boost` compilation. This is where we can take inspiration from the compilation flags discovered in step 2, such as the following:

   ❏ `-march=armv5te` to specify the target platform

   ❏ `-mthumb`, which indicates that generated code should use thumb instructions (`-marm` could also be used to use ARM instructions instead)

   ❏ `-Os` to enable compiler optimizations

   ❏ `-DNDEBUG` to request compilation in release mode

   Also include or tweak additional ones, such as the following:

   ❏ `-D__arm__`, `-D__ARM_ARCH_5__`, and so on, which help to determine the target platform from code

   ❏ `-DANDROID`, `-D__ANDROID__`, which help to determine the target OS

   ❏ `-DBOOST_ASIO_DISABLE_STD_ATOMIC` to disable the use `std::atomic`, which is buggy on Android (something that can be learnt only through (bad) "experience"...).

```
<compileflags>-march=armv5te
<compileflags>-mthumb
<compileflags>-mtune=xscale
<compileflags>-msoft-float
<compileflags>-fno-strict-aliasing
<compileflags>-finline-limit=64
<compileflags>-D__arm__
<compileflags>-D__ARM_ARCH_5__
<compileflags>-D__ARM_ARCH_5T__
<compileflags>-D__ARM_ARCH_5E__
<compileflags>-D__ARM_ARCH_5TE__
<compileflags>-MMD
<compileflags>-MP
<compileflags>-MF
<compileflags>-fpic
<compileflags>-ffunction-sections
<compileflags>-funwind-tables
```

```
<compileflags>-fstack-protector
<compileflags>-no-canonical-prefixes
<compileflags>-Os
<compileflags>-fomit-frame-pointer
<compileflags>-fno-omit-frame-pointer
<compileflags>-DANDROID
<compileflags>-D__ANDROID__
<compileflags>-DNDEBUG
<compileflags>-D__GLIBC__
<compileflags>-DBOOST_ASIO_DISABLE_STD_ATOMIC
<compileflags>-D_GLIBCXX__PTHREADS
<compileflags>-Wa,--noexecstack
<compileflags>-Wformat
<compileflags>-Werror=format-security
<compileflags>-lstdc++
<compileflags>-Wno-long-long
    ;
```

8. From a terminal pointing located in the boost directory, launch the compilation using the following command line. We need to exclude the **Python** module, which requires additional libraries not available on the NDK by default.

```
./b2 --without-python toolset=gcc-android4.6_armeabi link=static
runtime-link=static target-os=linux architecture=arm --
stagedir=android-armeabi threading=multi
```

Final static libraries are generated in `android-armeabi/lib/`.

Repeat the same steps for the ArmV7 and X86 platforms, creating a new configuration for each of them. The staging directory must be `armeabi-v7a` for ArmV7 and `android-x86` for X86.

 Final `user-config.jam` is provided with this book in the `Libraries/boost` directory.

What just happened?

We have customized the Boost configuration to use the raw Android GCC toolchain as a standalone compiler (that is, without the NDK wrappers). We have declared various flags to adapt compilation to Android target platforms. Then, we have built Boost manually using its dedicated building tool b2. Now, every time Boost is updated or modified, code has to be manually compiled again with b2.

We have also forced NDK-Build to generate verbose logs with the V=1 argument. This is helpful to either troubleshoot compilation issues or to get feedback on what and how NDK-Build is compiling.

Finally, we have enabled release compilation mode, that is, with code optimizations, by switching NDK_DEBUG to 0. This could have also been done by setting APP_OPTIM := release in jni/Application.mk. There are five main optimization levels in GCC, and they are as follows:

- **-O0**: This disables any optimization. This is automatically set by the NDK when APP_OPTIM is set to debug (more about this in the last part about Makefiles in this chapter).

- **-O1**: This allows basic optimizations without increasing compilation time too much. These optimizations do not require any speed-space tradeoffs, which mean that they produce faster code without increasing executable size.

- **-O2**: This allows advanced optimization (including -O1), but at the expense of compilation time. Like -O1, these optimizations do not require speed-space tradeoffs.

- **-O3**: This performs aggressive optimizations (including -O2), which can increase executable size, such as **function inlining**. This is generally profitable but, sometimes, counterproductive (for example, increasing memory usage can also increase cache misses).

- **-Os**: This optimizes compiled code size (a subset of -O2) before speed.

Although -Os or -O2 is generally the way to go for release mode, -O3 can also be considered for performance-critical code. The -Ox flags being shortcuts for the various GCC optimization flags, enabling -O2 and appending additional "fine-grain" flags (for example, -finline-functions), are an option too. Whatever option you choose, the best way to find the best choice is simply by performing benchmarking! To get more information about the numerous GCC optimization options, have a look at http://gcc.gnu.org/.

Now that the Boost module is prebuilt, we can embed any of its libraries in our application.

Time for action – compiling an executable linked to Boost

Let's use the Boost unit test library to build our own unit test executable through the following steps:

1. Still in the `boost` directory, create a new `Android.mk` file to declare the newly prebuilt libraries as Android modules and make them available to NDK applications. This file needs to contain one module declaration per library. For example, define one module `boost_unit_test_framework`:

   ❑ `LOCAL_SRC_FILES` reference the static library `libboost_unit_test_framework.a` we have built with b2.

   Use the `$(TARGET_ARCH_ABI)` variable to determine the right path to use, which depends on the target platform. Its value can be `armeabi`, `armeabi-v7a`, or `x86`. If you compile DroidBlaster for X86, the NDK will look for `libboost_unit_test_framework.a` in `androidx86/lib`.

   ❑ `LOCAL_EXPORT_C_INCLUDES` automatically appends boost root directory to the include file directory list of the including module.

   ❑ Indicate that this module is a prebuilt library with the `$(PREBUILT_STATIC_LIBRARY)` directive:

   ```
   LOCAL_PATH:= $(call my-dir)

   include $(CLEAR_VARS)

   LOCAL_MODULE:= boost_unit_test_framework
   LOCAL_SRC_FILES:= android-$(TARGET_ARCH_ABI)/lib/libboost_unit_
   test_framework.a
   LOCAL_EXPORT_C_INCLUDES := $(LOCAL_PATH)

   include $(PREBUILT_STATIC_LIBRARY)
   ```

   More modules can be declared in the same file with the same set of lines (for example, `boost_thread`).

    Final `user-config.jam` is provided with this book in the `Libraries/boost` directory.

2. Go back to the `DroidBlaster` project and create a new directory `test` containing the unit test file `test/Test.cpp`. Write a test to check the behavior, for example, of the `TimeManager`, as shown in the following code:

```
#include "Log.hpp"
#include "TimeManager.hpp"

#include <unistd.h>

#define BOOST_TEST_MODULE DroidBlaster_test_module
#include <boost/test/included/unit_test.hpp>

BOOST_AUTO_TEST_SUITE(suiteTimeManager)

BOOST_AUTO_TEST_CASE(testTimeManagerTest_elapsed)
{
    TimeManager timeManager;
    timeManager.reset();

    sleep(1);
    timeManager.update();
    BOOST_REQUIRE(timeManager.elapsed() > 0.9f);
    BOOST_REQUIRE(timeManager.elapsed() < 1.2f);

    sleep(1);
    timeManager.update();
    BOOST_REQUIRE(timeManager.elapsed() > 0.9f);
    BOOST_REQUIRE(timeManager.elapsed() < 1.2f);
}

BOOST_AUTO_TEST_SUITE_END()
```

3. To include Boost in an application, we need to link it with an STL implementation supporting exceptions and RTTI. Enable them globally in the `Application.mk` file, as shown in the following code:

```
APP_ABI := armeabi armeabi-v7a x86
APP_STL := gnustl_static
APP_CPPFLAGS := -fexceptions -frtti
```

4. Finally, open DroidBlaster `jni/Android.mk` and create a second module named `DroidBlaster_test` before the `import-module` section. This module compiles the additional `test/Test.cpp` test file and must be linked to the Boost unit test library. Build this module as an executable, and not a shared library, with `$(BUILD_EXECUTABLE)`.

Finally, import the `Boost` module itself in the import-module section, as shown in the following code:

```
. . .
include $(BUILD_SHARED_LIBRARY)

include $(CLEAR_VARS)

LS_CPP=$(subst $(1)/,,$(wildcard $(1)/*.cpp))
LS_CPP_TEST=$(subst $(1)/,,$(wildcard $(1)/../test/*.cpp))
LOCAL_MODULE := DroidBlaster_test
LOCAL_SRC_FILES := $(call LS_CPP,$(LOCAL_PATH)) \
    $(call LS_CPP_TEST,$(LOCAL_PATH))
LOCAL_LDLIBS := -landroid -llog -lEGL -lGLESv2 -lOpenSLES
LOCAL_STATIC_LIBRARIES := android_native_app_glue png box2d_static \
    libboost_unit_test_framework

include $(BUILD_EXECUTABLE)

$(call import-module,android/native_app_glue)
$(call import-module,libpng)
$(call import-module,box2d)
$(call import-module,boost)
```

5. Build the project. If you look into the `libs` folder, you should see one `droidblaster_test` file in addition to the shared library. This is an executable file that we can run on an emulator or a rooted device (given you have the right to deploy and change permission on a file). Deploy this file and run it (here on an Arm V7 emulator instance):

```
adb push libs/armeabi-v7a/droidblaster_test /data/data/
```

```
adb shell /data/data/droidblaster_test
```

```
packt@computer
Running 2 test cases...

*** No errors detected
```

What just happened?

We have created a fully native executable using a Boost prebuilt module and can run it on Android. Boost prebuilt static libraries have been "published" from the Boost `Android.mk` module file in the `Boost` directory.

Indeed, there exist four main ways to build a native library. We have already seen `BUILD_STATIC_LIBRARY` and `BUILD_SHARED_LIBRARY` in the Box2D part. Two more options coexist, which are as follows:

 ◆ `PREBUILT_STATIC_LIBRARY` to use an existing (that is, prebuilt) binary static library
 ◆ `PREBUILT_SHARED_LIBRARY` to use an existing binary shared library

These directives indicate that libraries are ready for linking.

Inside the main module file, as we have seen for Box2D, submodules linked need to be listed in:

 ◆ `LOCAL_SHARED_LIBRARIES` for shared libraries
 ◆ `LOCAL_STATIC_LIBRARIES` for static libraries

The same rule applies whether the library is prebuilt or not. Modules, whether they are static, shared, prebuilt, or built on-demand, must be imported in the final main module using the NDK `import-module` directive.

When a prebuilt library is linked to a main module, source files are not necessary. Include files are obviously still required. Thus, prebuilt libraries are an appropriate choice if you want to provide a library to third parties without releasing sources. On the other hand, on-demand compilation allows tweaking compilation flags on all included libraries (such as optimization flags, the ARM mode, and so on) from your main `Application.mk` project file.

To properly link with Boost, we have also enabled exceptions and RTTI on the whole project. Exceptions and RTTI are activated very easily by appending `-fexceptions` and `-frtti` to either the `APP_CPPFLAGS` directive in the `Application.mk` file or the `LOCAL_CPPFLAGS` file of the concerned library. By default, Android compiles with `-fno-exceptions` and `-fno-rtti` flags.

Indeed, exceptions have the reputation of making the compiled code bigger and less efficient. They prevent the compiler from performing some clever optimizations. However, whether exceptions are worse than error checking, or even no check at all, is a highly debatable question. In fact, Google's engineers dropped them in the first releases because GCC 3.x generated a poor exception handling code for ARM processors. However, the build chain now uses GCC 4.x, which does not suffer from this flaw. Compared to manual error checking and handling of exceptional cases, this penalty might not be so significant most of the time. Thus, the choice of exceptions is up to you (and your embedded libraries)!

> Exception handling in C++ is not easy and imposes a strict discipline! They must be used strictly for exceptional cases and require carefully designed code. Have a look at the **Resource Acquisition Is Initialization (RAII)** idiom to properly handle them. For more information, have a look at `http://en.wikipedia.org/wiki/Resource_Acquisition_Is_Initialization`.

Obviously, Boost provides much more interesting features than unit tests. Discover its full richness in its official documentation at `http://www.boost.org/doc/libs`. Beware, Boost is subject to regular breaking changes or bugs on Android since it is not very actively maintained and tested on that platform. Be prepared to investigate and fix problems directly in its code.

Now that we have seen in practice how to write module Makefiles, let's learn more about them.

Mastering module Makefiles

Android Makefiles are an essential piece of the NDK building process. Thus, to build and manage a project properly, it is important to understand the way they work.

Makefile variables

Compilation settings are defined through a set of predefined NDK variables. We have already seen the three most important ones: `LOCAL_PATH`, `LOCAL_MODULE`, and `LOCAL_SRC_FILES`, but many others exist. We can differentiate the following four types of variables, each with a different prefix:

- `LOCAL_` variables: These are dedicated to individual module compilation and are defined in `Android.mk` files.

- `APP_` variables: These refer to application-wide options and are set in `Application.mk`.

- ◆ NDK_ variables: These are mainly internal variables that usually refer to environment variables (for example, NDK_ROOT, NDK_APP_CFLAGS, or NDK_APP_CPPFLAGS). There are two notable exceptions: NDK_TOOLCHAIN_VERSION and NDK_APPLICATION_MK. The latter can be passed to the NDK-Build in parameter to define a different Application.mk location.

- ◆ PRIVATE_ prefixed variables: These are for NDK internal use only.

The following table contains a non-exhaustive list of LOCAL variables:

Variable	Description
LOCAL_PATH	To specify the root location of source files. Must be defined at the beginning of the Android.mk file before include $(CLEAR_VARS).
LOCAL_MODULE	To define module name, it must be unique among all modules.
LOCAL_MODULE_FILENAME	To override default name of the compiled module, which is: - lib<module name>.so for shared libraries. - lib<module name>.a for static libraries. No custom file extensions can be specified so that .so or .a remains appended.
LOCAL_SRC_FILES	To define the list of source files to compile, each separated by a space and relative to LOCAL_PATH.
LOCAL_C_INCLUDES	To specify header file directories for both C and C++ languages. The directory can be relative to the ${ANDROID_NDK} directory, but unless you need to include a specific NDK file, you are advised to use absolute paths (which can be built from Makefile variables such as $(LOCAL_PATH)).
LOCAL_CPP_EXTENSION	To change default C++ file extension, that is, .cpp (for example, .cc or .cxx). A list of file extensions separated by a space, can be specified. Extensions are necessary for GCC to determine which file is related to which language.
LOCAL_CFLAGS, LOCAL_CPPFLAGS, LOCAL_LDLIBS	To specify any options, flags, or macro-definitions for compilation and linking. The first one works for both C and C++, the second one is for C++ only, and the last one is for the linker.
LOCAL_SHARED_LIBRARIES, LOCAL_STATIC_LIBRARIES	To declare a dependency with other modules (not system libraries), shared and static modules, respectively. LOCAL_SHARED_LIBRARIES manage dependencies whereas LOCAL_LDLIBS should be used for declaring system libraries.

Variable	Description
LOCAL_ARM_MODE, LOCAL_ARM_NEON, LOCAL_DISABLE_NO_EXECUTE, LOCAL_FILTER_ASM	Advanced variables dealing with processors and assembler/binary code generation. They are not necessary for most programs.
LOCAL_EXPORT_C_INCLUDES, LOCAL_EXPORT_CFLAGS, LOCAL_EXPORT_CPPFLAGS, LOCAL_EXPORT_LDLIBS	To define additional options or flags in import modules that should be appended to client module options. For example, if a module A defines LOCAL_EXPORT_LDLIBS := -llog because it needs an Android logging module. Then, module B, that depends on module A, will be automatically linked to -llog. LOCAL_EXPORT_ variables are not used when compiling the module that exports them. If required, they also need to be specified in their LOCAL counterpart.

Documentation about these variables can be found at ${ANDROID_NDK}/docs/ANDROID-MK.html.

The following table contains a non-exhaustive list of the APP variables (all are optional):

Variable	Description
APP_PROJECT_PATH	To specify the root of your application project.
APP_MODULES	The list of modules to compile with their identifier. Dependent modules are also included. This can be used, for example, to force the generation of a static library.
APP_OPTIM	Set to release or debug to adapt compilation settings to the type of build you want. When not specified explicitly, the NDK determines the build type using the debuggable flag in the AndroidManifest.
APP_CFLAGS APP_CPPFLAGS APP_LDFLAGS	To globally specify any options, flags, or macro-definitions for compilation and linking. The first one works for both C and C++, the second one is for C++ only, and the last one is for the linker.
APP_BUILD_SCRIPT	To redefine the location of the Android.mk file (by default in project's jni directory).
APP_ABI	List of ABI (that is, "CPU architectures") supported by the application, separated by a space. Currently supported values are armeabi, armeabi-v7a, x86, mips, or all. Each module is recompiled once per ABI. So, the more ABI you support, the more time it will get to build.
APP_PLATFORM	Name of the target Android platform. This information is found by default in the project.properties file.

Variable	Description
APP_STL	The C++ runtime to use. Possible values are system, gabi++_static, gabi++_shared, stlport_static, stlport_shared, gnustl_static, gnustl_shared, c++_static, and c++_shared.

Documentation about these variables can be found at ${ANDROID_NDK}/docs/APPLICATION-MK.html.

Enabling C++ 11 support and the Clang compiler

The NDK_TOOLCHAIN_VERSION variable can be redefined in the Application.mk file to explicitly select the compilation toolchain. Possible values for the NDK R10 are 4.6 (now deprecated), 4.8, and 4.9, which simply correspond to GCC versions. Possible version numbers might change in future releases of the NDK. To find them, have a look at the $ANDROID_NDK/toolchains directory.

The Android NDK provides C++ 11 support, starting with the GCC 4.8 toolchain. You can enable it by appending the -std=c++11 compilation flag and activating GNU STL (STL Port is not supported and Libc++ only partially supported at the time this book was written) to get proper C++11 support. The following is an example of an Android.mk extract with C++11 activated:

```
...
NDK_TOOLCHAIN_VERSION := 4.8
APP_CPPFLAGS += -std=c++11
APP_STL := gnustl_shared
...
```

Switching to GCC4.8 and C++11 might not feel like a breeze. Indeed, the compiler, let's say, is a bit less permissive than before. In case you run into trouble when compiling legacy code with this new toolchain, try the -fpermissive flag (or rewrite your code!).

Moreover, beware, although C++11 support is quite large, you might still encounter a few problems or missing features.

To enable Clang, the LLVM-based compiler (famous for being used by Apple), in place of GCC, simply set NDK_TOOLCHAIN_VERSION to clang. You can also specify compiler version, such as clang3.4 or clang3.5. Again, possible version numbers might change in future releases of the NDK. To find them, have a look at the $ANDROID_NDK/toolchains directory.

Makefile Instructions

Makefile is a real language with programming instructions and functions.

Makefiles can be broken down into several sub-Makefiles, included with the `include` instruction. Variable initialization comes in the following two flavors:

◆ Simple affectation (operator `:=`), which expands variables at the time they are initialized

◆ Recursive affectation (operator `=`), which re-evaluates the affected expression each time it is called

The following conditional and loop instructions are available: `ifdef/endif`, `ifeq/endif`, `ifndef/endif`, and `for…in/do/done`. For example, to display a message only when a variable is defined, do:

```
ifdef my_var
    # Do something...
endif
```

More advanced stuff, such as functional `if`, `and`, `or`, and so on, are at your disposal, but are rarely used. Makefiles also provide some useful built-in functions, which are given in the following table:

`$(info <message>)`	Allows printing messages to the standard output. This is the most essential tool when writing Makefiles! Variables inside information messages are allowed.
`$(warning <message>)`, `$(error <message>)`	Allows printing a warning or a fatal error that stops compilation. These messages can be parsed by Eclipse.
`$(foreach <variable>, <list>, <operation>)`	Performs an operation on a list of variables. Each element of the list is expanded in the first argument variable, before the operation is applied to it.
`$(shell <command>)`	Executes a command outside of Make. This brings all the power of Unix Shell into Makefiles but is heavily system-dependent. Avoid it if possible.
`$(wildcard <pattern>)`	Selects files and directory names according to a pattern.
`$(call <function>)`	Allows evaluating a function or macro. One macro we have seen is `my-dir`, which returns the directory path of the last executed Makefile. This is why LOCAL_PATH `:= $(call my-dir)` is systematically written at the beginning of each `Android.mk` file to save in the current Makefile directory.

Custom functions can easily be written with the `call` directive. These functions look somewhat similar to recursively affected variables, except that the arguments can be defined: `$(1)` for first argument, `$(2)` for second argument, and so on. A call to a function can be performed in a single line, as shown in the following code:

```
my_function=$(<do_something> ${1},${2})
$(call my_function,myparam)
```

Strings and files manipulation functions are available too, as shown in the following table:

`$(join <str1>, <str2>)`	Concatenates two strings.

`$(subst <from>,`
 	
`<replacement>,<string>),`
`$(patsubst <pattern>,`
 	
`<replacement>,<string>)`
	Replaces each occurrence of a substring by another. The second one is more powerful because it allows using patterns (which must start with "%").

`$(filter <patterns>, <text>)` `$(filter-out <patterns>, <text>)`	Filter strings from a text matching patterns. This is useful for filtering files. For example, the following line filters any C file: `$(filter %.c, $(my_source_list))`
`$(strip <string>)`	Removes any unnecessary whitespace.
`$(addprefix <prefix>,<list>),` `$(addsuffix <suffix>, <list>)`	Append a prefix and suffix, respectively, to each element of the list, each element being separated by a space.
`$(basename <path1>, <path2>, ...)`	Returns a string from which file extensions are removed.
`$(dir <path1>, <path2>),` `$(notdir <path1>, <path2>)`	Extracts the directory and the filename in a path respectively.
`$(realpath <path1>, <path2>, ...),` `$(abspath <path1>, <path2>, ...)`	Return both canonical paths of each path argument, except that the second one does not evaluate symbolic links.

This is just really an overview of what Makefiles are capable of. For more information, refer to the full Makefile documentation available at `http://www.gnu.org/software/make/manual/make.html`. If you are allergic to Makefiles, have a look at CMake. CMake is a simplified Make system, already building many open source libraries on the market. A port of CMake on Android is available at `http://code.google.com/p/android-cmake`.

Have a go hero – mastering Makefiles

We can play in a variety of ways with Makefiles:

- Try the affectation operator. For example, write down the following piece of code, which uses the `:=` operator, in your `Android.mk` file:

```
my_value    := Android
my_message := I am an $(my_value)
$(info $(my_message))
my_value    := Android eating an apple
$(info $(my_message))
```

- Watch the result when launching compilation. Then, perform the same using `=`. Print current optimization mode. Use APP_OPTIM and the internal variable, NDK_APP_CFLAGS, and observe the difference between the `release` and `debug` modes:

```
$(info Optimization level: $(APP_OPTIM) $(NDK_APP_CFLAGS))
```

- Check that variables are properly defined, for example:

```
ifndef LOCAL_PATH
    $(error What a terrible failure! LOCAL_PATH not defined...)
endif
```

- Try to use the `foreach` instruction to print the list of files and directories inside the project's root directory and its `jni` folder (and make sure to use recursive affectation):

```
ls = $(wildcard $(var_dir))
dir_list := . ./jni
files := $(foreach var_dir, $(dir_list), $(ls))
```

- Try to create a macro to log a message to the standard output and its time:

```
log=$(info $(shell date +'%D %R'): $(1))
$(call log,My message)
```

- Finally, test the `my-dir` macro-behavior, to understand why LOCAL_PATH `:=` `$(call my-dir)` is systematically written at the beginning of each `Android.mk` file:

```
$(info MY_DIR    =$(call my-dir))
include $(CLEAR_VARS)
$(info MY_DIR    =$(call my-dir))
```

CPU Architectures (ABI)

Compiled native C/C++ code on current Android ARM devices follows an **Application Binary Interface** (**ABI**). An ABI specifies the binary code format (instruction set, calling conventions, and so on). GCC translates code into this binary format. ABIs are thus strongly related to processors. The target ABI can be selected in the `Application.mk` file with the `APP_ABI` variable. There exist five main ABIs supported on Android, which are as follows:

 ◆ **thumb**: This is the default option, which should be compatible with all ARM devices. Thumb is a special instruction set which encodes instructions on 16 bit, instead of 32 bit, to improve code size (useful for devices with constrained memory). The instruction set is severely restricted compared to ArmEABI.

 ◆ **armeabi** (Or Arm v5): This should run on all ARM devices. Instructions are encoded on 32 bit but may be more concise than Thumb code. Arm v5 does not support advanced extensions such as floating point acceleration and is thus slower than Arm v7.

 ◆ **armeabi-v7a**: This supports extensions such as Thumb-2 (similar to Thumb but with additional 32-bit instructions) and VFP, plus some optional extensions, such as NEON. Code compiled for Arm V7 will not run on Arm V5 processors.

 ◆ **x86**: This is for "*PC-like*" architectures (that is, Intel/AMD) and, more specifically, Intel Atom processors. This ABI provides specific extensions, such as MMX or SSE.

 ◆ **mips**: This is for MIPS processors developed by Imagination Technologies (which also produce the PowerVR graphics processors). Only a few devices exist at the time this book was written.

By default, the compiled binaries of each ABI are embedded in the APK. The most appropriate is selected at installation time. Google Play also supports the upload of different APKs for each ABI to limit application size.

Advanced instruction sets (NEON, VFP, SSE, MSA)

If you are reading this book, code performance is probably one of your main criteria. To achieve this, ARM created a SIMD instruction set (acronym Single Instruction Multiple Data, that is, process several data in parallel with one instruction) called NEON, which has been introduced along with the VFP (floating point accelerated) unit. NEON is not available on all chips (for example, Nvidia Tegra 2 does not support it), but is quite popular in intensive multimedia applications. They are also a good way to compensate the weak VFP unit of some processors (for example, Cortex-A8).

A NEON code can be written in a separate assembler file in a dedicated `asm` `volatile` block with assembler instructions, or in a C/C++ file or as intrinsics (NEON instructions encapsulated in a GCC C routine). Intrinsics should be used with much care as GCC is often unable to generate efficient machine code (or requires lots of tricky hints). Writing real assembler code is generally advised.

X86 CPUs have their own set of extensions that are different from the ARM ones: MMX, SSE, SSE2, and SSE3. SSE instruction sets are the Intel equivalent of NEON SIMS instructions. The latest SSE4 instructions are generally not supported on current X86 processors. Obviously, SSE and NEON are not compatible, which means that a code specifically written for NEON needs to be rewritten for SSE and reciprocally.

 Android provides a `cpu-features.h` API (with the `android_getCpuFamily()` and `android_getCpuFeatures()` methods) to detect available features on the host device at runtime. It helps in detecting the CPU (ARM, X86) and its capabilities (ArmV7 support, NEON, VFP, and so on).

NEON, SSE, and modern processors in general are not easy to master. The Internet is full of examples to get inspiration from. Reference technical documentation can be found on the ARM website at `http://infocenter.arm.com/` and the Intel developer manuals at `http://www.intel.com/`.

MIPS also has its own SIMD instruction set named MSA. It provides features such as vector arithmetics and branching operations, or conversion between integer and floating-point values. For more information, have a look at `http://www.imgtec.com/mips/architectures/simd.asp`.

All this stuff is interesting but it does not answer the question you are probably asking yourself: how hard it is to port code from ARM to X86 (or reciprocally)? The answer is "it depends":

- If you use pure C/C++ native code, without specific instruction set, code should be portable simply by appending `x86` or `mips` to the `APP_ABI` variable.
- If your code contains assembly code, you will need to rewrite the corresponding part for other ABI or provide a fallback.
- If your code contains specific instruction sets such as NEON (using C/C++ intrinsics or assembly code), you will need to rewrite corresponding part for other ABIs or provide a fallback.
- If your code depends on specific memory alignment, you might need to use explicit alignment. Indeed, when you compile a data structure, the compiler might use padding to align data in memory appropriately for faster memory accesses. However, alignment requirements are different depending on the ABI.

For example, 64-bit variables on ARM are aligned to 8, which means, for example, that double must have a memory address, which is a multiple of 8. X86 memory can be more densely packed.

> Data alignment is not an issue the vast majority of the time, except if you explicitly depend on data location (for example, if you use serialization). Even if you have no alignment issues, it is always interesting to tweak or optimize structure layouts to avoid useless padding and get better performances.

So, most of the time, porting code from one ABI to another should be rather simple. In specific cases, provide fallbacks when specific CPU features or assembly code is necessary. Finally, beware, some memory alignment issues might arise in some rare cases.

> As we have seen in the Prebuilding Boost part, each ABI has its own compilation flags to optimize compilation. Although the default GCC options used by the NDK are an appropriate basis, tweaking them can improve efficiency and performance. For example, you can use `-mtune=atom -mssse3 -mfpmath=sse` to optimize release code on X86 platforms.

Summary

This chapter introduced a fundamental aspect of the NDK: portability. Thanks to the recent improvements in the building toolchain, the Android NDK can now take advantage of the vast C/C++ ecosystem. It unlocks the door of a productive environment, where code is shared with other platforms with the aim of creating new cutting-edge applications efficiently.

More specifically, you learned how to activate the STL with a simple flag in the NDK makefile system. We have ported the Box2D library into an NDK module that is reusable among Android projects. You also saw how to prebuild Boost using the raw NDK toolchain, without any wrapper. We have enabled exceptions and RTTI and discovered in depth how to write module makefiles.

We have highlighted the path toward the creation of professional applications using the NDK as a leverage. But do not expect all C/C++ libraries to be ported so easily. Talking about paths, we are almost at the end. At least, this was the last chapter about DroidBlaster.

The next and last chapters will introduce RenderScript, an advanced technology to maximize your Android app performance.

10
Intensive Computing with RenderScript

If the NDK is one of the best tools to get a high performance on Android. It gives low-level access to the machine, gives you control on memory allocation, provides access to advanced CPU instruction-sets, and even more.

This power comes with a price: to get maximum performance on a key piece of code, ones need to optimize code for the many devices and platforms in the world. Sometimes, it is more appropriate to use CPU SIMD instructions, and other times, to perform computation on the GPU. You had better be experienced and have plenty of devices and time in front of you! This is the reason Google introduced RenderScript on Android.

RenderScript is a programming language specific to Android written with one goal in mind: *performance*. Let's be clear, applications cannot be entirely written in RenderScript. However, the critical parts, requiring intensive computations, should be! RenderScript can be executed from either Java or C/C++.

In this chapter, we will discuss these basics and concentrate our effort on its NDK binding. We will create a new project to demonstrate RenderScript capabilities by filtering images. More precisely, we will see how to:

- ◆ Execute the predefined **Intrinsics**
- ◆ Create your own custom **Kernels**
- ◆ Combine Intrinsics and Kernels together

By the end of this chapter, you should be able to create your own RenderScript programs and bind them into your native code.

What is RenderScript ?

RenderScript was introduced in Honeycomb in 2011 with a strong focus on graphics capabilities, hence the name. The graphics engine part of RenderScript has, however, been deprecated since Android 4.1 JellyBean. Although it has kept its name, RenderScript has deeply evolved to emphasize its "compute engine". It is similar to technologies such as OpenCL and CUDA, with an emphasis on portability and usability.

More specifically, RenderScript tries to abstract hardware specificities from the programmer and extract the maximum raw power from it. Instead of taking the least common denominator, it optimizes code according to the platform it executes on at runtime. The final code can run on either the CPU or GPU, with an advantage of automatic parallelization managed by RenderScript.

The RenderScript framework is composed of a few elements:

- A C-like language based on C99, which provides variables, functions, structures, and so on
- A **low level virtual machine** (**LLVM**) based compiler on the developer machine that produces intermediate code
- A RenderScript library and runtime that translates intermediate code to machine code only when the final program runs on the device
- A Java and NDK binding API to execute and chain computation tasks

Computation tasks are obviously the center of RenderScript. There are two kinds of tasks:

- Kernels, which are user-created scripts that perform a computation task using the RenderScript language
- Intrinsics, which are built-in Kernels to perform some common tasks such as blurring pixels

Kernels and Intrinsics can be combined together, the output of a program being linked to the input of another. From the complex graphs of computation tasks emerge fast and powerful programs.

However, for the moment, let's see what Intrinsics are and how they work.

Executing a predefined Intrinsic

RenderScript provides a few built-in functions, mainly dedicated to Image processing, called Intrinsics. With these, blending images, such as in Photoshop, blurring them, or even decoding raw YUV images from the camera, (see *Chapter 4, Calling Java Back from Native Code*, for a slower alternative) becomes simple and highly efficient. Indeed, Intrinsics are highly optimized and can be considered as one of the best implementations in their domain.

To see how Intrinsics work, let's create a new project that takes an input image and applies a blur effect to it.

 The resulting project is provided with this book under the name RenderScript_Part1.

Time for action – creating a Java UI

Let's create a new Java project with a JNI module.

1. Create a new hybrid Java/C++ project as shown in *Chapter 2, Starting a Native Android Project*:

   ❑ Name it RenderScript.

   ❑ The main package is com.packtpub.renderscript.

   ❑ minSdkVersion is 9 and targetSdkVersion is 19.

   ❑ Define the android.permission.WRITE_EXTERNAL_STORAGE permission in the AndroidManifest.xml file.

   ❑ Turn the project into a native project as already seen.

   ❑ Remove the native source and header files that have been created by ADT.

   ❑ Name the main Activity RenderScriptActivity and its layout activity_renderscript.xml.

2. Define the project.properties file as follows. These lines activate the RenderScript support library, which allows porting code to older devices until API 8:

```
target=android-20
renderscript.target=20
renderscript.support.mode=true
sdk.buildtools=20
```

3. Modify `res/activity_renderscript.xml` to make it look as follows. We will need:

- ❏ A `SeekBar` to define the blur radius
- ❏ A `Button` to apply the blur effect
- ❏ Two `ImageView` elements to display the image before and after the effect is applied.

```xml
<?xml version="1.0" encoding="utf-8"?>
<LinearLayout
  xmlns:a="http://schemas.android.com/apk/res/android"
  a:layout_width="fill_parent" a:layout_height="fill_parent"
  a:layout_weight="1" a:orientation="vertical" >
  <LinearLayout
    a:orientation="horizontal"
    a:layout_width="fill_parent" a:layout_height="wrap_content" >
    <SeekBar a:id="@+id/radiusBar" a:max="250"
      a:layout_gravity="center_vertical"
      a:layout_width="128dp" a:layout_height="wrap_content" />
    <Button a:id="@+id/blurButton" a:text="Blur"
      a:layout_width="wrap_content" a:layout_height="wrap_content"/>
  </LinearLayout>
  <LinearLayout
    a:baselineAligned="true" a:orientation="horizontal"
    a:layout_width="fill_parent" a:layout_height="fill_parent" >
    <ImageView
      a:id="@+id/srcImageView" a:layout_weight="1"
      a:layout_width="fill_parent" a:layout_height="fill_parent" />
    <ImageView
      a:id="@+id/dstImageView" a:layout_weight="1"
      a:layout_width="fill_parent" a:layout_height="fill_parent" />
  </LinearLayout>
</LinearLayout>
```

4. Implement `RenderScriptActivity` as shown below.

Load the `RSSupport` module, which is the `RenderScript` support library, and the `renderscript` module, which we are about to create in a static block.

Then, in `onCreate()`, load a 32-bit bitmap from an image placed in `drawable` resources (here, named `picture`) and create a second empty bitmap of the same size. Assign these bitmaps to their respective `ImageView` component. Also, define `OnClickListener` on the **Blur** button:

```
package com.packtpub.renderscript;
...
public class RenderScriptActivity extends Activity
```

```
implements OnClickListener {
    static {

        System.loadLibrary("renderscript");
    }

    private Button mBlurButton;
    private SeekBar mBlurRadiusBar, mThresholdBar;
    private ImageView mSrcImageView, mDstImageView;
    private Bitmap mSrcImage, mDstImage;

    @Override
    protected void onCreate(Bundle savedInstanceState) {
        super.onCreate(savedInstanceState);
        setContentView(R.layout.activity_renderscript);

        BitmapFactory.Options options = new BitmapFactory.Options();
        options.inPreferredConfig = Bitmap.Config.ARGB_8888;
        mSrcImage = BitmapFactory.decodeResource(getResources(),
                                R.drawable.picture, options);
        mDstImage = Bitmap.createBitmap(mSrcImage.getWidth(),
                                mSrcImage.getHeight(),
                                Bitmap.Config.ARGB_8888);

        mBlurButton = (Button) findViewById(R.id.blurButton);
        mBlurButton.setOnClickListener(this);

        mBlurRadiusBar = (SeekBar) findViewById(R.id.radiusBar);

        mSrcImageView = (ImageView) findViewById(R.id.srcImageView);
        mDstImageView = (ImageView) findViewById(R.id.dstImageView);
        mSrcImageView.setImageBitmap(mSrcImage);
        mDstImageView.setImageBitmap(mDstImage);
    }
...
```

5. Create a native function, `blur`, which takes in the parameter:

- ❑ The application cache directory for the `RenderScript` runtime
- ❑ The source and destination bitmaps
- ❑ The blur effect radius to determine the blur strength

Call this method from the `onClick()` handler using the seek bar value to determine the blur radius. The radius must be in the range [0, 25].

```
. . .
        private native void blur(String pCacheDir, Bitmap pSrcImage,
                                Bitmap pDstImage, float pRadius);

        @Override
        public void onClick(View pView) {
            float progressRadius = (float) mBlurRadiusBar.getProgress();
            float radius = Math.max(progressRadius * 0.1f, 0.1f);

            switch(pView.getId()) {
            case R.id.blurButton:
                blur(getCacheDir().toString(), mSrcImage, mDstImage,
                    radius);
                break;
            }
            mDstImageView.invalidate();
        }
    }
```

Time for action – running RenderScript Blur intrinsic

Let's create the native module that will generate our new effect.

1. Create a new file `jni/ RenderScript.cpp`. We will need the following:

- ❑ `android/bitmap.h` header to manipulate bitmaps.

- ❑ `jni.h` for JNI strings.

- ❑ `RenderScript.h`, which is the main `RenderScript` header file. This is the only one you should need. RenderScript is written in C++ and is defined in the `android::RSC` namespace.

```
#include <android/bitmap.h>
#include <jni.h>
#include <RenderScript.h>

using namespace android::RSC;
. . .
```

2. Write two utility methods to lock and unlock Android bitmaps as seen in *Chapter 4, Calling Java Back from Native Code*:

```
...
void lockBitmap(JNIEnv* pEnv, jobject pImage,
        AndroidBitmapInfo* pInfo, uint32_t** pContent) {
    if (AndroidBitmap_getInfo(pEnv, pImage, pInfo) < 0) abort();
    if (pInfo->format != ANDROID_BITMAP_FORMAT_RGBA_8888) abort();
    if (AndroidBitmap_lockPixels(pEnv, pImage,
            (void**)pContent) < 0) abort();
}

void unlockBitmap(JNIEnv* pEnv, jobject pImage) {
    if (AndroidBitmap_unlockPixels(pEnv, pImage) < 0) abort();
}
...
```

3. Implement the native method `blur()` using the JNI convention.

Then, instantiate the RS class. This class is the main interface, which controls RenderScript initialization, resource management, and object creation. Wrap it with the `sp` helper class provided by RenderScript, which represents a smart pointer.

Initialize it with the cache directory given in parameter, converting the string appropriately with JNI:

```
...
extern "C" {

JNIEXPORT void JNICALL
Java_com_packtpub_renderscript_RenderScriptActivity_blur
(JNIEnv* pEnv, jobject pClass, jstring pCacheDir, jobject pSrcImage,
        jobject pDstImage, jfloat pRadius) {
    const char * cacheDir = pEnv->GetStringUTFChars(pCacheDir, NULL);
    sp<RS> rs = new RS();
    rs->init(cacheDir);
    pEnv->ReleaseStringUTFChars(pCacheDir, cacheDir);
...
```

4. Lock the bitmaps we are working on using the utility methods we just wrote:

```
...
    AndroidBitmapInfo srcInfo; uint32_t* srcContent;
    AndroidBitmapInfo dstInfo; uint32_t* dstContent;
    lockBitmap(pEnv, pSrcImage, &srcInfo, &srcContent);
    lockBitmap(pEnv, pDstImage, &dstInfo, &dstContent);
...
```

5. Now comes the interesting part. Create a RenderScript **Allocation** from the source bitmap. This ALLOCATION represents the whole input memory area whose dimensions are defined by Type. The Allocation is composed of "individual" **Elements**; in our case, 32-bit RGBA pixels are defined as Element::RGBA_8888. Since the bitmap is not used as a texture, we have no need for **Mipmaps** (see *Chaper 6, Rendering Graphics with OpenGL ES*, about OpenGL ES for more information).

Repeat the same operation for the output ALLOCATION created from the output bitmap:

```
. . .
    sp<const Type> srcType = Type::create(rs, Element::RGBA_8888(rs),
            srcInfo.width, srcInfo.height, 0);
    sp<Allocation> srcAlloc = Allocation::createTyped(rs, srcType,
            RS_ALLOCATION_MIPMAP_NONE,
            RS_ALLOCATION_USAGE_SHARED | RS_ALLOCATION_USAGE_SCRIPT,
            srcContent);

    sp<const Type> dstType = Type::create(rs, Element::RGBA_8888(rs),
            dstInfo.width, dstInfo.height, 0);
    sp<Allocation> dstAlloc = Allocation::createTyped(rs, dstType,
            RS_ALLOCATION_MIPMAP_NONE,
            RS_ALLOCATION_USAGE_SHARED | RS_ALLOCATION_USAGE_SCRIPT,
            dstContent);
. . .
```

6. Create a ScriptIntrinsicBlur instance and the kind of elements it works on, which is again RGBA pixels. An Intrinsic is a predefined RenderScript function, which implements a common operation, such as a blur effect in our case. The **Blur Intrinsic** takes a radius as an input parameter. Set it with setRadius().

Then, specify the blur Intrinsic input, that is the source Allocation with setInput().

Apply the Intrinsic on each of its elements with forEach() and save it to the output Allocation.

Finally, copy the result to the destination bitmap with copy2DRangeTo().

```
. . .
    sp<ScriptIntrinsicBlur> blurIntrinsic =
            ScriptIntrinsicBlur::create(rs, Element::RGBA_8888(rs));
    blurIntrinsic->setRadius(pRadius);

    blurIntrinsic->setInput(srcAlloc);
    blurIntrinsic->forEach(dstAlloc);
    dstAlloc->copy2DRangeTo(0, 0, dstInfo.width, dstInfo.height,
            dstContent);
. . .
```

7. Don't forget to unlock the bitmap after the effect is applied!

```
...
    unlockBitmap(pEnv, pSrcImage);
    unlockBitmap(pEnv, pDstImage);
}
}
```

8. Create a `jni/Application.mk` file targeting the `ArmEABI V7` and `X86` platforms. Indeed, RenderScript currently does not support older `ArmEABI V5`. `STLPort`, and is also required by the RenderScript native library.

```
APP_PLATFORM := android-19
APP_ABI := armeabi-v7a x86
APP_STL := stlport_static
```

9. Create a `jni/Android.mk` file defining our `renderscript` module and listing `RenderScript.cpp` for compilation.

Make `LOCAL_C_INCLUDES` point to the appropriate RenderScript, including the file directory in the NDK platform directory. Also, append the RenderScript precompiled libraries directory to `LOCAL_LDFLAG`.

Finally, link against `dl`, `log`, and `RScpp_static`, which are required for RenderScript:

```
LOCAL_PATH := $(call my-dir)

include $(CLEAR_VARS)

LOCAL_MODULE      := renderscript
LOCAL_C_INCLUDES += $(TARGET_C_INCLUDES)/rs/cpp \
                    $(TARGET_C_INCLUDES)/rs
LOCAL_SRC_FILES := RenderScript.cpp
LOCAL_LDFLAGS += -L$(call host-path,$(TARGET_C_INCLUDES)/../lib/rs)
LOCAL_LDLIBS      := -ljnigraphics -ldl -llog -lRScpp_static

include $(BUILD_SHARED_LIBRARY)
```

What just happened?

Run the project, increase the `SeekBar` value, and click on the **Blur** button. The output `ImageView` should display the filtered picture as follows:

We embedded the RenderScript compatibility library in our project, giving us access to RenderScript down to the API 8 Froyo. On older devices, RenderScript is "emulated" on the CPU.

If you decide to use RenderScript from the NDK but do not want to use the compatibility library, you will need to embed the RenderScript runtime manually. To do so, remove all the stuff we added in the `project.properties` file in step 2 and include the following piece of code at the end of your `Android.mk` files:

```
...
include $(CLEAR_VARS)
LOCAL_MODULE := RSSupport
LOCAL_SRC_FILES := $(SYSROOT_LINK)/usr/lib/rs/lib$(LOCAL_MODULE)$(TARGET_SONAME_EXTENSION)
include $(PREBUILT_SHARED_LIBRARY)
```

Then, we executed our first RenderScript Intrinsic that applies a blur effect as efficiently as possible. Intrinsic execution follows a simple and repetitive pattern that you will see repeatedly:

1. Ensure that the input and output memory areas are exclusively available, for example, by locking bitmaps.
2. Create or reuse the appropriate input and output Allocation.
3. Create and set up the Intrinsic parameters.
4. Set the input Allocation and apply the Intrinsic to an output Allocation.
5. Copy the result from the output Allocation to the target memory area.

To understand this process better, let's dive a bit more into the way RenderScript works. RenderScript follows a simple model. It takes some data as the input and processes it to an output memory area:

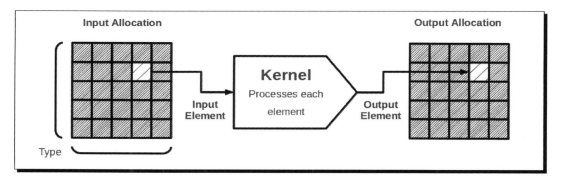

As a computing solution, RenderScript works with any type of data stored in-memory. This is an Allocation. An Allocation is composed of individual Elements. For an Allocation pointing to a bitmap, an element would typically be a pixel (which is itself a set of 4 `uchar` values). Among the large list of Elements available, we can cite:

Possible Allocation Elements		
U8, U8_2, U8_3, U8_4	I8, I8_2, I8_3, I8_4	RGBA_8888
U16, U16_2, U16_3, U16_4	I16, I16_2, I16_3, I16_4	RGB_565
U32, U32_2, U32_3, U32_4	I32, I32_2, I32_3, I32_4	RGB_888
U64, U64_2, U64_3, U64_4	I64, I64_2, I64_3, I64_4	A_8
F32, F32_2, F32_3, F32_4	F64, F64_2, F64_3, F64_4	YUV
MATRIX_2X2	MATRIX_3X3	MATRIX_4X4

U = unsigned integer, I = signed integer, F = float

8, 16, 32, 64 = byte count. For example I8 = 8-bits signed int (that is, a signed char)

_2, _3, _4 = Number of elements for vectors (I8_3 means vector of 3 signed int)

A_8 represents an Alpha channel (with each pixel represented as an unsigned char).

Internally, Elements are described with a **DataType** (such as UNSIGNED_8 for an unsigned char) and a **DataKind** (such as PIXEL_RGBA for a pixel). The DataKind is used with something called **Samplers** for graphics data that is interpreted on the GPU (see *Chapter 6, Rendering Graphics with OpenGL ES*, about OpenGL ES to better understand what is a Sampler). DataType and DataKind are for more advanced usage and should be transparent to you most of the time. You can have a look at the full list of elements at http://developer. android.com/reference/android/renderscript/Element.html.

Knowing the type of input/output Element is not enough. Their number is also essential, as this determines the whole Allocation size. This is the role of Type, which can be set up with 1 dimension, 2 dimensions (typically for bitmaps), or 3 dimensions. Some other information is also supported, such as the YUV format (NV21 being the default in Android as seen in *Chapter 4, Calling Java Back from Native Code*). So, in other words, Type describes a multi-dimensional array.

Allocations have a specific flag to control how Mipmaps are generated. By default, most Allocations will not need one (RS_ALLOCATION_MIPMAP_NONE). However, when used as the input of a graphics texture, Mipmaps are either created in script memory (RS_ALLOCATION_MIPMAP_FULL) or when uploaded to the GPU (RS_ALLOCATION_MIPMAP_ON_SYNC_TO_TEXTURE).

Once we create the Allocation from a Type and an Element, we can take care of creating and setting up Intrinsics. RenderScript provides a few of them, which are not many, but mainly focused on image processing:

Intrinsic	Description
ScriptIntrinsicBlend	To blend two Allocations together, for example, two images (we will see additive blending in the last part of this chapter).
ScriptIntrinsicBlur	To apply a blur effect on a Bitmap.
ScriptIntrinsicColorMatrix	To apply a color matrix to an Allocation (for example, to adjust image hue, change colors, and so on).
ScriptIntrinsicConvolve3x3	To apply a convolve matrix of size 3 to an Allocation (many image filters can be implemented with a convolve matrix, including blurring).

Intrinsic	Description
`ScriptIntrinsicConvolve5x5`	This is the same as `ScriptIntrinsicConvolve3x3` but with a matrix of size 5.
`ScriptIntrinsicHistogram`	This is used to apply a histogram filter (for example, to improve the image contrast).
`ScriptIntrinsicLUT`	This is used to apply a "Lookup Table" per channel (for example, to translate a given red value in a pixel to another predefined value in the table).
`ScriptIntrinsicResize`	This is used to resize a 2D Allocation (for example, to scale an image).
`ScriptIntrinsicYuvToRGB`	To translate YUV images coming, for example, from a camera to an RGB image (like we did in *Chapter 4, Calling Java Back from Native Code*). The binding of this Intrinsic in the NDK is bugged and, thus, unusable at the time this book was written. If you really need it, apply it from Java.

Each of these Intrinsics requires its own specific parameters (for example, the radius for a blur effect). Full Intrinsics documentation can be found at `http://developer.android.com/reference/android/renderscript/package-summary.html`.

Intrinsics require an input and output Allocation. It is technically possible to use an input as an output if the kind of function applied is appropriate. This is not the case, for example, `ScriptIntrinsicBlur` as a blurred pixel could be written at the same time it is read to blur other pixels.

Once Allocations are set, an Intrinsic is applied and performs its work. After that, the result must be copied to the output memory area with one of the `copy***To()` methods (`copy2DRangeTo()` for a bitmap, which has two dimensions or `copy2DStridedTo()` if there are gaps in the target area). Data copying is a prerequisite step before making use of the computation result.

 Some problems have been reported on some devices when the size of an image Allocation was not a multiple of 4. This will probably remind you of OpenGL textures, which have the same requirements. So, try to stick with dimensions that are multiples of 4.

Although the Intrinsics provided by RenderScript are really useful, you may want more flexibility. Maybe you need your own custom image filter, or a blur effect of more than 25 pixels, or maybe you do not want to process images at all. Then, RenderScript Kernels might be the right answer for you.

Writing a custom Kernel

RenderScript gives you the ability to develop small custom "scripts" instead of the built-in Intrinsics. These programs are called Kernels and are written in a C-like language. They are compiled to an intermediate language by the RenderScript LLVM-based compiler at build time. Finally, they are translated to machine code at runtime. RenderScript takes care of platform-dependent optimizations.

Let's now see how to create such a Kernel by implementing a custom image effect that filters pixels according to their luminosity.

 The resulting project is provided with this book under the name RenderScript_Part2.

Time for action – writing a luminance threshold filter

Let's append a new component to our UI and implement the new image filter.

1. Add a new **Threshold** SeekBar and Button in res/activity_renderscript. xml:

```xml
<?xml version="1.0" encoding="utf-8"?>
<LinearLayout
  xmlns:a="http://schemas.android.com/apk/res/android"
  a:layout_width="fill_parent" a:layout_height="fill_parent"
  a:layout_weight="1" a:orientation="vertical" >
  <LinearLayout
    a:orientation="horizontal"
    a:layout_width="fill_parent" a:layout_height="wrap_content" >
    ...
    <SeekBar a:id="@+id/thresholdBar" a:max="100"
      a:layout_gravity="center_vertical"
      a:layout_width="128dp" a:layout_height="wrap_content" />
    <Button a:id="@+id/thresholdButton" a:text="Threshold"
      a:layout_width="wrap_content" a:layout_height="wrap_content"/>
  </LinearLayout>
  <LinearLayout
    a:baselineAligned="true" a:orientation="horizontal"
    a:layout_width="fill_parent" a:layout_height="fill_parent" >
    ...
  </LinearLayout>
</LinearLayout>
```

2. Edit `RenderScriptActivity` and bind the **Threshold** `SeekBar` and `Button` to a new native method `threshold()`. This method is similar to `blur()`, except that it takes a threshold float parameter in the range [0, 100].

```
...
public class RenderScriptActivity extends Activity
implements OnClickListener {

    ...

    private Button mBlurButton, mThresholdButton;
    private SeekBar mBlurRadiusBar, mThresholdBar;
    private ImageView mSrcImageView, mDstImageView;
    private Bitmap mSrcImage, mDstImage;

    @Override
    protected void onCreate(Bundle savedInstanceState) {

        ...

        mBlurButton = (Button) findViewById(R.id.blurButton);
        mBlurButton.setOnClickListener(this);
        mThresholdButton = (Button)findViewById(R.id.thresholdButton);
        mThresholdButton.setOnClickListener(this);

        mBlurRadiusBar = (SeekBar) findViewById(R.id.radiusBar);
        mThresholdBar = (SeekBar) findViewById(R.id.thresholdBar);


        ...
    }

    @Override
    public void onClick(View pView) {
        float progressRadius = (float) mBlurRadiusBar.getProgress();
        float radius = Math.max(progressRadius * 0.1f, 0.1f);
        float threshold = ((float) mThresholdBar.getProgress())
                        / 100.0f;

        switch(pView.getId()) {
        ...

        case R.id.thresholdButton:
            threshold(getCacheDir().toString(), mSrcImage, mDstImage,
                    threshold);
            break;
        }
```

```
            mDstImageView.invalidate();
    }
    . . .


        private native void threshold(String pCacheDir, Bitmap pSrcImage,
                                Bitmap pDstImage, float pThreshold);
    }
```

3. Now, let's write our own `jni/threshold.rs` filter using the RenderScript language. First, use pragma directives to declare:

   ❑ The script language version (currently, only `1` is possible)

   ❑ The Java package name the script is associated with

   ```
   #pragma version(1)
   #pragma rs java_package_name(com.packtpub.renderscript)
   . . .
   ```

4. Then, declare an input parameter `thresholdValue` of type `float`.

   We also to need two constant vectors of 3 floats (`float3`):

   ❑ The first value represents a BLACK color

   ❑ The second value a predefined LUMINANCE_VECTOR

   ```
   . . .
   float thresholdValue;
   static const float3 BLACK = { 0.0, 0.0, 0.0 };
   static const float3 LUMINANCE_VECTOR = { 0.2125, 0.7154, 0.0721 };
   . . .
   ```

5. Create the root function of the script named `threshold()`. It takes a vector of 4 unsigned char, that is, an RGBA pixel in input, and returns a new one in output. Prepend `__attribute__((kernel))` to indicate that this function is the main script function, that is, the "Kernel's Root". The function works as follows:

   ❑ It converts the input pixel from a vector of char, with each color component in the range [0, 255], to a vector of float value with each component in the range [0.0, 1.0]. This is the role of the function `rsUnpackColor8888()`.

   ❑ Now that we have a float vector, some of the many mathematical functions provided by RenderScript can be applied. Here, a dot product with a predefined luminosity vector for the RGBA color space returns the relative luminosity of a pixel.

   ❑ With this information, the function checks whether a pixel's luminosity is sufficient according to the given threshold. If not, the pixel is set to black.

- ❏ Finally, it converts a pixel's color from a float vector to an unsigned char vector with `rsPackColor8888()`. This value will then be copied by RenderScript into the final Bitmap as we will see.

```
...
uchar4 __attribute__((kernel)) threshold(uchar4 in) {
    float4 pixel = rsUnpackColor8888(in);
    float luminance = dot(LUMINANCE_VECTOR, pixel.rgb);
    if (luminance < thresholdValue) {
        pixel.rgb = BLACK;
    }
    return rsPackColorTo8888(pixel);
}
```

6. To compile our new `threshold.rs` script, list it in the `Android.mk` file.

During the compilation process, `ScriptC_threshold.h` and `ScriptC_threshold.cpp` is generated in `obj/local/armeabi-v7a/objs-debug/renderscript`. These files contain the code to bind our code with the **Threshold Kernel** executed by RenderScript. So, we also need to append the directory to the `LOCAL_C_INCLUDES` directory:

```
LOCAL_PATH := $(call my-dir)

include $(CLEAR_VARS)

LOCAL_MODULE    := renderscript
LOCAL_C_INCLUDES += $(TARGET_C_INCLUDES)/rs/cpp \
                    $(TARGET_C_INCLUDES)/rs \
                    $(TARGET_OBJS)/$(LOCAL_MODULE)
LOCAL_SRC_FILES := RenderScript.cpp threshold.rs
LOCAL_LDFLAGS += -L$(call host-path,$(TARGET_C_INCLUDES)/../lib/rs)
LOCAL_LDLIBS    := -ljnigraphics -ldl -llog -lRScpp_static

include $(BUILD_SHARED_LIBRARY)
```

7. Include the generated header in `jni/RenderScript.cpp`.

```
#include <android/bitmap.h>
#include <jni.h>
#include <RenderScript.h>
#include "ScriptC_threshold.h"

using namespace android::RSC;

...
```

8. Then, implement the new method `threshold()`, respecting the JNI naming convention. This method is similar to `blur()`.

However, instead of instantiating a predefined Intrinsic, we instantiate a Kernel generated by RenderScript. This Kernel is named `ScriptC_threshold` according to our RenderScript filename.

The input parameter `thresholdValue` defined in our script can be initialized with `set_thresholdValue()` generated by RenderScript. Then, the main method `threshold()` can be applied using the generated method `forEach_threshold()`.

Once the Kernel has been applied, the result can be copied on the target bitmap, such as with Intrinsics, using `copy2DRangeTo()`:

```
. . .
JNIEXPORT void JNICALL
Java_com_packtpub_renderscript_RenderScriptActivity_threshold
(JNIEnv* pEnv, jobject pClass, jstring pCacheDir, jobject pSrcImage,
        jobject pDstImage, jfloat pThreshold) {
    const char * cacheDir = pEnv->GetStringUTFChars(pCacheDir, NULL);
    sp<RS> rs = new RS();
    rs->init(cacheDir);
    pEnv->ReleaseStringUTFChars(pCacheDir, cacheDir);

    AndroidBitmapInfo srcInfo;
    uint32_t* srcContent;
    AndroidBitmapInfo dstInfo;
    uint32_t* dstContent;
    lockBitmap(pEnv, pSrcImage, &srcInfo, &srcContent);
    lockBitmap(pEnv, pDstImage, &dstInfo, &dstContent);

    sp<const Type> srcType = Type::create(rs, Element::RGBA_8888(rs),
            srcInfo.width, srcInfo.height, 0);
    sp<Allocation> srcAlloc = Allocation::createTyped(rs, srcType,
            RS_ALLOCATION_MIPMAP_NONE,
            RS_ALLOCATION_USAGE_SHARED | RS_ALLOCATION_USAGE_SCRIPT,
            srcContent);

    sp<const Type> dstType = Type::create(rs, Element::RGBA_8888(rs),
            dstInfo.width, dstInfo.height, 0);
    sp<Allocation> dstAlloc = Allocation::createTyped(rs, dstType,
            RS_ALLOCATION_MIPMAP_NONE,
```

```
                    RS_ALLOCATION_USAGE_SHARED | RS_ALLOCATION_USAGE_SCRIPT,
            dstContent);

    sp<ScriptC_threshold> thresholdKernel = new ScriptC_threshold(rs);
    thresholdKernel->set_thresholdValue(pThreshold);

    thresholdKernel->forEach_threshold(srcAlloc, dstAlloc);
    dstAlloc->copy2DRangeTo(0, 0, dstInfo.width, dstInfo.height,
            dstContent);

    unlockBitmap(pEnv, pSrcImage);
    unlockBitmap(pEnv, pDstImage);
    }
    }
```

What just happened?

Run the project, increase the new `SeekBar`, and click on the **Threshold** button. The output `ImageView` should display the filtered picture with only luminous pixels as follows:

We have written and compiled our first RenderScript Kernel. Kernel scripts have a `.rs` extension and are written in a language inspired by C99. Their content starts with pragma definitions that bring additional "meta" information about them: the language version (which can be only 1) and the Java package. We can also use them to tweak the floating point precision for calculations with pragma directives (`#pragma rs_fp_full`, `#pragma rs_fp_relaxed`, or `#pragma rs_fp_imprecise`).

> The Java package is important for the RenderScript runtime, which needs to resolve compiled Kernels during execution. When using the RenderScript Compatibility library, scripts compiled with the NDK (that is stored in the `jni` folder) might not get resolved. In that case, a possible solution is to make a copy of the `.rs` files in the Java `src` folder in the appropriate package.

Kernels are, in a way similar, to Intrinsics. Indeed, once compiled, the same process applies to them: creating the allocations, the Kernel, setting everything up, applying, and finally, copying the result. When executed, a Kernel function is applied on each Element of the input and returned in the corresponding output allocation Element, in parallel.

You can set up a Kernel through the NDK binding API and an additional binding layer (more commonly called the **reflected** layer), which is generated at compile time. Each compiled script is "reflected" by a C++ class, whose name is defined according to the script filename prefixed with `ScriptC_`. The final code is generated in the **eponym** header and the source files in the `obj` directory, one for each per ABI. The reflected classes are your only interface with the script file, as a kind of wrapper. They perform some runtime checks on the kind of Allocation passed in the input or output of the Kernel to ensure their Element type matches what is declared in the script file. Have a look at the generated `ScriptC_threshold.cpp` in the project `obj` directory for a concrete example.

Kernel input parameters are passed from the reflected layer to the script file through global variables. Global variables correspond to all the non-`static` and non-`const` variables, for example:

```
float thresholdValue;
```

They are declared outside functions such as a C variable. Global variables are made available in the reflected layer through setters. In our project, the `thresholdValue` global variable is passed through the generated method `set_thresholdValue()`. Variables do not have to be primitive types. They can also be pointers, in which case the reflected method name is prefixed with `bind_`. and expects an Allocation. Getters are also provided in the generated classes.

On the other hand, static variables, declared in the same scope as global variables, are not accessible in the NDK reflected layer and cannot be modified outside of the script. When marked `const`, they are obviously treated as constants, like the luminance vector in our project:

```
static const float3 LUMINANCE_VECTOR = { 0.2125, 0.7154, 0.0721 };
```

The main Kernel functions, more commonly called **root functions**, are declared like a C function except that they are marked with `__attribute__((kernel))`. They take as parameter the Element type of the input Allocation and return the type of Element of the output Allocation. Both the input parameter and return value are optional but at least one of them must be present. In our example, the input parameter and the output return value is a pixel Element (that is, a vector of 4 unsigned char; 1 byte for each color channel):

```
uchar4 __attribute__((kernel)) threshold(uchar4 in) {
    ...
}
```

RenderScript root functions can be also given additional index parameters that represent Element position (or "coordinates") within its Allocation. For example, we can declare two additional `uint32_t` parameters to get pixel Element coordinates in `threshold()`:

```
uchar4 __attribute__((kernel)) threshold(uchar4 in, uint32_t x,
uint32_t y) {
    ...
}
```

Multiple root functions with different names can be declared in one script. After compilation, they are reflected in the generated class as functions prefixed with `forEach_`, for example:

```
void forEach_threshold(android::RSC::sp<const android::RSC::Allocation>
ain, android::RSC::sp<const android::RSC::Allocation> aout);
```

Before `__attribute__((kernel))` was introduced, RenderScript files could only contain one main function named root. This form is still allowed nowadays. Such functions take a pointer to the input, output Allocation in parameters, and do not allow return values. So the `threshold()` function rewritten as a traditional root method would look like the following:

```
void root(const uchar4 *in, uchar4 *out) {
    float4 pixel = rsUnpackColor8888(*in);
    float luminance = dot(LUMINANCE_VECTOR, pixel.rgb);
    if (luminance < thresholdValue) {
        pixel.rgb = BLACK;
    }
    *out = rsPackColorTo8888(pixel);
```

In addition to the `root()` function, a script can also contain an `init()` function with no parameter and return value. This function is called only once when the script is instantiated.

```
void init() {
    ...
}
```

Obviously, the possibilities of the RenderScript language are more limited and constrained than traditional C. We cannot:

◆ Allocate resources directly. The memory must be allocated by the client application before running the Kernel.

◆ Write low-level assembly code or do fancy C stuff. However, hopefully, plenty of familiar elements of the C language are available, such as `struct`, `typedef`, `enum` and so on; even pointers!

◆ Use C libraries or runtime. However, RenderScript provides a full "runtime" library with plenty of math, conversion, atomic functions, and so on. Have a look at `http://developer.android.com/guide/topics/renderscript/reference.html` for more details about them.

> A method provided by RenderScript that you may find particularly useful is `rsDebug()`, which prints debug log to ADB.

Even with those limitations, RenderScript constraints are still quite relaxed. A consequence is that some scripts might not benefit from maximum acceleration, for example, on the GPU, which is quite restricting. To overcome this issue, a limited subset of RenderScript called **FilterScript** was designed to favor optimization and compatibility. Consider it if you need maximum performance.

For more information about the RenderScript language capabilities, have a look at `http://developer.android.com/guide/topics/renderscript/advanced.html`.

Combining scripts together

Unity is strength could not be truer than with RenderScript. Intrinsics and Kernels alone are powerful features. However, combined together, they give its full strength to the RenderScript framework.

Let's now see how to combine the **Blur** and **Luminosity** threshold filters together with a blending Intrinsic to create a great-looking image effect.

 The resulting project is provided with this book under the name `RenderScript_Part3`.

Time for action – combining Intrinsics and scripts together

Let's improve our project to apply a new combined filter.

1. Add a new **Combine** Button in `res/activity_renderscript.xml`, as follows:

```
<?xml version="1.0" encoding="utf-8"?>
<LinearLayout
  xmlns:a="http://schemas.android.com/apk/res/android"
  a:layout_width="fill_parent" a:layout_height="fill_parent"
  a:layout_weight="1" a:orientation="vertical" >
  <LinearLayout
    a:orientation="horizontal"
    a:layout_width="fill_parent" a:layout_height="wrap_content" >
    . . .
    <Button a:"d="@+id/thresholdBut"on" a:te"t="Thresh"ld"
      a:layout_wid"h="wrap_cont"nt" a:layout_heig"t="wrap_cont"nt"/>
    <Button a:"d="@+id/combineBut"on" a:te"t="Comb"ne"
      a:layout_wid"h="wrap_cont"nt" a:layout_heig"t="wrap_cont"nt"/>
  </LinearLayout>
  <LinearLayout
    a:baselineAlign"d="t"ue" a:orientati"n="horizon"al"
    a:layout_wid"h="fill_par"nt" a:layout_heig"t="fill_par"nt" >
    . . .
  </LinearLayout>
</LinearLayout>
```

2. Bind the **Combine** button to a new native method `combine()`, which has the parameters of both `blur()` and `threshold()`:

```
. . .
public class RenderScriptActivity extends Activity
implements OnClickListener {
    . . .

    private Button mThresholdButton, mBlurButton, mCombineButton;
    private SeekBar mBlurRadiusBar, mThresholdBar;
```

```
private ImageView mSrcImageView, mDstImageView;
private Bitmap mSrcImage, mDstImage;

@Override
protected void onCreate(Bundle savedInstanceState) {
    ...

    mBlurButton = (Button) findViewById(R.id.blurButton);
    mBlurButton.setOnClickListener(this);
    mThresholdButton = (Button) findViewById(R.id.thresholdButton);
    mThresholdButton.setOnClickListener(this);
    mCombineButton = (Button)findViewById(R.id.combineButton);
    mCombineButton.setOnClickListener(this);


    ...
}


@Override
public void onClick(View pView) {
    float progressRadius = (float) mBlurRadiusBar.getProgress();
    float radius = Math.max(progressRadius * 0.1f, 0.1f);
    float threshold = ((float) mThresholdBar.getProgress())
                    / 100.0f;

    switch(pView.getId()) {
    case R.id.blurButton:
        blur(getCacheDir().toString(), mSrcImage, mDstImage,
            radius);
        break;

    case R.id.thresholdButton:
        threshold(getCacheDir().toString(), mSrcImage, mDstImage,
                threshold);
        break;

    case R.id.combineButton:
        combine(getCacheDir().toString(), mSrcImage, mDstImage,
                radius, threshold);
        break;
    }
    mDstImageView.invalidate();
```

```
        }
        ...

        private native void combine(String pCacheDir,
                                Bitmap pSrcImage, Bitmap pDstImage,
                                float pRadius, float pThreshold);
}
```

3. Edit `jni/RenderScript.cpp` and add the new `combine()` method, following the JNI convention again. The method performs similarly to what we saw previously:

- ❑ The RenderScript engine is initialized

- ❑ Bitmaps are locked

- ❑ The appropriate Allocation is created for the input and output bitmaps

```
    ...
    JNIEXPORT void JNICALL
    Java_com_packtpub_renderscript_RenderScriptActivity_combine
    (JNIEnv* pEnv, jobject pClass, jstring pCacheDir, jobject pSrcImage,
            jobject pDstImage, jfloat pRadius, jfloat pThreshold) {
        const char * cacheDir = pEnv->GetStringUTFChars(pCacheDir, NULL);
        sp<RS> rs = new RS();
        rs->init(cacheDir);
        pEnv->ReleaseStringUTFChars(pCacheDir, cacheDir);

        AndroidBitmapInfo srcInfo; uint32_t* srcContent;
        AndroidBitmapInfo dstInfo; uint32_t* dstContent;
        lockBitmap(pEnv, pSrcImage, &srcInfo, &srcContent);
        lockBitmap(pEnv, pDstImage, &dstInfo, &dstContent);

        sp<const Type> srcType = Type::create(rs, Element::RGBA_8888(rs),
                srcInfo.width, srcInfo.height, 0);
        sp<Allocation> srcAlloc = Allocation::createTyped(rs, srcType,
                RS_ALLOCATION_MIPMAP_NONE,
                RS_ALLOCATION_USAGE_SHARED | RS_ALLOCATION_USAGE_SCRIPT,
                srcContent);

        sp<const Type> dstType = Type::create(rs, Element::RGBA_8888(rs),
                dstInfo.width, dstInfo.height, 0);
        sp<Allocation> dstAlloc = Allocation::createTyped(rs, dstType,
                RS_ALLOCATION_MIPMAP_NONE,
                RS_ALLOCATION_USAGE_SHARED | RS_ALLOCATION_USAGE_SCRIPT,
                dstContent);
    ...
```

4. We will also need a temporary memory area to store the result of computations. Let's create a temporary allocation backed by a memory buffer `tmpBuffer`:

. . .

```
sp<const Type> tmpType = Type::create(rs, Element::RGBA_8888(rs),
        dstInfo.width, dstInfo.height, 0);tmpType->getX();
uint8_t* tmpBuffer = new uint8_t[tmpType->getX() *
        tmpType->getY() * Element::RGBA_8888(rs)- >getSizeBytes()];
sp<Allocation> tmpAlloc = Allocation::createTyped(rs, tmpType,
        RS_ALLOCATION_MIPMAP_NONE,
        RS_ALLOCATION_USAGE_SHARED | RS_ALLOCATION_USAGE_SCRIPT,
        tmpBuffer);
```

. . .

5. Initialize the Kernels and Intrinsics we need for the combined filter:

   - ❑ The `Threshold` Kernel
   - ❑ The `Blur` Intrinsic
   - ❑ An additional `Blend` Intrinsic that does not require parameters

     . . .

```
sp<ScriptC_threshold> thresholdKernel = new ScriptC_threshold(rs);
sp<ScriptIntrinsicBlur> blurIntrinsic =
        ScriptIntrinsicBlur::create(rs, Element::RGBA_8888(rs));
blurIntrinsic->setRadius(pRadius);
sp<ScriptIntrinsicBlend> blendIntrinsic =
        ScriptIntrinsicBlend::create(rs, Element::RGBA_8888(rs));
thresholdKernel->set_thresholdValue(pThreshold);
```

     . . .

6. Now, combine the multiple filters together:

   - ❑ First, apply the Threshold filter and save the result into the temporary allocation.
   - ❑ Second, apply the Blur filter on the temporary Allocation and save the result in the target bitmap Allocation.
   - ❑ Finally, blend both the source and the filtered bitmap using an additive operation to create the final image. Blending can be done "in-place", without an additional Allocation, since each pixel is read and written only once (to the opposite of the blur filter).

     . . .

```
thresholdKernel->forEach_threshold(srcAlloc, tmpAlloc);
blurIntrinsic->setInput(tmpAlloc);
blurIntrinsic->forEach(dstAlloc);
blendIntrinsic->forEachAdd(srcAlloc, dstAlloc);
```

     . . .

7. Finally, save the result and free resources. All values wrapped in a `sp<>` (that is, a smart pointer) template, such as `tmpAlloc`, are freed automatically:

```
...
    dstAlloc->copy2DRangeTo(0, 0, dstInfo.width, dstInfo.height,
            dstContent);

    unlockBitmap(pEnv, pSrcImage);
    unlockBitmap(pEnv, pDstImage);
    delete[] tmpBuffer;

}
...
```

What just happened?

Run the project, tweak the `SeekBar` components, and click on the **Combine** button. The output `ImageView` should display a "remastered" picture, where the luminous parts are highlighted:

We chained multiple Intrinsics and Kernels together to apply a **Combine** filter to an image. Such a chain is easy to put in place; we basically need to connect the output Allocation of one script to the input Allocation of the next. Copying data to the output memory area is really only necessary at the end.

 It's really sad but script grouping features are not yet available on the Android NDK API, only on the Java side. With the script grouping feature, a full "graph" of scripts can be defined allowing RenderScript to optimize the code further. If you need this feature, then you can either wait or go back to Java.

Hopefully, Allocations can be reused if necessary in multiple scripts, to avoid allocating useless memory. It is even possible to reuse the same Allocation in input and output, if the script allows "in-place" modifications. This is not the case, for example, of the **Blur** filter, which would rewrite blurred pixels while they are read to blur other pixels, resulting in weird visual artefacts.

 Speaking of reuse, it is good practice to reuse RenderSript objects (that is the RS context object, Intrinsics, Kernels, and so on) between executions. This is even more important if you repeatedly perform a computation, such as processing images from the camera.

Memory is an important aspect of RenderScript performance. Used badly, it can decrease efficiency. In our project, we provided a pointer to the Allocations we created it. This means that the Allocations we created in our project are "backed" with native memory, in our case, the bitmap content:

```
. . .
sp<Allocation> srcAlloc = Allocation::createTyped(rs, srcType,
        RS_ALLOCATION_MIPMAP_NONE,
        RS_ALLOCATION_USAGE_SHARED | RS_ALLOCATION_USAGE_SCRIPT,
        srcContent);
. . .
```

However, data can also be copied before processing from the input memory area into the allocation using the `copy***From()` methods, which are the pendant of the `copy***To()` methods. This is especially useful with the Java binding side, which does not always allow the use of "backed Allocation". The NDK binding is more flexible and input data copying can be avoided most of the time.

RenderScript provides others mechanisms to communicate data from a script. The first ones are the methods `rsSendToClient()` and `rsSendToClientBlocking()`. They allow a script to communicate a "command", optionally with some data, to the calling side. The latter method is obviously a bit more dangerous in terms of performances, and should be avoided.

Data can also be communicated through pointers. Pointers are dynamic memory that allows bi-directional communication between the Kernel and the caller. As indicated previously, they are reflected in the generated classes with a method prefixed with `bind_`. The appropriate getters and setters should be generated in the reflected layer at compile time.

However, the NDK RenderScript framework does not reflect structures declared in RenderScript files yet. So declaring a pointer to `struct` defined in a script file will not work for now. Pointers to primitive types work using Allocations though. Thus, expect annoying limitations on the NDK side on this subject.

Let's end on the subject of memory by saying that in case you need more than one input or output Allocations for a script, there is a solution, an `rs_allocation`, which represents an Allocation reflected through a getter and setter. You can have as many of them as you want. Then, you can access dimensions and elements through the `rsAllocationGetDim*()`, `rsGetElementAt*()`, `rsSetElementAt*()` methods, and so on.

For example, the `threshold()` method could be rewritten the following way:

 Note that since we do not pass an input Allocation in parameter, return one as usual

- The `for` loops are not implicit like it would be with an Allocation passed in parameter

- The `threshold()` function cannot be a Kernel root. It is perfectly possible to use input Allocation in conjunction with `rs_allocation` though.

```
#pragma version(1)
#pragma rs java_package_name(com.packtpub.renderscript)

float thresholdValue;
static const float3 BLACK = { 0.0, 0.0, 0.0 };
static const float3 LUMINANCE_VECTOR = { 0.2125, 0.7154, 0.0721 };

rs_allocation input;
```

```
        rs_allocation output;

        void threshold() {
            uint32_t sizeX = rsAllocationGetDimX(input);
            uint32_t sizeY = rsAllocationGetDimY(output);
            for (uint32_t x = 0; x < sizeX; ++x) {
                for (uint32_t y = 0; y < sizeY; ++y) {
                    uchar4 rawPixel = rsGetElementAt_uchar4(input, x, y);

                    // The algorithm itself remains the same.
                    float4 pixel = rsUnpackColor8888(rawPixel);
                    float luminance = dot(LUMINANCE_VECTOR, pixel.rgb);
                    if (luminance < thresholdValue) {
                        pixel.rgb = BLACK;
                    }
                    rawPixel = rsPackColorTo8888(pixel);

                    rsSetElementAt_uchar4(output, rawPixel, x, y);
                }
            }
        }
```

Also, the Kernel would be called in the following way. Note how the method that applies the effect is prefixed with invoked_ (instead of forEach_). This is because the threshold() function is not a Kernel root:

```
. . .
thresholdKernel->set_input(srcAlloc);
thresholdKernel->set_output(dstAlloc);
thresholdKernel->invoke_threshold();
dstAlloc->copy2DRangeTo(0, 0, dstInfo.width, dstInfo.height,
        dstContent);
. . .
```

For more information about the RenderScript language capabilities, have a look at http://developer.android.com/guide/topics/renderscript/advanced.html.

Summary

This chapter introduced RenderScript, an advanced technology to parallelize intensive computation tasks. More specifically, we saw how to use predefined RenderScript built-in Intrinsics, which are currently mainly dedicated to image processing. We also discovered how to implement our own Kernels with the RenderScript custom language inspired by C. Finally, we saw an example of an Intrinsics and Kernels combination to perform computations that are more complex.

RenderScript is available from either the Java or the native side. However, let's be clear, apart from the exception of Allocations backed by memory buffers (a rather important feature for performance though), RenderScript is still more useable through its Java API. Grouping is not available, `struct` is not reflected yet, and some other features are still buggy (for example YUV Intrinsics).

Indeed, RenderScript aims at giving tremendous computing power to the developers who neither have the time nor the knowledge to follow the native path. Thus, the NDK is not well-served yet. Although that will probably change in the future, you should be ready to keep at least parts of your RenderScript code on the Java side.

Afterword

Throughout this book, you learned the essentials to get started and overlooked the paths to follow to go further. You now know the key elements to tame these little powerful monsters and start exploiting their full power. However, there is still a lot to learn, but the time and space is not enough. Anyway, the only way to master a technology is to practice and practice again. I hope you enjoy the journey and that you feel armed for the mobile challenge. So my best advice now is to gather your fresh knowledge and all your amazing ideas, beat them up in your mind, and bake them with your keyboard!

Where we have been

We have seen concretely how to create native projects with Eclipse and the NDK. We learned how to embed a C/C++ library in Java applications through JNI and how to run native code without writing a line of Java.

We tested multimedia capabilities of the Android NDK with OpenGL ES and OpenSL ES, which are becoming a standard in mobility (of course, after omitting Windows Mobile). We have even interacted with our phone input peripherals and apprehended the world through its sensors.

Moreover, the Android NDK is not only related to performance but also portability. Thus, we reused the STL framework, its best companion `Boost`, and ported third-party libraries almost seamlessly.

Finally, we saw how to optimize intensive computing tasks with the RenderScript technology.

Where you can go

The C/C++ ecosystem has existed for several decades now and is full of richness. We ported some libraries, but a lot more are out there and waiting to get ported. Actually, many of them, which are listed as follows, work without the need of a full code revamp:

- Bullet (http://bulletphysics.org/) is an example of a physics engine that can be ported right away in a few minutes
- Irrlicht (http://irrlicht.sourceforge.net/) is one of the many 3D engines that can run on Android
- OpenCV (http://opencv.org/) is a computer vision and machine-learning library, which allows your application to "see" and understand the outside world through the camera
- GLM (http://glm.g-truc.net/) is a useful library for OpenGL ES 2 to handle matrix calculations in a fully C++ way
- Intel Threading Building Block library (https://www.threadingbuildingblocks.org/), or more commonly TBB, is an interesting library for those who need massive parallelization with their native code

Some libraries have been specifically designed for mobile devices such as:

- Unity (http://unity3d.com/), which is a great editor and framework that you should definitely have a look at if you want to write mobile games
- Unreal Engine (https://www.unrealengine.com/) is one of the most powerful engines and is now freely available
- Cocos2D-X (http://www.cocos2d-x.org/), which is a highly popular game engine used in many 2D games
- Vuforia (https://www.qualcomm.com/products/vuforia), which is an augmented reality SDK from Qualcomm

For those who would be tempted to get their hands dirty in the guts of Android, I encourage you to have a look at the Android platform code itself, which is available at http://source.android.com/. It is not a piece of cake to download, compile, or even deploy, but this is the only way to get an in-depth understanding of the Android internals, and also sometimes the only way to find out where these annoying bugs are coming from!

Where to find help

The Android community is really active, and following are the places to find useful information:

- The Android Google group (`http://groups.google.com/group/android-developers`) and the Android NDK group (`http://groups.google.com/group/android-ndk`), where you can get some help, sometimes from the Android team member.

- The Android Developer BlogSpot (`http://android-developers.blogspot.com/`), where you can find fresh and official information about Android development.

- Google IO (`https://www.google.com/events/io`) for some of the best Android video talks.

- The Intel Developer Site (`https://software.intel.com/en-us/android`) is full of interesting resources related to the NDK on x86

- The NVidia Developer Centre (`http://developer.nvidia.com/category/zone/mobile-development`) for Tegra but also general resources about Android and the NDK.

- The Qualcomm Developer Network (`https://developer.qualcomm.com/`) to find information about the NVidia main competitor. The Qualcomm's Augmented Reality SDK is especially promising.

- Stack Overflow (`http://stackoverflow.com/`), which is not dedicated to Android but you can ask questions and get accurate answers.

- GitHub (`http://github.com/`), which is full of NDK libraries and samples.

This is just the beginning

Creating an application is only part of the process. Publishing and selling is another. This is, of course, outside the scope of this book but handling fragmentation and testing compatibility with various target devices can be a real difficulty that needs to be taken seriously.

Beware! Problems start occurring when you start dealing with hardware specificities (and there are lots of them) like we saw with input devices. These issues are, however, not specific to the NDK. If incompatibilities exist in a Java application, then the native code will not do better. Handling various screen sizes, loading appropriately-sized resources, and adapting to device capabilities are things that you will eventually need to deal with. However, that should be manageable.

In short, there are a lot of marvelous but also painful surprises to be discovered. However, Android and mobility are still a fallow land that needs to be modeled. Look at the evolution of Android from its earliest version to the latest one to be convinced. Revolution does not take place every day so do not miss it!

Good luck!

Sylvain Ratabouil

Index

I

IDE (Integrated Development Environment) 2
instruction sets 424-426
Intel developer manuals
  URL 425
Intrinsics
  and scripts, combining 449-455
  URL 439

J

Java
  and native threads, synchronizing 144
  calling back, from native code 134, 138-141
  JNI method signatures, determining 134-137
  synchronizing, with JNI Monitors 155, 156
Java arrays
  in native store, handling 112-120
  managing 112
Java exceptions
  about 124, 125
  catching, in native store 125-128
  code, executing in Exception state 128, 129
  handling API 130
  raising, in native store 125-128
Java, interfacing with C/C++ code
  about 60
  C code, calling from Java 61, 62
Java Native Interfaces (JNI) 63
Java objects
  referencing, from native code 103
Java primitives
  in native store, handling 99-102
  passing 103
  passing, to native code 99
  returning 103
  types, URL 103
Java strings
  converting, in native code 91
Java UI
  creating 429-431
JetPlayer 291
JNI
  debugging 143
  in C 171, 172

  in C++ 171, 172
  methods 150
  Object, allocating with 144-151
  types 137
JNI library
  native JNI library, initializing 82
  native store, initializing 88-90
  simple GUI, defining 82-87
JNI method signatures
  determining 134-137
JNI Monitors
  Java, synchronizing with 155, 156
JNI Reflection API 142, 143
JNI specification
  URL 111
JNI String API 98, 99
Joypad
  Android device, turning into 355-362
JRE (Java Runtime Environment) 7

K

Kernel
  custom Kernel, writing 440
  luminance threshold filter, writing 440-448
Ketai
  URL 169
keyboard
  detecting 340
  handling 341-345
key event methods
  AKeyEvent_getAction() 346
  AKeyEvent_getDownTime() 346
  AKeyEvent_getFlags() 346
  AKeyEvent_getKeyCode() 346
  AKeyEvent_getMetaState() 346
  AKeyEvent_getRepeatCount() 346
  AKeyEvent_getScanCode() 346
Khronos
  URL 217, 299

L

legacy 73
Libc++ 367
Linux
  setting up 22

O

Object arrays 124
Objects
references, saving in native store 103-107
off-screen rendering
used, for adapting resolution 282-288
OpenGL ES
and GLSL specification, URL 290
buffers, clearing 223, 224
buffers, swapping 223, 224
documentation, URL 267
initializing 218-223, 247-267
releases 217, 218
OpenGL pipeline
about 225, 226
Fragment Processing 226
Pixel Processing 226
Primitive Assembly 226
Rasterization 226
Vertex Processing 225
OpenGL Texture
generating 240-243
Open Graphics Library for Embedded Systems.
See **OpenGL ES**
OpenSL ES
about 291
initializing 292
output, creating 293-298
OpenSL ES engine
creating 293-298
philosophy 298, 299
Oracle JDK 7
URL 4, 14
orthographic projection
URL 250
OS X
Android NDK, installing 17-21
Android SDK, installing 17-22
preparing, for Android development 13-16
setting up 13

P

particle effects
rendering 269, 270
star field, rendering 270-280

PID 71
PNG format
URL 240
PNG image
loading 234-240
point sprite 269
Portable Network Graphics (PNG) 227
predefined Intrinsic
executing 429
Primitive arrays
about 121, 122
other array types, handling 123
processor registers 72
Proguard 49
project files, NDK sample applications
build.xml 49
local.properties 49
proguard-project.txt 49
project.properties 50
project management capabilities, NDK sample applications
android create lib-project 51
android create project 50
android create test-project 51
android create uitest-project 51
android update lib-project 51
android update project 51
android update test-project 51
Pulse Code Modulation (PCM) 307

R

raw stack 72
raycasting 406
RDESTL
URL 382
references
saving, to Objects in native store 103-107
reflected layer 446
rendering pipeline
OpenGL.org wiki, URL 226
RenderScript
about 169, 427, 428
elements 428
language capabilities, URL 448, 456
tasks 428
URL 448

VFP 425
Virtual Machine 59
VS-Android
  URL 35

W

Weak references 110, 111
Windows
  Android development kit, installing 8
  Android NDK, installing 8-12
  Android SDK, installing 8-12
  preparing, for Android development 3-7
window surface
  accessing, natively 193
  dimensions 203
  Pixel format 202, 203
  raw graphics, displaying 193-203

X

X86 425
X86 processors 73

Y

YUV 157

Z

Z-buffer 221

Thank you for buying
Android NDK Beginner's Guide
Second Edition

About Packt Publishing

Packt, pronounced 'packed', published its first book, *Mastering phpMyAdmin for Effective MySQL Management*, in April 2004, and subsequently continued to specialize in publishing highly focused books on specific technologies and solutions.

Our books and publications share the experiences of your fellow IT professionals in adapting and customizing today's systems, applications, and frameworks. Our solution-based books give you the knowledge and power to customize the software and technologies you're using to get the job done. Packt books are more specific and less general than the IT books you have seen in the past. Our unique business model allows us to bring you more focused information, giving you more of what you need to know, and less of what you don't.

Packt is a modern yet unique publishing company that focuses on producing quality, cutting-edge books for communities of developers, administrators, and newbies alike. For more information, please visit our website at www.packtpub.com.

About Packt Open Source

In 2010, Packt launched two new brands, Packt Open Source and Packt Enterprise, in order to continue its focus on specialization. This book is part of the Packt Open Source brand, home to books published on software built around open source licenses, and offering information to anybody from advanced developers to budding web designers. The Open Source brand also runs Packt's Open Source Royalty Scheme, by which Packt gives a royalty to each open source project about whose software a book is sold.

Writing for Packt

We welcome all inquiries from people who are interested in authoring. Book proposals should be sent to author@packtpub.com. If your book idea is still at an early stage and you would like to discuss it first before writing a formal book proposal, then please contact us; one of our commissioning editors will get in touch with you.

We're not just looking for published authors; if you have strong technical skills but no writing experience, our experienced editors can help you develop a writing career, or simply get some additional reward for your expertise.

Android NDK Game Development Cookbook

ISBN: 978-1-78216-778-5   Paperback: 320 pages

Over 70 exciting recipes to help you develop mobile games for Android in C++

1. Tips and tricks for developing and debugging mobile games on your desktop.

2. Enhance your applications by writing multithreaded code for audio playback, network access, and asynchronous resource loading.

3. Enhance your game development skills by using modern OpenGL ES and develop applications without using an IDE.

Android Native Development Kit Cookbook

ISBN: 978-1-84969-150-5   Paperback: 346 pages

A step-by-step tutorial with more than 60 concise recipes on Android NDK development skills

1. Build, debug, and profile Android NDK apps.

2. Implement part of Android apps in native C/C++ code.

3. Optimize code performance in assembly with Android NDK.

Please check **www.PacktPub.com** for information on our titles

Android 4: New Features for Application Development

ISBN: 978-1-84951-952-6   Paperback: 166 pages

Develop Android applications using the new features of Android Ice Cream Sandwich

1. Learn new APIs in Android 4.

2. Get familiar with the best practices in developing Android applications.

3. Step-by-step approach with clearly explained sample codes.

Unity Android Game Development by Example Beginner's Guide

ISBN: 978-1-84969-201-4   Paperback: 320 pages

Learn how to create exciting games using Unity 3D for Android with the help of hands-on examples

1. Enter the increasingly popular mobile market and create games using Unity 3D and Android.

2. Learn optimization techniques for efficient mobile games.

3. Clear, step-by-step instructions for creating a complete mobile game experience.

Please check **www.PacktPub.com** for information on our titles

Printed in Great Britain
by Amazon